UNDERSTANDING THE NOVEL

A THEORETICAL OVERVIEW

UNDERSTANDING THE NOVEL

A Theoretical Overview

Albeena Shakil

PRIMUS BOOKS

PRIMUS BOOKS

An imprint of Ratna Sagar P. Ltd.
Virat Bhavan
Mukherjee Nagar Commercial Complex
Delhi 110 009

Offices at

CHENNAI LUCKNOW

AGRA AHMEDABAD BANGALORE COIMBATORE
DEHRADUN GUWAHATI HYDERABAD JAIPUR
JALANDHAR KANPUR KOCHI KOLKATA MADURAI
MUMBAI PATNA RANCHI VARANASI

First published 2015

ISBN: 978-93-84082-09-3

Published by Primus Books

Laser typeset in Bembo by Guru Typograph Technology
Crossings Republic, Ghaziabad 201 009

Printed and bound in India by Replika Press Pvt. Ltd.

For

AMMA

who was endlessly generous . . .

and

ABBU

for his unwavering commitment

to his daughter's education . . .

Contents

Acknowledgements

THIS STUDY HAS evolved over several years and I owe the completion of this book to the support and encouragement of many friends, well-wishers, teachers and family.

A large part of this book is based on my doctoral research at the Centre for English (formerly Centre for Linguistics and English), Jawaharlal Nehru University, done under the supervision of Professor G.J.V. Prasad, whose support has been important for the completion of this book. I must also thank Professors Udaya Kumar and M. Asaduddin whose comments helped in preparing the doctoral thesis for publication.

The research done during a one-year period at the Centre for Jawaharlal Nehru Studies, Jamia Millia Islamia, is the basis for one chapter on the novel in India. I am deeply thankful to all my former colleagues.

The book owes a great deal to many students, teachers, friends and comrades across disciplines from Jawaharlal Nehru University who unconditionally lent their ears and offered many insights. I am grateful to Anubhuti, who went through several drafts of the book and provided many useful suggestions. Jyotirmoy, Ena and Indranil must find special mention. The unfailing camaraderie of Ayesha Kidwai has been a source of constant motivation.

The cooperation extended by the staffs at Sahitya Akademi and Jawaharlal Nehru University libraries has been indispensable.

The interest taken by my teachers at Miranda House, University of Delhi, helped prepare the chapter on realism and the novel.

The fellowship provided by the Indian Institute of Advanced Study, Shimla, has also been crucial in the final stages.

I must especially thank Sehba Farooqui and Professors Biswamoy Pati and Amar Farooqui, without whom the publication of this book would not have been possible. The cooperation of my comrades in the women's movement and former colleagues at Bharati College was invaluable.

My family members have been extremely helpful and considerate. The invaluable support of Prasenjit through all the delays and difficulties helped to keep me on course and has been crucial in more ways than one.

ALBEENA SHAKIL

Introduction

THE NOVEL, AS a form of literary writing, has diversified and proliferated so extensively over time, that today, it is rarely discussed without referring to its subgenres and species like the epistolary novel, the sentimental novel, the Gothic, the propaganda, regional, psychological or thesis novel, the documentary or historical novel, the detective, crime, thriller, spy, or adventure novel, the satirical or allegorical novel, the science-fiction or fantasy novel, the anti-novel, the realist, modernist or postmodern novel, the national allegory or postcolonial novel, the graphic novel, etc. Its postmodern/postcolonial avatars like surfiction, metafiction, critifiction, historiographic metafiction, fabulations are no less in variety or numbers. However, knowledge of these subtypes usually seems to make us none the wiser about the overall nature of the novel. Despite proliferation, the death knell of the novel has been sounded several times—for instance, with the growth of cinema, with futurism and surrealism, with the avant-gardes, with the rise of the anti-novel or the nouveau roman, with the incredible spread of mass media, and more recently with debates about hypertexts on the Internet. The novel, however, has survived most of these predictions and its durability and profusion as a genre is intriguing with evermore novelists announcing their works as novels. It is this aspect of the novel that draws us to embark upon a more detailed study of the form in order to understand its generic fundamentals.

It is useful, at the very outset, to note that literary critics have rarely worked on the novel without simultaneously acknowledging the difficulty of defining or theorizing novels. Georg Lukács qualifies the novel as 'the most hazardous genre',[1] while M.M. Bakhtin observes that the 'utter inadequacy of literary theory is exposed when it is forced to deal with the novel'.[2] For Raymond Williams, the novel is 'not so much a literary form as a whole literature in itself';[3] while Fredric Jameson finds it to be more of an eclectic 'process' than a 'form'.[4] Christopher Gillie notes that, 'The novel, of course is a form that has always resisted definition',[5] while Lennard J. Davis concludes that the 'novel must always be thought of as ambivalent'.[6] Terry Eagleton also observes that, 'The point about the novel, however, is not just that it eludes definitions, but that it actively undermines them. It is less a genre than an anti-genre.'[7] Thanks to this difficulty, over time two divergent tendencies have developed in theoretical studies about the novel. One tendency is to argue that the novel as a genre is so exhaustive and complex that it cannot be studied in its entirety, and must be examined primarily through its subspecies or types. The other is to ignore the novel altogether in favour of employing more incorporative and inclusive conceptual categories like 'fiction', 'text' or 'narrative'. In bookstores as well as academic courses across the world, the novel is already referred to as fiction. As a subtext to this study, therefore, we shall try to examine the theoretical premises behind such views to investigate whether the 'novel' continues to remain a relevant and pertinent literary concept.

Before proceeding, however, let us briefly state that approaches to studying the novel can broadly be divided into three distinct categories. Some literary critics theorize the novel by identifying select novels and deriving the characteristics of the genre and its development through a detailed analysis of those works. There are those who first assume a working definition of the novel and develop theories by identifying novels according to the requirements of their working hypothesis; and then there are others whose studies are primarily theoretical. In this case, we shall primarily rely upon existing theoretical writings on the novel.

One of the most challenging aspects of studying the form is the novel's seemingly endless ability to incorporate formal and thematic features from other literary as well as non-literary genres within its fold. Two of the earliest theorists of the novel, namely, Georg Lukács and Mikhail Bakhtin, perceptively identified this characteristic in their analysis of the genre. In *The Theory of the Novel*, Lukács described the novel as a genre which is in a perpetual state of 'eternally existent becoming'. In 'Epic and Novel', Bakhtin identified 'plasticity' and 'hybridity' as the key tendencies of the novel wherein the genre parodies all other genres by critically incorporating them. Similar views have also been expressed by novelists. For instance, Zola wrote of the novel in the nineteenth century:

> The novel is no longer confined to one special sphere; it has invaded and taken possession of all spheres. Like science, it is the master of the world. It touches on all subjects: writes history; treats of physiology and psychology; rises to the highest flights of poetry; studies the most diverse subjects—politics, social economy, religion, and manners. Entire nature is its domain. It adopts the form which pleases it, taking the tone which seems best, feeling no longer bound by any limit.[8]

Projecting into the future of the novel ten or fifteen years thence, Virginia Woolf also observed, 'That cannibal, the novel, which has devoured so many forms of art will by then have devoured even more.'[9] Subsequent critics have also made similar observations. J.A. Cuddon remarks that the 'subject matter of the novel eludes classification, for it is the hold-all Gladstone bag of literature. No other literary form has proved so pliable and adaptable to a seemingly endless variety of topics and themes'.[10] Marthe Robert argues that the 'novel knows neither rule nor restraint. Open to every possibility, its boundaries fluctuate in all directions'.[11] Malcolm Bradbury calls the novel 'a loose and baggy monster, a form of fictional prose narrative that contains infinite variety'.[12] Edward Said characterizes it as 'an incorporative, quasi-encyclopedic cultural form'.[13] And, Allan H. Pasco emphasizes that '[n]ovels regularly infringe on other genres'.[14]

Despite such observations, to our knowledge, the reasons for the same have not been discussed or explained at any length. The flexibility of the novel is often taken for granted and ignored. One brief explanation was suggested by Terry Eagleton. In his 'Introduction' to *The English Novel*, he described the novel as 'an anarchic genre, since its rule is not to have rules' and linked the novel's anarchy to the ideology of the middle class that 'centres on a dream of total freedom from restraint'.[15] While one may not disagree with Eagleton on the relation between the novel and the middle class, his views on the 'anarchy' of the form and the 'dream of freedom' of the middle class are more difficult to concur with. As we shall discuss later at length, in our view, the middle class is not characterized in history by its firm defence of freedom but by its adeptness at ideologically negotiating both freedoms as well as unfreedoms. We propose that the roots of the incorporative form of the novel can be found in the emergence of the flexible and parasitic milieu of capitalism itself, which not only broke down the rigidities of the older feudal order but also heralded an era wherein strict codes and rules of literary decorum started to fade away. Rooted in the socially diverse and mobile antecedents of the middle class, the novel emerged as the first major literary genre to embody this incorporative, parasitic essence. In the course of this book, we shall try to argue that the apparent anarchy of the form of the novel actually conceals a broad pattern that can be traced by mapping the history of the middle classes in history.

Towards this end, our first chapter broadly surveys some key debates. The problems of existing definitions are discussed along with the divergence of views in tracing the emergence of the genre. The links drawn by different critics between the novel and epic, the novel and romances, and the novel and realism are examined. Related debates about modernism and postmodernism are also included in the investigation. Discussions about the novel vis-à-vis colonialism, nationalism, gender, ideology, print and other media are taken into account. So are the debates on the variable usages of 'novel' and/or 'fiction'. We, thus, try to set out the broad and paradoxical field of the theory of the novel, which provides the backdrop for our subsequent effort to sift out the nature of the genre from among these contesting views. In the same chapter, we also discuss our methodology in some detail, primarily making a distinction between historical and a-historical approaches to studying the genre and outlining the basic assumptions that we carry into this study.

The second chapter examines debates about the rise of the novel. Opinions about the novel's origin are divided between those who trace the novel to early eighteenth-century England and those who trace it to significantly earlier times and places, ranging from medieval Europe, Japan, China, to ancient Greece, Rome and Egypt. Obviously, all these opinions about the novel's rise cannot, simultaneously, be true. What is surprising, however, is the relative dearth of theoretical works that try to deal with this spectrum of irreconcilable views in order to resolve this dispute. We engage with these incompatible differences in order to investigate *when*, *where*, *why* and *how* the novel came up in history. This includes an examination of whether the novel emerged in continuation with earlier genres like epics and romances, or whether it was a significantly new literary genre.

Three texts, which are known to be classics on the rise of the novel, are taken up for this purpose, namely *The Theory of the Novel* (1920) by Georg Lukács, *The Dialogic Imagination: Four Essays* (1934–41) by Mikhail Bakhtin, and *The Rise of the Novel* (1957) by Ian Watt. The views of Marthe Robert, Lennard J. Davis, Nancy Armstrong, Michael McKeon, and Firdaus Azim are also examined. Rooted in different theoretical and historical assumptions, these critics arrive upon significantly different explanations for the emergence of the novel. Lukács argues that the novel came up as a new literary genre in the modern age because of the collapse of the earlier world of the epic. For him, the novel represents and embodies the lost totality and fragmentation of the new world, both in form and in content. Bakhtin traces the origin of the novel to ancient Greece and Rome, arguing that the modern triumph of the form of the novel can be attributed to the analogous development of dialogism and hybridity in the verbal-discursive universe, with the multilingual and polyglot form of the novel embodying this hybrid and dialogic essence. Watt attributes the rise of the novel to individualism, realism and the emergence of the English middle classes. As opposed to the unified worldview of the middle ages, the novel, according to him, is committed to expressing an aggregate view of the world, comprising of particular experiences of particular individuals at particular places in particular times. Robert employs psychoanalysis to link the novel to family romances. Davis associates the novel to the emergence of print culture and capitalism, Armstrong to gender and female individualism, McKeon to progressive and conservative ideological concerns involved in the transition from feudalism to capitalism, and Azim to questions of subjectivity and colonialism. All these debates are contextualized in the historical transition from feudalism to capitalism with reference to a few early English novels in order to draw our conclusions. We propose that any analysis that does not take into account the open-ended and incorporative character of the genre cannot do justice to the rise of the novel debate.

The third chapter is a study of the novel vis-à-vis realism. Realism has been used as an important concept to define, redefine, classify as well as periodize the novel. Many scholars claim that despite significant changes, the single most important characteristic of the novel remains realism, since the intentions of novelists remain wholly realist. They also argue that the novel has reinvented itself through radically different realisms like 'magic realism' and 'hyperrealism'. However, there are others who claim that realism is a dated concept which ran its course more than a hundred years ago—the time when anti-realist assertions began to be made by several modernist novelists. Over the last fifty years or so, several important theoretical works have emerged over the nature of realism as well as narratives wherein critics have argued that realist texts are necessarily fictive, and fictive texts inevitably represent a degree of reality. This chapter examines in detail some important writings, both by theorists of the novel as well as theorists of realism, to argue that the emergence and development of realism in the novel cannot be understood without linking the novel integrally to the changing consciousness and intellectual preoccupations of the middle classes in history.

For this, we first examine in some detail three important concepts, namely 'critical realism' by Lukács, 'mimesis' by Auerbach, and 'formal realism' by Watt. Lukács developed the concept of critical realism most elaborately in his book *Studies in European Realism* (1930), wherein he advocated critical realism as a desirable realist ethic for the novel. The central concept of critical realism for him was the 'type' which organically binds together both the general as well as the particular in creating characters as well as situations. In *Mimesis: The Representations of Reality in Western Literature* (1946), Auerbach developed his exhaustive thesis on the development of realism in the Western world. He examined the development of mimesis in writings ranging from *Odyssey* and *The Bible* (Old Testament) to modern novels by Virginia Woolf, by identifying and studying the development of two ancient styles of representing reality, 'separation of styles' and 'mixture of styles'. 'Separation of styles' is characterized by the belief that everyday reality can find description in literature only in comic, low or intermediary genres, whereas, 'mixture of styles' does not necessarily restrict realistic descriptions to low genres. Watt developed the concept of formal realism in *The Rise of the Novel* (1957) where he argued that the key thrust of formal realism is to embody the circumstantial view of life through the techniques of authentic reporting of human experience, detailing of story, individuality of actors, particularity of time and space, and referentiality of language. He proposed that formal realism is the lowest common denominator of the form of the novel and its temper is critical, anti-traditional and innovating. Along with these, some major debates about realism and the novel over the last century or so are also examined in this chapter in two sections: the period raging from 1880s to 1940s, and the period ranging from 1950s to contemporary times. Major modernist and postmodern debates about realism, including significant contributions made by Roland Barthes, Fredric Jameson, Linda Hutcheon and Jean Baudrillard are taken up—an appraisal that helps understand, that despite diverse claims, the evolution of positions on realism is perhaps not as radically different or sharp as is made out to be. The chapter is concluded by delineating the aesthetic and ethic of pro-realist positions and the premises behind relatively anti-realist positions.

The fourth chapter evaluates the development of the novel vis-à-vis both its 'external' as well as 'internal' history. As is known, the novel did not always enjoy the favour of the literary establishment. During its early years, the novel existed in considerable disrepute because of its controversial choice of subjects like prostitutes, thieves, social outcasts and other social misfits. The novel slowly gained in respectability over a period of time and it was only by the mid-twentieth century that it came to enjoy a central place in the literary establishment. But just about when the novel started gaining respectability in the literary canon, it also started getting divided into 'high' and 'low' novels, or what were considered as novels for the 'refined' taste as opposed to those for mass or popular consumption. Hence, only selective novels found a place in the corridors of culture. With the enormous spread of mass media over the past few decades, the primacy of the printed word itself stands challenged within the cultural field. By now, many critics have started calling the novel a minor cultural form compared to the film or the video. We seek to understand the reasons behind this interesting trajectory of the novel in the literary canon by examining developments in bourgeois culture in history.

Two interesting yet contradictory aspects of the development of the novel are taken up for discussion. While the novel has been continually plagued by predictions about its demise or death, it has simultaneously also been associated with a sense of constant newness. Novelists no less than Leo Tolstoy, Milan Kundera and V.S. Naipaul have predicted the end of the novel. On the other hand, the developing nomenclature of the novel exemplifies a sense of constant regeneration and novelty. For instance, that novel was first called 'Novel', literally meaning new, then 'New Novel' by Henry James at the turn of the twentieth century, then 'Nouveau Roman' or new novel by Robbe-Grillet and others in the mid-twentieth century, and subsequently 'New New Novel' by Philip Sollers by the late twentieth century. All these represent different stages in the development of the novel. We argue that the vacillation of the novel between these two extremes—of ever dying and ever rejuvenating—is linked to the print culture, the literary market and the modern era's fetish with the new on the one hand, and periodic challenges posed to middle class imaginings and value systems on the other. Additionally, specific aspects and reasons behind more contemporary notions of the exhaustion of the genre are examined alongside the theories of intertextuality, simulacra, etc., to locate this interesting paradox.

Next we study the novel through major developments in its techniques and themes alongside the evolution of its dominant typology of early, realist, modernist and postmodern novels. This involves the contentious area of debate between modernism and postmodernism. While some scholars like Jean-Francois Lyotard and Alex Callinicos argue that they represent the deepening of the same continuing essence, others like Brian McHale and David Harvey argue that they are fundamentally and integrally opposed to each other. Drawing attention to the complex and ideologically contested nature of the modernist movement as opposed to what is generally known today, we suggest that a more holistic view of modernist trends in art and literature is required to make more accurate assessments about both modernism and postmodernism.

The development of the techniques and themes of the novel are then traced with reference to the evolution of the increasingly fragmenting individual subject in the novel. The early novel was distinct from previous narrative forms because it was about the 'individual' subject delineated on the basis of personality traits or individual characteristics, as opposed to earlier 'heroes/heroines' known by their deeds, actions or station in life. Over time, this individual subject fragmented into stages of childhood, youth and old age. A sense of private and public selves also evolved followed by a more developed sense of the socio-historical context. Then the individual developed a sense of the psychological that paved way for depicting the interior as well as unconscious or subconscious life. In today's times, the individual has fragmented into many more phases of life like pre-teen or late teen years, midlife crisis, etc., alongside developing an acute sense of self-reflexivity about the 'act' of thinking, feeling, speaking, etc. Paranoia, schizophrenia, amnesia, etc., are often found to be more appropriate by novelists for depicting the nature of reality today. We trace this evolution of the fragmenting individual subject to understand the developments in the literary techniques and themes of the form over time.

In the last section of this chapter, we try to develop our most complex argument about the novel. While the novel is indeed characterized by an inclusive and incorporative tendency since the days of its inception and across its multifarious development and spread, just this hardly suffices as a suitable definitional characteristic. After all, the novel, if it were free to the point of arbitrariness and complete lack of restrictions, would cease to remain a genre and would become all literature in itself. Therefore, we try to discern a pattern in the generic incorporations made by the novel over time by delineating those literary genres and themes which the novel excludes, as well as those which it includes. The development of the novel is traced vis-à-vis the twin tendencies of centralization and fragmentation in modern history. We attribute some aspects of the novel to developments in the print industry and the centralized nature of the world under capitalism. Others are attributed to greater fragmentation in the consciousness of people. This dichotomy, the centralization of the world and the fragmentation of the individual subject, is then employed to examine a broad pattern of selective inclusions and exclusions vis-à-vis rural, folk, national, pan-European, colonial or postcolonial literary and cultural forms within the fold of the Western novel.

In the last chapter, we examine select aspects of the novel in India in its multilingual terrain. Theorists of the novel have pointed out that unlike the early European novel which was demarcated by the development of realism, the early novel in India was dominated by the melodramatic, sensational, didactic and historical modes. To understand this interesting feature, we devote some attention to tracing the evolution of the middle classes in India during the nineteenth century. We identify a two-fold process of evolution. First, as a nascent intellectual and professional class that arose through exposure to Western education and colonial administration, followed by a second phase of relatively rapid expansion during the second half of the nineteenth century reflected in the massive spread of education in the vernaculars. The second phase, we argue, was crucially propelled by the development of domestic industrialization within the colonial setup. This phase is the key to understanding the novel's popularity in various Indian languages after the 1860s. However, more than the timing, it is the nature of this development that explains the formal and thematic concerns contained within early novels in India. While the middle class arose in the West in the process of capitalist development that was essentially anti-feudal in its ethos, in India, domestic capitalism developed in an ethos that was anti-colonial, but not necessarily anti-feudal. This difference is examined at some length in the chapter to understand the notably different intellectual and cultural concerns of the Indian middle classes as well as their early preferences in novels.

We also examine the late development of the novel in colonial south India. It is significant that the region experienced an earlier introduction to print compared to the other regions of India. The Madras Presidency also had slightly better literacy records compared to the Calcutta or Bombay Presidencies. The region was also exposed to a much longer and diverse Western influence. However, despite a few notable early novels, the form took a considerable time developing and gaining in popularity in the four southern languages of Tamil, Malayalam, Kannada and Telugu. We try to locate this late development of the novel in the context of delayed development of industrial capitalism and bourgeois consciousness in the region.

This theme is carried further to explore the paucity of the novel form in Urdu. Despite a few outstanding early examples in the late nineteenth century, the novel form was overtaken by the Urdu short story after the 1930s. Since then, the short story has remained more central to Urdu fiction than the novel. To understand this interesting phenomenon, we first situate the Urdu language in context and then try to trace the colonial and postcolonial trajectory of the Urdu reading middle classes. We argue that the conditions conducive for the development of the novel in Urdu still do not exist.

The last section of this chapter is an examination of the continuing unease in India with Indian-English novels, particularly the globalized variety. Various factors have been invoked to articulate this discontent—the privileged status of English language, issues of location, content, postmodern moorings, ideology, etc. A contrast is often made vis-à-vis *bhasha* novels. After examining some notable views in this regard, we try to situate the arrival of the globalized Indian-English novel in the context of the period after the 1980s with the beginning of convergence between sections of the Indian middle classes and the West over neoliberalism. Three novels are examined in some detail, namely, *Midnight's Children* (1980), *The God of Small Things* (1997) and *Sea of Poppies* (2008), all of which belong to varying traditions of dissent with neoliberalism. Despite differences, we argue that the stratification of the middle classes in neoliberal India lies at the root of this deep unease. While some sections of the Indian middle classes are linked to the most advanced outposts of capitalism, others are still joining its ranks as relative newcomers to the class. The differences in the intellectual and cultural milieux of these different sections, we argue, can no longer be viewed in terms of simple linguistic differences between English and *bhasha* traditions. The need for addressing some of these differences more consciously is emphasized for better mutual evaluation and appreciation.

This book is necessitated by the fact that the field of theoretical studies of the novel today is divided mainly into two types of work. On the one hand are anthologies that contain excerpts by different theorists but leave the task of juxtaposing and discerning the nature of the novel from among these divergent views up to the reader; and on the other are detailed archival studies that focus on only particular aspects, periods or types of novels. For students of literature, this study may provide a useful overview of theoretical debates. Varying views are constantly juxtaposed to arrive upon conclusions. The reader may benefit from a critical evaluation of both—the development of the novel as well as the theories employed to understand the genre. In negotiating our way through various theoretical views, the attempt is to connect the dots and reconstruct a holistic sense of the genre from among these assorted views. While this may be easier said than done, we hope that the reader would gain from this approach to learn more about the novel, both in the West as well as in India.

Notes

1. Georg Lukács, *The Theory of the Novel*, tr. A. Bostock, London: Merlin Press, 1971, p. 73.
2. M.M. Bakhtin, 'Epic and Novel: Toward a Methodology for the Study of the Novel', in *Essentials of the Theory of Fiction*, ed. Michael J. Hoffman and Patrick D. Murphy, Durham and London: Duke University Press, 1988, pp. 53–4.
3. Raymond Williams, *The Long Revolution*, Westport, Connecticut: Greenwood Press Publishers, 1961, p. 278.
4. Fredric Jameson, *The Political Unconscious: Narrative as a Socially Symbolic Act*, Ithaca and New York: Cornell University Press, 1981, pp. 143, 151.
5. Christopher Gillie, *Longman Companion to English Literature*, London: Longman, 1972, p. 197.
6. Lennard J. Davis, *Resisting Novels: Ideology and Fiction*, New York and London: Methuen, 1987, p. 225.
7. Terry Eagleton, *The English Novel: An Introduction*, Malden: Blackwell Publishing, 2005, p. 1.
8. Emile Zola, 'Naturalism on the Stage', 1871, in *Modernism: An Anthology of Sources and Documents*, ed. Vassiliki Kolocotroni, Jane Goldman, and Olga Taxidou, Edinburgh: Edinburgh University Press, 1998, pp. 169–74.
9. Virginia Woolf, 'The Narrow Bridge Of Art', 1927, 1958, in *Modernism: An Anthology*, ed. Lawrence Rainey, Malden, MA and Oxford: Wiley-Balckwell, 2005, p. 907.
10. J.A. Cuddon, *The Penguin Dictionary of Literary Terms and Literary Theory*, London: Penguin Books, 1976, p. 600.
11. Marthe Robert, *Origins of the Novel*, 1972; tr. Sacha Rabinovitch, Sussex: The Harvester Press, 1980, p. 5.

12. Malcolm Bradbury, *The Modern British Novel*, London: Secker & Warburg, 1993, p. x.
13. Edward Said, *Culture and Imperialism*, New York: Vintage Books, 1994, p. 71.
14. Allan H. Pasco, *Inner Workings of the Novel: Studying a Genre*, New York: Palgrave Macmillan, 2010, p. 18.
15. Eagleton, *The English Novel*, p. 2.

CHAPTER ONE

Theories of the Novel

Some Debates

Problems of Definition

LET US FIRST look at some common definitions of the novel. *The Concise Oxford Dictionary of Current English* defines the novel as a 'fictitious prose narrative of book length portraying characters and actions credibly representative of real life in continuous plot'. As defined by *Encyclopaedia Britannica*, the novel is a 'genre of fiction (i.e. prose works created by the imagination), of considerable length and some complexity, in which characters (usually but not always human beings) interact with one another in a specific setting'; while *The Encyclopaedia Americana* explains the novel as a 'twentieth century generic term for any type of prose fiction of book length in which characters and actions are presented in a plot as if representing persons and events in real life'.

It can be argued, therefore, that the key features of the novel are 'prose', 'length', 'narrative', 'character', 'action', 'plot', 'realism' and 'fiction'. Examples, however, can always be cited of novels which are in verse (Vikram Seth's *The Golden Gate*, 1986), are relatively short (Ernest Hemingway's *The Old Man and The Sea*, 1952), openly profess lack of action and plot (as is found in modernist novels), avoid narrative and characterization (in postmodernist novels), rebel against realism (both modernist and postmodernist novels) or are non-fiction novels (Truman Capote's *In Cold Blood*, 1965; Primo Levi's *The Periodic Table*, 1975; or V.S. Naipaul's *Journey to Nowhere*, 1980).[1] As Mikhail Bakhtin says, 'experts have not managed to isolate a single definite, stable characteristic of the novel—without adding a reservation, which immediately disqualifies it altogether as a generic characteristic'.[2] *Collier's Encyclopedia* also notes that the novel 'has taken so many shapes, particularly in the last hundred years, that any more precise definition would eliminate a good proportion of works called by the name'.

Allan H. Pasco argues that 'The hope of contriving a definition of the novel that will be discrete and remain useful until the end of time will be possible only when the novel dies as a genre.'[3] Does it mean then, that while dealing with the novel we have to be content with the familiar maxim 'exceptions only prove the rule' and continue with, more or less, the same definition of the novel? Or, is it possible to identify certain key features, which can capture the difficult and dynamic nature of the novel within the bounds of classification? Defining the novel has become more difficult subsequent to modernist and postmodern innovations in the techniques of writing. The main approach towards understanding the genre, therefore, shall include looking at elements of continuity and change between early, realist, modernist and postmodern novels.

Emergence of the Novel

Let us, however, begin at the beginning. A sharp division exists among novel critics over the dating of the novel. Many agree that with the exception of Miguel de Cervantes' *Don Quixote* written in Spain in 1605, the novel arose in early eighteenth-century England with works such as *Robinson Crusoe* (1719) and *Moll Flanders* (1722) by Daniel Defoe, *Gulliver's Travels* (1726) by Jonathan Swift, *Pamela* (1740) and *Clarissa* (1747, 1748) by Samuel Richardson, *Joseph Andrews* (1742), *Jonathan Wild* (1743) and *Tom Jones* (1749) by Henry Fielding, etc.

Critics like Ian Watt in *The Rise of the Novel*, Michael McKeon in *The Origins of the English Novel 1600–1740*, Lennard J. Davis in *Factual Fictions: The Origin of the English Novel*, Marthe Robert in *Origins of the Novel* and Nancy Armstrong in *Desire and Domestic Fiction* offer very different theories about the origin of the novel but date it more or less to the same works. Jane Spencer in *The Rise of the Woman Novelist* traces the origin of the novel a little back to Aphra Behn's *Oroonoko* (1688) arguing that 'women's role in the novel's rise has been underestimated'[4] and that it were women, in fact, who pioneered the genre. Firdous Azim offers an interesting thesis in *The Colonial Rise of the Novel* arguing that the novel arose in the process of identifying/locating the European subject's 'self' vis-à-vis the colonial/racial/gendered 'other' at a time when intense debates were taking place in England about language and subjectivity. She, too, locates the rise of the novel to Behn's *Oroonoko*. Walter Allen in *The English Novel* traces the origin of the novel to John Bunyan's *The Pilgrim's Progress* (1678) arguing that it was 'not so different in form from the conventional picaresque novel'.[5]

Contrary to these critics, who share a consensus over the rise of the novel in modern England and have disputes only over a difference of a decade or two, there are those who trace the origin of the novel back to ancient Japan, China, Arabia, Greece and Rome. Gilbert Phelps, for instance, in *A Short Guide to the World Novel: From Myth to Modernism* argues that the novel has non-European origins in various national and linguistic cultures of the world, independent and in spite of the colonizers. He traces the novel to twelfth-century Japan and fifteenth-century China. Mikhail Bakhtin traces the origins of the novel to second century AD to Heliodorus's *Aethiopica*, Achilles Tatius's *Leucippe and Clitophon*, Chiriton's *Chareas and Callirhoe*, Xenophon of Ephesus's *Ephesiaca* and Longus's *Daphnis and Chloe*.[6] J.A. Cuddon traces the novel up to as far back as twelfth-century BC Egypt to works like *The Princess of Backstaw*, *The Pedestrian Prince* and *Sinuhe*.[7] A similar train of argument is provided by Margaret Anne Doody in *The True Story of the Novel*, wherein she traces the origin of the novel to ancient works like *Xenophon* (*c.* 428–*c.* 354 BC) and *Cyropaedia* (pre-354 BC) and also to early Chinese and Japanese novels. She argues that 'Romance' and 'Novel' are essentially the same narrative form and their distinction is a modern invention born out of a kind of British and European chauvinism in staking claims to the origin of the genre, obscuring the contributions of dark-skinned people, Muslims and others. She differs from the ancient emergence and modern re-emergence theory of Bakhtin, however, to propose that 'the Novel as a form of literature in the West has a continuous history of about two thousand years'.[8]

Thus, at two ends of the spectrum, critical opinions are separated by nearly three thousand years in tracing the origins of the novel. Walter Allen has a telling comment to make about this unsettling difference in his 'Introduction' to *The English Novel*:

> Literary historians, horrified it seems by the newness of the form, have commonly thought it necessary to provide the novel with a respectable antiquity. . . . In their eagerness to supply the novel with a dignified ancestry they have behaved rather like a man who, setting out to write a history of the motor-car, should think it proper to begin by devoting a third of his space to the evolution of the ox-cart.[9]

This great divide in tracing the origin of the novel is based upon how critics approach or define the novel, on why they include certain works within the novel genre and exclude certain others, and of course on how they deal with questions relating to the 'origin', 'beginning' or 'rise' of the novel. These three terms have slightly different connotations and have been employed differently by scholars for studying the novel. Let us broadly examine their variable usage.

'Origin'

The modern interest in the study of 'origins' gained currency at the beginning of the twentieth century, which saw tremendous advances in linguistics, sociology and anthropology as disciplines of study. These disciplines, along with psychoanalysis, emphasized discovering 'primitive' origins of language, literature, culture and society. Subsequent developments in new criticism and structuralism also led to a special interest in myths, storytelling, fables, modes, motifs, narratives and folktales as categories for understanding social phenomenon. Several major trends in linguistics, anthropology, psychoanalysis and structuralism involve a study of 'pre-historic' origins, which see development or history as a continuation or variation of essentially the same themes and features. A comprehension of origins and, thereby, the fundamental structures of society, for them, explains reality better than historicist or evolutionary accounts. Freud, for example, is invoked by Marthe Robert in *Origins of the Novel* in her argument that 'the Oedipus complex is a universal human phenomenon, all fiction, invention and image making express it more or less explicitly.... The novel is only one 'Oedipal' form among many others...'.[10] She goes on to argue that all writing is variation of the romance. The way that the novel is distinct is that it derives 'the violence of its desires and its irrepressible freedom from the Family Romance'[11] and, therefore, re-enacts the oedipal storyline. Gilbert Phelps employs the concept of 'myths' to understand the novel and its development across different civilizations and nations of the world. Tracing the development of the novel to ancient times Margaret Anne Doody explains, 'This book is an attempt to trace connections rather than to assert divisions.... If I emphasize continuities, it is because discontinuity, absolute division, has been harshly and hastily asserted before now. The fences have been too sturdy or too barbed—it is good sometimes to leap over fences, or even to break them down.'[12] Such critics, therefore, study 'origins' in order to discern some continuing structure or essence in the novel.

'Beginning'

'Beginnings' is a notion, which has been used by theorists like Michel Foucault and Edward Said in a slightly different sense than 'origins'. While they too view history as a continuum, instead of absolute origins, they look for discernible beginnings, ruptures or transformations in the 'knowable' past. This past can be grasped 'archeologically' through the study of 'discourse'. Discourse analysis is essential for interpreting or understanding all reality, particularly history. Nothing exists outside text and discourse, and neither does the novel. This approach, elucidated by Foucault in *The Archaeology of Knowledge* (1969) and *Discipline and Punish* (1975), and by Said in *Beginnings: Intention and Method* (1975), is invoked by Lennard J. Davis in *Factual Fictions*. Davis argues that while emerging in the early modern period, the novel is a discourse marked by a constitutive ambivalence towards fact and fiction. He links the beginning of the novel to journalistic writings, instead of romance, through an archaeological study of the discourse of journalism. He uses a method wherein the 'first and pre-eminent notion in any methodology of beginnings is that of the threshold',[13] and locates the emergence of the novel in the tensions and trends within journalistic writings. Roland Barthes, a structuralist and later post-structuralist theorist, in his famous essay 'Writing and the Novel' (1953) examines the novel as a narrative characterized by the 'serial story' or 'teleology', and the use of 'third person' account, which together creates a false sense of order, familiarity, universality and security among its readers. He argues that 'Narration is a form common to both the Novel and to History'[14] and discusses the similarities between them. Barthes, in fact, makes the claim that by virtue of sharing a basic narrative function of constructing false worlds, there exist practically no differences between cosmogonies, myths, histories or novels.

'*Rise*'

We come now to the third of the proposed concepts. Significantly different from these two notions of origin or beginning, is the notion of 'rise' used by historicists who reject timeless and universal standards in order to emphasize the periodicity of individuals, events, cultural phenomena, etc. They include a sense of process in understanding the past, and identify qualitative shifts. For them, literary texts make sense only when they are located in their contexts. Ian Watt in *The Rise of the Novel* argues that there exists a close social connection between the development of the novel and the English middle classes. He proposes that a wide range of factors like greater social mobility, urbanism, greater sexual equality, decline of feudal patronage, rise of publishing houses, growing rates of literacy, developing notions of private leisure as well as the influence of materialist writings of Locke and Descartes leading to the rise of formal realism and the ideology of secular individualism, were responsible for the rise of the novel.

While none of these concepts can simplistically be associated to some exclusive method, Frederic Jameson offers further insight into the concepts of looking at all things past in the 'Preface' to *The Political Unconscious*:

> ... traditional dialectics teaches us, the historicising operation can follow two distinct paths, which only ultimately meet in the same place: the path of the object and the path of the subject, the historical origins of the things themselves and that more intangible historicity of the concepts and categories by which we attempt to understand those things.[15]

The field of studying novels is similar—there is the history of the novel itself and the history of the concepts and theories employed to study novels. Sometimes they throw up unusual results. For instance, Mikhail Bakhtin in 'Forms of time and of the Chronotope in the Novel' (1937–8) uses Einstein's mathematical category of 'chronotope' to come to terms with the novel. He gives the name chronotope (time-space) 'to the intrinsic connectedness of temporal and spatial relationship that are artistically expressed in literature'.[16] Bakhtin views the chronotope as a formally constitutive category of literature that has intrinsic generic significance, gives character to each genre, defines it as well as distinguishes it from other genres. He studies different chronotopes of the novel like 'the road', 'the path of life', 'mystery', etc., which are produced in time and are reinforced by tradition. His approach can be located in the general temper of scientism prevailing in his times, when different critics sought to establish almost a science of the craft of literature.

The basic purpose of this brief discussion is to underscore the point that both novels as well as literary theories have a bearing on each other and a critical examination of both will be employed in resolving the debates about the rise and development of the novel. But before doing so, let us look at some other debates.

The Paradoxes

Epic and the Novel

One of the major trends in understanding novels is to compare them to epics. In the compilation of his lectures entitled *Aesthetics* (1842), G.W.F. Hegel argues that art forms characterize stages in the history of consciousness. While epic is an expression of an unorganized heroic age, symbolizing an organic unity between people, nature and society, the novel belongs to a later stage in which the symmetry between mind and matter is shattered. The novel, therefore, strives for a unity, which is denied to it by the very nature of reality. For Hegel, the modern age itself is antithetical to art. The novel embodies the contradiction between art and the modern world, or what he specifically calls the contradiction between 'the poetry of the heart and the opposing prose of circumstances and the accidents of external situations'.[17] Hegel suggests that the novel is a kind of 'modern popular epic', or a descendent of epic thereby, laying the foundation for future critics of the novel to see continuity as well as opposition between forms of the epic and the novel.

Using Hegelian categories, the pre-Marxist Georg Lukács employs a method in *The Theory of the Novel*, which he later called 'abstract synthesis' to come to terms with the novel. He finds it essential to compare the novel to the epic. Lukács argues that while in the epic, men are at home in the universe without having a sense of themselves as unique individuals, the novel is an expression of 'transcendental homelessness' or man's alienation or estrangement from the world. For Lukács, the 'novel is the epic of an age in which the extensive totality of life is no longer directly given, in which the immanence of meaning in life has become a problem, yet which still thinks in terms of totality'.[18] He further explains, 'The epic gives form to a totality of life that is rounded from within; the novel seeks, by giving form, to uncover and construct the concealed totality of life.'[19] Unlike the novel, the hero of the epic is never an individual in the strict sense and its theme is not about personal destiny but the destiny of a community. The material of the novel is of a 'discrete, unlimited nature' while that of the epic is a 'continuum—like infinity'.[20] The novel is the epic of a world which has been 'abandoned by God'[21] and which tells the adventures of interiority. Its hero is always a seeker who tries to reconcile the paradoxical nature of the world. Some great novels, he notes, have a tendency to overlap with the epic and capture its unity.

Mikhail Bakhtin in 'Epic and Novel' contrasts the epic, a genre which has completed its development, with the novel which is 'the only developing genre and therefore it reflects more deeply, more essentially, more sensitively and rapidly, reality itself in the process of its unfolding'.[22] He argues that the contrast between the epic and the novel has been made primarily to criticize 'epic heroization' on the one hand and to elevate the status of the novel vis-à-vis contemporary literature on the other. The epic world, for him, contains a single unified worldview, while the novel contains possibilities of multiple realities. The hero of the epic does not exist outside his destiny or fate, while the hero of the novel is an individual dealing with the 'inconclusive present-day reality'.[23] Bakhtin suggests that the novel and the epic are characterized by two rival impulses of 'novelness' and 'epicness' which can dominate literature from time to time and need not occur in any strict historical sequence.

Ralph Fox in *The Novel and the People* also compares the novel to the epic calling it 'The epic art form of our modern, bourgeois society.'[24] Christopher Hill, in *Writing and Revolution in Seventeenth Century England* (1985), observes that the 'novel is to bourgeois society what the epic had been to feudal society'.[25] The key values of the epic, for him, are military courage, honour and chivalry, and from the seventeenth century onwards, he argues that 'no significant poet' has written epics. Ian Watt in *The Rise of the Novel* devotes one whole chapter called 'Fielding and the Epic Theory of the Novel' to debunk Fielding's classification of *Joseph Andrews* as 'a comic epic poem in prose'. He disputes the tendency to read the novel vis-à-vis the epic:

> ... it is surely evident that ... the epic is, after all, an oral and poetic genre dealing with the public and usually remarkable deeds of historical or legendry persons engaged in a collective rather than an individual enterprise; and none of these things can be said of the novel.[26]

Franco Moretti, in *Modern Epic* (1996), uses Hegel's definition of the epic to argue that well known novels like *Ulysses* or *Hundred Years of Solitude* are, in fact, epics that have been wrongly classified as novels in a novel-centric literary world.[27] Joseph Frank in 'Spatial Form in Modern Novel' (1945) also classifies *Ulysses* and *A Portrait of the Artist as a Young Man* as epics.[28]

Thus, opinion is divided between those who view epics and novels as essentially similar or comparable, and those who view the two as clearly distinct. While most critics identify epics and novels as the narrative form of different historical ages, there are others who do not maintain such a distinction.

Romances and the Novel

Another theme in novel theory is that of reading the novel in relation to the romances. The term novel stabilized in common use only by the late eighteenth century. Before that, almost all early English novelists labelled their works differently, but defined them almost inevitably against the romance. For instance, Samuel Richardson writes, 'What a duce, do you think I am writing a Romance? Don't you see that I am copying Nature?....'[29] Or, Henry Fielding writes, 'I think it may very reasonably be required of every writer, that he keeps within the bounds of possibility....'[30] Clara Reeve in *The Progress of Romance Through Times, Centuries and Manners* (1785) explains that the word 'Novel' was first used to distinguish works of prose fiction from the 'Romance'. She elaborates that while the 'Romance' is a heroic fable, which deals with fabulous persons and things in lofty and elevated language, the 'Novel' presents a picture of real life and manners in contemporary times in order to deceive the readers into believing that everything is real.

Northrop Frye in *Anatomy of Criticism* also discusses the genre of the novel by counter posing it against the romance. He argues that the novel creates 'real people' while the romance gives rise to 'stylized figures which expand into psychological archetypes'.[31] According to him, this difference in the conception of characterization is the main difference between the novel and the romance. Undercutting all generic categories, however, he argues that 'there is hardly any modern romance that could not be made out to be a novel, and vice versa'.[32] This logic is carried forward by Hubert McDernott in *Novel and Romance* wherein he places the works of Richardson and Fielding in a continuing tradition of fiction, arguing against any break in the literary tradition of prose fiction. Geoffrey Day in *From Fiction to the Novel* also argues that unlike popular conception 'the Novel is but a modern modification of the same ingredients which constitute the romance . . .'.[33] While Marthe Robert observes that the novel has '*a compulsory content and an optional form*',[34] the compulsory content being that of Family Romances, Michael McKeon argues that the development of the novel follows the resolution of the romance genre into a contest between 'romance' and 'historical' elements, or what he calls 'the double reversal of romance idealism by naïve empiricism and of both by extreme scepticism'.[35] This dialectics, he proposes, brings about the historicist revolution and therefore, the tendency of accurate description in prose writing. Critics of the novel, therefore, either view the novel as a genre which develops in opposition to the themes and concerns of the romances and is, therefore, notably different from the romances, or they see a continuity between the novel and the romance and thereby, analyse their similarities.

Realism and the Novel

Another important factor in characterizing the novel is 'realism'. Ian Watt states that 'the lowest common denominator of the novel genre as a whole . . . [is] formal realism'.[36] For him, realism differentiates the novel from all previous fiction, and the novel as a form challenges all literary traditionalism, both of classicism and medievalism. Its new modern temper is critical, anti-traditional and innovating, its method—that of getting to the truth through individual experience. According to Watt, this individual experience or the circumstantial view of life, when expressed in a narrative, is called formal realism. Walter Allen also writes, 'From its very nature the novel demands a greater or less degree of realism, of fidelity to the facts of the world as men commonly see them.'[37] Henry James in 'The Art of Fiction' (1884) says that 'the air of reality (solidity of specification) seems to me to be the supreme virtue of a novel—the merit on which all its other merits . . . helplessly and submissively depend'.[38] Lionel Trilling in 'Manners, Morals, and the Novel' (1950) observes that 'The novel . . . is a perpetual quest for reality. . . .'[39] Realism, for Georg Lukács, is so crucial to the novel that in *Studies in European Realism* (1930) he practically studies all developments and trends in the novel through changes in approaches to realism. He treats realism as almost synonymous with a good novel, for it is, for him, a concept that can achieve a comprehensive description of the totality of society.[40]

Many critics, however, argue against studying the novel in terms of the concept of realism. Marthe Robert, for example, uses psychoanalysis to argue that the truth of the novel relies upon the success of the delusion/fantasy it can pass off as reality. With the development of narratology and deconstruction, more and more critics as well as novelists have been emphasizing that the deliberate techniques of creating realist texts are ultimately acts of subjective construction. However, despite fierce debates, realism has continued to be debated and asserted vis-à-vis the novel. Lucien Goldman in *Towards a Sociology of the Novel* (1964) criticizes Robbe-Grillet's ideas about nouveau romans to argue that writers like 'Nathalie Sarraute and Robbe-Grillet are among the most radically realistic writers in contemporary French literature'[41] because they seek to represent a new and distinct human reality of our times in self-admittedly different, rigorous and radical ways. David Lodge in *The Novelist at the Crossroads* (1971) insists on a precise overlap between realism and the novel.The novel, he asserts, is not dead therefore realism too lives on. George Levine in 'Realism Reconsidered' (1974) argues that despite claims to anti-realism, realism as a way of looking at the world, a kind of metaphysic continues to thrive in the modern novel. According to him, realism is a central mode of the novel that has been 'radically revised' by writers in response to new challenges and transformations.[42] Raymond Williams in *The Long Revolution* proposes a 'possible new meaning of realism'.[43] He argues that every day, ordinary reality is now conceived differently; and although new techniques have been developed to describe this new reality, the intentions of novelists remain wholly realist. It is also interesting to note that realism has often been employed in academic scholarship to both classify as well as periodize the novel. As a result, university papers all over the world are often classified into the early/proto-realist novel, the realist novel, the modernist and the postmodern novel.

Nation, Colonialism and the Novel

Critics also examine the novel vis-à-vis colonialism, imperialism, eurocentricism, racism, nationalism or orientalism. Marthe Robert in *Origins of the Novel* argues that the novel became a dominant genre 'mainly due to its encroachments on neighbouring territories it surreptitiously infiltrated, gradually colonizing almost all literature'.[44] As a result it is 'similar in many respects to the imperialistic society from which it sprang . . . it is irresistibly drawn towards the universal and the absolute, towards generalisation of events and ideas'.[45] Edward Said also claims in *Culture and Imperialism* that 'imperialism and the novel fortified each other to such degree that it is impossible . . . to read one without in some way dealing with the other'.[46] Benedict Anderson in *Imagined Communities* (1983) goes on to relate the rise of the novel to the rise of modern nationalism. The nation, he argues, acquires a historical place and status only after becoming conscious of nationalism. The novel, for Anderson, along with the newspaper, plays a significant role in 're-presenting' the imagined community of the nation. As a genre, it acquires a coherence, which is marked by its function in creating a 'nation-idea'.[47]

Over the past few decades, the postcolonial novel has received greater focus and attention. Salman Rushdie in his essay 'In Defence of the Novel, Yet Again' (1996) proposes, 'Might it not be simply that a new novel is emerging—a postcolonial novel, a decentred, transnational, interlingual, cross-cultural novel—and that in this new world order, or disorder, we find a better explanation of the contemporary novel's health?. . . .'[48] Eleanor McNees carries this idea further to observe in *The Development of the Novel* (2006)—'Recently, writers and critics have advocated the notion of the global novel, one that has shed its Anglo- and Eurocentric roots in favour of a broader cultural and aesthetic view. Significantly, many of the advocates of this new novel are not white Europeans or Americans.'[49]

Thus, while some theorists try to uncover the prejudices and stereotypes contained in novels, some others study the role played by the novel in building or subverting the nation or colonialism; yet others link the form of the novel to the 'form' of colonialism/imperialism, and some identify the postcolonial novel as the source of the contemporary novel's vigour.

Women and the Novel

The debates about the novel take another turn in relation to women. Feminist critics have explored the links between the novel and the role/status of women in history. Nancy Armstrong in *Desire and Domestic Fiction* (1987) argues that the novel arose in the modern age in an era of individualism, which, contrary to popular perception, was heralded by women. While men continued to retain their political/public identity, it were women who developed an individualism signified by differences in emotional natures. Armstrong argues that the rise of the novel was based 'upon a struggle to say what made a woman desirable'[50] and that the novel, during the early eighteenth century, forged the individuality of females. Rosalind Miles in *The Female Form* (1987) argues that 'women and the novel have been particularly important to one another',[51] because the novel is the only form in which women 'have contributed on anything like equal terms with men'.[52] She reiterates how the practice of the nineteenth century in which women writers had to disguise their female identity in order to make their novels acceptable, was, in fact, a reversal of the early eighteenth century practice when male authors did the same in order to get their novels published. From the 1960s onwards, feminist critics have taken a lot of interest in the novel arguing that the novel is a genre 'of', 'for' and 'by' women. Some important works in this regard are Elaine Showalter's *A Literature of Their Own* (1977), Sandra Gilber and Susan Gubar's *The Madwoman in the Attic* (1979), Patricia Stubbs—*Women and Fiction* (1979) and Terry Lovell's *Consuming Fiction* (1987).

There are debates and contrary views held, however, by feminist critics. For instance, Jane Spencer, in *The Rise of the Women Novelist*, accepts that women novelists played a very important and path-breaking role in the development of the novel. But, she argues that the proliferation of women writers did not necessarily mean greater powers for women in general. Giving an explanation, which she herself calls 'paradoxical', Spencer proposes that while women writers were rising in numbers in the eighteenth century their general condition was deteriorating—'Women's writing is not the same thing as women's rights.'[53] Countering critics like Armstrong and Spencer, Catherine Gallagher in *Nobody's Story* (1994) argues against the notion that 'women writers gained acceptance and prestige . . . only by constructing a discourse that 'reformed' women by locking them into a disciplinary domestic sphere'.[54] She forwards the thesis that 'many women writers emphasized their femininity to gain financial advantage and that, in the process, they invented and popularized numerous ingenious similarities between their gender and their occupation. Far from disavowing remunerative authorship as unfeminine, they relentlessly embraced and feminized it.'[55] Helene Moglen in *The Trauma of Gender* (2001) also underscores that 'It was in the novel, more than any other expressive form, that the social and psychological meanings of gender difference were most extensively negotiated and exposed.'[56] Thus, the novel and women have been seen as closely interrelated, with some critics focusing more on studying women writers and others on women subjects. But the main differences lies in assessing the impact of novels on the lives of women.

Print, Other Media and the Novel

Critics have also examined the development of literature in terms of media—oral, written, performance, print, radio, film and internet, with each affecting or contesting the other, throwing up its own genres and causing related mutations in the formal characteristics of those genres. There is a broader view that it is first and foremost the media and as a consequence the genre that dominates particular epochs, with other forms getting marginalized. The novel, therefore, is seen as a genre of the print culture of the modern age, coming into its own in the book form by the eighteenth century. Ralph Fox in *The Novel and The People* (1937) writes, '... the novel as an art in its own right, with its own rules, with its universal acceptance and appreciation, is a creature of our own civilization, *a creature, above, all, of the printing press*.'[57]

The institutional mechanisms of print have also been viewed as important. For instance, Pierre Bourdieu, in *The Field of Cultural Production* (1993), argues that literary works are produced in a 'complex institutional framework' comprising of publishers, critics, agents, and academics, etc., who collectively determine the creation of a work of art. A novel, therefore, according to him, must not be assessed 'internally' but in terms of these factors of literary 'production'.[58] John Sutherland in *Bestsellers* (1981) argues that more than two thousand new novels are put out in the British and American markets every year. An author in a market is 'merely a rate of production ... a brand-name [and a] standardized product'.[59] He argues that 'the novel is necessarily tied to the wheels of progressive technology, commercial management and the dictatorship of the consumer'.[60] Taking a more optimistic view, Dominic Head in *The Cambridge Companion to Modern British Fiction, 1950–2000* (2002) argues that 'it seems that the Internet, and the ebook, bucking the trend towards publishing conglomerates, could put publishing back into the hands of authors'.[61] Seymour Chatman, in *Coming to Terms: The Rhetoric of Narrative in Fiction and Film* (1990) compares the similarities between literature and cinema to propose that today it is essential to understand this commonality before the distinctiveness of the cinema or the literature of our times can be discerned. George P. Landow, in *Hypertext* (1992), argues that 'over the past several decades literary theory and computer hypertext, apparently unconnected areas of inquiry, have increasingly converged'.[62] He explains how the post-structuralist conceptions of Jacques Derrida or Roland Barthes about texts being open-ended, fluid, perpetually unfinished, mulitlinear, multisequential, intertextual, etc., have found their true form in the electronic medium of computer hypertexts. Page-bound texts in books, he feels, are no longer capable of giving expression to the de-centred multivocality of today's times. The new medium of the Internet is, therefore, throwing up its own new literary forms currently unfolding in the world around us.

Modernist and Postmodernist Novels

Another major typology for examining novels is that of modernist and postmodernist. The innovative themes and techniques of many modernist novels opposed traditional realism and its components like chronological plots, continuous narratives omniscient narrators, closed endings, etc., in favour of an emphasis on impression, subjectivity, point-of-view, stream of consciousness, non-chronological and discontinuous narratives, fragmented forms, and self-reflexivity. Frederic Jameson in 'Beyond the Cave: Demystifying the Ideology of Modernism' writes:

> [T]he target of their [the modernists'] attack becomes the very concept of reality itself...The objection is thus, clearly, a critique of something like an *ideology of realism*, and charges that realism, by suggesting that representation is possible ... tends to perpetuate a preconceived notion of some external reality to be imitated ...[63]

Subsequently, towards the second half of the twentieth century, the 'postmodern' novel emerged as a further reaction against realism. In 1955, through his essays, in *Pour un Noveau Roman* French writer Robbe-Grillet announced a new type of writing called the Nouveau Roman, rejecting previous kinds of writings. He argued for the death of plot, action, narrative, character, author's privilege, etc., and said that such things had no place in the novel. Writers like Italo Calvino, Umberto Eco, Marquez and others have written novels, which have variably been called magic-realist, new fiction, anti-fiction, metafiction, surfiction or postmodern fiction. Postmodern novelists carry a deep scepticism towards all truth claims, grand or meta-narratives, and totality. Employing a playful or ironic tone they often revel in black humour, parodies, pastiche, collage, etc. The collapse of the distinction between 'high' and 'low' culture, too, is characteristic of postmodern fiction.

Brian McHale, in *Postmodernist Fiction* (1987), suggests a possibility of mimetic relations between forms of postmodernist fiction to advanced, late capitalist systems. Frederic Jameson, too, calls postmodernism 'the cultural logic of late capitalism' in a book by the same name, although he argues that the novel is the weakest of the newer cultural areas and is considerably excelled by narrative counterparts in film and video.[64] McHale differentiates between modernist and postmodernist fiction by arguing that:

> ...the dominant of modernist fiction is *epistemological*. That is, modernist fiction deploys strategies which engage and foreground questions such as.... How can I interpret this world of which I am a part? And what am I in it? ...What is there to be known; Who knows it; How do they know it, and with what degree of certainty?'[65]

Whereas:

> ...the dominant of postmodernist fiction is *Ontological*.... That is, postmodernist fiction deploys strategies which engage and foreground questions like ... which

world is this? What is to be done in it? Which of my selves is to do it ... what is a world? What kinds of worlds are there, how are they constituted, and how do they differ?[66]

Critics also argue that postmodernism did not necessarily develop in opposition to modernism. Brian McHale in a later work called *Constructing Postmodernism* (1992) writes that 'modernism and post-modernism are not successive stages in some inevitable evolution from less advanced aesthetic forms, but rather alternative contemporary practices, equally "advanced" or "progressive", equally available, between which writers are free to choose'.[67] Elizabeth Dipple in *The Unresolvable Plot* (1988) notes that 'the difference between modernism and postmodernism remains obscurely difficult to talk about'[68] and in fact continuities and similarities between the two merit that the development of the novel be viewed in only two phases, i.e. the realist and the experimental.

Raymond Federman, a novelist and critic, discussed more in recent times for his assertions about the 'Death or End of Postmodernism', writes in *Critifiction: Postmodern Essays* (1993) that postmodernism is 'all about: A Supreme Indecision!'[69] which turns its back on the representation of 'Reality', 'Life', and 'Man'. However, Brian Mchale, in his essay 'What Was Postmodernism?' (2007), advocates greater caution towards Federman's assertion that we may have already moved beyond postmodernism.[70] On the other hand, Bran Nicol in *The Cambridge Companion to Postmodern Fiction* (2009) notes that postmodernism is 'a thing of the past' for many and that there are advantages to discussing postmodernism 'retrospectively'.[71]

A remarkable overlap between theory and fiction is also notable in postmodern times. Michael Greaney in *Contemporary Fiction and the Uses of Theory* (2006) observes:

> On reviewing the literary careers of novelist-theorists like Eco or Kristeva, it seems reasonable to ask whether what we are dealing with here is a question not of influence of theory on fiction, but of a new confluence between the two—a creative intermingling of discourses that dissolves the traditional boundaries between literary text and critical metalanguage.[72]

Greaney argues that theory and fiction have not 'entirely' collapsed or merged into each other but have fortified and fashioned each other more consciously and self-referentially in the postmodern era.

Thus, while some critics emphasize continuities between modernist and postmodern novels, others see the two as distinct and different, and yet others are engaged in discussions over whether postmodernism too might have come to its end.

Ideology of the Novel

Critics have also examined the novel, as a genre, 'ideologically'. Walter L. Reed in *An Exemplary History of the Novel* (1981) argues that the novel resists institutionalization or incorporation into the official systems of genres. 'The novel,' for Reed, 'is a deliberate stranger to literary decorum; it insists on placing itself beyond the pale of literary tradition. Its ethos of opposition is fundamental and should not be ignored.'[73] Reed singles out the novel's sense of itself as an 'outsider' to be one of its most basic features. Lennard J. Davis in *Resisting Novels* notes that out of 'the million titles that have no doubt been printed since the beginning of the eighteenth century, only a handful come to mind as being capable of fostering social change'.[74] The novel, he contends, has had no radical political effect and has completely failed the working classes because it is incapable of representing groups or collectives. It is strongly oriented towards the isolated person, whether in character, dialogue, plot or in the process of reading itself. This politically conservative nature of the novel, in his view, can be changed only by the readers, and 'resisting' the novel is one step towards 'reforming' the novel.

Michael McKeon takes a more nuanced view towards the ideology of the novel in *The Origins of the English Novel: 1600–1740*. For him, the novel is an early modern cultural instrument that mediates and records the confrontation between progressive and conservative ideologies involved in the transformation from 'status' orientation in social relations to 'class' orientation, the decisive rise of the individual and the development of autonomy of the self away from society, alongside the slow separation of history from literature. Nancy Armstrong in *How Novels Think* argues that 'The novel of course was not made to think beyond the individual, but neither, on the other hand, was it made to reproduce the status quo.'[75] Allan H. Pasco in *Inner Workings of the Novel* proposes that the novel 'continues to serve as a foil for rebellion or as a comfortable form that can be exploited for almost any aesthetic purpose'.[76]

Fiction and/or the Novel

In present times, the study of literature through the category of 'genres' itself is disputed. Many trends within literary theory emphasize the study of novels in terms of features or themes that are unique not only to the novel but can also be found in other prose writings (both fiction and non-fiction) produced in different times and places in history. Rather than the genre of the novel, therefore, it is these features and themes, which have become the main object of study for many contemporary literary critics. Such critics also often border on a-historicism or a kind of universalization.

For instance, liberal humanists tend to find permanence in 'human values' in all literature. Structuralists, new critics or stylists stress upon slightly more complex yet eternal or universal categories, like 'myths', 'narratives', 'discourse', etc., for studying the novel. Anti-genre tendencies have been further strengthened by developments in myth-criticism, post-structuralism and narratology. The strongest attack against genre-criticism came in the mid-twentieth century from Northrop Frye in *Anatomy of Criticism* (1957). Frye argues that all prose genres in literature, including the novel, must be dealt within a single category of prose fiction. To this end, he employs concepts like 'myths', 'modes', 'symbols' and 'archetypes'. Frye advocates that fiction must be studied as a form instead of the novel. Fiction, he states, has four strands binding it together, namely novel, confession, anatomy and romance; and a 'novel-centered view of prose fiction'[77] must be replaced by a more 'relative' view of forms as a complex combination of these various strands. Wyne C. Booth in *The Rhetoric of Fiction* (1961) and David Lodge in *Language of Fiction* (1966) also prefer the concept of fiction in comparison to the novel. Booth examines novels in terms of subtle differences in rhetorical functions like 'authoritative telling', 'impersonal narration', 'author's voice', etc.[78] Lodge, for his part, argues that a novelist is a 'verbal artist' whose basic medium is language, therefore, any understanding of the novel requires a detailed study of the language of prose fiction.[79]

Today, historicist critics, i.e. those who view historical development as a progress over the past, with discernible and classifiable stages of development, find it practically impossible to study the novel without first asserting the importance of studying genres. Frederic Jameson in *The Political Unconscious* (1981) finds it essential to outline two incompatible tendencies of genre criticism before devoting his attention to the study of novels. He calls these tendencies, the *semantic* and the *syntactic*, respectively—the semantic being one in which a given genre is understood in terms of some ultimate vision or essence and the syntactic approach being one, which tries to understand a genre in terms of its laws and limits or as a model. The former tries to emphasize the 'why' of a genre while the latter tries to emphasize its 'how'. Discussing the shortcomings of both these tendencies, Jameson underscores the importance of inventing new ways of using historically reflexive categories that will both classify as well as describe. Michael McKeon in his anthology, *Theory of the Novel: A Historical Approach* (2000), argues that his main purpose for putting together an entire collection of important essays on novel theory is to 'rectify' the imbalance created by literary theory over the past few decades in undermining history as well as literary categories, so much so, that 'in common academic usage there's a tendency to conflate "the novel" not only with "fiction" but also with "narrative"'.[80] Critics of the novel can thus broadly be subdivided into those who accept the novel as a genre and those who are anti-genre and therefore study all prose fiction as a single category.

Approaches to the Novel

As is evident, the novel is shrouded in many such paradoxical, irreconcilable and opposing views. Clearly, all these views cannot simultaneously be true. In the course of this study, therefore, we shall try to sift out the nature of the novel from among these conflicting views. However, it is first important to take into account a few aspects regarding our basic approach and methodology.

Despite differences, the basic purposes of both creative arts and academic scholarship converge in trying to make sense of the world, in finding some meaning in life. For this, both rely on abstractions of the world—the more accurate the abstraction, the more meaningful or enduring the work of art or scholarship. Each abstraction in turn is premised upon a set of assumptions. In mathematical theorems, this sequence is stated explicitly—if this and this is true then the given reasoning or proof is correct. If the assumption is changed then the same reasoning does not hold. Humanities and social sciences, too, follow the same approach, albeit in a more nuanced or implicit manner.

More than a method, therefore, we have some basic assumptions. At the outset we seek to join issues with a-historical approaches to studying the novel which suffer from some crucial methodological flaws. By focusing on elements of continuities in history, they pay comparatively less attention to factors that undergo change. Systems of thought such as religion, liberal humanism, psychoanalysis, structuralism, myth-criticism, etc., have strong a-historical undercurrents and display remarkable ease in answering questions relating to origins or beginnings. Almost all religious ideologies, for instance, offer detailed descriptions of the origin of the universe or of human beings, with greater confidence than any scientific method. Sociologists or anthropologists often explain the social and historical relevance of these religious accounts by arguing that they are 'allegorical' rationalizations of history. The relevance of myths, too, is understood in similar terms; Freudian psychoanalysis often comprehends individuals and their relationships through the application of the same concept of Oedipal myth. Methods such as narratology or stylistics also use universally applicable categories like language, narrative and rhetoric to understand all literature. But, a-historical accounts display severe shortcomings in explaining or coming to terms with developments or changes, and exhibit a marked weakness in drawing up classificatory distinctions.

For instance, Freudian application of the Oedipal myth does not necessarily require taking into account the changes brought about in the development from pre-agrarian communes to joint family set-ups to nuclear families or to its more fragmented current *avatars*. Edward Said's new-critical work, *Orientalism*, does not explain the links between the historical spread of colonialism and the discourse of 'orientalism'. Rather, Said offers a sweeping account of orientalism as employed in pre-colonial times up to contemporary times, by non-colonial as well as colonial/imperialist powers like the United States and Europe. In his essay 'Writing and the Novel', the structuralist and later post-structuralist critic, Roland Barthes underscores the lack of any fundamental difference between genres as diverse as 'cosmogonies', 'myths', 'histories' or 'novels' because he finds them similar in their basic rhetorical function as narratives. Linda Hutcheon, in *Narcissistic Narrative: The Metafictional Paradox*, discusses recent writers like Italo Calvino, Salman Rushdie, Timothy Findley, Gabriel Garcia Marquez and others to suggest, 'The one thing, however, that we must never forget is that metafiction is not new . . . Rather it is part of a long novelistic tradition. . . .'[81] Or, while delineating narcissism as an important component of contemporary novels, she concludes, '. . . narcissism can be argued to be, not an aberration, but the "original condition" of the novel as a genre'.[82] *Thus, a-historical views of history suffer from the fatal methodological flaw of being unable to adequately explain change or to demarcate or classify differences.*

On the other hand, historicists approach the rise or emergence of any phenomenon in society in fundamentally different ways. Broadly speaking, they tend to explain origins by detailing tendencies and trends that demarcate development and change. For instance, in order to understand 'free verse' it would be important for historicists to understand preceding genres like 'lyric poetry' and 'dramatic monologue' as well as the broader histories of those times. They try to examine the 'why' of all changes, since they view the movement of history as having a complex logic of cause and effect. Instead of focusing on 'absolute' origins, however, they often focus upon 'historical' origins. Historicists, for instance, do not date capitalism or nationalism to any precise year or decade, rather, taking a cross section of time as their template they focus upon detailing and demarcating the distinctive characteristics and factors associated with the rise of the two. Similarly, with regard to the novel, historicists are relatively more comfortable in dealing with a 'set' of tendencies and a 'range' of early works, instead of any precise 'first' novel or a generically 'perfect' novel.

The problem of whether they should first assume certain works as novels and then study their characteristics, or first fix the characteristics of the novel and subsequently study specific literary works, is a perpetual methodological problem for historicists. This predicament finds appropriate expression in the 'chicken and egg' maxim. Historicists often solve this problem by approaching history 'dialectically', i.e. treating the movement of history as an outcome of contradictory social and historical forces, or through a process of what is commonly understood in Hegelian terms as a 'synthesis' of 'thesis' and 'anti-thesis'. Of course, historicists have their own differences and disagreements, and do not see eye to eye on all issues. All historicists, for instance, do not believe that historical developments have a dialectical basis or that dialectics has a material basis. For instance, Raymond Williams' concept of the dynamics of 'residual', 'dominant' and 'emergent' forces in society offers a model for understanding as well as classifying the process of historical change, but it is not exactly based on dialectics. Mikhail Bakhtin's concept of 'dialogism' comes close to the Marxist concept of 'dialectics'; but is focused more upon the dialogic movement of history based on the development of 'discourse' rather than of 'material forces'. *To put it briefly, we can say that origins for historicists are always linked to understanding developments, while developments are understood by a-historicists often through the essence of origins.*

As far as we are concerned, we shall try to understand the novel by situating its rise and development in a materialist conception of history. However, materialism is not an easy given in our times and stands challenged in many fundamental ways. It is argued that the ways to know the world are mediated through language and discourse. However, all discourses are contrived, subjective, ideological and selective. As Derrida said, 'there is nothing outside the text' and textual meaning itself is produced through *différance*, i.e. a number of heterogeneous signifiers that govern its production and also defer its significance. Following this chain of logic, one is left with no option but to engage with the labyrinth of endless deconstruction to gain some elusive meaning which in any case is contingent upon individual consciousness, which too is conditioned by various subjective and historical factors. The task of making sense, therefore, has become a process without an end.

Over the past few decades, the effort of much scholarship and artistic creation has converged on trying to self-reflexively show that theorizations and creations are ultimately abstractions and therefore partial, provisional, contingent or ideological. Considerable creative and intellectual energies have been spent in trying to impress upon the literary world the sheer impossibility or difficulty of making sense of the world.

Despite contributions to the advancement of knowledge, the task of scholarship or art cannot be to endlessly obscure matters, cannot be to lead the reader or student on an arduous journey only to reveal that the path does not reach anywhere in particular.

Critics of the novel are also conscious of the difficulties posed by both novels and literary theories in recent decades. For instance, Bran Nicole in the 'Preface' to *Postmodern Fiction* (2009) recognizes that readers must struggle and be challenged to get some meaning out of postmodern fiction; and that they must give up the assumption that 'A novel should be something accessible, easy to read.'[83] In the 'Introduction' to *The Novel* (2006), Dorothy J. Hale explains, 'My classroom experience has taught me that many students are intimidated by literary theory. They regard it almost as a foreign language, riddled with ugly jargon and originating from esoteric philosophical homelands to which they feel they have been given no intellectual passport.'[84] As a solution, she offers the limited relief of learning to 'work through difficult theoretical texts as they would any difficult piece of literature'.[85] And yet, as Allan H. Pasco says in *Inner Workings of the Novel* (2010)—'whatever the emphasis, all or almost all, novels are easily recognized as novels'.[86] As far as we are concerned, our efforts would involve trying to understand the genre as well as the tools employed to understand them in more simple ways.

The other intellectual challenge in the post-Foucauldian era is of retaining a sense of proportion while making assessments. Foucault's detailed discussions on power and discourse vis-à-vis madness, sexuality, discipline and punishment, etc., have no doubt greatly expanded the frontiers of knowledge in our world. Yet, despite the advocacy—'do not become enamoured of power'—his legacy often leaves us gasping for breath in a complex web of power relations. With power-power everywhere, we no longer know what to fight or where to escape. In combination with the other prevalent tendency of abandoning the study of the 'whole' by tarnishing it as 'totalitarian', we are currently witnessing two types of resultant distortions in scholarship—making a mountain out of a molehill or missing the woods for the trees. The impact of this trend in literary studies is simultaneously fruitful and damaging. On the one hand, we have gained fresh insights into several neglected aspects of the novel through detailed archaeological and archival studies about particular aspects, periods and types; on the other, scores of studies end up devoting endless attention to what may at best be considered marginal aspects of the novel.

In the course of this study, therefore, our principal challenge is to try to understand the form and development of the novel by examining various theoretical reflections, and in the process, make sense of the genre as a whole with the hope to reach some conclusions without losing our sense of proportion. For this we will rely upon a historicist and materialist approach for caution. And last but not the least, this study is also informed that by the motivation that by comprehending the novel better we would also understand the world around us better, and vice-versa. The linkages between the two must never be lost sight of.

Notes

1. See John Russel, *Reciprocities in the Non-fiction Novel*, Athens and London: The University of Georgia Press, 2000. Russel examines the non-fiction novel by connecting this genre to New Journalism.
2. Mikhail Bakhtin, 'Epic and Novel: Toward a Methodology for the Study of the Novel', 1941; Hoffman, Michael J. and Patrick D. Murphy, eds., *Essential of the Theory of Fiction*, Durham and London: Duke University Press, 1988, p. 54.
3. Allan H. Pasco, *Inner Workings of the Novel: Studying a Genre*, New York: Palgrave Macmillan, 2010, p. 13.
4. Jane Spencer, *The Rise of the Woman Novelist*, Oxford and New York: Basil Blackwell, 1986, p. viii.
5. Walter Allen, *The English Novel*, 1954; London: Penguin Books, 1991, p. 132.
6. M.M. Bakhtin, 'Forms of time and of the Chronotope in the Novel',1934–8, *The Dialogic Imagination: Four Essays*, ed. Michael Holquist, tr. Caryl Emerson and Michael Holquist, Austin: University of Texas Press, 1981, pp. 86–7.
   See Bakhtin, 'Epic and Novel', p. 65. Bakhtin argues that the ultimate roots of the novel lie in the folklore. He argues that the novel was formed in the era of classic antiquity and Hellenism though it found its true expression in the new world during Late Middle Ages and Renaissance.
   See also Arthur Heiserman, *The Novel before the Novel*, Chicago and London: Chicago University Press, 1977; Ernest A. Baker, *The History of the English Novel*, London: H.F.G. Witherby, 1924; J.J. Juserand, *The English Novel in The Times of Shakespeare*, New York: A.M.S. Press, 1965.
7. J.A. Cuddon, *The Penguin Dictionary of Literary Terms and Literary Theory*, London: Penguin Books, 1991, p. 601.
8. Margaret Anne Doody, *The True Story of the Novel*, New Brunswick and New Jersey: Rutgers University Press, 1996, p. 1.
9. Allen, op. cit., p. 13.
10. Marthe Robert, *Origins of the Novel*, 1972; tr. Sacha Rabinovitch, Sussex: The Harvester Press, 1980, p. 31.
11. Ibid., p. 32.
12. Doody, op. cit., pp. xvii–xviii.
13. Lennard J. Davis, *Factual Fictions: The Origins of the English Novel*, Philadelphia: University of Pennsylvania, 1983, p. 2.
14. Roland Barthes, 'Writing and the Novel', 1953; Hoffman, Michael J. and Patrick D. Murphy, eds., *Essentials of the Theory of Fiction*, Durham and London: Duke University Press, 1988, p. 145.

15. Frederic Jameson, *The Political Unconscious: Narrative as a Socially Symbolic Act,* Ithaca and New York: Cornell University Press, 1981, p. 9.
16. Bakhtin, 'Chronotope', p. 84.
17. G.W.F. Hegel, *Aesthetics*, 1842; tr. K.M. Knox, London: Oxford University Press, 1975, p. 1092.
18. Georg Lukâcs, *The Theory of the Novel*, tr. A. Bastock, London: Merlin Press, 1971, p. 56.
19. Ibid., p. 60.
20. Ibid., p. 81.
21. Ibid., p. 88.
22. Bakhtin, 'Epic and Novel', p. 53.
23. Ibid., p. 66.
24. Ralph Fox, *The Novel and the People*, Moscow: Foreign Language Publishing House, 1956, p. 72.
25. Christopher Hill, *Writing and Revolution in Seventeenth Century England,* Brighton: The Harvester Press, 1985, p. 324.
26. Ian Watt, *The Rise of the Novel*, London: Penguin Books, 1968, pp. 249–50.
27. See Franco Moretti, *Modern Epic*, tr. Quintin Hoare, London and New York: Verso, 1996.
28. See Joseph Frank, 'Spatial from in Modern Novel', in Hoffman and D. Murphy, eds., 1945, pp. 85–100.
29. Correspondence of Samuel Richardson with Miss Mulso in 1762, Qtd. in Miriam Allott, *Novelists on the Novel*, London and Hexley: Routledge and Kegan Paul, 1980, p. 41.
30. Correspondence of Samuel Richardson with Miss Mulso in 1762, Qtd. in Allott, p. 42.
31. Northoop Frye, *Anatomy of Criticism: Four Essays*, Princeton and New Jersey: Princeton University Press, 1957, p. 304.
32. Ibid., p. 305.
33. Geoffrey Day, *From Fiction to the Novel*, London and New York: Routledge and Kegan Paul, 1987, p. 4.
34. Robert, p. 32.
35. Michael McKeon, *The Origins of the English Novel: 1600–1740*, Baltimore: The John Hopkins University Press, 1987, pp. 63–4.
36. Watt, op. cit., p. 35.
37. Allen, op. cit., p. 23.
38. Henry James, 'The Art of Fiction', in Hoffman and D. Murphy, eds., 1884, p. 18.
39. Lionel Trilling, 'Manners, Morals, and the Novel', in Hoffman and D. Murphy, eds., 1950, p. 122.
40. See Georg Lukàcs, *Studies in European Realism*, 1930; tr. Alfred Kazin, New York: The Universal Library, 1964.
41. Lucien Goldman, *Towards a Sociology of the Novel*, 1964; tr. Alan Sheridon, London: Tavistock Publications Ltd., 1975, p. 140.

42. George Levine, 'Realism Reconsidered', in Hoffman and D. Murphy, eds., 1974, p. 346.
43. Raymond Williams, *The Long Revolution,* Westport and Connecticut: Greeenwood Press Publishers, 1961, p. 346.
44. Robert, op. cit., p. 4.
45. Ibid.
46. Edward Said, *Culture and Imperialism*, New York: Vintage Books, 1994, pp. 70–1.
47. See Benedict Anderson, *Imagined Communities: Reflections on the Origin and Spread of Nationalism*, London: New Left, 1983.
48. Salman Rushdie,'In Defense of the Novel,Yet Again', 1996, in *The Development of the Novel: Literary Sources and Documents*, ed. Eleanor McNees, East Sussex: Helm Information, 2006, p. 349.
49. McNees, op. cit., p. 29.
50. Nancy Armstrong, *Desire and Domestic Fiction: A Political History of the Novel*, New York and Oxford: Oxford University Press, 1987, pp. 4–5.
51. Rosalind Miles, *The Female Form: Women Writers and the Conquest of the Novel*, London and New York: Routledge and Kegan Paul, 1987, p. 2.
52. Ibid., p. 2.
53. Spencer, op. cit., p. xi.
54. Catherine Gallagher, *Nobody's Stories: The Vanishing Acts of Women in the Marketplace 1670–1820*, Berkeley and Los Angeles: University of California Press, 1994, p. xx.
55. Ibid., p. xiii.
56. Helene Moglen, *The Trauma of Gender: A Feminist Theory of the Novel*, Berkeley and Los Angeles, London: University of California Press, 2001, p. 4.
57. Fox, op. cit., pp. 51–2.
58. See Pierre Bourdieu, *The Field of Cultural Production: Essays on Art and Literature*, Cambridge: Polity Press, 1993.
59. John Sutherland, *Bestsellers: Popular Fictions of the 1970's*, London, Boston and Henley: Routledge and Kegan Paul, 1981, p. 12.
60. Ibid.
61. Dominic Head, *The Cambridge Companion to Modern British Fiction, 1950–2000*, Cambridge: Cambridge University Press, 2002, p. 5.
62. George P. Landow, *Hypertext: The Convergence of Contemporary Critical Theory and Technology*, Baltimore and London: The John Hopkins University Press, 1992, p. 2.
63. Fredric Jameson, 'Beyond the Cave: Demystifying the Ideology of Modernism', 1975, in *Contemporary Marxist Literary Criticism*, ed. Francis Mulhern, London and New York: Longman, 1992, p. 174.
64. Frederic Jameson, *Postmodernism, or, The Cultural Logic of Late Capitalism*, London, New York: Verso, 1991, p. 298.

    Frederic Jameson elaborates on late capitalism as a phase which witnesses the domination of multinationals and transnationals. internationalization of business and finance, proliferation of media products embodying capitalist values, automation and computerization, etc. However, his main emphasis, while explaining postmodernism, is on the cultural impact of all these developments on the lives of individuals. He differentiates between the 'fragmentation' of the postmodern subject from the 'alienation' of the modern subject. He identifies postmodern aesthetics as flat, and lacking in both depth and substance.

65. Brian McHale, *Postmodernist Fiction*, London and New York: Routledge, 1987, p. 9.
66. Ibid., p. 10.
67. Brian McHale, *Constructing Postmodernism*, London and New York: Routledge, 1992, p. 207.
68. Elizabeth Dipple, *The Unresolvable Plot*, New York and London: Routledge, 1988, p. 10.
69. Raymond Federman, *Critifiction: Postmodern Essays*, New York: State University of New York Press, 1993, p. 106.
70. Brain McHale, 'What Was Postmodernism?' http://www.electronicbookreview.com/thread/fictionspresent/tense
71. Bran Nicole, *The Cambridge Introduction to Postmodern Fiction*, Cambridge: Cambridge University Press, 2009, p. xv.
72. Michael Greaney, *Contemporary Fiction and the Uses of Theory*, Hampshire and New York: Palgrave Macmillan, 2006, p. 3.
73. Walter L. Reed, *An Exemplary History of the Novel: The Quixotic Versus the Picaresque*, Chicago and London: The University of Chicago Press, 1981, p. 3.
74. Lennard J. Davis, *Resisting Novels: Ideology and Fiction*, New York and London: Methuen, 1987, p. 227.
75. Nancy Armstrong, *How Novels Think: Limits of Individualism from 1719–1900*, New York: Columbia University Press, 2005, p. 25.
76. Pasco, op. cit., p. 156.
77. Frye, op. cit., p. 304.
78. See Wyne C. Booth, *The Rhetoric of Fiction*, Chicago and London: The University of Chicago Press, 1983.
79. David Lodge, *Language of Fiction*, London: Routledge and Kegan Paul, 1966, p. 30.
80. Michael McKeon, *Theory of the Novel: A Historical Approach*, Baltimore and London: The John Hopkins University Press, 2000, p. xiii.
81. Linda Hutcheon, *Narcissistic Narrative: The Metafictional Paradox*, New York and London: Methuen, 1980, p. xix.
82. Ibid., p. 8.
83. Nicole, *Postmodern Fiction*, p. xiii.
84. Hale, *The Novel*, p. 1.
85. Ibid.
86. Pasco, op. cit., p. ix.

CHAPTER TWO

Rise of the Novel

AMONG THE FIRST few questions that need to be resolved about the novel are—when, where, why and how did the form come up in history. As we have already gathered, views on this issue vary quite dramatically, both in relation to the temporal dating of the novel as well as the spatial location of its rise. Differences over the dating of the early novel range up to three thousand years and differences about its location span practically all continents of the globe. Various critics have various stories to tell on this matter; while most share a consensus over dating the beginning of the genre to the modern age—more specifically to early eighteenth-century Europe—some trace its origin to significantly different times and places in history like ancient Greece, Rome, Arabia, Egypt, to medieval Japan, China, Spain or France. Even among those who agree that the main benchmark of the rise of the novel is modern Europe, there appear significantly divergent views over delineating the key characteristics of the novel as well as the factors responsible for its rise. The form of the novel seems to almost lend itself to these multiple, ambiguous and often contradictory explanations. Notwithstanding the diversity and nuances of these viewpoints, it cannot be the case that the novel arose in twelfth century BC Egypt as well as in modern Europe. Or that ancient Greek writers like Heliodorus and Achilles Tatius as well as modern English writers like Richardson and Fielding were collectively the innovators of the genre.

What is surprising in the area of novel theory, however, is that not many critics directly engage with these incompatible and irreconcilable opinions in order to resolve the dispute. In this chapter, therefore, while dealing with debates about the rise of the novel, we shall also try to engage with the questions arising out of the evident diversity of views on this matter, and to understand the generic characteristics of the novel better. Questions relating to the origin as well as the form of the novel are inexorably linked to each other, and improving our understanding about one can serve as a means to refine and fine-tune our understanding about the other. As far as finding answers to questions about the rise of the novel are concerned, we shall try to understand why the novel arose when it did, how the novel came up where it did, and what the definitional features of the novel are, in other words, the '*what*', '*why*', '*when*', '*where*' and '*how*' of the novel. These aspects are related to each other and we shall work on the premise that it is not possible to throw light on one without simultaneously taking into account the others.

For this, we will first begin by examining the views of a few chosen critics like Georg Lukács, Mikhail Bakhtin, Ian Watt, Marthe Robert, Lennard J. Davis, Nancy Armstrong, Michael McKeon and Firdaus Azim, all of whom have reflected extensively on the rise of the novel. Among them, Lukács is particularly noteworthy because historically he is the first critic to develop a comprehensive theory of the novel. He studies the novel by contrasting it to the earlier form of the epic. He also examines in detail, albeit in highly symbolic and evocative terms, the historical factors responsible for the rise of the novel. Mikhail Bakhtin adopts a somewhat different approach. His focus of study is not on socio-historical factors, but the verbal discursive universe. Bakhtin examines the origin of the novel as part of a long novelistic literary tradition, which is traced to ancient times. Ian Watt, on the other hand, neither focuses his study upon demarcating the novel from other genres, nor on the socio-historical features of earlier times. Rather, he delineates the literary characteristics of novelists like Defoe, Richardson and Fielding by linking them to the socio-historical-philosophical debates of their times, and vice-versa. Marthe Robert employs psychoanalysis and post-structuralism to study the novel. She traces its development to the long line of 'family romances'. Lennard J. Davis first uses the Foucauldian method of discourse analysis and subsequently shifts to Marxism. He locates the roots of the novel to changes in print technology, and later to conceptual developments associated with capitalism. Nancy Armstrong uses feminism to link the emergence of the novel to changing notions of gender and sexuality during the early eighteenth century. Michael McKeon employs Marxism to describe the novel as a genre which gives voice to the ideological concerns of the English middle classes. Firdaus Azim applies postcolonial theories to insist that it is impossible to understand the rise of the novel without taking into account colonialism.

The rise of the novel will be examined by us by emphasizing an important though theoretically neglected generic aspect of the novel, i.e. its open-ended and all-inclusive form which allows the novel to incorporate a range of themes, techniques and genres within its fold. Early novel theorists like Lukács and Bakhtin made important observations in this regard. Lukács argued that the novel is only 'half-art' because as 'form, the novel establishes a fluctuating yet firm balance between becoming and being'.[1] According to him, the novel exists in a state of 'eternally existent becoming,' and is unlike other genres because it is by nature not a 'closed' genre.[2] Subsequently, Bakhtin reiterated this point with greater emphasis, 'The novel parodies other genres (precisely in their role as genres); it exposes the conventionality of their forms and their language; it squeezes out some genres and incorporates others into its own peculiar structure, reformulating and re-accentuating them.'[3] After Lukács and Bakhtin, it is only of late that this aspect has returned to discussions about the novel (this development can be attributed to the theoretical popularity of Bakhtin since his translation from Russian, into French and English). Nevertheless, to our knowledge, no critic has tried to explain in detail the possible reasons behind the same.

In this study, we shall try to locate how and why the novel became the first major literary genre to develop an open, flexible and incorporative form. This aspect of the novel is different from other preceding forms of other genres like epics and romances, which were constrained by relatively fixed literary rules and codes relating to their themes and techniques. For instance, epics could only be about gods or demi-gods, not about ordinary people. Similarly, romances could only be about aristocratic or noble characters governed by the codes of chivalry. Mystery, miracle and supernatural elements played an important part in the plots of both the genres. Their narratives were necessarily about the past, rather than about contemporary times. Literary genres generally considered 'low', like lampoon, comedy, burlesque or picaresque were never integrally incorporated into the 'high' epics and romances. In the course of this chapter, therefore, we shall try to investigate the possible reasons behind the emergence of an incorporative and inclusive genre like the novel. We shall try to argue that the roots of this generic feature of the novel can be traced to the emergence of the flexible and incorporative system of capitalism, which in turn, led to associated changes in literature as well as other cultural forms which saw a breakdown of rigid codes, with the novel becoming the first major literary genre of print to exhibit this tendency in an explicit and pronounced manner.

Georg Lukács

Let us begin by examining an extremely influential book written by young Georg Lukács during 1914–15, *The Theory of the Novel.*[4] The book was written before his engagement with Marxism.[5] It occupies a unique place in the history of the novel, for it is the first critical text of its kind devoted exclusively to analysing the genre of the novel.

Lukács explains the emergence of the novel by pitting it against the 'totality' of an earlier form—the epic.[6] He attributes the epic's totality to the fact that it belonged to an earlier 'integrated civilization' wherein there was no difference between the self and the world, there was no interiority or exteriority, and there was no sense of otherness. The soul completely lacked self-consciousness and reflexivity and did not require them either, because it was at once one with the world. He argues that in the new world of the novel, man is solitary and the old totality or natural unity is exhausted. The modern world of the novel is much larger and richer than the rounded epic world of the Greeks, but there is no transcendental essence present to guide life anymore. Therefore, both the world as well as its forms, most notably the novel, are fragmentary in nature.

Lukács argues, however, that in spite of being new, the form of the novel is not fundamentally different from the earlier form of the epic because the intention of their creators is the same—to capture totality. However, the novel is somewhat different because, 'The novel is the epic of an age in which the extensive totality of life is no longer directly given, in which the immanence of meaning in life has become a problem, yet which still thinks in terms of totality.'[7] No matter how hard the author of the novel tries, it is pre-given that he/she would never be able to capture the elusive totality of the new world within the bounds of a novel. Thus, the novel for Lukács is only a 'half-art' which does not have a finished form and always '*appears as something in the process of becoming*'.[8] Its problematic form is an expression of 'transcendental homelessness'. Unlike the 'organic totality' of the world of the epic, the totality of the world of the novel is a 'concealed totality' which the authors as well as the hero creatively seek to uncover. The fragmentary nature of this world is carried into the world of the novel and its form, a new world in which it is no longer possible to write epics because the intention of capturing totality can no longer be realized. Thus, the epic disappears to give way to the new form of the novel.

Lukács discusses several important generic characteristics of the novel. The heroes of novels are always seekers. Unlike epic heroes they have interiority and are problematic. They have to always undertake measures of their own to find themselves because they belong to a world which has been abandoned by God. Unlike the self-assured heroes of epics, they have no assurance from God. They are left to their own devices. The heroes of novels are 'problematic individuals' who represent personal destinies, while epic heroes represent the destiny of communities. This is why epic heroes are kings whose individual destinies are linked to a totality, while the heroes of novels are commoners whose actions do not have a necessary bearing upon the rest of the world. The experiences of these latter individuals are important however, because they become the means through which the author tries to organize the world. That is why the outward form of the novel is usually biographical. It gives a sense of unity and roundedness to the world, where there is none. The subjectivity or 'ethical intention' of the author of a novel to organize the concealed totality of the world gives shape to the content of the novel and penetrates its very form. Lukács explains that the individuality of the heroes of novels is a product of 'estrangement' or 'alienation' from the outside contemporary world of man-made constructs. The second nature or nature of man-made structures is not homogenous and lacks real substance since it only represents senseless necessities. 'Estrangement from nature (the first nature), the modern sentimental attitude to nature, is only a projection of man's experience of his self-made environment as a prison instead of as a parental home.'[9]

In such a world, irony, or what Lukács calls '. . . the normative mentality of the novel'[10] becomes the means through which the author of a novel tries to impart self-correction on a fragmented world. Irony acts as a kind of tact to achieve balance in the content of the novel. 'Irony, the self-surmounting of a subjectivity that has gone as far as it was possible to go, is the highest freedom that can be achieved in a world without God.'[11] In this new world, ideas no longer 'penetrate' reality; systems of ideas only 'regulate' reality. That is why the reality in novels is never immanently obvious but always strained. Linking this to the question of whether prose is the most important signifier of the novel form, he says that while '. . . in verse, everything hidden becomes manifest . . .',[12] in prose, meaning appears naked because prose is more deliberate. Therefore, verse and prose suit the forms of the epic and the novel, respectively. However, he also clarifies that verse and prose are not the be-all and end-all of determining the differences between the epic and the novel. Lukács further elaborates that in the novel, time is dealt with as a duration or real time, while in the epic time is static and inevitably the action is located in the past. Moreover, memory does not have the power to change the past in the epic, while in the novel memory acts as a creative and transformative force, which can transform the past.

In the process of outlining such characteristics, Lukács also builds a typology of the development of the form. He asserts that the key impulse behind the emergence of the novel is the world abandoned by God. This, in turn, leads to two types of distortions in the world—the world of the novel either becomes 'narrower' than the outside world, or it becomes 'wider' than the outside world. This is a consequence of the soul itself becoming narrow or wide. The soul becomes narrow when the problematic individual of the novel believes in the idea of a rounded and ideal reality with an authentic and unshakable faith, when he underestimates its problematic nature. But upon finding that reality is contrary to his beliefs, he decides to redeem it by fighting evil forces, which he thinks have created this incommensuration. Such a novel is the novel of 'abstract idealism' and its best example is *Don Quixote* by Cervantes. In such a novel, the hero's interiority does not have an inner problematic or conflict. An unquestioning interiority projects its own version of reality on to the real world, which in turn leads to novelistic action. Elaborating upon the nature of the world in *Don Quixote*, Lukács writes:

> Thus the first great novel of world literature stands at the beginning of the time when the Christian God began to forsake the world.... Cervantes lived in the period of the last, great and desperate mysticism, the period of a fanatical attempt to renew the dying religion from within; a period of a new view of the world rising up in mystical forms; the last period of truly lived but already disoriented, tentative, sophisticated, occult aspirations.[13]

For Lukács, *Don Quixote* represents the battle between an unblemished interiority, and an increasingly prosaic and vulgar outer world. In his view, different writers employ different tactics to come to terms with this. Dickens, for instance, seems flat and moralistic because he makes his heroes respond to a prosaic bourgeois society by creating a false, artificial and inadequate poetic effect. Balzac, on the other hand, manages to attain a genuine epic significance, by situating the subjective-psychologism of the hero within a world peopled by similar subjective-psychologist human beings, thereby, obtaining a strange, boundless and immeasurable essence of reality.

According to Lukács, another type of distortion starts manifesting itself by the nineteenth century—this one between the soul and the world. Now, the soul becomes larger than life and interiority gets transformed into a self-sufficient cosmos, at rest with itself. As a consequence, the form of the novel disintegrates into a random reflection of moods, and the novel's action gets replaced by psychological analysis. Reflexion and mood become an end and lead to the destruction of form. Unlike the earlier novel, in which interiority was rounded and the outward world failed to correspond to its idea of a rounded world, now '[a]n interiority denied the possibility of fulfilling itself in action turns inwards, yet cannot finally renounce what it had lost forever; even if it wanted to do so, life would deny it such a satisfaction; life forces it to continue the struggle and to suffer defeats which the artist anticipates and the hero apprehends'.[14] Lukács provides an example of such a novel—Flaubert's *L'Educationsentimentale*—where 'the hero's inner life is as fragmentary as the outside world'.[15] Yet, the novel manages to attain true epic objectivity by using real-life time to bring order to chaos. Such a novel is the novel of 'disillusionment' which reflects an impotent sorrow and a process of decomposition. He opines that the novel as a genre witnesses no innovations after the novel of 'disillusionment', and that there seem to be no signs of that happening either because contemporary literature is just an imitation of earlier works. Although there is a requirement to renew the form of the epic, art will never be able to restore the lost totality of the epic on its own, because the limits of art are always defined by the limits of the existing world. Art will, therefore, only reflect the world, but never change it.

Lukács argues that the paradoxical form of the novel borders on certain inherent dangers. On the one hand it has a tendency to overlap with the epic and on the other hand it can also get reduced to mere entertainment. It might also disintegrate and become formless due to continuous fragmentations. 'The novel,' he says, 'remains a beautiful yet unreal mixture of voluptuousness and bitterness, sorrow and scorn, but not a unity; a series of images and aspects, but not a life totality.'[16] Or, further, '[t]he novel is the form of the epoch of absolute sinfulness, as Fichte said, and it must remain the dominant form so long as the world is ruled by the same stars'.[17] Lukács also elaborates that after Homer, only a few artists managed to retain a sense of epic totality and roundedness in the new world. They are Giotto (painter and architect) and Dante (poet), Wolfram von Eschenbach (poet) and Pisano (sculptor), St. Thomas and St. Francis.

The overall method of young Georg Lukács, in this formative work, remains obscure. He draws his conclusions mainly on the basis of what he, in his 1962 preface to this book, called—'intuition'. Lukács betrays different theoretical tendencies in the course of his book. Sometimes he is an idealist, sometimes a materialist; at times he argues like a historicist but mostly he remains an a-historicist. He argues that the main task of true philosophy is to draw the 'archetypal map' of the world and discern the impulse of 'eternity' in literature. Explaining how new literary genres come into being from older ones, he asserts that there exist three 'timeless paradigmatic forms of world literature: epic, tragedy, philosophy'[18] which have a 'home' or a-priori origin. Mostly only superficial changes take place in these genres, while their original form-giving principle remains the same. Sometimes, however, their all-determining genre-creating principle itself undergoes a change. It is at such times that new genres, whose intention and aim is different from earlier genres, come into being. The novel is a product of such an overall transformation.

On the whole, the nodal points of the theory of the novel for Lukács are: *fragmentation as opposed tototality, emergence of the problematic individual, absence of god, diminishing link with nature, increasing subjectivity tending towards complete interiority, alienation, irony, depiction of the common man as subject, use of real-life and contemporary time, a state of 'eternally existent becoming' and most important of all, the transformation of the real world into a prosaic one.* Lukács suggests that most aspects of the form of the novel are linked to the condition of the new world. However, the causality of many of his observations remains obscure and difficult to grasp. For instance, Why does the world lose its 'totality' at about a certain point of time? Why does God abandon the world? What are the factors responsible for making the world more prosaic? What gives rise to alienation and acute subjectivity? Was the world of Homer as unified as Lukács says it was? Do concepts like the soul becoming narrower or wider, hold water as valid concepts to model the typology of the novel on? The answers to many such questions remain shrouded in the evocative symbolism of Lukács.

In spite of claiming the contrary, Lukács dwells mostly in the 'idealist' realm and only occasionally ventures to draw 'material' links between the world and literature. He does not, therefore, draw any overt connections between the emergence of the novel in the new world and major historical transformations that were taking place in Europe at the same time, i.e. a transition from feudalism to capitalism, the advent of the industrial revolution, the ideas of rationality, secularism, equality, democracy and liberty associated with the Enlightenment, growing nationalism, individualism, etc. Almost forty years later, reviewing *The Theory of the Novel* as a Marxist, Georg Lukács criticized his own work for the lack of any coherent theoretical principle. In the course of our study, we shall examine the usefulness and validity of his important work in the light of what other critics of the novel have to say about the nature of the form.

An important observation made by Lukács about the novel is that it progressively loses its grip on totality and becomes more and more fragmented. We shall examine this opinion in a subsequent chapter about the development of the novel. In this chapter, we shall devote our attention to examining Lukács' definition of the novel as a form which is always in a state of eternally existent becoming, i.e. getting formed but never quite complete. We shall examine the possible reasons behind the emergence of such a form, and why this definition of the novel seems to fit the bill better than most other common definitions of the novel. For the time being, however, let us just underline that Lukács, one of the earliest scholars of the novel, characterizes the novel as an open-ended form.

Mikhail Bakhtin

Another important critic who has fascinated generations of literary critics through his remarkable insights is Mikhail Bakhtin.[19] Here, we shall examine three important essays on the novel written by Bakhtin, namely

'Discourse in the Novel' (1934–5), 'Forms of Time and Chronotope in the Novel' (1937–8), and 'Epic and Novel' (1941). The point of crucial difference between Bakhtin and Lukács is that the former traces the origin of the novel to folklore rather than to the epic. As far as we are concerned, the most notable aspect of Bakhtin's views on the novel is that he describes the novel as a hybrid, ever regenerative and all-inclusive genre, which refuses to get canonized or establish fixed rules of writing.

In 'Discourse in the Novel' Bakhtin distinguishes the novel from other literary genres by arguing that the novel has a predominantly verbal genealogy and must be studied as a 'verbal art'. Unlike other genres it exists outside the scope of the artist's study in the context of 'open public spaces of public squares, streets, cities and villages'.[20] Its development involves many extra-artistic dimensions. The discourse of the novel is unique because it is 'multiform in style and variform in speech and voice'.[21] That is why the novel must not be approached in some abstract 'formal' or 'ideological' way. Rather, its form and content must be studied in an integrated manner. According to Bakhtin, 'diversity of voices', 'heteroglossia' or 'simultaneity in dialogues' are the distinguishing features of the novel. These features are evident from the diverse compositional unity of the novel, which he breaks down into the following:

1. Direct authorial literary-artistic narration (in all its diverse variants);
2. Stylization of the various forms of oral everyday narration (skaz) [to tell];
3. Stylization of various forms of semi-literary (written) everyday narration (the letter, the diary, etc.);
4. Various forms of literary but extra-artistic authorial speech (moral, philosophical or scientific statements, oratory, ethnographic descriptions, memoranda and so forth);
5. The stylistically individualized speech of characters.[22]

Bakhtin argues that in ancient times, too, certain double-voiced prose genres had come into being, but they could not achieve the status of the novel. Earlier, only single voiced or monologic narratives were dominant. Multi-voiced elements remained scattered and occasional, and they were viewed as belonging to 'low' rather than to 'acceptable' genres. No ancient genre could ever become completely hybrid or dialogic in nature, and dialogism could offer no challenge to the prevalence of monologism. Explaining this further, Bakhtin claims that over time discourse has undergone many changes and its dialogic essence has deepened. This growing dialogism is an outcome of the tussle between two kinds of forces. On the one hand are 'the forces that serve to unify and centralize the verbal-ideological world',[23] on the other are the forces that seek to decentralize and disunify the world. The development of the novel in history, according to Bakhtin, is a function of this deepening dialogic essence wherein decentralizing forces seek to destabilize the centralizing forces.

Bakhtin argues that the novel is fundamentally different from 'poetic' genres. Poetic genres require a pre-requisite unity of the language system and of the poet's individuality. Novelistic genres on the other hand make the most of 'the internal stratification of language, of its social heteroglossia and the variety of individual voices in it'.[24] By heteroglossia, Bakhtin means, the coexistence of different speeches or varieties within a single language; for instance, the speech of the author, narrator, character, etc. He explains that the novel does not spring from 'poetic activity' but emanates from pure 'rhetoric'. It has an orientation towards the listener. In the novel, the forces of centralization and decentralization or unification and disunification, which Bakhtin also calls centrifugal and centripetal forces respectively, intersect in the utterance of the speaking subject. The representation of the unique discourse of each speaking subject criss-crossing with those of others, distinguishes the novel from other genres. There are two stylistic lines of development in the novel—one that approaches heteroglossia from above, while the other approaches it from below. The novel is engaged in an uninterrupted relationship with both living rhetorical genres, which are journalistic, moral, and philosophical, as well as with artistic genres like the epic, drama or lyric. This finds reflection in the genre of the novel in the tendency of hybridity:

> The novel permits the incorporation of various genres, both artistic (inserted short stories, lyrical songs, poems, dramatic scenes, etc.) and extra-artistic (everyday, rhetorical, scholarly, religious genres and others). In principle, any genre could be included in the construction of the novel, and infact it is difficult to find any genres that have not at some point been incorporated into the novel by someone.[25]

According to Bakhtin, the printing of books, too, plays a decisive role in the history of the novel. It serves 'to shift discourse into a mute mode of perception'[26] and turns the novel into the folk literature of the reading public. Distinguishing the novel from the epic, Bakhtin says that the idea of testing the hero radically distinguishes the novel from the epic. In the epic world 'an atmosphere of doubt surrounding the hero's heroism is unthinkable'[27] whereas in the novel the heroism of the hero is mostly yet to be seen.

Bakhtin develops his concept of 'novelness' in this essay as a combination of dialogism, heteroglossia and hybridity and uses it to distinguish the novel from all other genres which have more centralizing tendencies. He traces novelness in the literature of ancient times, and argues that it has taken time to come into its own in order to become the novel. He vaguely calls different works 'more' or 'less' novelistic, since different literary works are to different extents dialogic or hybrid. He holds earlier scholars responsible for having deliberately ignored verbal and rhetorical genres as well as the concept of novelness in developing their theories about different genres. In our view, Bakhtin's concept of novelness effectively ends up having a wide range of connotations that can be applied to different kinds of genres—poetic and prosaic, literary as well as non-literary, because many literary as well as non-literary genres show the tendency of hybridity, i.e. a tendency to mix various forms and discourses within their fold. Bakhtin does not explain why the progressive mixture of styles and discourses is unique to the novel, how it starts taking place in the form of the novel, and why this hybridity eludes other literary genres.

Bakhtin identifies the novel for its distinctly democratic essence. While implying a progressive democratization of the world of discourses, however, Bakhtin does not draw any links with the democratization of society. It has been argued by many historians, that the development of human society across history is one of progress and freedom, in which 'slave' societies paved way for the relatively better condition for 'serfs' under feudalism, and for 'workers' under capitalism. Bakhtin does not link the two processes of democratization—in society and in the realm of discourses. Unlike Lukács, however, Bakhtin does not bear a gloomy picture about his contemporary times; rather he sees his present as relatively free from top-heavy ideologies, as having a space for the clown, the buffoon, folksayings and anecdotes. Bakhtin evocatively calls the novel a folk art of the reading public. However, if Bakhtin is celebrating the novel for its increased readership as compared to the restricted readerships of manuscripts, then the novel can only be dated to the period after the print revolution in Europe, i.e. only after the fifteenth century. If Bakhtin is characterizing the novel by its generic affinity to folk forms of art, particularly oral narrative forms, then the association of the novel to the reading public becomes difficult because the development of print culture in history was simultaneously accompanied by the destruction of folk and oral forms of art. However, if the novel is more about its popularity with the reading public and therefore, its more democratic consumption, then, it becomes all the more difficult to understand what Bakhtin exactly means by 'folk'. Perhaps, the suggestion is to the humble origins of the novel.

In his essay 'Forms of Time and Chronotope in the Novel', Bakhtin borrows the concept of 'chronotope' from Einstein and develops it further to classify novels. The chronotope simultaneously denotes both time and space. Bakhtin argues that chronotopes can be used to define as well as differentiate between different genres. He traces the beginnings of the novel to ancient times and studies a variety of 'novels' ranging from *Aethiopica* (second century AD) by Heliodorus, to works by Stendhal,

Balzac, Flaubert and Tolstoy, in order to elaborate upon his theory of the chronotope. He chooses to bypass 'all questions dealing with the origin of these types [of novels] in history',[28] and provisionally calls the first type of ancient novel—*adventure novel of ordeal.* Doing so, he outlines various novelistic chronotopes like adventure chronotope, chronotope of the road, chronotope of the Greek Romance, etc. The second type of ancient novel, he calls *adventure novel of everyday life*, and includes in it ancient Roman works like *Satyricon* and *The Golden Ass*. He examines these works through the chronotope of the path of life. He calls the third and last type of ancient novel *ancient biography and autobiography*, and examines it through the folkloric chronotope. He outlines a typology for the novel which is difficult to exactly understand. For instance, the chronotope of the Greek Romance occurs in ancient works like *Daphnis and Chloe*, and also in the novels of Sir Walter Scott. Chance plays an important role in these works wherein things happen suddenly, coincidences occur and the resolution of the plot depends upon the vagaries of destiny. Similarly, 'whole' individuals who are fully exteriorized and lack interiority are represented in the works of Plato, Socrates, and St. Augustine, and also in the works of Rabelais and Goethe. Bakhtin makes many such observations about different chronotopes and novels in this essay.

At this juncture, perhaps it is useful to consider Bakhtin's views about the development of literary genres in another book, *Problems of Dostoevsky's Poetics*:

> . . . a literary genre, by its very nature, reflects the most stable . . . tendencies in literature's development. Always preserved in a genre are undying elements of the archaic. True these archaic elements are preserved in it only thanks to their constant renewal, which is to say, their contemporization. A genre is always the same and yet not the same, always old and new simultaneously.[29]

In his essays, Bakhtin succeeds more in demarcating continuities rather than change, archaic elements rather than their renewal or contemporization. As a result, literary phenomena in widely separate periods of time tend to coexist simultaneously. Taking time as the primary category of literature, he outlines various characteristics of different types of novels. In the 'adventure novel of ordeal' time is static and immobile. In spite of many adventures, no individual undergoes any change. In the 'adventure novel of everyday life' some changes or transformations take place in the individual; however, the world remains unchanged. Such novels depict exceptional or unusual moments of crisis or change. In 'ancient biography or autobiography' on the other hand, the individual passes through biographical time and shows signs of a public self-consciousness. After the Renaissance, time starts developing a sense of moving forward, especially in the novels of Rabelais, although it does not yet get divided into a distinct past, present and future. Slowly, time becomes irreversible and realistic, and individualism starts coming into being. By contrast, the time in the epic always exists in the absolute past, never in the present day. Bakhtin expresses his distinct preference for folkloric time because in it the individual is truly integrated with his present.

On the one hand, Bakhtin proposes that the notion of time changes in history, and he associates different notions of time with different types of novels; yet, on the other, types of novels do not change in his conception of history. He argues that different types of novels have existed in the realm of literature since ancient times. He pays attention in great detail to how the treatment of time and individual subjectivity varies in different works of literature, but does not engage with explanations for 'why' the notions of time or individualism undergo changes. Moreover, he does not explain why the changing treatment of time is exclusively linked only to the novel as a genre and not to other genres. In the course of our study, we shall try to argue that the notions of time and individual subjectivity, in fact, underwent radical changes during the modern age. And therefore, it makes more sense to associate particular types of narratives as novels, rather than many types of fictional narratives as novels.

Bakhtin's essay is remarkable for its broad sweep of literary history, in which Bakhtin explains how literary works develop over earlier works and change into more sophisticated and complex forms. However, even after many readings, Bakhtin's concept of the chronotope remains undefined and difficult to grasp. As Michael Holquist says in *Dialogism: Bakhtin and his world*, 'at the conclusion of the 200-page monograph on the chronotope—a small book really—many readers will find themselves hard pressed to answer the question, "What exactly is the chronotope?"'[30] Is it a motif, a symbol, a type of plot, a notion of time or a kind of subjectivity? In 1971, over thirty years after writing this essay, Bakhtin said that contrary to his proposition, he had by and large studied only temporal relationships in novelistic chronotopes—therefore, a study of the spatial aspects of novelistic chronotopes still remained to be conducted. However, without going into further discussions about this essay, let us just say that this essay is significant for us because in it Bakhtin traces the origin of the novel to ancient times. It is also significant because like Lukács, Bakhtin too argues that the concept of subjectivity is important for understanding the development of the novel. We shall follow this lead later in a subsequent chapter on the development of the novel. Despite many details, however, what exactly Bakhtin means by the novel remains elusive.

The third essay under consideration, 'Epic and Novel', was written under the distinct influence of Georg Lukács' *Theory of the Novel*. Bakhtin is different from Lukács in that he traces the origin of the novel to folklore instead of the epic. This is his most comprehensive essay on the genre of the novel, which includes many points from his earlier essays, although there are arguments here that also contradict some of his earlier observations. Bakhtin argues that the epic is an antiquated genre that has completed its development, unlike the novel which is a still developing genre. The novel gets along poorly with other genres for it has a tendency to parody them, especially the dominant or fashionable genres; 'it exposes the conventionality of their forms and their language; it squeezes out some genres and incorporates others into its own peculiar structure, reformulating and reaccentuating them'.[31] Whenever the novel becomes dominant, it 'novelizes' all remaining genres. The novel also has a remarkable ability to parody its own popular types, and thereby, criticize itself. Therefore, no novel emerges as a model for other novels, and the novel as a genre never gets antiquated or canonized. Bakhtin, in fact, calls it the only genre born out of this new world, having a deep affinity with it, which reflects its reality more integrally, rapidly and sensitively in its process of unfolding. The novel exists 'in the zone of direct contact with inconclusive present-day reality'.[32] It has an integral relation with ideological genres, and genres of everyday life, so its boundaries fluctuate between fiction and nonfiction, literature and non-literature. The novel also marks 'a radical re-structuring of the image of the individual',[33] who instead of becoming a whole finished man, develops endless possibilities and potentials. The individual in the novel develops a tension between the external and internal man, and his destiny or future opens up. Bakhtin argues that the emergence of the 'present, in all its open-endedness . . . is an enormous revolution in the creative consciousness of man'.[34] The novel finds expression due to the destruction of older hierarchical temporalities. This happens 'on the boundary between classic antiquity and Hellenism, and in the new world during the late Middle ages and Renaissance'.[35] The Renaissance is important because it marks a very specific rupture in the history of Europe. It is during the Renaissance that Europe emerges 'from a socially isolated and culturally deaf semipatriarchal society . . . [and enters] into international and interlingual contacts and relationships'.[36] The availability of a multitude of different cultures, times and languages creates the ground for 'polyglossia' or multilingualism, which thereby further develops the form of the novel. The Renaissance is also important because for the first time in history a concept of the future comes in and a new heroic beginning is made, which develops a greater kinship to the future than to the past.

Bakhtin criticizes the comparison of the novel to the epic which, in his view, is nothing but an attempt to falsely elevate the status of a self-conscious genre like the novel. In ancient times, too, the novel had existed unofficially, outside the order of high literature, except that genre theorists of the time like Aristotle, Horace or Boileau ignored it because they took into account only those genres which could be organized into a harmonious whole. It was in the nineteenth century that scholars started taking the novel into cognizance. They gave it recognition, however, without having a proper understanding about the philosophy of the novel. They just included the novel into the formal list of genres with a view to completing a maximal anthology rather than taking into account its ultimate roots in folklore.

On the whole, the nodal points of Bakhtin's theory of the novel are *heteroglossia, dialogism, hybridity, novelness, print, parody, polyglot discourse, folklore, decentralizing tendency in discourse, changing individuality, use of present day inconclusive time, orientation towards the future and an ever-regenerative all-inclusive form*. The basic approach of Bakhtin remains rooted in the study of discourse in history. He elucidates at length 'how' discourses change in history and yet can be found across time. He painstakingly details changes that lead to the true blooming of the genre of the novel, but argues that the novel had always existed and its emergence after the Renaissance has got as much to do with its discovery as with the actual revolutionizing of discourse by writers like Rabelais, etc. On the whole, Bakhtin invokes many different categories to understand the novel. But in spite of the details, many of his categories as well as his concept of the novel remain elusive. While studying discourse, he does not seek to link changes in the discursive universe with material changes. In spite of repeatedly attributing immense importance to the Renaissance, he again and again goes back in time while tracing individual aspects of the novel. So it remains difficult to understand whether Bakhtin traces certain discursive tendencies to ancient times or to the novel as such. Both remain interchangeable concepts in his writings.

Ian Watt

Let us now examine *The Rise of the Novel* (1957) by Ian Watt—a text that is considered a benchmark in the rise of the novel debate. Ian Watt begins by first identifying Defoe, Richardson and Fielding as the earliest innovators of the novel during the early eighteenth century. He argues that the key to comprehending the emergence of the novel can only be found in a proper understanding of the favourable literary and social conditions responsible for the emergence of these three talented writers simultaneously. In the course of this book, he examines and outlines the main characteristics of their writings in order to understand the form of the novel. Watt starts by first trying to establish a working definition of the novel which must be 'sufficiently narrow to exclude previous types of narrative and yet broad enough to apply to whatever is usually put in the novel category'.[37] However, he notes that establishing such a working definition is difficult because writers like Defoe, Richardson and Fielding are very different from each other. They do not view themselves as similar to each other; rather their only similarity is that they write in opposition to earlier genres and possess a sense of creating something new.

Watt identifies 'formal realism' as the defining characteristic of the novel. He argues that realism in the novel is characterized not by its predominant treatment of 'low' subjects as is commonly perceived, but by the 'way' in which novels present life. Whereas the earlier realists of the Middle Ages believed in finding realities in universal abstractions, the realists of the modern age, particularly novelists, believe that realities reside in particular concrete objects of sense perception, which are discovered by individuals through their senses. The novel borrows this 'provisional' temper or method of investigation from the 'philosophical realism' of Descartes and Locke, who develop entirely new conceptions of the individual. They do not accept anything on trust, and emphasize the importance of finding things on one's own. Instead of conforming to tradition, they believe in having a distinct break from the past. Their philosophy is anti-traditional, critical and innovating. They argue that an individual investigator is more likely to arrive upon the truth if he chooses to consciously depart from previous assumptions. Watt identifies individualism and innovation as the benchmarks of philosophical realism. This individualist and innovating tendency of philosophy, he argues, is best reflected in literature in the form of the novel.

Distinguishing the novel from earlier literary forms, Watt elaborates that the plots of classical or Renaissance epics were based upon past history or fable, and their writers were judged on the basis of their adherence to received literary decorum. However, the novel as a form challenges this logic by placing unprecedented value on originality and novelty. It becomes a vehicle for a cultural tendency that believes in the uniqueness of each individual experience. Watt notes that the 'critical tradition in the early eighteenth century was still governed by the strong classical preference for the general and universal'.[38] The emergence of the novel marks a rejection of this classical past that seeks to universalize reality. The novel now resorts to 'particularity of description'. Novels like *Robinson Crusoe* by Defoe and *Pamela* by Richardson are provided as examples of this type of narrative. These novels focus upon characterization and the presentation of background for achieving particularity of description.

The link between proper names and individual identity becomes very important. These early novelists devote considerable attention to naming characters appropriately and giving proper names and surnames to major as well as minor characters. Watt discusses the unique styles of Defoe, Richardson and Fielding in this regard.

He points out that 'time' becomes an essential and important category in the novel. Time is always treated as 'duration' linked to the flow of experience. In earlier literary genres, timeless stories were told to mirror unchanging moral values. Now, novels show a distinct logic of cause and effect, wherein the past feeds into the future for developing novelistic action. Novelists reject the outlook of earlier fiction which is based on an 'abstract continuum of time and space'.[39] He draws parallels between the principal of 'individuation' put forward by John Locke and the creation of characters by novelists. According to Locke, an object could become individualized only if it was placed against a backdrop, which was particular, both in time as well as in space. 'Particular space' gains in importance in the narrative of novels, in contrast to earlier tragedies, comedies and romances in which 'place' was represented as something general and vague. Watt further explains that as a correlative of time, detailed description of 'space' becomes essential to creating a picturesque and vivid social setting. He elaborates how, along with a more serious treatment of time, the novels of Defoe like *Robinson Crusoe* and *Moll Flanders* also start depicting some of the most visual scenes of all literature.

Watt also draws a parallel between the 'language or semantics' of novelists and the philosophers of the early eighteenth century who seek to find links between words and real objects. Novelists depict this link by following styles of representation in accordance with their subjects. Augustan prose traditions are rejected by them in order to create an easy and realistic prose style, appropriate for the natural diction of under-educated characters like Moll Flanders or Pamela Andrews in *Moll Flanders* (1722) and *Pamela: Or Virtue Rewarded* (1740), respectively. Thus, novelists become the pioneers of a new and different kind of literary prose. Their language becomes more referential than the language of other literary forms and 'works by exhaustive presentation rather than by elegant concentration'.[40] Watt discusses how writers like Defoe and Richardson criticized many of their well-educated colleagues for indiscriminately using highly polished prose, which was often completely inappropriate for their subjects.

He, however, also argues that it should not be assumed that realism in philosophy directly leads to realism in the novel. The relationship between the two is not very overt because 'philosophy is one thing and literature is another' and they should at best be viewed as 'parallel manifestations of larger change'.[41] This larger change is the transformation of Western civilization after the Renaissance, wherein a unified world picture of the Middle Ages is replaced by an aggregate picture 'of particular individuals having particular experiences at particular times and at particular places'.[42] Apart from philosophy and literature, other fields of thought also start displaying this tendency. For instance, the juries in law courts start taking the circumstantial view of life into account. The novel takes on an air of authenticity and aims to depict 'a close correspondence between life and art'.[43] However, he notes that this claim to authenticity also creates the maximum controversies for the novel with many arguing that the novel does not produce endearing realities.

While Watt characterizes 'formal realism' as the most distinctive characteristic of the genre of the novel, constituted by a combination of many elements, he argues that it was not the invention of eighteenth-century novelists. Traces of formal realism could also be found in the works of Homer, or in works like *The Golden Ass*, and in the writings of Chaucer and Bunyan. But unlike modern writings, they did not assimilate the aim of verisimilitude very deeply in their works. The novel is noteworthy because it is the first literary genre that fully rejects all non-realist conventions in order to embrace realism completely. Watt identifies writers ranging from Richardson to James Joyce for their use of formal realism in their novels.

Watt goes on to explain why the novel emerged first of all in England. He attributes its rise to the rise in the reading public wherein the ability to read became a necessary accomplishment for the rapidly rising middle classes of eighteenth-century England. The rural and urban poor also started getting access to education, though they faced many social impediments, the most important one being their poverty. In spite of rapid increase, however, the size of the reading public largely remained restricted, and the most substantial additions to the buying-public were drawn from well-to-do merchants, shopkeepers, and important tradesmen, 'rather than from the impoverished majority of the population'.[44] Although a variety of printed material became available in the market, the cost of books remained very high. Cheap forms of printed entertainment like ballads, chapbooks containing abbreviated versions of chivalric romances, stories of criminals, etc., became the most popular. Some newspapers started carrying short stories or novels in serialized form. But in terms of sales and accessibility, the novel—a medium-price range literature—did not become the most popular form of literary entertainment.

Watt argues that by the 1740s circulating libraries became very popular whose main attraction were novels, especially among women. In a context where the nobility and the gentry were facing a steady cultural retreat, women from the upper and middle classes started witnessing an increased participation in the field of literature. The availability of a great deal of leisure time played a key role in making women voracious readers. Even less well-to-do women ended up having more leisure time than before, because traditional household duties like 'spinning and weaving, making bread, beer, candles, and soap, and many others, were no longer necessary, since most necessities were now manufactured and could be bought at shops and markets'.[45]

This process of social change, according to Watt, was not very smooth because the upper classes actively opposed the spread of education among the poor. They also sought to deny access to cheap literary entertainment to them. Many advocated that leisurely pursuits were the prerogative of only the leisured classes, and the labouring classes must not be distracted from their labour. Measures were taken by employers to deny leisure time to their employees by increasing their working hours and duties. The scarcity of private space for reading also became another factor that made reading a difficult activity. Even leading writers of the day could not boast of a private writing place due to overcrowding in London. However, in spite of this, for the first time in the history of literature 'the centre of gravity of the reading public'[46] started shifting towards the middle classes. This sparked off debates of all kinds, for instance, between 'critical reading' and 'reading for pleasure', wherein many classicists argued in favour of the former. The changing composition of the reading public directly impacted the content of novels. Popular periodical essays, newspapers and journals also made their own contributions to shape the novel. A new public taste which preferred informative literature, improvement literature, and entertainment literature in the form of easy reading, came into being. Watt elaborates that the biggest volume of books published during the eighteenth century were religious books. Novelists like Richardson and Defoe carried the piety of religious tracts into the field of fiction. Simultaneously, an increased tendency towards secular tastes and values also became notable.

Elaborating further, Watt outlines that the decline of patronage by the court and the nobility led to many serious changes in the establishment of literature. An important place between the author and the reader now came to be occupied by middlemen. These middlemen primarily engaged in the trade of 'manufacturing and selling the products of the printing press'.[47] The *Gentleman's Magazine*, whose main contributors were hacks and amateurs, replaced periodicals like the *Spectator* and the *Tatler*, which had writers like Steele and Addison writing for them. Booksellers now achieved a financial and social standing as never before, and became important determinants of literary taste and public opinion. These powerful booksellers influenced both the authors as well as the readers. Many writers started complaining about 'the effect of turning literature itself into a mere market commodity'.[48] Watt quotes Defoe on this matter—'Writing . . . is become a very considerable Branch of the English Commerce. The Booksellers are the Master Manufacturers or Employers. The several Writers, Authors, Copyers, Sub-writers, and all other Operators with Pen and Ink are the workmen employed by the said Master Manufacturers.'[49] Watt also quotes complaints by writers like Goldsmith, Pope and Fielding about this growing mechanization and commodification of literature at the hands of traders.

This, Watt argues, explains part of the novel's association with the debased considerations of booksellers. However, writing as a profession became lucrative in this bargain. Richardson, Fielding, Johnson and many other writers were able to earn considerable money through writing. Watt argues that a major technical innovation of 'particularity' of description and explanation in the novel was possibly a contribution of the laws of the market place that required writers to write books that were easy to understand for the reading public. In this new milieu, a writer's success started depending upon his ability to please the readership rather than a patron or the literary elite. In this competitive milieu, writers also started accusing each other of writing for economic rather than artistic reasons.

On the question of prose and poetry, Watt argues that the 'economic' criterion was the primary reason behind an increased favour for prose. Instead of wasting time on creating 'verbal grace, complication of structure, concentration of effect'[50] of verse, writers now preferred to write verbose prose, because they got paid on the basis of per sheet; the more the pages, the higher the wage. In this new era of writing, writers without any formal training in classical rules of literature became major writers. Defoe and Richardson were two of the best examples of good writers who had had no formal training. Their lack of familiarity with the baggage of past literature was a major reason responsible for the originality of their writings. Because of their unique social position, early novelists were able to respond to the needs of their audiences better.

On the whole, the nodal points of the theory of the novel for Ian Watt are: *formal realism, individualism, novelty, anti-traditionalism, description, characterization, representation of background, proper names, time and space, prose, rise in the reading public in England, growing literacy, leisure time for women, growth of the middle classes, increasing secularization, decline of feudal patronage, emergence of the marketplace, proliferation of entertainment literature, and professionalism among writers.* Watt primarily attributes the rise of the novel to interlinked changes in the literary, philosophical, social and economic fields. He outlines structural parallels between developments in these fields. Writing during the time that he did, Watt's thesis was remarkable for its ability to sift out and link the details of the specific conditions prevailing in eighteenth-century England to the rise of the novel. His' was the first major study of the novel that attributed changes in the literary realm directly to specific developments in the socio-historical realm. Unlike Lukács or Bakhtin, however, Watt did not seek to understand the novel in terms of its core 'genre giving' principle. He looks more at the surface of discernable changes. He focuses upon 'formal realism' as the main genre giving principle of the novel, but it is easy to say today that if it were indeed the main feature of the novel as a genre, then either the novel has become a marginal genre for the last century or so, or Ian Watt is not entirely right in making this observation. We shall discuss his specific views on realism in the next chapter. At this juncture, we can safely say that the views of subsequent critics revolve around the framework laid down by these three critics. Without any further ado, therefore, let us move on to examining some other influential views on this issue.

Contemporary Opinions

An important critic who approaches the question of the rise of the novel by combining psychoanalysis with literary theory is the French post-structuralist critic Marthe Robert. In her book *Origins of the Novel* (1980), she traces the roots of the genre to its 'psychological origins' to note—'notwithstanding the distinguished and historically acknowledged ancestry it claims, [the novel] is a newcomer to the literary scene'.[51] She notes that during its early years, it was held in much disrepute, and early writers like Defoe and Diderot took pains to argue that they were not novelists. And yet, within a century the situation changed considerably and Balzac could claim—'*la Comédiehumaine* was no less important than Napoleon's heroic exploits'.[52] Writing about his achievements Balzac declared his unquestionable superiority over scholars—'I have excelled the historian, I am freer.'[53] Robert argues that the novel is a form that is publicly condemned but secretly enjoyed. The 'devastating success' of the novel is based upon its basic parasitic nature wherein it appropriates all modes of writing in order to 'monopolize' the entire literary heritage. Encroaching upon other literary forms, it gradually infiltrates and colonizes almost all other literature. 'With the freedom of a conqueror who knows no law other than that of his unlimited expansion, the novel has abolished every literary caste and traditional form.'[54] The novel is able to draw upon all kinds of subjects and styles. It borrows from drama, essay, commentary, monologue, conversation, fable, history, parable, romance, chronicle, story, or epic. It even includes poetry sometimes by being simply poetic. Unlike traditional genres, the novel has no 'prescriptions or proscriptions'. It mirrors the 'inventiveness, restlessness and vitality'[55] of modern societies in its form. It follows no rules, and its power lies in its total freedom. In fact, it gets more and more intricate, elusive and anarchic with time. In Robert's view, it is the critics who feel a 'need to constrain it within the boundaries of law and order . . . to restrict, if not deny its freedom'.[56] But the novel thrives undisciplined and licentious. Yet it is plagued by guilt because it evades one form of tyranny only to succumb to another.

Robert argues that 'realism' or 'subject matter' can never be the main criteria for classifying the novel because novelists are demarcated by their intention to necessarily invoke or activate some degree of illusion through their writings. For a writer to be successful with this illusion, he/she inevitably requires the complicity of the reader. While some writers try to create an illusion of reality, many also emphasize the fictive nature of their writings. They either choose to 'ring true' or they choose to flout reality and create delusions in the name of truth. Robert particularly identifies Swift, Hoffmann and Kafka for their writings and infers, 'the genre's originality and paradox consist in thus "trying to make us believe" . . . for the sole purpose of deceiving'.[57] The plea for sincerity employed by many novelists is not born out of a desire for clarity but from an uneasy desire for self-justification. 'The novel's truth is never more than its greater ability to delude.'[58] Although, the novel merely seems to imitate reality, its effort to do so is not entirely without meaning. The novel's basic impulse lies in its endeavour to transform reality. 'Indeed, by virtue of its initial plan of conquest, it can only be simultaneously democratic and conservative; . . . dare devil and thrusting; . . . liberated and dyspotic, typically middle-class, order loving and restless.'[59]

In order to draw the links between this transformative desire and the novel, Robert digs into Freud's classification of 'the family romance of the neurotic'. Each child, when he is born starts idolizing his parents. However, with time the child realizes that he is no longer the object of their undivided attention. He also comes to realize that there are many other parents in the world. He wishes for the eternity of his outgrown beliefs, and upon discovering its impossibility, takes refuge in a world of imaginary parental idyll. He invents his family romance in order to 'overcome the first disappointment whereby his parental idyll is in danger of foundering'.[60] Feeling estranged from his parents he nurtures a feeling of rebellion and dissent. Over time, this feeling changes into a vague desire for freedom. Robert argues that it is this basic conflict and crisis of humanity that manifests itself in the novel: 'During the whole of its history the novel has derived the violence of its desires and its irrepressible freedom from the . . . Family Romance.'[61] Providing a description for the form of the novel she says:

> . . . it is the genre, with all its, inexhaustible possibilities and congenital childishness, the faults, frivolous, grandiose, mean, subversive and gossipy genre of which each of us is indeed the issue (to his shame, say the philosophers; to his delight, say the novelist, speaking for himself and for his readers) and which, moreover, recreates for each of us a remnant of our primal love and primal reality.[62]

The novel, for Robert, simply has its own *psychology*. However, it is only one Oedipal genre among many others. It is different from other genres because it does not have any fixed codes or directions. It follows no hard and fast rules, neither classical nor modern. The novel has 'a compulsory content and an optional form'.[63] The content of the novel is necessarily that of the family romance, while its form is ambiguous and elastic. 'Thus, the childhood Family Romance determines the novel's lack of generic feature—its notorious inconsistency—and more specifically, the endeavour to be realistic which, oddly enough it considers as a proof of its reality.'[64] Its primitive desire is to recast life under ideal circumstances. The novel can follow only two major directions—'. . . the way of the realistic Bastard who backs the world while fighting it head on; and the way of the Foundling who, lacking both experience and the means to fight, avoids confrontation by flight or rejection.'[65] Thus, Marthe Robert traces the origins of the novel to an essential Freudian impulse while employing a wide variety of interesting adjectives to describe the novel, like upstart, newcomer, colonizer, monopolist, free, anarchic, etc.

Unlike Robert, who links the origin of the novel to family romances, Lennard J. Davis in *Factual Fictions: The Origins of the English Novel* (1983) links the roots of the form to journalism and history. A student of Edward Said, Davis adopts the Foucauldian method of 'discourse analysis.' He argues that the emergence of any new phenomena in history is linked to particular power relations and the propagation of certain ideologies. Therefore, the novel, too, must be serving certain ideological ends. All early novelists claimed to be writing factual accounts rather than fictional ones. Therefore, the key to the mystery of the form of the novel must lie in this paradox of fact and fiction.

He first of all examines *Don Quixote* to argue that it suffers from a crucial deficiency that it is not self-conscious, therefore, it cannot be considered a novel. It does not involve the reader actively into its craft. In Cervantes' work, characters are involved in fabrications or are duped by other people's fabrications, but the reader is never involved in such an activity. In the works of novelists like Defoe or Fielding, however, the reader is 'him-or herself involved in the con game ostensibly perpetrated by the author who maintains that the novel is not fiction but fact'.[66] Distinguishing the novel from the romance, he says that the latter necessarily has a backward glance which links it with the classical tradition. It is targeted at the wealthy and aristocratic readership. It uses the authority of 'history' in its narrative, but does not invoke the authority of 'fact'. Romance adheres to the codes of decorum and good manners, wherein nothing vulgar finds mention. Its action is set in the distant past rather than in more recent times. Its location is exotic and its protagonist aristocratic. It values the preservation of virtue and chastity, while the novel, by contrast, has no hesitation in dealing with illegal and forbidden activities. Unlike the novel, the romance is much longer in length and is never written in the first person or epistolary form. Davis argues that, 'The recurrent code embedded in the novelistic prestructure is one of rupture with the past, with the romance tradition, with stories about the distant past.'[67] This discontinuity, however, is not simply one of reaction against the romance, but its reasons lie primarily in the non-literary realm. The emergence of the novel must, therefore be studied in the context of micro developments in the particular national context of England. Its emergence must also be studied in the context of the discourse of prose narratives in print. Davis argues that the technology of print plays a crucial role in deciding and shaping the content of the novel, not because print changes the kind of literature that is written, but because it makes circulation of literature much faster. As a result, content based on more immediate happenings or seemingly immediate happenings begins to gradually find preference. The main feature of prose narrative in print is that it develops a journalistic character, that is, a tendency to report things immediately. Forms like periodicals, newspapers and novels share this common function and basis.

However, Davis also argues that the trajectories of the development of the newspaper and the novel do not exactly overlap. The specific nature of laws regarding licensing in England during the seventeenth and eighteenth centuries made newspapers and 'news' controversial. The Licensing Act lapsed in 1695 and by 1712 the government decided to impose a kind of censorship on news by making it taxable through the Stamp Act. This became a major turning point in the history of the discourse of prose narrative. A 'previously intact discourse—narrative—[got divided] into the taxable (news) and the untaxable (fiction, history).'[68] On the whole, Davis argues that the novel is characterized by an ambivalent attitude towards fact and fiction. It comes 'into being as a form of defence against censorship, power, and authority'.[69] However, it also helps to support and establish the very same power relations. It conveys its meaning to the reader through a relationship of voyeurism between the reader and the text. He also argues that the emergence of the novel should not be linked to the rise of the middle classes. 'The weakness of the middle-class hypothesis is not that it is incorrect but only that it is incomplete. Why should a rising middle class necessarily lead to a 250-page book about a man on an island or a young girl who resists the seduction of her master?'[70]

Four years after writing this book, Lennard J. Davis wrote another book on the origin of the novel called *Resisting Novels: Ideology and Fiction* (1987). Through this book, he rejected the methodologies of new criticism and post-structuralism. He rebelled against his teacher Edward Said to come closer to Marxism. Davis changed most of his earlier conclusions about the novel and modified his entire framework for discussing novels to argue that the form is based on four major components—location, character, dialogue and plot. A combination of these components, he argues, come into being in the form of the novel due to changing political and economic relations in Europe heralded by emergent capitalism and colonialism. Under capitalism, all relationships start getting defined in terms of exchange value. This leads to a social and cultural obsession with 'descriptions of all objects', since everything gets objectified. The new form of the novel becomes a cultural bearer of this ideology wherein questions of 'space' as well as 'property' become more important than ever before. This results in unprecedented importance being accorded to the description of location in each novel.

Davis, like his predcessors, differentiates between the characters of epics and the characters of novels. He argues that the former exist without subjectivity, while the latter exist as individuals with subjectivity. This development takes place in the context of a world plagued by alienation. Characters of novels always fit into a pattern of behaviour that makes sense, while in the real world people can be quite arbitrary and strange. By becoming familiar with the decodable characters of novels, it becomes possible for readers of novels to feel that they know or are familiar with characters in a novel as well or even better than people in the real world. Davis elaborates that 'the coherence of character can be a kind of substitute for the formlessness or irrational nature of modern consciousness and culture'.[71] The novel, therefore, becomes a means of conditioning individual social beings into devoting their attention to understanding other individuals instead of the mechanisms of the entire society.

Davis argues that contrary to the claims made by Bakhtin, conversations and dialogues in novels represent forces of centralization rather than the forces of decentralization. The persona of the author always tells his tale in a civilized, literate and cultured language. As a consequence, the language that is closer to the actual speech of speaking subjects becomes deviant or unusual because of its representation on the printed page of the novel through abbreviations or contractions. He also argues that the emergence of thick plots in novels reflects the objectification and commodification of 'lived experience and daily life'[72] whereby the lives of people work out in front of the reader's eyes. Thus, the action of the novel is separated from life itself. Contrary to general assumptions about the democratic and universal appeal of the novel, the novel actually serves the purpose of preparing the reading public to adjust to regressive political ideologies by reinforcing property relations.

Along with Davis, studies by Nancy Armstrong and Michael McKeon also came out in the same year. Nancy Armstrong adopted a different approach to both the rise of the novel debate as well as European history in her book *Desire and Domestic Fiction: A Political History of the Novel.* She argues that the explanations that are available for why a majority of novelists during the eighteenth century were women are woefully inadequate. Countering existing views, she contends Ian Watt's view that somehow the feminine sensibility was more suited to express the intricacies of personal relationships in novels. She also finds inadequate, Sandra Gilbert and Susan Gubar's engagement with the lives of early women writers in *Madwoman in the Attic* that only showed how they subverted and conformed to patriarchal standards in a world that was largely determined by men. Armstrong proposes that women writers played an active role in giving shape to the modern individual and society. The production of a new female ideal, the rise of the novel as well as the rise of the middle classes in England were all intricately linked with each other. She insists that the history of the novel cannot be understood without taking the history of sexuality into account. Invoking Foucault's *History of Sexuality* and *Discipline and Punish*, she claims that changing sexual relations provided the site for negotiating the changing power equations between classes, cultures, genders and generations. 'My study of the novel will demonstrate that, with the formation of a modern institutional culture, gender differences—though one of the many possible functions of sexuality—came to dominate the functions of generation and genealogy, which organized an earlier culture.'[73] This gendering of human identity during the early eighteenth century, in her view, is one of the key developments of the modern age which produced 'a woman whose value resided chiefly in her femaleness rather than in traditional signs of status'.[74]

Armstrong insists that the modern individual is first and foremost a woman. Unlike men, she is not known by her birth, title or status, rather, she becomes known in terms of the qualities of the mind, or the more subtle nuances of behaviour and psychology indicating what she is 'really' worth. It is the emergence of such an individual which shapes individualism of the modern variety, wherein people learn to relate to each other as individuals. She argues that domestic fiction becomes the main form of the novel and functions as a means of reordering society. The middle class struggle for dominance is fought on the domestic front, even more so than in the courts or the marketplace. The middle class gendered female comes into being initially against the aristocratic woman and then against the disorder of the working classes. It is during the early eighteenth century that 'people began to understand social relations in terms of the modern class society . . .'.[75] At this moment in history, the tradition of the novel gets established through collections like Walter Scott's *The Novels of Daniel Defoe* (1809–10) which exclude *Roxana* and *Moll Flanders*, Mrs. Barbauld's fifty volumes of *The British Novelists; with an Essay; and Prefaces Biographical and Critical* (1810), Mudford's *British Novelists* (1810–17) and Scott's *Ballantyne's Novelist's Library* (1821–4). The novel is regarded by Armstrong as both a document and an agency of cultural history.

Armstrong maps how this change is mediated through language. Instead of signifying history in terms of older kinship relations, now, a new feminine discourse comes into being which divides the universe into the masculine and feminine spheres. This discourse gives rise to the first comprehensive theory of psychology. The details of what is meant by being a woman, get written about in novel after novel. Armstrong argues that 'the rise of the novel hinged upon a struggle to say what made a woman desirable'.[76] Simultaneously, what a woman should desire and which desires she should repress, etc., also get defined. The novel becomes a site of silent and covert struggle for more power for women. In times when intense social upheavals were taking place and a class conscious society was coming into being, the proliferation of personal histories or stories about courtship and marriage become a manifestation of displacing an entire body of political fiction. Important drama gets enacted within the domestic realm wherein class identity is formed through the institution of marriage. Initially women marry into wealth, but soon the figure of sexual exchange is turned against itself. New boundaries are marked against the earlier fantasy of watching class lines dissolve within marriage.

Conduct books, that seek to educate the reader about social norms, and an obsession with sexual purity feed into the content of novels because of a social conviction that women's leisure activities requires supervision. Through conduct books women are schooled into the differences between the country and the city and the creation of a domestic ideal. Their labour gets shaped into domestic duty, the economy into household expenditure and a feminization of the domestic takes place wherein the mother emerges at the centre of the nuclear family. Armstrong maps how the upheavals or changes of history find reflection within the changing narratives about domestic life, desirable women and the desires of women. Therefore, the form of the novel 'redefines what men were supposed to desire in women and what women, in turn, were supposed to desire to be'.[77] Armstrong concludes that the novel arose and developed in the context of a 'decisive shift in the number of those [books] devoted to making women desirable rather than telling men how to assume a high position in life'.[78] Thus, writing by, for and about women occupied a central position in history wherein the power of domestic clichés was given to women as well as exercised by them. In her subsequent book written in 2005, *How Novels Think: Limits of Individualism from 1719–1900*, Nancy Armstrong modified this argument to make a more fundamental point about individuals and novels. She argued that 'the history of the novel and the history of the modern subject are, quite literally, one and the same'.[79] The 'ideological core' of the novel is that novels presuppose individuals and think about how individuals can fulfill themselves in respective socio-historical conditions. Only a genuine alternative to the individual can fundamentally alter the narrative core of the novel.

Michael McKeon, in *The Origins of the English Novel: 1600–1740*, begins by proposing 'that genre theory cannot be divorced from the history of genres, from the understanding of genres in history . . . that the theory of genre must be a dialectical theory of genre'.[80] He uses Marx's concept of 'simple abstraction' to approach the question of the origin of the novel:

> By the middle of the eighteenth century, the stabilizing of terminology—the increasing acceptance of 'the novel' as a canonic term, so that contemporaries can 'speak of it as such'—signals the stability of the conceptual category and of the class of literary products that it encloses. My procedure in this study will be to work back from that point of origin to disclose the immediate history of its 'pre-givenness.'[81]

McKeon begins by distinguishing his methodology from previous theorists of the novel—Ian Watt, Claude Lévi-Strauss and Northrop Frye, and Mikhail Bakhtin. He argues that Watt's concept of formal realism provides an inadequate explanation for the persistence of romance and anti-individualistic elements in the novels of Fielding. He finds Watt's thesis of the 'dominance' of the middle classes in early eighteenth century problematic especially in relation to the novels of Fielding which reflect a sympathy with the declining gentry rather than the emerging middle classes. McKeon engages with Strauss's 'normative mythic modal' and Frye's 'archetype' to argue that their methods evacuate the historical process from the analysis of how genres come into being. For them, a new literary form consists of nothing but the old and its process is not of transformation but of 'calcification'. McKeon differentiates Bakhtin from the archetypalists in that he appears to free the novel from a deadly ossification; but in ways also presents a mirror inversion of Frye's archetypalism. 'Bakhtin digs an implausible gulf between the "rigid", "fixed", "sealed-off", "straight-forward", closure of traditional genres and the "openended flexibility" and "indeterminacy" of "the novel".'[82] Thus, instead of a relatively determinate literary form the novel becomes a generalized aura and an ethos of that form.

McKeon argues that the novel as a form bears the unique distinction of being the genre that 'internalizes the emergence of the middle class'[83] and its concerns. The early eighteenth century is a time when Europe as a whole and England in particular, face simultaneous social and intellectual crises due to intense class struggles in society. In such a context, the novel becomes an 'early modern cultural instrument' to confront this crisis. He locates the origin of the English novel to the dialectical fluidity between the 'naive empiricism' of the claim to historicity and documentation of authentic truth, and its demystification by 'extreme scepticism' as mere romance. Instead of focusing upon the similarities between early English novelists, McKeon emphasizes the differences between writers like Richardson and Fielding who bear completely different ideological views on preceding literary genres as well as their contemporary times. Yet, they become the innovators of the same genre because of the various important transformations that were taking place in social values. One is the move towards secularization, wherein society starts facing a crisis of faith and begins looking for alternate secular sources of spiritual and moral authority. Against this backdrop, art begins to replace religion, and narrative begins to replace drama. The criterion of class also begins to gradually replace the status criteria based on birth and kinship. The notion of social hierarchy having a basis in 'Natural' laws takes a serious drubbing wherein the culture of lineage and kinship relations starts destabilizing. The double standards involved in the requirements of female chastity from gentlewomen, where the transmission of property is more of an issue than among those lower down in the social order starts becoming apparent. The themes of forced marriage to an aristocrat or the threat of aristocratic rape continue to recur. Moneyed interests slowly gain acceptance as opposed to landed interests. The relation between capitalist ideology and Protestant reform starts becoming evident.

In such fluid times, two distinct ideological tendencies come into being. McKeon calls these the 'progressive' and 'conservative' ideologies, respectively, that is, ideologies that support the commoner as opposed to those which support the aristocracy. Reason, social instrumentality and usefulness are employed by both sides. In early modern England, the novel thus emerges as a means to mediate, represent and conceal the social and ethical problems involved in the gradual discrediting of the aristocracy. Established literary forms no longer serve this purpose as they lack conviction in carrying these ideological concerns. The novel's most frequented theme becomes that of 'questions of virtue' through which both sides seek to claim virtuosity and superiority. Virtues, their identification and definitions become a site for continuous conflict, and gradually envelope in an allegorical way the questions of politics, gender, class, history, language, etc. Both romance and the aristocracy slowly get replaced. Unlike Davis, McKeon argues that the novel is not an outcome of an insulated national culture but a composite culture of print, wherein different types of fiction translated from French or Spanish, contribute to shaping the style of English novels. He identifies the complex nature of this ideological terrain in the writings of Richardson and Fielding who seem to reconcile both progressive and conservative ideologies as well as naive empiricism and extreme scepticism in the course of their careers. He argues that the dialectics between progressive and conservative ideologies is not very simple and that progressive ideology seems to have an inherent tendency towards conservatism, and vice versa, especially, as evidenced in novels.

Another critic who throws some light on the rise of the novel debate is Firdous Azim. In *The Colonial Rise of the Novel* (1993) Azim locates her study of the English novel in the terrain of post-colonial pedagogy wherein questions of language and canon interact with postcolonial subjectivities of class, race and gender. She employs a wide range of insights offered by critics as diverse as Bhabha, Fanon, Gauri Viswanathan, Watt, Barthes, Lennard Davis, Marthe Robert, Terry Lovell, Spivak, Derrida, Levi-Strauss, Lukács, etc., to examine the formation of the 'central narrating subject' in novels. Her choice of novels for close textual analysis is based on pushing the limits of feminist analysis to include a view of imperialism—not merely through the explicit theme of colonialism, but also in the formation of subject-positions and the formation of the pedagogic subject. She argues that the origin of the English novel cannot be understood without taking into account 'the European colonial project, and the ideological and political implications of the dissemination of the novel as literature and its function in the creation of the colonial terrain'.[84] She examines *Oroonoko* as a first person account of the life of a Black prince through a female narrator/author—Aphra Behn. Her next study is of Daniel Defoe's *Roxana* as an account of a female life within a more domestic European setting, written by a male author through a female narrator. She interrogates the novels of Charlotte Brontë for a 'rereading of feminism's texts'. Her central effort is to map the formation of '...a coherent, consistent narrating subject, often female, who was constructed by the effacement of *Other* subjects'.[85]

Azim argues that eighteenth-century England deeply engages with questions of human subjectivity. The search for understanding subjectivity takes English narrative forms into the terrain of travel narratives. Cultural encounters become the recurrent theme of the novel right from its inception, be it with Man Friday in *Robinson Crusoe* or the adventures in different travel tales. She analyzes Aphra Behn's novel, *Oroonoko*, as a means of defining as well as differentiating the identity of a white prosperous English woman from that of a black Surinamese prince/slave. However, Imoinda, the slave woman remains a 'vague and hazy figure'.[86] As the Other, she is forcefully eradicated and obliterated both by the colonizers as well as Oroonoko who himself transforms from a prince to a trader on the colonizer's side, to a class conscious slave, to a tourist guide and entertainer, to an impractical rebel, to a broken and defeated man who first kills Imoinda and his unborn child, and is then dismembered, tortured and destroyed.

However, Azim argues that it is not in only in travel novels that colonialism occurs as an overt theme and actor, but also in the novels located in more European and domestic settings. For instance, the 'Other' in *Roxana* occupies fluctuating positions. The split narrating subject of Roxana recounts her life, loves and many guises. Her origins are ambiguous. She is told that she was born in France and her parents came to England fleeing religious persecution. Her subject position develops in relation to the class position of Amy, her maid. Her accidental name Roxana is acquired from her costume bought from a Turkish slave who remains an invisible presence in the novel. 'Roxana's sexual career is accompanied by an amassing of wealth, making her the prototype of the capitalist woman, whose entry into the expanding commercial world is effected through the decoration of her body with foreign goods.'[87] Another 'Other', her daughter Susan (who shares her mother's real name), threatens her subsequent life as a respectable married woman. Susan's search for her mother/origin represents a threat and is effaced through murder. It is essentially in relation to these other women that the subjectivity of Roxana gets formed.

Azim examines the writings of Charlott Brontë, particularly *Jane Eyre* in which the figure of Bertha Mason becomes the representative of the dark sexuality, savagery, madness of the colonial other, and presents a mirror/mimetic image of Jane's own psyche. She is obfuscated by a female narrator/author. Azim discusses themes in the juvenile writings of Brontë like sexuality, racial difference, displacement, travel and conquests. The language of imperialism finds its way into negotiating different subjectivities in *The Professor.* Themes of sexual irregularity and transgression of the Gothic novels find resonance in Brontë's novels and take endangered femininity through tensions and travails to find resolution in true romantic love associated with dominant notions of female passivity. The strain of locating the origin of the novel to the Gothic marks another domain of understanding the novel. In a novel like *Shirley* which is about industrial strife, both rebellious femininity and the striking worker are domesticated and contained through a colonial position that 'veers' somewhere in between.

Azim argues that the 'central narrating subject' is the main formal feature of the novel. This narrating subject comes into existence in the backdrop of the discourse of Western Enlightenment in which philosophers seek to create citizens. This narrating subject is rooted in the 'inauguration of the bourgeois democratic order, based on the notion of the rights and sovereignty of the human individual'.[88] The novel occupies an ambiguous and anomalous place in this project. On the one hand, it wages struggle against the master narratives of other genres, on the other, it tries to get recognition from the very culture that scorns it. Azim claims that it is significant that the novel is given a 'very reluctant status as literature, and was not even included in the Oxbridge literature syllabus until the 1930s'.[89] Dichotomy or paradox are the key characteristics of the novel, where the encounter of the self with the other becomes extremely important. The birth of realism in the novel is linked to this subject-object dichotomy, as reality is 'something *external* to the narrating subject'.[90] Females or feminine viewpoints within the novel confront or bring within their ambit the brutality and violence accompanying the process of colonialism. The novel, therefore, becomes the key genre through which many subject positions are worked out. '[I]mperialism does not remain limited to colonialism as a *theme* in the novels, but becomes part and parcel of the genre itself.'[91] Azim concludes that the novel is 'an imperialist project, based on the forceful eradication and obliteration of the Other'.[92]

On the whole, there are different versions and explanations about the rise of the novel. Let us briefly recall the main views studied so far. For Lukács the main reason for the rise of the novel lies in the emergence of a new world in which an earlier totality and wholesomeness are lost. In this new world the harmonious epic gives way to the 'transcendental homelessness' of the novel. For Bakhtin, the rise of the novel is rooted in the ever-increasing dialogism and hybridity of the verbal-discursive universe, which progressively finds true expression in the polyglot or multilingual form of the novel. For Ian Watt, the most important factor is that an aggregate view of the world, comprising of particular experiences of particular individuals at particular places in particular times replaces the unified worldview of the Middle Ages. The novel, for Watt, is the best exponent of this provisional, critical and anti-traditional temper represented through the technique of 'formal realism'. Marthe Robert argues that the elastic and ambiguous form of the novel mirrors the inventiveness, restlessness and vitality of modern colonial societies, even while its content continues to reflect the primordial essence of 'family romances'. In his two separate explanations, Lennard J. Davis first argues that the novel is a product of an express print culture which overhauls and updates all literary themes, especially in opposition to the romances. Later, he argues that the novel is a deeply ideological form which reinforces the new capitalist order by propagating notions of private property through its narratives and themes. For Nancy Armstrong, the most important factor behind the rise of the novel is the emergent primacy of individualism, propelled by a modern emphasis on the social category of gender, which shifts the focus of the middle classes away from class to domesticity. The novel, according to Michael McKeon, is the literary form of the emergent middle classes, which represents progressive as well as conservative ideological concerns involved in the transition of society from feudalism to capitalism, especially those associated with 'virtue'. Firdaus Azim argues that the novel is the product of a new colonial world which encounters several 'others'; in such a context, the novel provides a narrative site where questions of identity and subjectivity are resolved. While there exist many more views and variations to the rise-of-the-novel debate, we will restrict ourselves to the above critics because they represent some key contours of the debate over the rise of the novel. The main questions that emerge from this appraisal are:

1. Why does an 'elastic', 'plastic', 'parasitic', 'hybrid', 'inventive' or 'unfinished' genre like the novel come up in literature? What are the historical factors that explain the rise of such a form?
2. Why does 'totality' in literature collapse at the turn of the modern age, and why does god abandon the world at about the same point of time? What is the link between these developments and the emergence of fragmented and subjective narratives?
3. Which historical processes explain the democratization of discourse and its special link to the novel?
4. What is the link between capitalism, individualism and the middle classes? What is their link to the novel?
5. Why do questions of subjectivity, gender, the 'other' become so important in the novel?

Impact of Social Transformations

To find answers to these questions, let us revisit the process of the historical transition from feudalism to capitalism and its impact on popular imagination and literature. The rise of a plastic, elastic, inventive, parasitic, unfinished and ever-regenerative form like the novel can be understood only if it is located in the context of the emergence of a plastic, elastic, inventive, parasitic, unfinished and regenerative system of capitalism. The change also impacted the arts and literature, which under feudalism, were based on strict rules as well as a hierarchical system of genres. Adhering to decorum, conventions and codes in themes and composition was important. In fact, historically, the literary and academic interest even in 'folk' or people's art began only by the eighteenth century when feudalism was already on its way out.[93] Before that, a largely rigid division existed between different arts based on their social origins. The rigidity was broken perhaps only during fairs or religious pageants when some ground for interface was created between different social classes. The novel and several other new literary forms broke new grounds in this context.

This historical transition was embedded in many conflicts, tensions and shifts in the intellectual, moral and conceptual terrain. The socially rigid system of feudalism, organized on the basis of inviolable kinship relations of station by birth, structured around a hierarchical 'chain of being' gave way to greater social mobility and individualism under capitalism. Unlike before, when an individual, more often than not, died in the same social position that he/she was born into, very often in the same village or parish as well, because of inviolable ties to land,[94] emergent capitalism generated professions that required mass scale migration and uprooting, eroding the kingship and land based old order. The reasons for this lay in the dynamism generated within the capitalist economy, wherein, instead of hoarding surplus, earnings were now reinvested into the economy to generate greater profits. This led to many innovations in production techniques. The stagnation of feudalism paved way for a constant flow of capital. The income generated in the new economy by entrepreneurs could now exceed the entire wealth accumulated over generations by the old nobles. Even the new Protestant ethnic taught that wealth should not be dissipated, but ploughed back into business.[95] Acquiring private property received a new impetus, colonial exploits gathered momentum, and the accumulation and circulation of capital became a continuous process. Upward mobility now became possible. A new class of people like '... the mercantile circles and economically enlightened landlords, financiers, scientifically-minded economic and social administrators, the educated middle class, manufacturers and entrepreneurs,[96] made the most in the new system. The old feudal form of small-scale subsistence agriculture gave way to a large-scale capitalist mode, in which land, too, became a commodity like any other.[97] Religious institutions, which were deeply entrenched in feudal social codes and a hierarchical social order, also started facing a crisis of legitimacy. These changes, however, did not happen overnight, but were part of a slow and passionately resisted process of change.

The ensuing conflict involved all walks of life—religion, art, literature, science, agriculture, politics, state, family, marriage, etc., and led to significant shifts in worldview. The ideas of freedom, equality and fraternity emerged on the European social scene. Large-scale questioning of social hierarchies took place, not merely among the educated or intellectual circles, but also at the popular level. New ideas of equality found their most powerful exposition in the French Revolution (with the 'Declaration of the Rights of Man and the Citizen'), although revolutions, both before and after, kept on happening in different countries of Europe. Powerful arguments for the equality of women in society were also articulated. The likes of Mary Astell, who wrote *A Serious Proposal to the Ladies for the Advancement of their True and Greatest Interest* (1694), and later, Mary Wollstonecraft, with her *A Vindication of the Rights of Woman* (1792), broke new grounds for the cause of women through advocacy for women's education and equality with men. These were also times when large-scale colonial encounters as part of capitalist expansion were taking place. Slave trade became a major occupation. Many anti-slavery tracts were written as part of the anti-slavery movements.[98] 'Citizenship', an idea in which each individual was seen to be equal before the state, evolved and was popularly embraced both by the French and the American Revolutions. The concept of a 'democratic' form of government now challenged the older 'aristocratic' form of government. The first major example of this change, although partial, took place in England through the Glorious Revolution of 1688, when the powers of the parliament over the monarchy were ensured.

Another major change based on technological innovations and enterprise, was the Industrial Revolution. Within a short span of time, various path-breaking and dramatic advancements took place. Britain was the first country where many new productive forces were unleashed. It is important to delineate here that the Industrial Revolution was not merely a product of path-breaking technological advances, as is popularly thought, but that path breaking technological advances were as much an outcome of the capitalist mode of production, wherein profits were reinvested to devise means for generating greater profits. As Eric Hobsbawm says, 'Whatever the British advance was due to, it was not scientific and technological superiority.'[99] France was far ahead of England in the natural sciences and produced more original inventions, and Germany, by far, excelled Great Britain in technical knowledge. 'But the right conditions were visibly present in Britain, where more than a century had passed since the first king had been formally tried and executed by his people, and since private profit and economic development had become accepted as the supreme objects of government policy.'[100]

A major impact of the Industrial Revolution and the rapid advancement of technology was an accompanying sense of 'progress' over the past; a sense that the new was better than the old, that the earlier times were not the most venerable, and that it was the future which was worth looking forward to. Value came to be invested in innovation and novelty, instead of that which was ancient or traditional. Innovation became the ideology of the new market. The entire way of looking at earlier times changed. The past became more removed from the present. It is not a coincidence, therefore, that 'history' as a serious and important discipline also developed at the same point of time.

Along with the new-found power of technology and an unprecedented confidence in the future, came a new sense of control over 'nature'. At this point in history, people came to entertain a sense of dominance over nature. Before, right from pre-agrarian hunter-gatherer communes to feudalism, nature was always perceived as a formidable force. But now, people came to experience a sense of confidence in dealing with the challenges thrown by nature, be it bad weather, storm, disease or illness. It is significant that the ideas of secularism also gained ground in European societies around the same point in time. As sociologists and theologians like Max Weber and P. Tillich have argued, the origin of religion in society lay in the sense of powerlessness and inability of people to explain natural phenomenon, particularly those related to birth, sickness or death. Now, instead of blaming the vagaries of nature upon the supernatural force of 'God', there was an effort to discern and understand the underlying principles of nature. What was simultaneously witnessed was an unprecedented enthusiasm over the power of science. It is not a coincidence that England, the first European country to separate religion from the state as well as the first to form the Royal Society[101] of London in 1660, was also the first to develop capitalism, the first to have a democratically elected government, the first to have a major revolution in 1688, as well as the first to have the Industrial Revolution. Although the Royal Society failed to achieve many of its lofty goals, i.e. unravel all the laws of nature, their confidence was particularly noteworthy. It is important to note that though all these changes took place in England over a prolonged period of time in history, they were closely and dialectically linked to each other.

A significant outcome of the new historical sense of progress, the delegitimization of religious authority, the accompanying technological advancement, and vice versa, was the popular emergence of reason and rationality as an ethic as well as a governing principle for capitalist societies. The logic of 'cause and effect' came to dominate thought and philosophical systems. A new belief developed in the agency or will of human beings. Descartes in *Meditationes de prima Philosophia* (1641) and *Regulae ad directionem ingenii* (1684), Antoine Arnauld and Pierre Nicole in *Logic, or, The Art of Thinking* (1662), Baruch Spinoza in *Ethics* (1677), John Locke in *An Essay concerning Human Understanding* (1689) and Hume in *Treatise of*

Human Nature (1739) argued for the primacy of reason, logic and rationality as supreme social virtues. In fact, the social vacuum created by the absence of religion in governance, was filled by a new secular code of reason. It became important to discern what was reasonable. Rationality emerged in a significant way as an important human faculty as opposed to emotion. However, for a society or a nation to be rational, it was also important for its constituent individuals to be rational and reasonable. As per the new doctrine of Protestantism, it became important that an individual negotiate his/her own relationship with god based upon what was reasonable, instead of depending upon the church.

Individualism, too, emerged as an important ideology. It became economically important for an individual to make maximum profits on the basis of individual enterprise. With this came the urge to rise above the constraints of community and kinship ties, to maximize individually owned private property. Individualism also emerged as an alternative to class/community based understanding of society. Nationalism emerged in place of the older authority of religion and kinship ties. For the first time in history, the view of society as an aggregate of individuals got evolved. It slowly became important for the state to work for the benefit and development of individual citizens. The new political theory of 'liberalism' emerged, which sought to protect the rights and liberties of individuals vis-à-vis governments. Individualism became an important ethic as well as virtue under capitalism, wherein if an individual made profits then it reflected his inner virtue, and the nation and people as a whole benefited from him. Another reason for the development of individualism was the collapse of old community ties. As Ian Watt says:

> For those fully exposed to the new economic order, the effective entity on which social arrangements were now based was no longer the family, nor the church, nor the township, nor any other collective unit, but the individual: he alone was primarily responsible for determining his own economic, social, political and religious roles.[102]

The old joint family setup started breaking up in order to make way for the new nuclear family. The nuclear family was 'free of wider kinship ties, . . . more geographically and socially mobile, . . . [gave] greater emotional support via the unconstrained choice of marriage partners, and . . . [permitted] occupational roles to be filled by achievement criteria, all requirements of industrial society'.[103] The notion of love marriage as opposed to arranged marriage started gaining popularity. Apart from its progressive aspect, the notion of free choice in marriage also went hand-in-hand with the aspiration for improving one's social standing by marrying into money.

In this ethos of individualism, a new kind of subjectivism developed. Individuals became more self-conscious about others as well as themselves and questions of subjectivity gained importance. Lives of individuals got sharply divided between the hierarchically rated private and public realms, with a new work ethic expecting minimum overlap and interference between the two. Multiple subjective selves of individuals became a popular point of discussion for leading philosophers of these times—Diderot talked about the 'complexity of personhood' while Adam Smith discussed the 'nature of sympathy'. The faculties of feeling and thinking within the same being were slowly separated. This new subjective consciousness intensified due to the expanding colonial project, which brought Europeans into contact with people of different races, regions, language, religion and culture, and made them acutely conscious of their own identities.

The colonial project was integrally tied up with the development of capitalism. Capitalism explored new worlds in search of more lands, new markets as well as cheap labour. As a system it was antithetical to the existence of autonomous, insulated or self-sustaining economic units, as under feudalism. Its predatory nature required the engulfing of all economies of the world into its own. Capitalism as an economic system showed tremendous flexibility and adaptability when brought into contact with other modes of production. While its history in Europe involved a conflict with the old feudal system, its trajectory in the colonies displayed a profit based reconciliation with, and appropriation of, all other pre-capitalist modes of production. As Prabhat Patnaik opines:

> [Capitalism breaks] down the insulation of existing pre-capitalist societies, it does ruthlessly draw them into the vortex of its own accumulation process, but not necessarily by creating within them, in dominant form, the structures of the bourgeois mode of production itself. They are transformed by, and hegemonized by, metropolitan capitalism, but they themselves never get transformed into bourgeois societies.[104]

Thus, capitalism, while trying to gain a foothold as a new system in Europe, entailed certain radicalism and a critical-oppositional approach towards many aspects of the existing feudal setup. But simultaneously, while branching off into the colonies, it showed the remarkable ability of making everything a part of its own vortex of profit generation without confronting all reminiscent features of other modes of production. While it promoted nationalism on the one hand, it remained international in its character on the other. As Eric Hobsbawm says, '. . . it was easier to link distant capitals than country and city'.[105] Urban centres slowly became the locus of all activities—political, economic, artistic and scientific.

The shift from feudalism to capitalism led to the emergence of another key factor, i.e. the rise of the middle classes. The middle classes made a living out of transactions, in which they were neither the producer/worker nor the owner of the means of production. Instead, they occupied an intermediary position and performed all kinds of specialized as well as odd jobs. The growing members of this upwardly mobile class thronged to the urban centres. With the development of capitalism, this class grew on a massive scale. In the emergent phase, it was this class that provided the key ideological, moral and intellectual impetus to the rise of capitalism. However, the role played by this class was most unusual. Neither did it bear the political and economic power of the capitalist class to pioneer capitalism, nor did it bear the democratic power of the workers and peasants, who with their aspiration to break free from feudal exploitation, participated in popular uprisings and continuous revolutions. The middle classes were influential or decisive in neither of these ways, yet it was always they who bore the entire moral and ethical burden of change. Historically, they often sided with the powerful. If revolution were imminent, they would champion equality, democracy and freedom; if it were crushed they would reconcile with the inevitability of inequality and exploitation. On their own, they were not powerful enough to decide the course of history, but they always pretended as though they were.

All these changes, however, did not happen unproblematically. Capitalism did not emerge unchallenged; rather its rise was fiercely contested and resisted. There were two kinds of debates and oppositions to the spread of capitalism. On the one hand, there was stiff resistance from the old feudal and monarchical order, which lost out on its old privileges and fought with all its might against capitalism based on the ideological use of 'convention' and 'tradition'. On the other hand, there was growing criticism against the glaring shortcomings of capitalism like its overcrowded cities, brutality toward the working classes, cruelty toward child workers and slaves, breakdown of social cohesion, lack of community feeling, cold materialism, profit or money becoming the new god, increased alienation and fragmentation, commodification of everything, destruction of nature. This criticism was also often aimed at transcending capitalism without returning to the old system. Thus, the critique of capitalism happened from two different quarters, the conservative and the progressive.

This critique became manifest in the dominant debates of those times. The 'ancients' clashed with the 'moderns' arguing about value being invested in the old instead of in the new. 'The battle of the books' took place at the time in which thinkers either sided with modernity arguing that it entailed progress, or they went against it declaring that the future signified deterioration.[106] The literary and philosophical worlds saw a return to classicism or neoclassicism, in which ancient forms and thought were revived. Decorum became an important ingredient of literature, i.e. a belief that 'literary genres, characters and styles were all ordered in hierarchies, or "levels", from high through middle to low, and had to be matched to one another'.[107] The 'cult of antiquity' in which 'classical manuscripts were collected and printed ... and ... [t]he study of Greek and Latin ... entrenched as the essential of polite learning in schools and universities'[108] was established. English literature of the eighteenth century witnessed a domination by the 'Augustans', i.e. writers like Oliver Goldsmith, Dryden, Johnson, Pope and Swift, who resurrected and reinvented the writing styles of Roman writers like Virgil, Ovid and Horace. Considerable lament was expressed over the decline of the nobility and monarchy. A lot of hue and cry about growing immorality and licentiousness in society was also voiced. This was partly due to the marginalization of the church as the main source of moral authority, and partly because of increased social mobility, especially that of women. The need for following strict moral codes became a social obsession. Chapbooks, sermons and instruction-books providing guidance and advice about right virtues became the most widely circulated forms of literature.

New literary forms like the essay and the satire came into being for carrying out many of these debates. Popular forms like newspapers, pamphlets, periodicals and ballads, popularized these debates. University 'wits' carried the limits of reason and rationality to new heights. Disagreements regarding the relative values of intuitive knowledge as opposed to rationalist knowledge also took place. Debates revolving around the theme of 'nature' became central to much of literature. A return to nature through the gothic emphasized the dark yet powerful side of nature. On the one hand, the gothic became a means to critique the dangers involved in trying to control nature, on the other, the uncontrolled wilderness of nature only made the requirement for pruning and careful cultivation all the more urgent. Nature also became a means to argue for the equality of all beings and the artificiality and falsity of social hierarchy. The inherent harmony, order and intelligibility of nature were emphasized. The notions of 'natural law' and 'natural religion' came up. The cult of the 'noble savage' or the natural man provided another argument for the universality of all human beings. A new social fascination with the 'child' also developed at the same time. The inherent goodness, sensitivity and innocence of children were emphasized to underscore the equality of all human beings by birth. Many also argued to the contrary by opining that some children were, in fact, 'special' and not like others. The importance of imparting suitable education in order to build good citizens was debated, especially with the path-breaking works of John Locke and later Jean Jacques Rousseau.[109]

A new persona emerged powerfully at this time. This was the genius, romantic artist, who created spontaneous/natural art, without bothering for money, payment, publication or fame. This was in complete contradiction to the emergence of professionalism among artists who made a living by selling their artistic goods in the new literary market, or what was popularly called the Grub Street. By the time the Romantic persona of the anguished artist developed, the Grub Street had been already operating in full force for nearly a century, both as a metaphor as well as an actual hub of commercial writers. Most trends within Romanticism, which were coterminous with the French Revolution, became part of the progressive critique of capitalism. The search for utopias or new perfect societies became important. However, the fact that the objectives of the French Revolution were not carried to their logical conclusion led to widespread disillusionment among many Romantic artists who vacillated from extreme left to extreme right positions within their lifetimes, some prominent examples being Wordsworth, Coleridge and Victor Hugo.[110]

Ethnographies and travelogues that provided a window to new places and people became popular. Stories of common people became the subject of many new genres. New literary forms exploded on the European scene, like the essay, newspapers, periodicals, dictionaries, encyclopaedias, letters, characters, travelogues, utopias, ballads, sermons, diaries, etc. The most important factor about all these genres was that they were not rule bound or code bound. They did not follow any old convention or decorum. In fact, their entire rhetoric was that of the new. Most of these genres were aimed at the new middle class readership, made possible by the expansion of literacy and print. Many such forms intentionally focused upon 'low' subjects and themes for their content.

It is only if we take into account this entire backdrop of changes involved in the transformation from feudalism to capitalism, that we would be able to understand the emergence of the novel better. Obviously, this shift took place over a prolonged period of time, starting from the sixteenth century and continuing well into the nineteenth century. Many of the trends and tendencies that we have outlined did not become evident simultaneously, in fact, their moments of eminence varied over several decades. Today, we are able to appreciate the link between them only because of the advantage of hindsight. But as we have tried to argue, they were all deeply and intrinsically related to each other and symptomatic of the same essential transition and transformation, i.e. from feudalism to capitalism.

Conclusion

The above appraisal helps explain how the emergence of novel was indeed linked to individualism, democratization, anti-traditionalism and subjectivity. It also involved a greater role for women, as well as for the colonial and racial 'other'. Moreover, the novel was integrally tied up with the emerging middle classes. However, to argue that the changing role of women or the development of individualism was singularly the most important factor responsible for the emergence of the novel would, in our view, be reductive. We would also argue that the emergence of these factors, in turn, can be understood if we look at an entire and interlinked process of historical change. Therefore, the emergence of the novel can be best understood if the total process of transition from feudalism to capitalism is kept in mind. In fact, if we take a look at a few early novels, it immediately becomes evident that the novel as a genre displays an exhaustive range, both in its choice of themes, as well as in its choice of forms. It cannot, therefore, be restricted or tied down only to one or the other factor.

For instance, the form of Aphra Behn's *Oroonoko* (1688) is a combination of *medieval romances, ethnographies, travel tales and allegories*. It is located in the 'exoticized' locales of Africa and South America. Oroonoko the black prince/slave is sentimentalized almost as a gallant with Restoration virtues like 'true honour', 'wit', 'sweet and diverting conversation', 'civility of well-bred man', etc., becoming almost an allegory for the Stuart Kings. Oroonoko is the only humanized slave among the mass of slaves, so it is never easy to understand if his virtues lie in his royal origins or if he seems royal because of his virtues. The narrator as well as the narration is deliberately subjectivized and dramatized. The female narrator/author narrates her travel adventures to describe the brutality of colonialism, the process of psychological colonization, the workings of plantation economies, the clash between British and Dutch colonizers, the cult of the noble savage, and the novel mirrors or perhaps predates anti-slavery tracts. The novel engages with debates about religion—both pagan and Christian—and the true meaning of 'virtue'. It invokes the traditions of *history writing* to describe ethnographic details (albeit erroneous) with authority, and the female subjectivity of the narrator is employed to both subvert as well as reinforce colonial, national and gender dynamics.

Another early novel, Daniel Defoe's *Robinson Crusoe* (1719) borrows extensively from genres like *travel tales, church sermons, letter writing and journals*. It contains painfully long descriptions of Crusoe's travels and adventures. The action of the novel is justified by the means of Crusoe's rationalizations through religion, but Crusoe does not require the church or any other institution to do so. He interprets the will of god all by himself. The story itself is like an allegorical rendition of the civilizational progress of man starting from the original sin to modernity. Robinson Crusoe keeps a journal during his long stay at the island, so that some parts of the novel are narrated through journal entries. He represents the *homo economicus* (an economic being who seeks to maximize individual profit and consumption) and accomplishes all his deals through contracts and extensive bookkeeping. The novel represents the development of a nationalist discourse through the clash between different national interests over colonization and slave trade. It also reflects the new Calvinist ethic, with an emphasis on predestination and bourgeois profit. It embodies the new individualistic ethic of capitalism and demonstrates the evolution of a new selfhood defined through commodity value, i.e. the 'worth' of an individual as measured in terms of money and property rather than in more esoteric categories. This individualism of Crusoe is also forged in contrast to the racial and colonial 'other'—Man Friday. The novel is an early narrative about the essential capitalist logic, i.e. how to make crass profits without disturbing the conscience too much.

Another early novel, Jonathan Swifts' *Gulliver's Travels* (1726) is a *mock-travel tale and a mock-utopia.* It delves deep into the debate between the ancients and the moderns, and engages with questions of rationality, logic, science, liberty, religion, morality, governance, empire, anti-colonialism, etc. Through the journeys to Lilliput, Brobdingnag, Laputa, Balnibarbi, Luggnagg, Glubbdubdrob, Japan and the country of the Houyhnhnms over a period of sixteen years, Gulliver, a surgeon, encounters various types of peoples, cultures and governments. These encounters become Swift's way of reflecting upon emotion, human nature, knowledge, rationality, individual and society in England. From an enthusiastic traveller, Gulliver returns to become a recluse at his home, alienated from both family and society. By the end, questions of nationalism and patriotism seem strangely irrelevant as Gulliver starts thinking about England from the point of view of Houyhnhnmland with Englishmen seeming as Yahoos. The novel touches upon many major historical debates of its age. It employs *satire* and displays the celebrated wit and rationality of the Augustan age. *Gulliver's Travels* also borrows form from the narrative techniques of *ethnography, journal, fantasy, allegory, adventure tale, letter writing and history writing.*

Samuel Richardson in *Pamela: or Virtue Rewarded* (1740) utilizes *letter writing* techniques to evolve the epistolary form of the novel, giving a day-by-day, minute-by-minute account of the fifteen year old Pamela's life through her letters to her parents describing how she resists the advances of her master Mr B to safeguard her virginity till he ultimately surrenders before her superior virtue and proposes marriage to her. From a servant girl, thus, Pamela becomes an upper class wife. Through this novel, Richardson brings into play issues of virtue, psychology, individuality, class, gender, aristocracy, social mobility, status, education and sexuality. The novel caused quite a stir in its times. Like the famous Cinderella story (usually dated to 1697), this novel provides one of the first versions of the new myth of social mobility for women under capitalism, i.e. through love marriage in which a rich man marries a poor but virtuous and really worthy woman in spite of her poverty and low social origins. This modern myth, like the Robinson Crusoe myth for men, has seen innumerable adaptations and re-workings in modern literature.

Henry Fielding in *Joseph Andrews* (1742) lampoons Richardson's novels using the techniques of *burlesque and the picaresque*. The novel is *mock-heroic* and *neoclassical* in its style and narrates the adventures of Joseph Andrews, who suffers assaults on his virtue by Lady Booby. He leaves for London along with his simpleton companion Parson Adams so that he can earn the means to live comfortably with his childhood love, Fanny. The plot is full of chance elements from the *romance* tradition. Fielding borrows extensively from *drama*, wherein his narrator makes interludes in the narration through the figures of the chorus, the curtain raiser and as a member of the audience. Through the various episodes, Fielding deals with questions of virtue, hypocrisy, religion, literature, crime, trade, rustic values, philosophy and classicism. He calls his novel a 'comic epic poem in prose' admittedly seeking to recreate adventures parallel to those in the Homeric and Virgilian *epics*. It is also significant that Fielding calls himself 'the founder of a new province of writing'.[111] Fielding ties the end of the novel to Richardon's *Pamela* wherein Joseph emerges to be the brother of Pamela, with both Joseph and Fanny discovering their true parentage to ultimately be happily united in marriage.

Lawrence Sterne's *The Life and Opinions of Tristram Shandy* (1759–67) is a remarkably different and whimsical novel, which employs dashes, catalogues, illustrations, blank pages and blank chapters in its narration. It is full of bizarre action and is an emphatic statement against the logic of cause and effect, the notion of rationality and reasonability, and the sense of historical progress. It defies all these concepts by constantly being random and deliberately unintelligible, both in form as well as in content. Sterne's novel makes allusions to the writings of Cervantes, Rabelais, Bacon, Burton, Pope, Locke, Swift and others. Highly self-reflexive, it is the autobiography of Tristram Shandy who cannot narrate his life in a simple, linear or chronological plot. Rather, he digresses into lengthy discussions on philosophy, science, religion, his father's quaint beliefs, etc., to explain events in his life that are too few and far between in the novel. In his times, Sterne was criticized for being bawdy, even accused of plagiarism, but over time, especially lately, the novel has been appreciated for being aware of the problems of representation and narration throughout its nine volumes.

Even a cursory look at these early novels reveals how they are all deeply embedded in the debates of their times, i.e. debates that particularly engaged the educated/literate middle classes. The common factor in their themes is the rejection of older kinds of protagonists, i.e. those coming from the nobility or the aristocracy in favour of upwardly mobile men and women from humble origins. All these novels include fleshed out individual characters as well as dramatized narrators. Their action is always located in the present-day, contemporary, inconclusive time, instead of in the past. But the most remarkable thing is that even authors like Fielding, who claim to be following conventions, flout all acceptable and known rules of writing, that too, in so many different ways that no set pattern or formula can be attributed to their novels. The novelists borrowed from every conceivable genre in sight, particularly contemporary genres. However, as a major literary genre of print, the novel took time to come into its own. In fact, it took over two hundred years of innovations in new genres of print literature to finally give birth to the novel. We shall discuss the particular link of the novel to the print medium in a subsequent chapter along with the link of the novel to the loss of totality and growing fragmentation in modern times.

Right now, without discounting many of the things that different critics of the novel have argued, we would only like to reiterate the important but neglected aspect of the rise-of-the-novel debate, i.e. its plastic, elastic, inventive, parasitic, unfinished and ever-regenerative nature, both in terms of form as well as theme. This aspect of the novel, in our view, is essential for developing any theory of the rise of the novel. As we have mentioned before, important critics like Lukács and Bakhtin made this significant observation about the nature of the genre. The emergence of this flexible aspect of the novel can be attributed to the fact that an entire literary ethos that preferred the creation of genres on the basis of rules and decorum declined with the decline of feudalism. With capitalism, the new form of the novel emerged to give expression to the diverse imaginative concerns of the people, particularly the educated middle classes. The middle classes, by virtue of the fact that they were situated in the middle and because of their diverse social origins, were intensely involved in these debates. The flexible form of the novel came up with the rise of the flexible and dynamic form of capitalism itself, which advocated against the rigidity of fixed rules, especially during its early phase. Obviously there existed some elements of continuity in the novel with past genres, but the elements of difference and distinction both in terms of form, themes or the treatment of themes were much greater. It is also significant that before this time, no other literary genre displayed the same flexibility in form. It is only by this anti-traditional logic that a much earlier work of literature, i.e. Cervantes' *Don Quixote* (1605) that borrows from the romances but essentially lampoons their entire universe, can be called a novel.

However, if the roots of 'flexibility' of form lie in the essence of capitalism, then an obvious question also arises. Why do flexibility in form and complete breakdown of rule-bound writing affect only the novel and not other genres as well? Obviously this question merits further study and exploration vis-à-vis transitions in drama, poetry and other non-literary genres. It is common knowledge, however, that radical changes in drama and poetry through the emergence of 'realist drama' or 'free verse' happened only at the turn of the twentieth century. Perhaps, being older forms steeped in tradition, they took their own time to change and imbibe the new ethos within them. That is why instead of seeking the roots of the novel in forms like the epic or the romances, it is more appropriate to view the novel as a new genre. The emergence of the novel lies in the genesis of a new middle class with the emergence of capitalism itself, wherein the inherent referential character of prose helps to concretize an ethos of making sense through the logic of cause and effect. As Philip Henderson says, 'Prose, we may say . . . is primarily an instrument of the rational intelligence'.[112] It is through prose that greater objectivity and particularity of description become the dominant mode of these times instead of the concentrated and covert meanings of verse.

Getting back to our main task, let us now try to answer the basic questions about the rise of the novel—'Why', 'where', 'when' and 'how' did the novel come up in history? The novel arose accompanying the historical transition from feudalism to capitalism. Among the various modern classes that emerged with the rise of capitalism, the novel was the expression of middle class imaginings and concerns. Rather than a collective class based view of the world, it preferred and devoted a great deal of attention to devising the individual as its subject. Although the entire transition was spread over several centuries in Europe, the tide started turning in England during the late seventeenth century when the dominance of capitalism over feudalism seemed imminent. The new form of the novel came up by embodying in its content and form, the key tendencies and trends involved in this transition. Views that attribute the rise of the novel only to the questions of gender, otherness, individualism or discourse, undoubtedly represent only partial truths about the rise of the novel, as many of these changes were inter-related and caused by the more enduring transition to a capitalist mode of production. The nature of the genre of the novel is best represented by its nomenclature itself, i.e. the 'new' or the 'novel'. The novel was aimed at a new class of people, i.e. the middle classes and it was one of the first few important genres of the new medium of print as opposed to the old manuscript. Therefore, tracing the beginnings of the genre of the novel to ancient or medieval times or to non-European societies, which did not witness the same breakdown of social codes and rigidities required to pave way for an incorporative and flexible genre like the novel would be, in our view, erroneous and incorrect.

Notes

1. Georg Lukács, *The Theory of the Novel*, tr. A. Bastock, London: Merlin Press, 1971, p. 73.
2. Ibid., p. 74.
3. Mikhail Bakhtin, 'Epic and Novel: Toward a Methodology for the Study of the Novel', 1941; Hoffman, Michael J. and Patrick D. Murphy, eds., *Essentials of the Theory of Fiction*, Durham and London: Duke University Press, 1988, p. 51.
4. This book is a product of the philosophical tradition of pessimism prevalent among many intellectuals and artists of Europe during the war-ravaged years of the First World War. It is apparent from the book that Lukács shares with many of his contemporaries a very poor opinion about the path tread by advanced capitalist nations. He looks towards the past for catching a glimpse of lost civilizational wholeness and unity. In the early twentieth century, many artists and thinkers belonging to various ideological hues were trying to do the same by making an effort to recover a lost 'completeness' or 'wholeness' through conceptions of cultures other than Europe, or times other than their own. T.S. Eliot looked for it in *The Upanishads*; W.B. Yeats took refuge in the Celtic legends; E.M. Forster pursued it to an ancient Indian cave; Conrad sought it in the margins of the colonies; and D.H. Lawrence searched for it in the symbolism of a no longer possible 'uncorrupted nature'. None of them could pinpoint the exact nature of this vague 'wholeness', but they all bore a sense of a loss with them, as though they had to pay the price for eating the apple of knowledge. For Lukács, the 'epic' symbolizes a similar lost wholeness.
5. This book was translated into French only in 1963 and into English in 1971. Thus, it took a long time for Lukács early views on the novel to be known across the entire European literary scene. Today, it is an essential part of all reading lists on the theory of the novel.
6. Lukács borrows heavily from Hegel's landmark work *Aesthetics* (1842), where Hegel argues that the epic is an expression of an early stage of the history of consciousness in which only minimal separation exists between mind and things, or thought and matter. The epic for Hegel characterizes the unorganized, heroic age, symbolizing an organic unity between people, nature and society. Next comes the middle stage, symbolizing harmony and a visible balance between things and activities of the mind. The later stage is the stage of the novel, in which the symmetry between mind and matter gets shattered.

   Unlike the idealist philosopher Hegel, who argues that early consciousness was 'integrated' and contemporary consciousness has become 'problematic', Lukács argues that a change in consciousness takes place precisely because the earlier material world was integrated and the contemporary world has become problematic, and that consciousness does not have an independent movement of its own, but depends upon and reflects the state of the real world.

7. Lukács, *Theory*, p. 56.
8. Ibid., pp. 72–3 (emphasis mine).
9. Ibid., p. 64.
10. Ibid., p. 84.
11. Ibid., p. 93.
12. Ibid., p. 56.
13. Ibid., pp. 103–4.
14. Ibid., p. 118.
15. Ibid., p. 124.
16. Ibid., p. 120.
17. Ibid., p. 152.
18. Ibid., p. 35.
19. Bakhtin had a remarkable history as a philosopher. He remained in obscurity for several decades in the Soviet Union. He suddenly emerged on the European intellectual scene after his discovery by a group of young students. He was translated from Russian into French during the late 60s when structuralism was at its peak within the academia, and into English by the early 1980s. Bakhtin became an immediate sensation in Europe due to his affinity to the philosophical fundamentals of structuralism. Today, in spite of being methodologically difficult to pin down, Bakhtin enjoys tremendous popularity with literary critics and theorists, and his essays on the novel have become practically impossible to ignore. Some of his works, however, remain disputed on the authorship question.
20. Mikhail Bakhtin, 'Discourse in the Novel', 1934–5, *The Dialogic Imagination: Four Essays*, ed. Michael Holquist, tr. Caryl Emerson and Michael Holquist, Austin, University of Texas Press, 1981, p. 259.
21. Ibid., p. 261.
22. Ibid., p. 262.
23. Ibid., p. 270.
24. Ibid., p. 264.
25. Ibid., pp. 320–1.
26. Ibid., p. 379.
27. Ibid., p. 388.
28. Mikhail Bakhtin, 'Forms of Time and of the Chronotope in the Novel' (1934–8), in *The Dialogic Imagination: Four Essays*, ed. Michael Holquist tr. Caryl Emerson and Michael Holquist, Austin: University of Texas Press, 1981, p. 86.
29. Mikhail Bakhtin, *Problems of Dostoevsky's Poetics*, 1929; ed. and tr. Caryl Emerson, United Kingdom: Manchester University Press, 1984, p. 106.
30. Michael Holquist, *Dialogism: Bakhtin and his World*, London and New York: Routledge, 1990, p. 109.

31. Ibid.
32. Bakhtin, 'Epic and Novel', p. 66.
33. Ibid., p. 62.
34. Ibid., p. 65.
35. Ibid.
36. Ibid., p. 57.
37. Ian Watt, *The Rise of the Novel*, 1957; London: Penguin Books, repr. 1968, p. 9.
38. Ibid., p. 16.
39. Ibid., p. 24.
40. Ibid., p. 31.
41. Ibid., pp. 31–2.
42. Ibid., p. 32.
43. Ibid., p. 34.
44. Ibid., p. 42.
45. Ibid., p. 46.
46. Ibid., p. 49.
47. Ibid., p. 54.
48. Ibid., p. 55.
49. Ibid., p. 55.
50. Ibid., p. 59.
51. Marthe Robert, *Origins of the Novel*, 1972; tr. Sacha Rabinovitch, Sussex: The Harvester Press, 1980, p. 3.
52. Ibid., p. 4.
53. Ibid., p. 14.
54. Ibid., p. 4.
55. Ibid., p. 5.
56. Ibid., p. 10.
57. Ibid., p. 15.
58. Ibid., p. 16.
59. Ibid., p. 19.
60. Ibid., p. 22.
61. Ibid., p. 31.
62. Ibid.
63. Ibid., p. 32.
64. Ibid., p. 32.
65. Ibid., p. 37.
66. Lennard J. Davis, *Factual Fictions: The Origins of the English Novel*, Pennsylvania. 1983, p. 21.
67. Ibid., p. 38.
68. Ibid., p. 97.
69. Ibid., p. 222.
70. Ibid., p. 43.
71. Lennard J. Davis, *Resisting Novels: Ideology and Fiction*, New York and London: Methuen, 1987, p. 114.

72. Ibid., p. 202.
73. Nancy Armstrong, *Desire and Domestic Fiction: A Political History of the Novel*, New York and Oxford: Oxford University Press, 1987, p. 12.
74. Ibid., p. 20.
75. Ibid., p. 37.
76. Ibid., p. 4.
77. Ibid., p. 257.
78. Ibid., p. 258.
79. Nancy Armstrong, *How Novels Think: Limits of Individualism from 1719–1900*, New York: Columbia University Press, 2005, p. 3.
80. Michael McKeon, *The Origins of the English Novel, 1600–1740*, Baltimore: The John Hopkins University Press, 1987, p. 1.
81. Ibid., p. 19.
82. Ibid., p. 13.
83. Ibid., p. 22.
84. Firdous Azim, *The Colonial Rise Of The Novel*, London and New York: Routledge, 1993, p. 15.
85. Ibid., p. 88.
86. Ibid., p. 51.
87. Ibid., pp. 81–2.
88. Ibid., p. 215.
89. Ibid., p. 10.
90. Ibid., p. 20.
91. Ibid., p. 89.
92. Ibid., p. 37.
93. See Eric Hobsbawm, *The Age of Revolution 1789–1848*, London: Abacus, 2002.
94. See Peter Burke, 'Folklore', in *The Penguin Dictionary of Eighteenth Century History*, ed. Jeremy Black and Roy Porter, London: Penguin Books, 1994, p. 254.
95. See Roy Porter, 'Capitalism', Black and Porter, eds., pp. 118–19.

    See also Max Weber, *The Protestant Ethic and the Spirit of Capitalism*, tr. Talcott Parsons and Anthony Giddens, London and Boston: Unwin Hyman, 1930.
96. Hobsbawm, op. cit., p. 34.
97. Christopher Hill, *Writing and Resolution in Seventeenth Century England*, Brighton: The Harvester Press, 1985, p. 319.
98. Thomas Clarkson and William Wilberforce were two outstanding English figures who campaigned against slavery during the late eighteenth century.
99. Hobsbawm, op. cit., p. 45.
100. Ibid., p. 46.
101. The Royal Society was dedicated to Baconianism, i.e. a disregard for tradition, emphasis on empiricism, on humanistic belief in progress, on improvement of human life through scientific control of nature. The presidentship of Newton signified its most eminent phase.

102. Watt, op. cit., p. 63.

103. See 'Nuclear Family', in *The Penguin Dictionary of Sociology*, ed. Nicolas Abercoombie, Stephen Hill and Bryan S, Turner, London: Penguin Books, 1994, pp. 288–9.

    See also Lawrence Stone, *The Family, Sex and Marriage in England, 1500–1800*, London: Weidenfeld & Nicolson, 1977, and 'Family', in Williams, *Keywords*, pp. 131–4.

104. Prabhat Patnaik, 'The Concept of the Mode of Production and the Theory of Imperialism', in *The great Divergence: Hegemony, Uneven Development, and Global Inequality*, ed. K.S. Jomo, New Delhi: Oxford University Press, 2006.

    See also Paul Sweezy and Paul Baran, *Monopoly Capital*. '. . . only a few countries—most of Western Europe (including Britain), Japan, Canada, Australia, New Zealand, possibly South Africa—can conceivably follow in the footsteps of the United States. In the rest of the capitalist world scores of colonies, neo-colonies, and semi-colonies are doomed to remain in their degraded condition of under-development and misery.' Calcutta: K.P. Bagchi & Co., 1994, p. 12.

105. Hobsbawm, op. cit., p. 22.

106. William Temple in *Essay upon the Ancient and Modern Learning* (1690) argued for the superiority of Greek philosophy and science, while William Wotton in *Reflections upon Ancient and Modern Learning* (1694) argued that the moderns were superior to the Greeks in at least the sciences. Francis Bacon (1561–1626), a major philosophical figure, stood clearly in favour of modernity.

107. M.H. Abrams, 'Decorum', in *A Glossary of Literary Terms*, New Delhi: Macmillan, 2004, p. 40.

108. See 'Cult of Antiquity', in *The Peuguin Dictionary of Eighteenth-Century History*, ed. Jeremy Black and Roy Porter, London: Penguin Books, 1994, p. 31.

109. It is notable, however, that over the last decade we are experiencing a slew of fictional creations revolving around the view that behind their apparent innocence, children are evil.

110. Hobsbawm, op. cit., pp. 307–35.

111. Henry Fielding, *The History of Tom Jones, A Foundling*, 1749; Wordsworth Classics, 1999, pp. 7–8.

112. Philip Henderson, 'The Function of the Novel' (1936), in *Modernism: Critical Concepts in Literary and Cultural Studies*, ed. Tim Middleton, vol. 2, 1935–1970, London and New York: Routledge, 2003, p. 22.

CHAPTER THREE

The Realism Controversy

Novelists and critics have crucially employed 'realism' to *define, re-define, classify* as well as *periodize* the novel. So much so that, literary critics have rarely theorized the novel without, in some way, dealing with realism, and those working on realism have seldom managed to develop comprehensive theories by sidestepping the novel. When early writers of the English novel like Aphra Behn, Daniel Defoe, Samuel Richardson or Henry Fielding began writing something 'new', they did so by making claims to copying nature, presenting a picture of real life or of writing histories. These claims were often coupled with a stated opposition to either the prevalent romances or the epics, or to both.

The emergence of the novel and/or realism in literature is attributed to a range of factors that we have already discussed: the rise of the middle classes, development of the printing press, individualism, etc., which were analogous to the development of the culture of Enlightenment, wherein ideas of reason, secularization, freedom and equality made unprecedented breakthroughs in eighteenth-century European society and polity. The novel, in its early experimental phase, emerged by borrowing extensively from various forms of writings like travelogues, letters, picaresque, newspapers, chronicles, satires, pamphlets, essays, characters, sermons, chapbooks, diary entries, journals, pastoral and even drama, epics and romances. And, over time, it has charted out a complex history for itself, incorporating techniques not only from other literary genres, but also from painting, photography, film, radio, television and the Internet within its narrative fold. The peak of the realist novel, however, was during the nineteenth century, with subsequent stages being characterized more by anti-realist proclamations and assertions. Contemporary writers have departed significantly from earlier realist conventions to create anti-novels, metafiction, surfiction, etc., and realism has become a pejorative term in most critical and literary circles. Yet, realism in some form or the other still looms large on the novel, with the novel reinventing itself through radically different and innovative realisms like 'magic realism' or 'hyperrealism'. In spite of over a hundred years of attacks and controversies, realism still forms one of the nodal points of most theorizations of the novel. Opinions are divided between those who favour realism and those who treat it with contempt; those who find all novels realist and those who find no narrative realist. Many recent critics have also started emphasizing that all realist narratives are fictive by nature, and that all fictional representations are inevitably real. In the course of this chapter, therefore, we shall deal with the realism debate at some length in order to interrogate the relevance and usefulness of 'realism' in understanding the novel.

Before getting into the thick of the debate, however, it is useful to start by making some broad observations about the different ways in which the term realism has been employed in literary studies about the novel. In a general sense, realism has been used to denote ways of presenting or capturing the lives of people in fiction which is so evocative that it seems quite lifelike. In a more specific sense, realism has been used as a period concept to denote particularly those fictive techniques which were used by nineteenth-century novelists to consciously depict the lives of ordinary, common, poor or socially marginalized people in their novels. In the former sense, realism is applicable to literatures of almost all types and times, reminiscent of the age-old 'mimesis' debates; while in the latter sense, it is largely applicable to novelists like Balzac, Flaubert, Zola, Dickens, Dostoevsky, Tolstoy, etc. Novelists have more frequently put the former sense of verisimilitude to use while critics have usually employed realism in the latter sense, especially for classifying the novel. The most common outcome of its use by critics is the classification/periodization of the novel into *early/proto-realist*, *realist*, *modernist* and *postmodern* novels.

This classification does not cover the entire diversity or range of works produced or consumed in the name of novels. Its validity can be put to test through alternative categories of classification like realist and experimental novels, women's and men's novels, national and/or postcolonial novels, high or mass and fine or popular novels, etc. Yet, these classificatory departures also do not entirely do away with realism while theorizing the novel. For instance, realism remains the benchmark to contrast the anti-realist experimental techniques of 'modernist' and 'postmodern' novels with the conventional realist techniques of 'popular' or 'mass' fiction. Postcolonial critics also use realism to explain the development of the novel. Kwame Anthony Appiah in his essay 'Is the Post- in Postmodernism the Post- in Postcolonial?' argues that the conventional chronology of the first-world novel is 'traditional-modern-postmodern', while that of the third-world novel is 'traditional-colonial-postcolonial'.[1] The postcolonial African novel, he argues, can be sub-divided into the 'realist-nationalist' and 'postrealist-postnationalist' phase. Feminist critics also find realism useful for theorizing women's writings. For instance, Elaine Showalter, in *A Literature of Their Own*, argues that there are three distinct phases in the development of women's writings, the *feminine* phase from 1840 to 1880, the *feminist* phase from 1880 to 1920, and the *female* phase from 1920 to the present. The first phase is a 'prolonged phase of *imitation* of the prevailing modes of the dominant tradition ...'[2] in which women writers from Jane Austen to George Eliot develop 'an all-inclusive female *realism*, a broad, socially informed exploration of the daily lives and values of women within the family and the community'.[3] The second phase is that of 'protest' and 'advocacy', and the third phase is that of 'self-discovery'.

Basic definitions of the novel also enlist realism as an important ingredient of the genre. Our main effort in this chapter, therefore, shall be to find out whether realism (in all its different *avatars*) constitutes an integral generic component of the novel, or is it expendable when it comes to understanding the genre? To find an answer to this question, we shall discuss both theorists of the novel as well as specialist theorists of realism. But before doing that, let us first examine the views of a few novelists on this matter.

Novelists on Realism

Major novelists across different periods and styles have commented upon realism in the novel. For instance, Aphra Behn, an early innovator of the novel, demarcated her novel from the romances in the 'Epistle Dedicatory' to *Oroonoko*:

> This is a true story.... If there be anything that seems romantick I beseech your Lordship to consider these countries do, in all things, so far differ from ours that they produce unconceivable wonders, at least, so they appear to us, because new and strange. What I have mentioned I have taken care shoud be truth, let the critical reader judge as he pleases.[4]

Behn gave her tale a ring of truth through the devise of the persona of a dramatized narrator who was the confidante of Oroonoko, and hence, privy to an authentic account of his travails and sufferings. Daniel Defoe in the 'Preface by Editor' and the 'End Account' of *Robinson Crusoe* took great pains to dispel doubts about the plausibility of Crusoe's experiences. He used various journalistic and historiographic narrative techniques to provide intricate details of Crusoe's activities over a period of twenty-four years. Samuel Richardson also made his preference for authenticity as opposed to artifice in literature known. The full title of his novel *Pamela, or*

Virtue Rewarded: A narrative which has its foundations in Truth and Nature . . ., itself stands testimony to his intention. Similarly, Henry Fielding in his famous 'Preface' to *The History of the Adventures of Joseph Andrews, and of his Friend Mr Abraham Adams*, distinguished his novel 'from the productions of romance writers on the one hand, and burlesque writers on the other'.[5] He explained his 'comic epic poem in prose' by contrasting it with the romances which offered 'very little instruction or entertainment' and dealt only with the highest of characters instead of containing the possibility of 'introducing persons of inferior rank, and consequently of inferior manners'.[6] Lawrence Sterne in *A Sentimental Journey* (1768), also invited his reader to get 'as close to life as we can'.[7]

Walter Scott, in a review written in 1815, appreciated the quality of verisimilitude in the writings of Jane Austen to argue that 'the art of copying from nature as she really exists in the common walks of life, and presenting to the reader, . . . a correct and striking representation of that which is daily taking place around him'[8] was an advisable literary goal. Charles Dickens went a step further to defend the inherent merit of representing the lives of people who came from the seamier side of life. Defending the characters of his novel, *Oliver Twist*, who were often thieves, pickpockets or prostitutes he wrote, 'It appeared to me that to draw a knot of such associates in crime as really do exist . . . to show them as they really are . . . would be a service to society.'[9] Through his *Realist Manifesto* written in 1856, Louis-Edmond Duranty advocated realism for all the arts, 'Realism . . . means the frank and complete expression of individuality; what it attacks is precisely convention, imitation, all types of school.'[10] He also argued that a writer must focus on the present rather than on representing a mystical past. During the late nineteenth century, Emile Zola gave a new twist to this debate by pioneering the scientific technique of 'Naturalism', i.e. a . . . return to nature and to man, direct observation, exact anatomy. . . . No more abstract characters in books, no more lying inventions, no more of the absolute; but real characters, the true history of each one, the story of daily life.'[11] For Zola, a return to nature involved not just reporting facts as a novelist observed them, but that a novelist like a scientist introduced an experiment in which he/she 'sets his characters going in a certain story as to show that the succession of facts will be such as the requirements of the determinism of the phenomena under examination call for'.[12] The character was now determined by a set of givens—family lineage/traits plus the socio-historical context.

After Zola, the tide in novel writing started turning against realism. In 1884, Joris-Karl Huysmans, a follower of Zola, broke away from the naturalist school by writing his novel *Against Nature.* Thomas Hardy also argued against the possibility of any 'Science of Fiction' and called naturalism an error. He explained:

> To advance realism as complete copyism, to call the idle trade of storytelling a science, is the hyperbolic flight of an admirable enthusiasm, the exaggerated cry of an honest reaction from the false, in which the truth has been impetuously approached and overleapt in fault of lighted on . . . perhaps, true novelists, like poets, are born, not made.[13]

This argument was carried forward by Henry James in his 1894 essay, 'The Art of Fiction', where he claimed that a 'sense of reality' was absolutely essential for good novels but, 'Humanity is immense, and reality has myriad forms; the most one can affirm is that some of the flowers of fiction have the odour of it, and others have not.'[14] E.M. Forster in *Aspects of the Novel* reinterpreted the meaning of realism to write, '[A] novel is a work of art, with its own laws, which are not those of daily life, and that a character in a novel is real when it lives in accordance with such laws',[15] not as in daily life. Emphasizing the same provisional or relative nature of the 'real' in fiction, D.H. Lawrence explained, 'Everything is true in its own time, place, circumstance, and untrue outside of its own time place circumstance. If you try to nail anything down, in the novel, either it kills the novel, or the novel gets up and walks away with the nail.'[16]

By Samuel Beckett's time, the scepticism about capturing reality in fiction grew to such an extent that reality became almost impossible to grasp. Beckett argued in his 1929 essay 'Dante . . . Bruno . . . Vico . . . Joyce', 'We only wish everyone was as sure of anything in this watery world as we are of everything in the newlywet fellow that's bound to follow . . .'[17] or, 'Reality, whether approached imaginatively or empirically, remains a surface, hermetic.'[18] Albert Camus in *The Myth of Sisyphus* (1942) took this argument further to declare that the world lacked immanent meaning yet humans always needed to make sense of things or have some purpose in life. He called this disjunction between reality and desire the 'Absurd'. Through an interjection by the dramatized narrator/author in *The French Lieutenant's Woman* (1969), John Fowles proposed that 'We are all in flight from the real reality. That is a basic definition of *Homo sapiens*.'[19] Umberto Eco in *Reflections on The Name of The Rose* (1985) elaborated that '. . . The ideal postmodernist novel will somehow rise above the quarrel between realism and irrealism . . .'.[20] Elsewhere, while discussing the impossibility of locating 'meaning', he argued, 'Let us be realistic: there is nothing more meaningful than a text which asserts that there is no meaning.'[21]

This short appraisal of a few views on realism by a few novelists demonstrates the divided house over realism. It also shows that realism forms an important concern in the philosophy of writing novels for different novelists. Let us now return to our initial task of examining some significant theoretical views on realism and the novel.

'Critical Realism'

Georg Lukács wrote three important works on the novel, *The Theory of the Novel* (1920), *Studies in European Realism* (1930) and *The Historical Novel* (1937).[22] Among these, it is his book *Studies in European Realism* that encompasses the most detailed discussions on realism and the novel. Lukács both discusses the uses of realism by great novelists of nineteenth-century Europe, as also develops a realist 'aesthetic' for assessing literature. Being acutely critical of his contemporary modernist novelists, he wries, 'Never in all history did mankind so urgently require a realist literature as it does to-day.'[23] For Lukács, a truly great, profound and all-embracing realism has the capacity to educate the people and transform public opinion. He calls this type of realism 'critical realism' and defends it in opposition to subsequent trends of naturalism and modernism, as well as the Soviet prescriptions for socialist realism.

The central category and criterion of realist literature for Lukács is 'the "type", a peculiar synthesis which organically binds together the general and the particular both in characters and situations'.[24] A type is a three-dimensional, all-rounded way of presenting a complete human personality, both through depiction of a psychological inner life as well as the representation of its organic link to social and historical factors. Lukács argues that such a representation is possible only if a writer manages to capture the key contradictions of an epoch or age within the scope of his work. This work may be a historical novel, as in the case of Walter Scott, who depicts the unfolding reality of medieval England accurately in his novels, or it may be a novel about contemporary times, as in the case of the great realist writer Balzac. Writers who are unable to understand the social problems or human conflicts of their times, end up either leaving out the most decisive social elements from their plots, or situate their imperfectly crafted characters against 'merely "sociologically" or impressionistically-psychologically conceived *milieu*'.[25] Lukács elaborates that the type does not represent merely a social average or a profoundly conceived individual. Rather, types are 'figures of exceptional qualities, who mirror all essential aspects of some definite stage of development, evolutionary tendency or social group'.[26] That is why the characters created by great realist novelists like Balzac or Stendhal have an independent life of their own. They are governed by an 'inner dialectic of their social and individual existence',[27] rather than by the will of the author. Lukács argues that a 'ruthlessness towards their own subjective world-picture is the hall-mark of all great realists'.[28]

Lukács appreciates the writings of 'true' realists like Balzac, Goethe, Tolstoy, Scott, Gorky and Thomas Mann. He admires Balzac's understanding of the specific conditions governing French capitalist development. Unlike in England, where the social compromise struck between aristocratic landowners and bourgeois capitalists became the basis of social evolution, in France, the landed aristocracy was doomed and was standing on the brink of an economic ruin. Lukács recounts that in his novel, *The Peasants*, Balzac depicts this historical evolution of French society from the French Revolution of 1789 to 1848, i.e. the year of great revolutions all over Europe. Balzac's own sympathies lie with the moribund French aristocracy and Roman Catholicism. However, Balzac doesn't let that come in the way of accurately describing the break up of the feudal estate, set against the backdrop of capitalist transformation and growing secularization of France. Although Balzac is deeply tormented by the transition to capitalism, he presents it as a social and historical inevitability, and doesn't tamper with the story to create some desired picture. Neither does he choose to ignore and escape this immense social upheaval. Accordingly, he manages to sophisticatedly represent both the morally debased as well as the socially progressive character of this paradoxical transition. His skill of narration lies in the fact that though he manages to represent all significant aspects involved in the decline of feudalism and the advent of capitalism in France, the action of his novel never moves out of a particular fictional estate and its neighbouring small town.

Elaborating upon the development of the narrative styles of the novel, Lukács explains that after the 'realism' of Balzac, Stendhal, and Hugo in France comes the 'naturalism' of Emile Zola. He attacks the 'exclusive extraversion' or 'pseudo-objectivism' of naturalism for its treatment of the socio-historical as mere background. Lukács argues that the 'trivial photographic naturalism' of Zola distorts reality and presents it as just a lifeless average. Severely criticizing naturalism, he states:

> Zola's method, which hampered not only Zola himself but his whole generation, because it was a result of the writer's position as solitary observer, prevents any profoundly realistic representation of life. Zola's 'scientific' method always seeks the average, and this grey statistical mean, the point at which all internal contradictions are blunted, where the great and the petty, the noble and the base, the beautiful and the ugly are all mediocre 'products' together, spells the doom of great literature.[29]

Looking into the reasons for the development of naturalism, it is Lukács' proposition that after the revolutions of 1848 throughout Europe, the hitherto seemingly progressive bourgeoisie abandons its conflict with the nobility for a struggle against the proletariat. This causes widespread pessimism among radicals and intellectuals. Instead of seeking to capture this 'totality' in their novels, novelists resort to looking at just aspects or facets of the real. Thus, while Zola was a left-wing progressive, and authors like Goethe, Walter Scott, Tolstoy and Thomas Mann were on the wrong side of history because they sided with the nobility, the landlords or the bourgeoisie, the latter were the truly great realist writers because they captured the key contradictions of their times more accurately and profoundly in their works.

Tracing out the further progress of the novel, Lukács seeks to demonstrate how naturalism gave way to another kind of 'distortion' of reality, i.e. the 'mirage-subjectivism' or 'exclusive introspection' of the psychologist or abstractly formalist modernism. The depiction of reality gets mutilated into an individual principle, which dissolves itself into nothingness. The false extremes of representing conversations without beginnings or ends, chance fragments, or incoherent slices of life, portray not a new kind of near-realism or realism, but false subjectivism or an impoverishment of reality. Lukács argues that such a fragmentary representation developed in the twentieth century due to an apparently fragmented or disrupted nature of capitalism, but beneath its surface of autonomies, separations and disunity, existed an 'essential' unity. True realism or critical realism requires that an author not only portray segments or aspects of reality that are immediately obvious, but also those that are permanent and objectively more significant. For Lukács, modernism, like naturalism, is a reflection of alienation under capitalism, when the writer increasingly gets reduced to a mere spectator rather than a participant in the workings of society and the making of history.

Thus, Lukács differentiates between realism and anti-realist modernism in his work. His main emphasis remains upon delineating the merits of good realism and the demerits of anti-realism. Good realism or critical realism, according to him, has the potential to educate people about their own societies and histories. In Lukács' view, realism in the novel is integrally linked to the consciousness of the middle classes across modern European history. As long as the middle classes play a progressive social role in the unfolding contradiction between feudalism and capitalism, realist preoccupations remain their priority. However, as soon as capitalism becomes a triumphant force by the mid-nineteenth century, the middle classes become preoccupied with the workings of the 'mind' rather than the workings of 'society' and become anti-realist. For Lukács, questions pertaining to the *form* of the novel are never as important as those relating to the *content* of novels. Any technique which reflects reality accurately is good; however, no technique that seeks to escape material reality can be credited for its style. A good novel is like a good book of sociology or history or philosophy, which educates people about their societies. Good novels can contribute to building a more progressive and just social order. On the whole, Lukács makes a case for imbibing realism and its virtues in literature and in this regard appreciates great realist writers like Balzac and Tolstoy. He does not generically associate realism with the novel, i.e. he does not consider realism to be an integral part of the genre of the novel. Realism for him is simply defined as the dominant preoccupation of early novels, while anti-realism is the dominant preoccupation of modernist novels.

Lukács' celebration of realism and his disapproval of the modernist turn is attacked by Bertold Brecht, giving rise to the famous Brecht–Lukács debate.[30] Brecht questions the veracity of the argument that nineteenth century bourgeois artists could provide a right model for the new modern age. Reality changes, therefore, the modes of representation must also change. Although, Brecht does not deal directly with the novel, he develops his 'epic' or 'dialectical' theatre against naturalist drama. Brecht views naturalism as a continuation of realism. He argues that naturalism persuades audiences to identify so fully with characters and situations that they unquestionably accept what they perceive. Brecht does not want his audiences to suspend all disbelief; rather to recognize the constructedness of representation and to realize that things could have been otherwise. By making everything seem strange, he seeks to expose everything as artificial and ideological. He is critical of Lukács' exclusive interest in the novel, which he calls 'narrowly prescriptive'. He also disagrees with Lukács for his 'empty formalism' and eulogization of the old. Thus, for Brecht, nineteenth-century realism is a historically dated concept which cannot and must not be resurrected in modern times.

'Mimesis'

Eric Auerbach shared Lukács' distaste for modernism and his preference for French Realism. His exhaustive study, *Mimesis: The Representations of Reality in Western Literature* (1946), is a powerful book which demolishes monolithic conceptions about realism. Auerbach does not focus his study solely upon the novel form. Instead, he examines different types of writings in history in their uses of realism and mimetic techniques. He begins his study with Homer's *Odyssey* and *The Bible* (Old Testament) and goes on to eventually examine the novels of Virginia Woolf. Homer's *Odyssey*, he argues, has significant sections that are very evocative and picturesque, where the descriptions are such that everything seems right in front of one's eyes—visible. This 'mimesis', however, is characterized by an *action* that is limited only to the lives of the ruling classes, *emotions* that alter and change but cause no psychological development in the characters, treatment of *time* that is legendary, and *descriptions* that are detailed but fully externalized. Similar yet different is the mimesis or realism of the *Old Testament* which explores various levels of conflicting consciousness simultaneously existing within the human soul. The *Old Testament* treats time historically, deals with nomadic or half-nomadic tribal leaders, and represents action that is largely confined to the domestic realism of daily life. It invokes a multiplicity of meanings and a need for constant interpretation and re-interpretation.

Auerbach treats the *Odyssey* and the *Old Testament* as literary prototypes. He goes on to map the slow evolution of mimetic/realistic representations in subsequent literary works such as the Greco-Roman writings of Petronius and Tacitus, historical accounts of fourth century AD, *The Confessions of St. Augustine,* poems like *Chanson de Roland* or *Chanson d'Alexis,* twelfth century courtly romances like Chrétien de Troyes' *Yvain* or plays like *Mystèred'Adam,* Dante's *Inferno,* Boccaccio's *Decameron,* fifteenth-century novellas, Rabelais's adventure tales, Montaigne's *Essais,* Shakespeare's plays, Cervantes's *Don Quixote,* La Bruyère's *Caractères,* early eighteenth-century novels, Schiller's *Luise Millerin,* Stendhal's novels, works by Flaubert, Balzac, and Zola, plays by Ibsen, etc., right up to Woolf and Joyce. Auerbach explicates that very complex and intricate uses of realism existed in literature since time immemorial in prose, poetry as well as drama. Through this discussion he explains how different mimetic techniques have become more refined and evolved with time, and how in different successive ages they reflect the changing preoccupations of their own times.

The crucial categories for Auerbach, however, for examining the development of realism are two ancient styles of representing reality, the 'separation of styles' and the 'mixture of styles'. Separation of styles is characterized by a belief that everyday reality can find description in literature only in comic, low or intermediary genres. Whereas, mixture of styles does not necessarily restrict realistic descriptions to low genres but seeks to altogether do away with rigid hierarchies, rules or codes of high and low forms. Auerbach begins by expounding that classical theorists of literature like Plato, etc., advocated a rigid separation of styles and viewed mixture as sacrilege. Plato in Book 10 of *The Republic* ranked mimesis third after truth. Auerbach argues that throughout literary history a conflict can be discerned between these two styles of representation. But sometime after the Renaissance, 'mixture of styles' starts turning the tables on 'separation of styles'. The decisive moment comes with the rule of Louis XIV in France when the French nobility and the elite start considering their culture at par with the ancients, a belief that betrays their anxieties about the changing status quo, at a time when their supremacy was being challenged by many. In doing so, they also revert to a strict imposition of the separation of styles method through the copy of the ancients. This neo-classicism causes subsequent writers to rebel against its artificiality; this is also because the profile of society itself starts undergoing a dramatic change after the French revolution, though, it is yet some time before 'tragic seriousness and everyday reality could again meet'.[31] For Auerbach, writers like Stendhal and Balzac are notable for breaking away completely from the classical rules of distinct levels of styles. They complete a development which had long been in preparation, by becoming the creators of modern realism. Auerbach explains that throughout the nineteenth century, France played a far more important role than England or Germany in the rise and development of modern realism. In his opinion, writers like Dickens or Thackeray, who were the best of the English realists, were deficient because their novels did not manage to capture the fluidity of their political or historical background within their work. Auerbach describes the modern realism of the French realists as follows:

> The serious treatment of everyday reality, the rise of more extensive and socially inferior human groups to the position of subject matter for problematic-existential representation, on the one hand: on the other, the embedding of random persons and events in the general course of contemporary history, the fluid historical background—these, we believe, are the foundations of modern realism, and it is natural that the broad and elastic form of the novel should increasingly impose itself for a rendering comprising so many elements.[32]

According to Auerbach, while subsequent writers like Flaubert and Zola continued this holistic realism, their works suffered from a 'certain dryness, excessive clarity, almost inhumanity in it'.[33] This was because by the decade of the 1850s, while the economy continued to grow at a rapid pace in France, the ideas of the Enlightenment and the Revolution became merely passé; two tendencies which until now had gone hand in hand. Unlike Hugo and Balzac, who tried to intervene in the events of their times by trying to influence the moral, political and practical lives of their urban middle class readership, Flaubert and Zola were more preoccupied with questions of style. Auerbach emphasizes that the impulse behind their mixed-style-realism became aesthetic rather than social. By the last decade of Zola's life, whom he calls '. . . the last of the great French realists',[34] the anti-naturalist movement grew quite strong and gave way soon after to modernism. Being critical of modern novelists and differentiating them from their predecessors, Auerbach writes, 'It is all, then, a matter of the author's attitude toward the reality of the world he represents.'[35] Unlike the objective assurance found in Goethe, Keller, Dickens, Meredith, Balzac or Zola, the modern writers seem to abdicate their position and authority as bearers of objective truth. They 'hesitate to impose upon life . . . an order which it does not possess in itself'[36] and emphasize its arbitrary nature. But, argues Auerbach, through our acts of story telling we 'are constantly endeavouring to give meaning and order to our lives in the past, present, and the future, to our surroundings, the world in which we live . . .'.[37] The attempt by the moderns to merely grasp the random moment, therefore, poses 'a challenge to the reader's will to interpretive synthesis'.[38]

According to Auerbach, writers like Virginia Woolf display the distinctive characteristics of 'realistic' novels written between the two world wars—'multipersonal representation of consciousness, time strata, disintegration of the continuity of exterior events, shifting of the narrative viewpoint'.[39] These characteristics indicate certain needs and tendencies of both the authors as well as the reading public of the twentieth century to try to come to terms with their changing realities. Auerbach argues that by the time of the First World War, society became so complicated that a writer, engaged in representing reality, could no longer rely on the old criteria of a 'clearly formulable and recognized community of thought and feeling'.[40] With rapid but unevenly distributed advances made in the areas of science, technology and economics, the world became a smaller place in which the differences between different people or different strata of the same people were more acutely visible. Auerbach claims that during the early twentieth century all sources of authority, be it religion, philosophy, ethics, economics, or the ideas of the Enlightenment, democracy, liberalism, and even socialism were eroded in a violent and disaster-prone world, caught in the midst of heterogeneous ways of life overflowing with unsettled ideologies. This led to the development of the literary method of dissolving 'reality into multiple and multivalent reflections of consciousness . . . But [this] method is not only a symptom of the confusion and helplessness, not only a mirror of the decline of our world . . .',[41] but a great deal more. It carries with it an atmosphere of universal doom, blatant and painful cynicism, uninterpretable symbolism, vague indefinability of meaning, confusion, hopelessness, and hostility to the very reality it represents. This seemingly unprejudiced and exploratory type of representation, with its emphasis on random occurrence, however, does not make obvious to the reader the other side of the coin. Auerbach compellingly argues:

> Beneath the conflicts, and also through them, an economic and cultural levelling process is taking place. It is still a long way to a common life of mankind on earth, but the goal begins to be visible. . . . So the complicated process of dissolution which led to fragmentation of the exterior action, to reflection of consciousness, and to stratification of time seems to be . . . the first forewarnings of the approaching unification and simplification.[42]

Merely representing fragmentation and not representing the ongoing simultaneous process of unification for Auerbach is an incomplete representation of reality. On the whole, he argues that similar kinds of realisms occur across genres in particular ages. He values 'mixture of styles' as the most important breakthrough in the literary history of realism. He doesn't view modernism as completely unrealistic, but, as a modified or degraded form of realism in which the author is no longer able to represent the complete entirety or totality of the world within the framework of his work. He does see, however, a basic conflict between realism and modernism and views the latter as a departure from the former. He does not view the novel form as being too crucial for the development of 'mixed-style-realism', nor does he see 'mixed-style-realism' as being too important for the novel form. Auerbach just finds the two mutually compatible.

'Formal Realism'

Unlike both Lukács and Auerbach, who do not integrally associate realism with the genre of the novel, Ian Watt argues that realism, in fact, is the most important feature of the novel. In *The Rise of The Novel* (1957) he notes that historians of the novel often see realism as the main feature which differentiates the novel from previous fiction. He proposes that '...the lowest common denominator of the novel genre as a whole, is formal realism'.[43] Being critical of the assertions made by French Realists like Flaubert, etc., of representing low subjects in their novels, he argues that such assertions have created distortions in the very concept of realism. The result of this distortion is that '...the "realism" of the novels of Defoe, Richardson, and Fielding, is closely associated with the fact that Moll Flanders is a thief, Pamela a hypocrite, and Tom Jones a fornicator'.[44] However, 'the novel's realism does not reside in the kind of life it presents, but in the *way* it presents it'.[45] Although the French Realists insist upon scientific objectivity as the way/method to capture reality, it is obvious that scientific objectivity 'certainly cannot be realized in practice'.[46] It is precisely the air of total accuracy and authenticity claimed by the French Realists which has created a general distaste for realism today. According to Ian Watt, the unique realism of the novel can only be understood by tracing out its correspondence with 'philosophical realism', i.e. with the views held by philosophers like Descartes or Locke who were the originators of modern realism and whose philosophical ideas had a profound influence upon the development of different features of the novel. Watt sums up their ideas as follows:

The general temper of philosophical realism has been critical, anti-traditional, and innovating; its method has been the study of the particulars of experience by the individual investigator, who, ideally at least, is free from the body of past assumptions and traditional beliefs; and it has given a peculiar importance to semantics, to the problem of the nature of the correspondence between words and reality.[47]

This formal realism of the novel, for Watt, mainly involves a narrative method that embodies a circumstantial view of life. It is 'formal' because it has nothing to do with 'any special literary doctrine or purpose, but only ... [with] a set of narrative procedures which are so commonly found together in the novel, and so rarely in other literary genres, that they may be regarded as typical of the form itself'.[48] In the novels of Defoe or Fielding, this formal realism comes into effect through the simultaneous use of the following techniques—authentic reporting of human experience, detailing of the story, individuality of actors, particularity of time and space, and referentiality of language. He argues that literary forms other than the novel also imitate reality, but the specialty of formal realism in the novel is that it allows '... a more immediate imitation of individual experience set in its temporal and spatial environment ...'[49] and involves a distinctive break with tradition and convention both in the choice of story and plot, as well as in the ways to narrate it. It is deeply linked both to the development of individualism and the rise of the middle classes.

Nineteenth-century French realists are obviously not the particular favourites of Ian Watt, but neither is his position an anti-realist one. He views realism—an anti-traditional, innovating realism—as the chief characteristic of the novel. Apart from tracing the origin of the novel to the materialist writings of Locke and Descartes which consequently lead to the development of secular individualism, displaying a preference for a circumstantial and experiential view of life and its meaning, Watt also links the origin of the novel to a new sense of understanding history, i.e. a sense wherein the present is viewed not merely as part of an a-historical continuum but as a progress over the past. He expounds that it is not the case that realism did not exist in the middle ages, only that the realists of the middle ages believed in representing reality in their stories through 'universal abstractions', as opposed to particular, objective, sense-perception based realities of the modern realists.

Although the focus of Watt's study are Defoe, Richardson and Fielding, as the first three genius innovators of the novel, he also notes the obvious 'technical weaknesses' of their works in comparison to the works of subsequent novelists like Balzac or Jane Austen, who were able to evolve novelistic techniques much further. Remarking on the pre-eminence and the generally acknowledged supremacy of the early

English novel, Watt simultaneously notes that eighteenth-century French novelists like Stendhal and Balzac stood unchallenged by their English contemporaries. This, he argues, was because early French novelists enjoyed three additional advantages over their English counterparts. One, they did not have to invent the novel but inherited novelistic techniques from their English predecessors; two, the force of the French Revolution of 1789, which brought the middle classes into social and literary power was far more immediate and dramatic for the French than the hundred-year-old Glorious Revolution of 1688 was for the English novelists; and three, the critical culture of Romanticism prevalent in France at the time of the origin of the French novel was far more favourable for the development of 'formal realism', than the neo-classicism prevalent in England just before the development of the English novel.[50] On the whole, Ian Watt argues that realism is crucial to the form of the novel, but he also emphasizes the differences between realism as employed in other genres, the realism of the genre of the novel and the specific realism of late nineteenth-century French novelists.

Realism Debates: 1880s to 1940s

While Lukács, Auerbach and Watt defend and appreciate the merits of realist novels, especially those written during the early nineteenth century, not all critics hold similar views. If we examine the debates about realism chronologically, we find that by the late nineteenth century realism begins to get explicitly contentious. Simultaneously, the novel also starts becoming more problematic. As Henry James notes in his 1884 essay called 'The Art of Fiction':

> During the period I have alluded to there was a comfortable, good—humoured feeling abroad that a novel is a novel, as a pudding is a pudding, and that our only business with it could be to swallow it. But within a year or two, for some reason or other, there have been signs of returning to animation—the era of discussion would appear to have been to a certain extent opened.[51]

In the same essay, James also notes, 'The only reason for the existence of a novel is that it does attempt to represent life.'[52] However, in another important essay, 'The New Novel', written in 1914, James distances himself from this earlier opinion and attacks the common literary level of contemporary English novels which pretend to be in the 'state of knowing all about whatever it may be'.[53] Criticizing the 'cheap gift' of the democratic model he says, '...prose fiction now occupies itself as never before with the "condition of the people"'.[54] The realist novelists of the nineteenth century wrote what was suitable and innovative for their own times, but for modern novelists to continue practising the same technique is not at all appropriate. He attacks the very claim of capturing reality by asking, 'How can a slice of life be anything but illustrational of the loaf, and how can illustration not immediately bristle with every sign of the extracted and related state?'[55] There is no universal reference or illustration, and even the most closely or vividly covered canvas is relational and depends entirely upon recognition by the reader. All representation depends upon 'selection'; therefore, the reader must not assist the author in comfortably creating an illusion of truth. James argues against all prescriptions and recommendations made by other authors about realism. He takes an ideological position wherein he draws an association between the 'derogatory' form of realism and growing democracy in society.

Unlike James, who argues for creating new styles for the new novels of a new age, the modern movement of surrealism, symptomatic of its extreme positions, calls not only for a change in the form of the novel, but also for the abolition of the very form of the novel. André Breton in the *First Manifesto of Surrealism* written in 1924 sharply attacks 'the realist attitude' contained in the form of the novel to say, 'I have a disdainful prejudice against the novel.'[56] He calls the novel an inferior genre because it flatters public opinion in its lowest taste through the style of pure information. Criticizing the classic realist novel he expostulates, 'The intractable mania that consists in reducing the unknown to the known, to the classifiable, lulls minds.'[57] That is why realist novels leave him with 'no other discretionary power than to close the book, which I do not neglect to do somewhere about the first page'.[58] André Breton's case is for the liberation of the mind from the domination of logic, rationalism, as well as notions of civilization and progress. He asserts that 'our mental world which we pretended not to be concerned with any longer'[59] is far more important than the material world. Through the surrealist movement, Breton seeks to reclaim imagination to its rightful place by arguing that 'the marvellous is always beautiful, anything marvellous is beautiful, in fact only the marvellous is beautiful'.[60] He classifies surrealism as a kind of absolute reality, or a resolution of the two states of dream and reality. More precisely, he defines it as, 'Psychic automatism in its pure state, by which one proposes to express—verbally, by means of the written word, or in any other manner—the actual functioning of thought. Dictated by thought, in the absence of any control exercised by a reason, exempt from any aesthetic or moral concern.'[61] Thus, the Surrealists redefine realism to mean exactly the opposite of what it had signified so far. From an emphasis on the description of the material world based upon assumptions of rationality, the logic of cause-and-effect, and the progress of history through a clear distinction between the past, the present and the future, they now modify its meaning to signify the arbitrary expression of a fragile reality of life and an equally fragile working of the mental world through imagination, unrestricted language, nonconformism and fancy.

The same year as Andre Breton's scathing attack on the novel, Virginia Woolf wrote her famous essay, 'Mr Bennett and Mrs. Brown'. Through this essay, she countered social and historical writers like Arnold Bennett, John Galsworthy and H.G. Wells, i.e. the Edwardians. Woolf argued that these writers wrote incomplete books, which required 'that the reader should finish them, actively and practically, for himself'.[62] 'In order to complete them it seems necessary to do something—to join a society, or, more desperately, to write a cheque. That done, the restlessness is laid, the book finished; it can be put upon the shelf, and need never be read again.'[63] Criticizing Arnold Bennett for maintaining that Georgian writers were unable to create 'real characters' she says, 'But, I ask myself, what is reality? And who are the judges of reality? A character may be real to Mr Bennett and quite unreal to me.'[64] Therefore, like Henry James, she too insists upon the relative or provisional nature of truth/reality. She condemns writers who imagine or present a complete or deliberately reasoned picture of life, who pretend to authoritatively narrate truths in their works. Woolf accuses them of denying relativity, deluding and misleading the readers, and pretending to be more authoritative sources of knowledge than they actually were. She advocates 'that writers shall come down off their plinths and pedestals'.[65] Describing the shortcomings of the reading public, she says, 'In England it is a very suggestible and docile creature, which, once you get it to attend, will believe implicitly what it is told for a certain number of years.'[66] She insists that the readers must stop thinking that they know any less than the writers. Stressing upon technique and style, Woolf adds that it is essential to bring about a change in the conventional 'tools' of writing. New methods should report accurately and describe in detail the 'impression' created by a character or scene, instead of trying to give it a larger meaning by 'describing' in detail a background, a location, an occupation, a complete family history, etc. While distancing herself from the Edwardians, Woolf also distances herself from modernist innovators like James Joyce and T.S. Eliot. She calls their methods 'indecent' and 'obscure', respectively. She argues that though Joyce and Eliot are innovators who break away from past inadequacies, their experiments represent nothing but 'failures and fragments'. After all, 'where so much strength is spent on finding a way of telling the truth, the truth itself is bound to reach us in rather an exhausted and chaotic condition'.[67]

Expressing similar views in another essay, 'Modern Fiction', written a few years earlier in 1919, she says, '[I]t is difficult not to take it for granted that the modern practice of the art is somehow an improvement upon the old.'[68] In truth, art is all about 'a circular tendency', where no one writes better but just moves on. Woolf attacks her immediate predecessors for completely disappointing her generation of writers by trying to label certain methods as superior. On the contrary, according to her, the main merit of the English tradition lies in the fact that, 'no "method" no experiment, even of the wildest—is forbidden'.[69] Arguing against the tendency to represent the seamier side of life in fiction she asserts, '"The proper stuff of fiction" does not exist; everything is the proper stuff of fiction.'[70] She calls writers like Bennett and Galsworthy materialists who take upon themselves the work that ought to be discharged by government officials. Criticizing them she asserts:

> Life is not a series of gig-lamps symmetrically arranged; life is a luminous halo, a semi-transparent envelope surrounding us from the beginning of consciousness to the end. Is it not the task of the novelist to convey this varying, this unknown and uncircumscribed spirit, whatever aberration or complexity it may display, with as little mixture of the alien and the external as possible?[71]

Woolf urges that writers must have the courage to acknowledge their true point of interest, rather than meekly following conventions. Going a step further, she writes that the main point of interest for the moderns very likely lies in the 'dark places of psychology'. It is the inner life which, according to Woolf, is as important or perhaps more, than the outer life. She argues for the amalgamation of outer and inner realities within the scope of the novel and claims that spiritualists like Lawrence Sterne, James Joyce or Marcel Proust are far superior to materialists like H.G. Wells or John Galsworthy. Elaborating upon the nature of reality in her novel *A Room of One's Own*, she says, '[Reality] would seem to be something very erratic, very undependable—now to be found in a dusty road, now in a scrap of newspaper in the street, now a daffodil in the sun.'[72] It is not simple or systematic; rather it is fluid and bafflingly complex. Although she insists that it is the business of a writer to find reality, collect it and communicate it to the rest of humankind, reality is something that resides under the skin or surface of life; it is a pure truth, a great abstraction and closely related to ideas and feelings within the intense life of the mind. Thus, Virginia Woolf, as a writer, does not differentiate between realism and anti-realist modernism; she just redefines realism to mean the representation of what she calls the more enduring aspect of reality, i.e. the interiority of the mind, instead of just an outer reality.

With the Russian Revolution of 1917 serving as a backdrop, the debate over realism became more ideologically pitched. Taking their respective sides in this debate, critics argued for either the primacy of representing socio-historical reality in literature, or the realities of the functioning of the mind. Elizabeth Drew, in her book, *The Modern Novel* (1926), intervened in this ongoing tussle between the Edwardians and the Georgians, or the realists/pragmatists and the moderns to indict the 'egotistical' moderns who are 'a good deal more interested in their own psychology and environment than in general human life'.[73] Elaborating upon this view she writes, 'There is no reason why subconscious life should be any more "true" or "essential" than conscious life, the ingredients of a pudding are no more "true" or "essential" than the pudding itself when it is cooked.'[74] Also, the entire purpose of art is 'to bring order out of chaos, to impose form on being'.[75] Therefore, to criticize art for making life more intelligible is completely erroneous on part of the moderns.

Jose Ortega y Gasset, a major early twentieth-century Spanish critic, essayist and philosopher, however, shared the disdain of James and Woolf for the deliberate representation of the bleak side of life in fiction. In his book *The Revolt of the Masses* published in 1929, he lamented new social changes taking place in the modern life of the West, in which the mass or the average man appear in the highest seats of power—political, economic, moral, intellectual, religious and cultural power. He classifies the dynamic unity of society into two main factors—the minorities and the masses. The minorities represent 'especially qualified individuals and groups' and the masses represent the multitude, the social animal or the average type who are not particularly qualified. Ortega expresses his disapproval for this 'depressingly ordinary' or ungifted mass-man becoming the 'qualitative determinant'. Earlier, the minorities practised democracy through the liberal principle and judicial norm. Now, the masses have caused a lawless 'triumph of hyperdemocracy'. Launching a scathing attack on the historical changes taking place in modern times, he writes:

> The characteristic note of our time is the dire truth that the mediocre soul, the commonplace mind, knowing itself to be mediocre, has the gall to assert its right to mediocrity, and goes on to impose itself wherever it can.... The mass crushes everything different, everything outstanding, excellent, individual, select, and choice. Everybody who is not like everybody else, who does not think like everybody else, runs the risk of being eliminated.[76]

In his other work, *Mediations on Quixote* (1914), Ortega states that the difficult task of transforming illusion into reality is what characterizes *Don Quixote*, a novel which evolves many techniques of the modern novel. In his famous work, *Dehumanisation of Art and Ideas About The Novel (1925*), Ortega predates Lévi-Strauss and Roland Barthes in arguing that the novel has exhausted itself. Like many other modernists, he places greater emphasis upon *form* rather than *content*. He argues that modern realism is all about relating things from a certain distance. Ortega makes an important paradoxical remark when he says, 'Precisely because it is a preeminently realistic genre [the novel] is incompatible with outer reality.'[77] His presupposition is that no writer can be called a novelist unless he possesses the gift of forgetting, and thereby making us forget the reality beyond the walls of his novel. Consequently, in order to establish its own inner world, the novel necessarily must dislodge and abolish the surrounding one. In such a context then 'description interests us in the novel precisely because we are not actually interested in what is described. We disregard the objects which are placed before us in order to pay attention to the manner in which they are presented.'[78] Things seem realistic because 'we do not consider real what actually happens but a certain manner of happening that is familiar to us'.[79] Ortega contends that it is the content, not the form or structure of the novel which stands considerably depleted because of the novel's attempt to meet its reader's expectation of realistic content. The novel, he asserts, has become a victim of its own success.

In 1934, Andrey Alexandrovich Zhdanov of the Union of Soviet Writers addressed the debate over realism in the first meeting of the union. He took an emphatic position against bourgeois realism and argued for embracing 'socialist realism' as the mantra of writing fiction. Demarcating the tasks of this new literary aesthetic, he states:

> [Socialist realist literature must organize] the toilers and oppressed for the struggle to abolish once and for all every kind of exploitation and the yoke of wage slavery . . . [base] the subject matter of its works on the life of the working class and peasantry and their fight for socialism . . . [defend and uphold] the principle of equal rights for the toilers of all nations, the principle of equal rights for women . . . [smash] every kind of obscurantism, every kind of mysticism, priesthood and superstition . . .[80]

He proposes that socialist realism must become the main method of both literature as well as literary criticism.[81]

Philip Henderson in his essay, 'The Functions of The Novel' (1936), criticizes the inverted or interiorized preoccupation of modern writers and critics. Giving vent to his disappointment he laments, '[C]riticism has retired from the world at large to the "inner world" of the psychiatrist's consulting-room and the novel itself has come to be regarded as primarily the tool of self-analysis.'[82] Modern writers 'dare not look too closely at social reality lest it lead them to unwelcome conclusions. Their art being based . . . upon compromise and evasion, however brilliantly they may juggle with their unresolved perplexities, can never achieve greatness . . . because it has lost touch with the basic realities of the world which sustains [them].'[83] Henderson also disapproves of the popular novels of writers like Galsworthy and Wells which confirm 'familiar feelings' and keep life on a 'safe dead level'. Asserting that all works are political and biased even if the authors deny so, Henderson advocates that there is nothing wrong in politics, for 'everyone must believe in something, otherwise there would be no point in living at all'.[84] It is this belief or worldview that a writer must bring to bear upon the specific fragment which forms his immediate theme. He labels novels which do so as 'vital novels', which always serve the purpose of changing society. It is this noble function that is the duty of all sensitive writers who must honestly try to explore and explain the painful issues of life.

While Ortega opposes mass culture from a conservative position, a major modernist thinker, Theodore Adorno, of the Frankfurt school, engages in its criticism for entirely different reasons. He argues that mass art represents a degraded culture, not because it represents the low taste of the masses or the multitude, but because it represents the deliberately produced 'rubbish' of the bourgeois order. Mass art, according to him, is completely controlled by the *culture industry.* In a landmark work, *The Dialectic of Enlightenment* (1944), written jointly with Horkheimer, Adorno posits the view that modern society is dominated by monopoly capitalism. Under monopoly capitalism, not only goods but also culture are turned completely into a commodity. Culture now caters to the manufactured needs of the modern society; commodified artworks are manufactured and distributed by big culture monopolies. Serious art or fine art, on the other hand, has to counter and resist the power of the culture industry because the people at the top of the culture industry seek to mould the spontaneity of the public into conformity and passivity. Reiterating this view in a subsequent article, 'Culture Industry Reconsidered' (1975), he argues, 'The customer is not king, as the culture industry would like us to believe, not its subject but its object.... The masses are not the measure but the ideology of the culture industry.'[85] Through mass reproductions and formula, the culture industry deliberately standardizes all art, produces conformism, disseminate norms, promotes status quo and, generates dependence and servitude among all in their opinions about culture. Modern society, which is dominated by monopoly capitalism, is a society in which consciousness gets completely reified or commodified. In such a context, Adorno privileges non-realist art. He defends modernism by arguing that modernist forms are non-representational in nature. Rather than communicating an unambiguous content, they foreground the processes of literary production. Content and subject matter are not as important as they are made out to be, because art is never a reproduction of the real, but an aesthetic representation or an image of it.[86] It is precisely the distance or gap between artwork and reality that permits art to contradict and even critique the real. Art, Adorno famously observes, is the 'negative knowledge of the world'. Thus,

Adorno keeps his primary focus on elements of form, style and technique. For Adorno, however, the key distinction is not between realism and modernism but between fine art and mass art. He defends fine art since it resists appropriation by the market. It is vital to do so, he asserts, in order to prevent the masses from joining 'the progress of barbaric meaninglessness'.

Realism Debates: 1950s to Contemporary Times

By the turn of the century, the most notable features of the realist novel like the omniscient narrator, the attempt to capture something like a totality within its content, an emphasis on plot with a beginning, middle and end, development of character, description of the socio-historical, etc., were beginning to get replaced by new features of the modernist novel, which favoured impressionism, symbolism, subjectivity, interiority, point-of-view, stream-of-consciousness, non-chronological and discontinuous narratives, fragmented forms and self-reflexivity. It is surprising, therefore, that during the fifties and sixties when French authors like Alain Robbe-Grillet, Michel Butor, Claude Ollier, Nathalie Sarraute, Robert Pinget, Claude Simon and Marguerite Duras announced the Nouveau Roman or the new novel, they did so not in opposition to its immediate predecessor—the modernist novel—but against the realist writings of Balzac, who wrote over a hundred years ago. In an important collection of essays on the new novel titled *For A New Novel* (1963), Alain Robbe-Grillet announced that his novels like *The Erasures* (1953), *The Voyeur* (1955) and *Jealousy* (1957) were meant against omniscient narration, rounded characterization, the all-embracing totality and linearity of closed narratives of nineteenth-century novels, particularly those written by Balzac. Explaining his new philosophy of writing novels, he writes:

> Today we are, in fact, witnesses of a new development that separates us radically from Balzac ... it is the abandonment of the old myth of 'depth'.
>
> We know that the entire literature of the novel was based on such myths, and on them alone. The role of the author traditionally consisted in mining the depths of Nature, descending as far as possible, in order to reach increasingly deeper layers, and then finally bringing to light some fragment of a disturbing secret.... And the sacred vertigo the reader suffered on these occasions, far from causing anguish or nausea, would, on the contrary, reassure him of his power to dominate the world ... *but we no longer even believe in its depth.*[87]

He warns that the novel must immediately innovate and rejuvenate, otherwise it will die of stagnation. The new novel, he asserts, must lack any 'analysis' by the author, and must involve the reader into thinking about fresh ways of reading and viewing the world around him. In another significant essay from the same school of writers, 'What I am seeking to do' (1971), Nathalie Sarraute argues that imagination can give rise to an infinite mass of possible situations, none of which can claim to be greater, more real or superior to the other. An author must not try to intervene and establish an artificial order upon the universe. The construction of characters in novels should be such that they remain fluid instead of getting enclosed or contained in some fixed mould. The narrative must be 'formless', 'shaking' and 'trembling'; that is the only way to write novels in present times.

While the innovators of the nouveau roman made anti-realist proclamations, in his essay, 'The *Nouveau Roman* and Reality', the French Marxist thinker, Lucien Goldmann, analyses their writings in another light:

> ... while many critics and a large section of the public see in the *nouveau roman* a set of purely formal experiments and generally speaking, an attempt to evade social reality, two of the principal representatives of this school [Nathalie Sarraute and Alain Robbe-Grillet tell] ... that their work was born out of an effort, as rigorous and as radical as possible, to grasp, in its most essential way, the reality of our time.[88]

Goldmann offers another kind of explanation to the innovations happening in the writing of novels. He asserts that the essence of human reality changes through history, therefore, it is no longer possible to write like Balzac, Flaubert or Stendhal. The nouveau roman is an outcome not merely of a wish to create something new in opposition to the old, but actually of the very nature of a different reality that we live in. Describing this new reality with the help of the concept of commodity-fetish or reification, Goldmann argues that in the era of market economies, autonomous objects 'are the sole concrete reality and outside which human realities and feelings can have no autonomous existence'.[89] Robbe-Grillet, in his novels, manages to capture precisely this process of reification, which he makes the center of his artistic creation. But, argues Goldmann, Robbe-Grillet is also conscious of differentiating himself from obvious similarities with the Marxists in their opposition to such dehumanization. Goldman cites him, 'Marxists ... are people who take up a position, I am a realist, objective writer; I create an imaginary world that I do not judge, that I neither approve nor condemn, but whose existence I record as an essential reality.'[90]

In another essay, 'Interdependences Between Industrial Society And New Forms of Literary Creation' written in 1965, Goldmann explains that the New Novel presents a picture of a 'universe where man is entirely subordinate to things and whose structure and mechanisms ... [the New Novel analyses] realistically and pitilessly, but almost without anguish.'[91]

It is this lack of anguish and the presence of 'hope' that distinguishes Robbe-Grillet from his predecessors and makes the nouveau roman remarkable. Talking about the role of literary creations in social life, he says that literary works must not merely record reality or reflect collective consciousness. Rather, literature has and must continue to fulfil two basic functions of social life: on the one hand, make people aware of 'their own affective, intellectual, and practical aspirations' and, on the other hand, simultaneously give individuals as group members 'a satisfaction on the imaginary plane which can and must compensate for . . . multiple frustrations . . . which reality imposes'.[92] Goldmann, therefore, defends the function of literature of providing imaginary relief to its readers and does not view it as a vice as long as the other function of making the reader aware is also fulfilled. He views Robbe-Grillet as an important writer, who, in a society with 'inauthentic' human existence, brings to 'anxiety-prone novels', an element of hope.[93]

Sharing Goldmann's basic view that reality changes and therefore its modes of representation must also change, Raymond Williams in the short essay 'Realism and the Contemporary Novel' in his book *The Long Revolution* (1961) argues that realism is not an 'object' but a 'method', which denotes different things. In its simplest usage, it is a term that invokes descriptive precision or vividness of some observed detail in fiction. Right from the beginning, its most straightforward definition has been that 'of an ordinary, contemporary, everyday reality, as opposed to traditional heroic, romantic, or legendary subjects'.[94] He explains that since the Renaissance, it has been associated with the rising middle classes or the bourgeoisie. From an initial 'domestic' content, however, it changed to depicting the 'startling', i.e. showing the unpleasant, the poor and the sordid. Starting as a bourgeois form, it gradually developed into an anti-bourgeois form that made further selections from ordinary material. With the advent of naturalism, it moved on to Zola's 'technical' and 'offensive' accounts. Srindberg further refined its meaning to juxtapose natural with the 'supernatural'. In the twentieth century again, its focus changed to representing 'psychological reality'. The advent of Soviet socialism gave rise to the differentiation between socialist realism and bourgeois realism. Williams argues that though it is usually said that the psychological novel of the twentieth century is opposed to the realist novel, it can also be argued that in spite of different techniques of narration, the intentions of writers still remain wholly realistic.

Describing the development of the modern novel, Williams proposes the classification of the 'social' novel and the 'personal' novel, which can be further sub-divided into social documentary and social formula, and personal descriptive and personal formula novels. 'In the social novel there may be accurate observation and description of the general life, the aggregation; in the personal novel there may be accurate observation and description of persons, the units.'[95] Social documentary novels focus upon a general way of life of the community, while social formula novels, instead of having a descriptive tenor, prioritize an abstracted pattern from the sum total of social experience. Personal descriptive novels deliberately dwell upon personal experience, with society being usually outside the people, while personal formula novels deal with the abstracted pattern of the sum total of individual experience rather than that of societies. Williams proposes this four-fold classification for the novel and insists that these forms have replaced the older realist novel to reflect the 'crisis of our society', which is searching for relationships of a 'whole kind'. Like Lukács, Williams too develops a realist aesthetic, although a slightly different one. Elaborating upon a desired form of realism, Williams explains:

> . . . a valuing of a whole way of life, a society that is larger than any of the individuals composing it, and at the same time valuing creations of human beings who, while belonging to and affected by and helping to define this way of life, are also, in their own terms ends in themselves. Neither element, neither the society nor the individual, is there as priority.
>
> . . . In the highest realism, society is seen in fundamentally personal terms, and persons, through relationships, in fundamentally social terms.[96]

Williams argues that distortions in realism amount to the privileging of one aspect versus the other. The modern novel can possibly be divided into the polarizations of 'object-realist and subject-impressionist' novels. The older form of realism, he states, is dead and impossible to recreate now. We can no longer go back to the simple idea of the old observer who is blissfully unaware of the problems of perception and communication. The absence of balance between the individual and the social in the contemporary novel, however, reiterates the need for achieving a new creative realism. The shortcomings of the contemporary novel are both a warning as well as a challenge for the contemporary writer.

In the late 1960s, another kind of realism, i.e. 'magic realism', started making its presence felt in the world of fiction. Writers like Gabriel García Márquez, Julio Cortázar and Carlos Fuentes brought it to the centre stage of literary discussions through their novels like *One Hundred Years of Solitude* (1967), *Hopscotch* (1963) and *The Death of Artemio Cruz* (1962), respectively. Their novels effortlessly combine the representation of everyday mundane reality with elements of fantasy, folktale, myth and magic. The content of their novels completely upsets the familiar rationalist logic of cause and effect. Yet, the author/narrator narrates his/her story without any awkwardness about unusual events. Magic realist writers assert that in their societies magic is very much a part of the everyday real life and consciousness of the people. That is why they see no reason to emulate the scepticism of the Europeans towards magic or myth; and that by making the supernatural an integral part of their stories, they are only making their narratives more natural and real. Subsequently, magic realism came to be associated with many non-Latin-American writers like Günter Grass, Italo Calvino and Salman Rushdie. Although the practitioners of magic-realism wrote no manifesto on their style of writing, the sheer success of their novels has kept magic realism in the hub of debates about realism, especially in theories about postcolonial literature.[97] Debates over what kind of reality magic realist novels represent, however, are far from being resolved, with critics arriving at contesting and often irreconcilable views. As Franco Moretti writes in *Modern Epic: The World-System from Goethe to García Márquez*:

> *Lo real maravilloso*. Not magical *realism*, as it has unfortunately been translated ... but marvelous *reality*. Not a poetics—a state of affairs.... It is an everyday, collective fact, which restores reality to modernist techniques: which takes the avantgarde, and sets it feet back on the ground.... And after half a century of enigmas, there is always a great need for explanations ... [a need to s]et modernism's feet back on the ground.[98]

The magic realist novel, Moretti elucidates, has reality seeping out from every aspect, the reality of wars, revolutions, trade, invention, religion, gypsies, military revolts, etc., things which the West has been shying away from looking straight in the eye. In its content 'if there is any nostalgia, it is *nostalgia for disorder*. The world was beautiful when ... it was formless, composite, unstable',[99] implying, thereby, that the contemporary world is highly ordered and regimented. In order to seek disorder, magic realism takes recourse to the past. However, unable to resolve the true meaning of magic realism for the people of the third world, Moretti writes:

> A backward-looking myth, or one hope of freedom. For now, let us leave the matter in suspense. What is certain is that myth ... is the sign and instrument of a *symbolic resistance* to Western penetration.... For rewriting an event in mythical form is tantamount to making it *meaningful*: freeing it from the profane world of cause and effect, and projecting into it the symbolic richness of the archetype.[100]

Being relatively clearer about the significance of magic realism for the West, he says that magic realism fulfils 'the desire for "meaning", imagination, re-enchantment'.[101] It reaches Europe during the decade of the sixties when the long phase of colonial conquest comes to an end and the colonial powers withdraw from Africa.

Marthe Robert has another take on the ever-recurring debate over realism. She claims in *Origins of The Novel* (1972) that there exists a generic commonality between realist and non-realist narrative techniques in the novel right from the days of its inception and 'Whether the subject is based on reality or is purely fictional is not what makes a novel.'[102] Realism in the novel is not a period concept as is commonly perceived; in fact, the novel manages to appropriate every traditional form and all modes of expression within its boundaries—'Fantastic or realistic, utopian or naturalistic, "fictitious" or true, whatever relation it may claim to have with reality, a novel's subject matter can thus never provide a reliable criterion for defining the genre.'[103] It is not the case that every writer prefers to create an illusion or an effect of reality; rather, there are many novelists who emphasize the fictive nature of their novels. Describing the simultaneous interplay between reality and fiction in the narrative techniques of the novel, Robert writes:

> [T] he genre's originality and paradox consist in . . . 'trying to make us believe'; in the willful delusion always created in the name of truth but for the sole purpose of deceiving . . . the novel is neither true nor untrue but merely creates the illusion of being one or the other. In other words it can only choose between two ways of deceiving, between two kinds of deceit which exploit the readers gullibility in unequal proportions. . . . The novel's truth is never more than its greater ability to delude. Doubtless according to popular opinion the novel is no better nor worse than reality. But neither is it a pointless imitation of reality.[104]

It is Robert's belief that the novel has this twin ability of representation, and all novelists are always torn between these two tendencies. Novelists like Balzac, Hugo, Tolstoy, Dostoevsky, Proust, Faulkner and Dickens try to be true to life by being engaged writers; while Cervantes, Hoffman, Jean-Paul, Novalis, Kafka or Melville fly in the face of reality and ignore history. According to Robert, these two trends constitute the ways in which novels negotiate reality.

Roland Barthes, in his work *S/Z* written in 1973, takes the critique of realism a step further by criticizing what he calls the 'reality effect' created by readerly texts, i.e. most realist or classic texts which ascribe to the reader the role of a passive consumer who is constantly reassured by familiar and predictable representation of character and plot. Barthes advocates for the creation of writerly texts, i.e. texts that shake the assumed stability of meaning and involve the reader as a collaborator in breaking racial and gender stereotypes created by classic realist texts in the guise of objectivity and '. . . the goal of work (of literature as work) is to make the reader no longer a consumer, but a producer of the text'.[105] He elaborates:

> The writerly is the novelistic without the novel, poetry without the poem, the essay without the dissertation, writing without style, production without product, structuration without structure. But the readerly texts? They are products (and not productions), they make up the enormous mass of our literature.[106]

Doing a detailed structural study of Balzac, he says that two types of empirical codes participate closely in creating the reality effect, the code of actions, and the cultural or referential code. The former operates by creating a structure of intelligibility through a sequence of action, like answering a knock on the door, while the latter operates through several connotations or explicit/implicit references that create the fullness of a familiar social reality through received and available knowledge which is cultural, proverbial, commonsensical, general, stereotypical, based on school gossip, etc. These codes are 'already-written, already-seen, already-read, already-done'.[107] Barthes argues that writerly texts lend themselves to evaluation and interpretation to reveal a plurality of meanings. It is important to write writerly texts, but it is also possible to find writerly qualities in readerly texts if the reader so applies herself. He, therefore, reads Balzac's short story *Sarraisine*, a readerly text, as a writerly one. Barthes also proposes that the task of a critic is not merely to discern the common elements or codes of literature, but also to appreciate their differences.

In his essay, 'Beyond the Cave: Demystifying the Ideology of Modernism' (1975) and also in his book *The Political Unconscious* (1981), Fredric Jameson offers the view that realism is inseparable from the development of capitalism. He believes that it is the rising bourgeoisie and its ideologues that created the movement of Enlightenment in which they set out to destroy religion and superstition. In this phase, the novel performs an extremely important historical task in the bourgeois cultural revolution by systematically undermining and demystifying pre-existing inherited traditions. It helps in the 'immense process of transformation whereby populations whose life habits were formed by other, now archaic, modes of production are effectively reprogrammed for life and work in a new world of market capitalism'.[108] It does so by creating a referent, i.e. a newly quantifiable space of extension and market equivalence, a 'disenchanted' object of the secular world of commodity system, along with a 'centred subject', 'closure' and 'description':

> And when in our own time the bourgeoisie begins to decay as a class, in a world of social anomie and fragmentation, then that active and conquering mode of representation of reality which is realism is no longer appropriate; indeed, in this new social world which is ours today, we can go as far as to say that the very object of realism itself—secular reality, objective reality—no longer exists either.[109]

Jameson states that modernism is that stage in the development of bourgeois ideology, which comes after the stage of realism. The middle classes now seek to repress reality, not so much out of false consciousness or a distortion of reality stemming from outright cynicism or lies, but as a part of careful preparation to prevent certain questions from being asked. Modernism, thus, is an entirely ideological practice that seeks to make people look away, forget, ignore or lose interest in the strategic realities of their lives.

Jean-Francois Lyotard in *The Postmodern Condition* (1979) talks about how realism creates mass conformism through a style that relies on unity, simplicity, and communicability. Realism seeks to represent an uncritical and oversimplified picture of the world. Lyotard argues that the present society is a post-industrial, knowledge based, computerized society in which knowledge is power. This knowledge is conveyed through narrative and language. He attacks the very veracity of narrative knowledge because narratives always illustrate how they are to be applied. 'They thus define what has the right to be said and done in the culture in question, and since they are themselves part of that culture, they are legitimated by the simple fact that they do what they do.'[110] All knowledge in society is quintessentially some or the other form of narrative knowledge. But narrative knowledge causes legitimation especially because it is based upon claims of representing reasonable reality. He insists that instrumental conceptions of reason and belief in totalities, and systematic metaphysical systems produce totalitarianism and reigns of terror. Lyotard welcomes the collapse of grand theory and meta-narratives in the postmodern society, claiming that modernism cannot exist without the shattering of belief, without the discovery of the lack of reality of 'reality', together with the invention of other realities. Modernity places an emphasis on the powerlessness of the faculty of representation, on the nostalgia for the presence felt by the human subject. The postmodern, he says, is part of this modernity:

> The postmodern would be that which, in the moderns puts forward the unrepresentable in presentation itself; that which denies itself the solace of good forms, the consensus of a taste which would make it possible to share for new presentations, not in order to enjoy them but in order to impart a stronger sense of the unrepresentable.... Let us wage a war on totality; let us be witness to the unrepresentable; let us activate the differences and save the honor of the name.[111]

Unlike in the early twentieth century, when people developed nostalgia for lost narratives, in the postmodern era people lose the nostalgia for lost narration. They become aware of the fact that legitimation can occur only through their own linguistic practice and communicational interaction, but that there is nothing much that they can do about it. This, he argues, is 'the harsh austerity of realism'.[112] The validity of narrative knowledge can no longer be judged since, 'All we can do is to gaze in wonderment at the diversity of discursive speeches.'[113]

Linda Hutcheon in *Narcissistic Narrative: The Metafictional Paradox* (1980) defines metafiction as a new kind of contemporary 'fiction that includes within itself a commentary on its own narrative and/or linguistic identity'.[114] It involves the reader as a collaborator instead of a consumer. Metafiction challenges its own textual autonomy by constantly pointing out that it is only a construct in which the artist is not a god-like creator but a maker of a social product. She emphasizes that this self-awareness in literature is similar to the Brechtian technique of defamiliarization, wherein the reader/audience is made acutely aware of the constructedness of literary creations. Tracing the genealogy of the novel she writes:

> [W]e could say that the poetics of Romanticism involved a concentration on the author and his biography, that realism then brought social and historical reference to the fore, that modernism proceeded to orient critics and readers formally and formalistically toward the closed text and its difficulties, then it would seem that the poetics of postmodernism has been responsible for continuing the work. . . .[115]

Hutcheon argues that narcissist metafiction is different from modernist fiction in that it 'tends more to play with the possibilities of meaning . . . and form'.[116] A different kind of mimesis takes place in the contemporary novel in which the *product mimesis* of nineteenth century is replaced by the *process mimesis* of the late twentieth century. It is the act of reading itself, which is now imitated by the novel. The novel today is '. . . self-referring and autorepresentational: it provides within itself, a commentary on its own status as fiction and language, and also on its processes of production and reception'.[117] The referents of the novel, in her view, no longer refer to the real world, but to a fictive verbal universe.

Countering the critique of nineteenth-century realists, George Levine in *The Realistic Imagination* (1981) denounces this entire attack as unfounded. He argues that nineteenth-century writers were never so naïve about the problems of representation as they are made out to be. Studying writers like the Brontes, Dickens, Eliot, and Hardy, Levine explains that their perception of reality is filtered through the ideas of Romanticism, along with those of the Enlightenment, in which a 'sympathetic imagination' is often regarded as a more reliable means to understand and represent elements of reality than 'rational objectivity'. Their multiple sense of reality is also informed by popular literary traditions of fairy tales, melodrama, religious and radical discourse, etc., which strengthen the impulse to question dominant perspectives. Levine proposes that the English realists were alert to 'the possibilities of indeterminate meaning" and 'the arbitrariness of the reconstructed order to which they point'.[118] He particularly gives the example of *Wuthering Heights* to show how the great novelists of the nineteenth century were never simply 'deluded into believing that they were in fact offering an unmediated reality' and that they tried to transcend the limitations of language.

Another scholar who makes important contributions to the realism debate is Jean Baudrillard. In his influential book, *Simulations* (1983), he elaborates upon the concept of 'simulacrum' or the fact that everything is simulated, calling it the defining feature of our age. In an age of frantic reproduction and reduplication of art works '... the real is not only what can be reproduced, but *that which is always already reproduced.* The hyperreal'.[119] In this culture of hyperreality, models replace the real and determine the real. Reality utterly disappears. Baudrillard argues that hyperrealism is the end of the real as well as the end of art because now representation itself is part of the real. He states that in postmodern times we live in an 'esthetic' hallucination of reality where guilt, anguish, death can be replaced by the signs of guilt, anguish, despair, 'Reality no longer has the time to take on the appearance of reality ... The principle of simulations wins out over the reality principle....'[120] We experience fake things as real and reality as fake, as for instance we watch the reality television show *Big Brother* as if it were real and view the bombing of the WTC towers as though it were a Hollywood film. Baudrillard says, '[A]rt is everywhere, since artifice is at the very heart of reality.'[121]

Raymond Federman, a novelist and critic, who coined the term 'surfiction' for contemporary novels, writes in his book *Critifiction: Postmodern Essays* (1993) that fiction today has become a pursuit of non-knowledge:

> Much of contemporary fiction does not relate the reader directly to the external world (reality), nor does it provide the reader with a sense of lived experience (truth), instead contemporary fiction dwells on the circumstances of its own possibilities, on the conventions of narrative, and on the openness of language to multiple meanings, contradictions, paradoxes, and irony.[122]

Federman protests that to write simply to reveal the difficulty or impossibility of writing is hardly a worthwhile enterprise. The more we read postmodern novels the less we seem to know. Instead of proposing the 'limitations of the possible', writers dwell more upon the lack of 'limits for the impossible'. It is due to these reasons that contemporary novelists are socially or politically not engaged. The act of creating fiction today is an act of transforming reality; it is also, simultaneously, an act of abolishing reality and the notion of its truth. He argues that contemporary fiction proposes that it must not be judged; rather, it should be allowed to just simply 'BE'. That is why contemporary fiction by any name, be it New Fiction, Antifiction, Metafiction, Postmodern fiction or Surfiction, is absurd and must be 'questioned, challenged, undermined, and even rejected'.[123]

Bran Nicol in the introduction to *Postmodernism and the Contemporary Novel* (2002) echoes Baudrillard as he says:

> Reality is no longer something we can take for granted, but is something that we suspect is continually organized and constructed for us by the twin apparatuses of the mass media and the global capitalist economy. . . . In postmodernity we are no longer able to appreciate the particularity of our historical location. We can no longer create original works of art, we live and work in 'virtual' space rather than reality.[124]

Nicol's subsequent book *Postmodern Fiction* (2009) carries forward the view that postmodernism is no longer the hot topic of debate among academics and may be discussed in a retrospective sense. However, he also argues that one of the most significant aspects of postmodernism is 'an implicit (or sometimes explicit) critique of realist approaches both to narrative and to representing a fictional "world"'.[125] Without the 'starting-point' of comparison to realism, particularly the nineteenth-century novel, Nicol concludes that it is not possible to understand the postmodern fiction of today.

Conclusion

As can be seen, realism in the novel has continued to inspire many strong opinions both among novelists as well as critics. The debate is very high pitched, with critics and novelists not merely defining their own versions of realism, but also ridiculing and attacking others for being pro or anti-realist, as well as claiming to be more real than the others. Those who favour realism, argue that it offers a better understanding and comprehension about the world, especially with its emphasis on the socio-historical. Those who attack realism, do so on the grounds that it offers the false comfort of understanding and comprehension, while in fact the world is too complicated to comprehend. Their argument is that the realists do not take into account the fact that there are no absolute truths in this world, and that everything is relative; that what is true for one may not be so for the other, and that it is impossible to find objectivity in any account. Narrative cannot but be subjective, because the process of narration necessarily involves a process of selection and extraction from specific points of view. Realist narratives, according to them, impose an artificial sense of order, logic, rationality, familiarity and symmetry upon the world. This, in turn, blunts critical thinking among the readership because it reassures the mind into passive acceptance. The complexities of interiority are completely ignored by the realists. Additionally, the realists are accused of being blissfully unaware of the problems of representation, which among other things include the fact that even the language of narration is already historically and textually constituted. Therefore, according to the anti-realists, the claim of presenting a neutral, objective account through any kind of discursive practice is entirely erroneous and the problem and process of representation must itself be highlighted. While the main emphasis of their attack remains on the question of form rather than content, some also attack the realists for their deliberate choice of low subjects, and attribute it to the distortions of democracy/hyperdemocracy.

While most realists and anti-realists attribute these respective literary trends to particular periods in history, there exist a few exceptions to this tendency. For instance, Marthe Robert is partially right in pointing out that some anti-realist tendencies in the novel can be traced back to the days of the novel's inception, to writers like Cervantes, Hoffman and Sterne, and that there is no monolithic period of realism in the novel. However, we do not think that this offers a very valid explanation for concluding the debate on realism in the novel. Fredric Jameson in *Postmodernism, or, The Cultural Logic of Late Capitalism* emphasizes that in order to understand any cultural or literary phenomenon we must first identify the 'cultural dominant' of an age which '. . . allows for the presence and coexistence of a range of very different, yet subordinate, features'.[126] This helps explain why certain artistic-intellectual-ideological practices come to occupy the dominant space of culture and its critical debates in certain times and ages. The cultural dominant is not merely reflective of an autonomous artistic/literary development, but is always constituted in a complete historical totality. By this logic, it can be argued that the anti-realist techniques practised by some novelists during the eighteenth and nineteenth centuries were not the cultural dominants of their age. At best, novelists like Sterne, who are today being celebrated as the precursors to postmodern fiction, represent an occasional, marginal and exceptional tendency of the literature of their times. Using this conceptual category, we can say that the cultural dominant of the novel can be divided into two distinct phases—the realist and the anti-realist, the former being the cultural dominant of the novel during the eighteenth and nineteenth centuries, and the latter occupying the same position during the twentieth and twenty-first centuries. This does not mean that other trends in novel writing did not exist simultaneously; only that, they were not the dominant trends of their times. Of course, it is also significant to keep in mind that the 'cultural dominant' is not some steady marker of a long phase of the novel. As Raymond Williams says, there is a trajectory of emergent, dominant and residual trends at different points of time in the development of the novel.

In the realist phase, the novel largely engages the reader in a process of discerning the logic of cause and effect behind the movement of plot, behaviour of characters, etc. The subsequent anti-realist phase is characterized by the absence of such invocation. For instance, Jane Austen's novels involve the reader in a process of trying to understand why certain characters behave the way they do, why certain characters fall in love, how family equations operate, etc. However, similar questions are not invoked about characters and action in the novels of Gabriel Garcia Marquez or Salman Rushdie. In the anti-realist phase, things are just given, and even if readers are involved in an elaborate process of unravelling motivations, as in Joseph Conrad's *Lord Jim* or E.M. Forster's *A Passage to India*, it is a foregone conclusion that they would *never* be able to do so.

Let us now get back to the question that we began with—*does realism constitute an integral generic component of the novel, or is it expendable when it comes to understanding the genre?* Some would definitely answer this question in the affirmative. They would argue that almost all novelists at least claim to represent reality. Besides, if we were to take a closer look at the world around us, we would find that it does not have a semblance of any kind of order. Therefore, to give it a chronological, well ordered, unproblematic structure within a narrative is, in fact, far less realistic than representing its randomness and arbitrariness through non-chronological, illogical, diverse points-of-view. To make the world of the novel seem reasonable is to impose artificiality upon it. They would seek to remind that in the real world, life does not have a distinct beginning, middle and end. There is no plot, no fathomable characters. In real life, even the closest people we know are never as familiar or logical in their actions and behaviour, as characters in a novel. Therefore, the sophisticated techniques evolved by modernist and postmodern novelists to represent narratives without plot, character, chronology, action, and even authorial privilege, tend more towards the real than the so called realists. While this argument merits serious consideration and cannot be simplistically dismissed, we would like to reason to the contrary.

As many have done before us, we would also argue that creating any form of art is basically an effort to extract some kind of meaning from the world and communicate it to others. To assume that there is no logic to social organization and that the world is completely random and its workings are entirely accidental is a deeply ideological position that seeks to deny human agency in creating or changing the world. The anti-realists today, at the most, seek to grasp fleeting moments of truth residing in mere fragments of social reality and neither wish to look at the total picture, nor to decode it and convey it to the reader. Whatever they do convey, they undermine it themselves by simultaneously arguing that their understanding is only as good or bad as anyone else's. However, even if we were to cast a cursory glance at the development of the novel in Europe and subsequently in the colonies,[127] we would find a particular pattern to exactly when 'realism' becomes an important preoccupation for novelists, and exactly when doubts regarding the reality of realist representations start getting expressed.

As we have underscored in the previous chapter, the rise of the novel was particularly tied to the development of capitalism. Historically, the peak of realism in the European novel occurred during the first half of the nineteenth century. By the late nineteenth century, doubts regarding the shortcomings of 'realism' started coming to the fore. As far as the development of the novel in the colonies is concerned, it was during their national liberation movements that the novel witnessed the peak of realism, and almost without fail, started suffering from a crisis of realism in post-independence days when the era of disillusionment with the objectives of the national liberation movements started setting in. The common element in both these developments is that the novel is realist when the middle classes are involved in the forward march of progressive social movements, while it becomes anti-realist when the same middle classes start suffering from disillusionment and begin to adjust to the injustices of the world.

Lukács, Jameson and others have powerfully argued the middle class thesis in their theories about the novel. The main proposition in this chapter also is that *the novel is basically a genre of the middle classes, and reflects closely, integrally and accurately the dominant cultural and intellectual moorings of this class. Instead of seeing 'realism' as a crucial feature of the genre of the novel, it makes more sense to use it as a concept for classifying stages and types in the development of the genre.* Let us examine this point in greater detail. As is common knowledge, right from the days of its inception, the novel derived its readership from the middle classes. The main reason for this was the integral dependence of the novel on the ability to read for its consumption. As Eric Hobsbawm says, '... the chief indicator of social membership [of the middle classes] increasingly became, and has remained, formal education'.[128] Even though the novel has expanded its scope and circulation since the days of its inception, it has not transcended the middle classes as its readership. Neither is the novel elite enough to belong only to ruling classes, nor is it popular enough to go beyond the scope of the middle classes to become a genre of the underclasses, unlike cinema, which has always had a more cross-class character. Though its circulation is nowhere close to that of newer forms like television or film, the novel has not seen any decline in sales. The spread of the novel has almost paralleled the spread of the middle classes, who came into being with the advent of capitalism, and by now have become an enormous and growing global class.

To make our point, let us digress a bit to outline a few features of this class. As we have detailed in the previous chapter, the middle classes, with all their moral and ethical preoccupations, came into existence with the advent of capitalism. In the initial stages, as a modern class they were involved in fighting the old feudal system in the process of transition to capitalism as a dominant economic and political system. In Europe, the bulk of this process was accomplished by the mid-nineteenth century, mostly though popular rebellions and revolutions. A large section of the masses participated in these movements motivated by the ideas of equality, democracy, secularism, progress, etc. However, once this task was accomplished, and capitalism did, in fact, emerge as a dominant system, the bourgeoisie was no longer interested in carrying forward these ideological positions any further. In fact, after the mid-nineteenth century, the bourgeoisie 'had no great difficulty in organizing itself as an elite, . . . [using] methods very similar to those used by aristocracies, or even—as in Great Britain—the actual mechanisms of aristocracy'.[129] New notions of exclusivity started developing. The bourgeoisie became more interested in demarcating itself from its erstwhile allies, the poor and the working classes. A new contradiction began to occupy the political centre stage, that between the bourgeoisie and the yet aspiring working classes. This was also a moment of crisis for the middle classes. As Eric Hobsbawm says:

> [By the turn of the century] . . . the middle classes of Europe were uneasy . . . They had lost their historic mission. The most heartfelt and unqualified praise of the benefits of reason, science, education, enlightenment, freedom, democracy and progress of humanity which the bourgeoisie had once been proud to exemplify, now came . . . from those whose intellectual formation belonged to an earlier era and had not kept up with the times. It was the working classes and not the bourgeoisie . . .[130]

This crisis was reflected in the worlds of art and literature as well. While the new elites looked for more exclusive cultural status symbols, the middle classes were torn between carrying forward their earlier mission and abandoning it all together. The arts of the early twentieth century displayed both these trends. On the one hand were those who still fought for adherence to realism with its focus on representing the lives of the common folk and making sense of this world. On the other were those who took a strong position against realism and argued that the world was not intelligible. Therefore, to make distinctions between 'progressive' and 'conservative', 'right' and 'wrong' or 'good' and 'bad' was completely meaningless. We shall not enumerate the specific instances of this debate again. We shall only point to the fact that at the turn of the last century this battle of ideas was almost evenly divided. However, after the Second World War, the arts came to be completely dominated by the latter trend. The innovators of the *new novel* during the mid-twentieth century did not hold a debate with their 'non-existent' realist contemporaries, but went considerably back in time to attack the nostalgia of the realism of Balzac. To quote Hobsbawm again, 'All "postmodernisms" had in common an essential scepticism about the existence of an objective reality, and/ or the possibility of arriving at an agreed understanding of it by rational means. All tended to a radical relativism.'[131]

However, this shift in ideological position was not a very comfortable one. The entire intellectual and artistic movement had to confront their own guilty conscience. The loss of meaning in the world was accompanied by a deep sense of anguish. The more the world became unintelligible, the greater was there a sense of nihilism and torment. This tendency intensified and led to the depths of despair visible during the existentialist crisis of the mid-twentieth century Europe, beyond which an ironic playfulness came to become the dominant aesthetic of this anti-realist trend. This playful attitude was related, among many other things, to the post-war economic boom of 1950–73 in the developed world, in which the middle classes benefited enormously. To use a phrase popularly used in those times, the middle classes 'never had it as good'. This newfound economic and material prosperity of the middle classes was unlikely to go hand in hand with extreme social depression; perhaps that is why the middle classes just started looking up. As Hobsbawm says, 'The old moral vocabulary of rights and duties, mutual obligation, sin and virtue, sacrifice, conscience, rewards and penalties, could no longer be translated into the new language of desired gratification.'[132]

If we examine the trajectory of the development of realism in the novel of the colonies, there exists a striking resemblance with its European counterpart. The middle classes in the colonies emerged with the development of capitalism which, on the one hand, was an outcome of colonialism; on the other hand, it also had its own independent and domestic character. The colonial middle classes initially championed many values that the middle classes of Europe had stood for at an earlier historical juncture, although to varying degrees and with many contradictions, i.e. the values of equality, liberty, women's emancipation, democracy, secularism, reason and rationality. Once the middle classes became involved in their respective national liberation movements, the novel witnessed the peak of the realist form. However, the post-liberation disillusionment brought the same questions regarding the intelligibility of the world to the fore, and the realist novel ran into a crisis, leading to the evolution of techniques of writing, both similar as well as different from to those of Western modernism and postmodernism.[133]

To return to our original point of inquiry, we can say that 'realism' is both an aesthetic as well as an ethic. It is a particular kind of representation that places an emphasis, both on an engagement with the common people as well as upon comprehending the society as a whole. The realist aesthetic believes that the 'whole' can be understood. It places a special emphasis on understanding individual life as part of socio-historical realities. We would, therefore, disagree with critics who say that the novel is always realist, as well as with those who say that the novel is never so. It is difficult to associate this concept integrally with the intention of the genre of the novel, because if realism were indeed to be associated intrinsically with the genre of the novel, then most anti-realist fiction written over the last hundred years or so would merit a name other than that of the novel. Therefore, keeping realism at the diagnostic core of understanding the genre of the novel is incorrect. On the contrary, the best insights into the genre of the novel can be gained by viewing the novel essentially as a genre that exhibits the consciousness of the middle classes. It is the middle classes that the novel has remained true to, across its multifarious development and spread. Different dominant and marginal concerns of the middle classes have all found reflection in the form and content of the novel.

Realism in the novel is not just a matter of subjective concerns or individual intentions of authors. There are many who continue to write in the realist mode even today, however, despite the best of intentions, it cannot be said that they are writing novels that are making much headway either in uncovering the great mysteries of the socio-historical realities of our times or with the reading public. The inability to capture contemporary 'totality' arises from the conditions produced by capitalism which have increasingly led authors to grasp at fragments and make connections with the reading public based on those fragments. We shall discuss this aspect of the development of the novel in greater detail in the next chapter. Let us, for the time being, just conclude by reiterating that realism is not a generic feature of the novel, but a stage in its development. It is a very important stage nevertheless; important enough to remain the intellectual point of departure for defining all subsequent stages, but its relevance for the novel can only be understood if the middle classes and their histories are kept in view.

Notes

1. See Kwame Anthony Appiah, 'Is the Post- in Postmodernism the Post- in Postcolonial?', 1991; *Contemporary Postcolonial Theory: A Reader*, ed. Padmini Mongia, Delhi: Oxford University Press, 1997, pp. 55–71.

   See also Kwame Anthony Appiah, 'The Postcolonial and the Postmodern', 1992; *The Post-Colonial Studies Reader*, ed. Bill Ashcroft, Gareth Griffiths and Helen Tiffin, London and New York: Routledge, 2003, pp. 119–24; McKeon, *Theory*, p. 854.

2. Elaine Showalter, *A Literature of Their Own: British Women Novelists From Bronte to Lessing*, Princeton and New Jersey: Princeton University Press, 1977, 1999, p. 13.
3. Ibid., p. 29 (emphasis mine).
4. Aphra Behn, *Oroonoko or, The History of the Royal Slave*, 1688, ed. Maureen Duffy, London: Metheun, 1986, p. 25.
5. Henry Fielding, *Joseph Andrews*, 1742; London: Penguin Books, 1985, p. 30.
6. Ibid., pp. 25–6.
7. Lawrence Sterne, *A Sentimental Journey*, 1768; ed. Graham Petrie, London: Penguin Books, 1986. A novel much discussed in contemporary times for being a predecessor to the anti-realist techniques of the postmodern novel.
8. Walter Scott, 'The art of copying from nature', 1815; in *European Literature from Romanticism to Postmodernism: A Reader in Aesthetic Practice*, ed. Martin Travers, London and New York: Continuum, 2001, p. 85. It is significant to note that Scott wrote historical novels in the image of medieval romances.
9. Charles Dickens, 'These melancholy shades of life', 1841; in Travers, ed., p. 95.
10. Louis-Edmond Duranty, 'Demanding from the artist useful truth', 1856; in Travers, ed., p. 101.
11. Emile Zola, 'Naturalism on the Stage', 1871; Vassiliki Kolocotroni, Jane Goldman, and Olga Taxidou, eds., *Modernism: An Anthology of Sources and Documents*, Edinburgh: Edinburgh University Press, 1998, pp. 169–74.
12. Emile Zola, 'The Experimental Novel', 1893; in *The Nineteenth-Century Novel: A Critical Reader*, ed. Stephen Regan, London and New York: The Open University, 2001, p. 108.
13. Thomas Hardy, 'The Science of Fiction', 1891; in Kolocotroni, Goldman and Taxidou, eds., pp. 120–3.
14. Henry James, 'The Art of Fiction', 1884; Hoffman, Michael J. and Patrick D. Murphy, eds., *Essentials of the Theory of Fiction*, Durham and London: Duke University Press, 1988, pp. 147–50.
15. E.M. Forster, *Aspects of the Novel*, Harmondsworth: Penguin Books, 1964, p. 69.
16. D.H. Lawrence, 'Morality and the Novel'; qtd. in K.K. Sharma, *Tradition in Modern Novel-Theory,* New Delhi: Abhinav Publications, 1978, p. 22.
17. Samuel Becket, 'Dante . . . Bruno . . . Vico . . . Joyce', 1929; in Kolocotroni, Goldman and Taxidou, eds., p. 450.
18. Samuel Becket, 'Proust', 1931; in Kolocotroni, Goldman and Taxidou, eds., p. 454.
19. John Fowles, 'Fiction is woven into all', 1969, in Travers ed., p. 300.
20. Umberto Eco, 'Postmodernism, Irony, The Enjoyable', 1985; Bran Nicole, ed., *Postmodernism and the Contemporary Novel: A Reader*, Edinburgh: Edinburgh University Press, 2002, p. 112.

21. Umberto Eco, 'Introduction', in *The Limits of Interpretation*, Bloomington and Indianapolis: Indiana University Press, 1990, p. 7.
22. It is to be noted that most of Lukács works were translated and published into English much later.
23. Georg Lukács, *Studies in European Realism*, tr. Alfred Kazin, New York: The Universal Library, 1930, repr. 1980, p. 18.
24. Ibid., p. 6.

    Lukács borrows the idea of the 'type' from Friedrich Engles, who in a letter wrote, 'Realism, to my mind, implies, besides truth of detail, the truthful reproduction of typical characters under typical circumstances,' 'Letter to Margaret Harkness', 1888, in Travers, ed., p. 123.
25. Ibid., p. 176.
26. Ibid., p. 71.
27. Ibid., p. 6.
28. Ibid., p. 11.
29. Ibid., p. 91.
30. Bertold Brecht, 'The Modern Theatre is The Epic Theatre', 1930, in Kolocotroni, Goldman, and Taxidou, eds., pp. 465–9.

    Also see Moyra Haslett, 'A Question of Form: the Realism/Modernism Debates', in *Marxist Literary and Cultural Theories*, London: Macmillan Press Ltd., 2000, pp. 86–124.
31. Eric Auerbach, *Mimesis: The Representation of Reality in Western Literature*, 1946; tr. Willard R. Trask, Princeton, New Jersey: Princeton University Press, 1974, p. 394.
32. Ibid., p. 491.
33. Ibid., p. 510.
34. Ibid., p. 515.
35. Ibid., p. 535.
36. Ibid., p. 548.
37. Ibid., p. 549.
38. Ibid.
39. Ibid., p. 546.
40. Ibid., p. 550.
41. Ibid., p. 551.
42. Ibid., pp. 552–3.
43. Ian Watt, *The Rise of The Novel: Studies in Defoe, Richardson and Fielding*, London: Penguin Books, 1957, 1968, p. 35.
44. Ibid., p. 11.
45. Ibid., p. 11 (emphasis mine).
46. Ibid.
47. Ibid., pp. 12–13.
48. Ibid., p. 32–3.
49. Ibid., p. 33.
50. Ibid., p. 312–13.
51. James, 'The Art of Fiction', p. 147.

52. Ibid.
53. Henry James, 'The New Novel', 1914; Tim Middleton, ed., *Modernism: Critical Concepts in Literary and Cultural Studies*, vol. 1, London and New York: Routledge, 2003, p. 67.
54. Ibid., p. 60.
55. Ibid., p. 74.
56. André Breton, 'First Manifesto of Surrealism', in *Surrealism and the Novel*, ed. J.H. Matthews, Ann Arbor: The University Of Michigan Press, 1966, p. 1.
57. Ibid., p. 4.
58. Ibid., p. 3.
59. Andre Breton, 'The First Manifesto of Surrealism', 1924, in Kolocotroni, Goldman, and Taxidou, eds., p. 308.
60. Ibid., p. 309.
61. Ibid.
62. Virginia Woolf, 'Mr Bennet and Mrs. Brown', 1924, in Hoffman and Murphy, eds., p. 33.
63. Ibid., p. 33.
64. Ibid., p. 31.
65. Ibid., p. 39.
66. Ibid., p. 36.
67. Ibid., p. 38.
68. Virginia Woolf, 'Modern Fiction', 1919, in Middleton, ed., vol. 1, p. 110.
69. Ibid., p. 115.
70. Ibid.
71. Ibid., p. 113.
72. Virginia Woolf, *A Room of One's Own*, 1928; hp://gutenberg.net.all/ebooks02/020079/h.htm/.
73. Qtd. in Robert Morss Lovett's 'The Novel To-Day', which is a review of Elizabeth Drew's *The Modern Novel*, in Middleton, ed., vol. 1, pp. 227–8.
74. Robert Morss Lovett, 'The Novel To-Day', in Tim Middleton, ed. *Modernism: Critical Concepts in Literary and Cultural Studies*, vol. 1, London and New York: Routledge, 2003, p. 227.
75. Ibid., p. 228.
76. Jose Ortega y Gasset, 'The Crowd Phenomenon', an extract from his book *The Revolt of The Masses*, 1929, in Middleton ed., vol. 1, pp. 253–4.
77. Jose Ortega y Gasset, 'From Mediations on Quixote', 1914 and 'Notes on the Novel', 1925; Michael McKeon, *Theory of the Novel: A Historical Approach*, Baltimore and London: The John Hopkins University Press, 2000, p. 265.
78. Ibid., p. 265.
79. Ibid.
80. Andrey Alexandrovich Zhdanov, 'On Socialist Realism', 1934, in Travers, ed., pp. 224–5.
81. Socialist realism became a major conceptual force in many colonized nations where its development coincided with developing national liberation

movements which found the notion of commitment embedded deeply in the concept of socialist realism very attractive.

82. Philip Henderson, 'The Function of the Novel', 1936, qtd. in Middleton, ed., vol. 2, p. 7.
83. Ibid., pp. 7–8.
84. Ibid., p. 8.
85. T.W. Adorno, 'Culture Industry Reconsidered', 1975; *The Study of Popular Fiction: A Source Book*, ed. Bob Ashley, London: Pinter Publishers, 1989, pp. 52–9.
    See also Theodor W. Adorno and Max Horkheimer, *The Dialectic of Enlightenment*, London: Verso, 1944.
86. Haslett, op. cit., pp. 99–108.
    See also Martin Jay, *The Dialectical Imagination: A History of the Frankfurt School and the Institute of Social Research 1923–1950*, Heinemann and London: Heinemann Educational Books, 1973, pp. 173–218.
87. Alain Robbe-Grillet, 'Towards a New Novel', 1963; Travers, ed., pp. 302–3 (emphasis mine).
88. Lucien Goldmann, *Towards a Sociology of the Novel*, 1964; tr. Alan Shoriden, London: Tavistock Publications Ltd., 1975, p. 132.
89. Ibid., p. 146.
90. Ibid., p. 47.
91. Lucien Goldmann, *Cultural Creation in Modern Society*, 1971; tr. Bart Grahl, Oxford: Basil Blackwell, 1977, p. 84.
92. Ibid., p. 77.
93. It is to be noted that Goldmann is writing in times that have just seen the pits of the hopelessness of the Absurd movement and the existentialist crisis.
94. Raymond Williams, The *Long Revolution*, Westport, Connecticut: Greenwood Press Publishers, 1961, p. 274.
95. Ibid., p. 280.
96. Ibid., pp. 278–87.
97. Initially the term was used during the 1920s for denoting a dream-like quality in painting. In 1943, Cuban writer Alejo Carpentier applied it to Latin-American fiction for the first time in the Prologue to his novel *The Kingdom of This World*. Since then magic-realism has been seen as a fictional assertion made by the erstwhile colonies over the literature of the West.
    See also, Ashcroft, Griffiths and Tiffin, eds., *The Post-Colonial Studies Reader*, London and New York: Routledge, 2003.
98. Franco Moretti, *Modern Epic: The World System from Goethe to Garcia Marquez*, tr. Quintin Hoare, London and New York: Verso, 1996, pp. 234-5.
99. Ibid., p. 241.
100. Ibid., pp. 247–8.
101. Ibid., p. 249.
102. Marthe Robert, *Origins of the Novel*, 1972; tr. Sacha Rabinovitch, Sussex: The Harvester Press, 1980, p. 8.

103. Ibid.
104. Ibid., pp. 15–17.
105. Roland Barthes, *S/Z,* 1973, tr. Richard Miller, Malden, MA: Blackwell Publishing, 2002, p. 4.
106. Ibid., p. 5.
107. Ibid., p. 262.
108. Fredrick Jameson, *The Political Unconscious: Narrative as a Socially Symbolic Act,* Ithaca and New York: Cornell University Press, 1981, p. 152.
109. Fredrick Jameson, 'Beyond the Cave: Demystifying the Ideology of Modernism', 1975; Francis Mulhern, ed., *Contemporary Marxist Literary Criticism*, London and New York: Longman, 1992, p. 176.
110. Jean-Francois Lyotard, 'From Postmodern Condition: A Report on Knowledge' in *Postmodernism and the Contemporary Novel: A Reader*, ed. Bran Nicol, Edinburgh: Edinburgh University Press, 2002, p. 80.
111. Jean-Francois Lyotard, 'Answering the Question: What is Postmodernism', in *Modern Literary Theory*, ed. Philip Rice and Patricia Waugh, London and New York: Arnold Publishers, 2002, p. 337.
112. Ibid., p. 87.
113. Ibid., p. 83.
114. Linda Hutcheon, *Narcissistic Narrative: The Metafictional Paradox*, New York and London: Methven, 1980, p. 1.
115. Ibid., p. xiii.
116. Ibid.
117. Ibid., p. xii.
118. George Levine, *The Realist Imagination: English Fiction from Frankenstein to Lady Chatterley*, Chicago and London: University of Chicago Press, 1981, p. 4.
119. Jean Baudrillard, *Simulations*, tr. Paul Foss, Paul Patton and Philip Beitchman, New York: Semiotext[e], 1983, p. 146.
120. Ibid., p. 152.
121. Ibid., p. 151.
122. Raymond Federman, *Critifiction: Postmodern Essays*, New York: State University of New York Press, 1993, p. 2.
123. Ibid., p. 3.
124. Nicol, *Postmodernism*, p. 5.
125. Bran Nicol, *Cambridge Introduction to Postmodern Fiction*, Cambridge: Cambridge University Press, 2007, p. xvi.
126. Frederic Jameson, *Postmodernism, or, The Cultural Logic Late Capitalism,* London and New York: Verso, 1991, p. 4.
127. We largely mean Asia and Africa, not Latin America, because there, the sales of novels were often banned under several kinds of regimes for various political reasons. As a result the novel has had an entirely different kind of development in that continent.
128. Eric Hobsbawm, *The Age of Empire: 1875–1914*, London: Abacus, 1987, p. 174.

129. Ibid., p. 176.
130. Ibid., pp. 190–1.
131. Eric Hobsbawm, *Age of Extremes: The Short Twentieth Century—1914–1991*, London: Abacus, 1994, p. 517.
132. Ibid., p. 338.
133. See any introduction to the development of the novel in different countries, continents or linguistic cultures. The same holds true for the Russian novel as well, which was realist during the phase when its middle classes were committed to building a better social order, starting from anti-serfdom struggles till the Russian Revolution. Gogol, Turgenev, Dostoevsky and Tolstoy, all wrote during this stretch of history.

CHAPTER FOUR

Development of the Novel

THE GENRE OF the novel has undergone many changes and modifications since the days of its emergence. Novelistic plot, character, narrative and theme have all undergone major transformations. In its history, the novel often developed by announcing itself against its predecessors. So much so that Frank Kermode comments that 'the history of the novel is a history of anti-novels'[1] while Wallace Martin explicates that, "the novel" cannot be defined because its defining characteristic is to be unlike a novel'.[2] Walter L. Reed says that 'the novel . . . has delighted in flouting its own conventions'.[3] And Lorna Martens argues that 'if we say that the novel changes, what we mean is that the word "novel" remains the same, while this word is used to designate a multitude of different phenomenon'.[4] Indeed, it is quite difficult to capture the novel within the bounds of classification. Its development, too, remains difficult to catalogue.

The history of the novel is very chequered, alternating between mind-blowing success to apocalyptic predictions of demise and death. Yet the novel has somehow managed to repeatedly reinvent itself like a phoenix. It is not a coincidence, therefore, that many contemporary critics have become deeply uneasy about the nomenclature of the 'novel' for describing much of prose fiction. Many have shifted almost entirely to the use of more incorporative terms like 'fiction' or 'narrative', and some use even more specialized terms like 'metafiction', 'surfiction', 'fabulation', 'narcissist narrative', 'historiographic metafiction', etc. In fact, one of the first questions to confront any student of the novel is what exactly are the features that have prevailed in the novel across its multifarious development and spread? We have argued in an earlier chapter that, among other things, an important (though theoretically neglected) generic feature of the novel is its plastic and elastic form, which allows it to incorporate a wide range of formal and thematic elements and concerns within its fold. In this chapter, we would test the veracity of this hypothesis by studying the trajectory of the development of the novel from its inception to contemporary times.

However, the definition of the novel cannot be that it has no boundaries or limits. Therefore, we would explore whether there exists any pattern or logic to the generic incorporations made by the novel.

There are two broad approaches to understanding the development of the novel. One is by studying changes in the general perceptions or opinions about the genre in history, i.e. how the novel is positioned at different points of times. The other is by studying the development of its techniques and themes, i.e. its internal growth as a literary genre. In this chapter, we shall strive to understand the novel through both these approaches, and in the process also try to ascertain the structural parallels between these trajectories. We shall first study the external growth of the novel, and only later move on to examining the content and techniques of early, realist, modernist and postmodern novels. This, we believe, will help us locate the internal development of the novel in, what Pierre Bourdieu calls *the field of literary production* of the novel. But before all of that, let us first delve into the debate over genres.

The Question of 'Genre'

This is not for the first time in Western literary history that 'genres' have come to occupy the centre stage of literary contemplation. Classical genre theory, starting from Plato to Aristotle, to Horace's *Arspoetica*, was considerably important. Neoclassical genre theory resurrected by Dryden and others in the beginning of the eighteenth century was also very influential.[5] However, these earlier periods were distinct from the current period in one major respect. While the earlier debates about genre were all about establishing the primacy and centrality of genres and codes in literature, today's debates challenge the reliability of the concept of genres as an analytical category. Critics and thinkers like Northrop Frye, Jacques Derrida, Hayden White, Roland Barthes and Gérard Genette have contributed significantly to weakening the notion of genres, particularly the novel, by arguing for the use of 'fiction', 'text' or 'narrative' as alternative interpretive categories instead. As Wallace Martin says, 'During the past fifteen years, the theory of narrative has replaced the theory of the novel as a topic of central concern in literary study.'[6] This broad sweep of employing concepts and categories can be unsettling. Umberto Eco makes the following observation in a different discussion about classification:

> Unfortunately, 'postmodern' is a term *bon à tout faire*. I have an impression that it is applied today to anything the user happens to like. Further, there seems to be an attempt to make it increasingly retroactive: first it was apparently applied to certain writers or artists active in the last twenty years, then gradually it reached

the beginning of the century, then still further back. And this reverse procedure continues; soon the postmodern category will include Homer.[7]

This a-historical tendency, however, is not unique to postmodernism alone. E.M. Forster argues in *Aspects of the Novel*, that the classification of the novel 'by chronology' is silly, but classification by 'subject matter' is 'sillier still'.[8] He explicates the similarities between novelists like, Samuel Richardson and Henry James, Charles Dickens and H.G. Wells, and Lawrence Sterne and Virginia Woolf, who seemingly do not fall into similar literary categories. Doing so, he poses the main question of his study and attempts to answer it as he states:

How then are we to attack the novel—that spongy tract, those fictions in prose of a certain extent which extend so indeterminately? Not with any elaborate apparatus. Principles and systems may suit other forms of art, but they cannot be applicable here.... And I have chosen the title 'Aspects' because it is unscientific and vague ...[9]

Forster's views can be easily understood the moment we take into account his main thesis about the nature of all art—'History develops, Art stands still.'[10] He emphatically reiterates this point both in the introduction as well as the conclusion of his book.

The attack on the category of genres, however, does not arise merely out of this inability to demarcate historical differences, but also from a deeper ideological point of view. Ralph Cohen, for instance, explains in his essay 'Do Postmodern Genres Exist?', that contemporary postmodern writing deliberately and self-consciously claims that it 'blurs genres, transgresses them, or unfixes boundaries that conceal domination or authority, and that "genre" is an anachronistic term and concept'.[11] Elaborating on this postmodern malady, he writes:

Postmodern critics have sought to do without a genre theory. Terms like 'text' and 'écriture' deliberately avoid generic classifications. And the reason for this are to abolish the hierarchies that genres introduce, to avoid the fixity of genres and the social as well as literary authority such limits exert, to reject the social and subjective elements in classification.[12]

Cohen argues, however, that contrary to such popular postulations, which are quite reductive in nature, genres do not serve only one single purpose; in fact, they serve multiple ends depending upon how they are employed. Apart from 'classifying' literary types, they also serve to clarify, describe, theorize, analyse and interpret literature without necessarily making prescriptions or proscriptions. Hence, postmodern arguments for the dissolution of genres are not merely a call for doing away with hierarchy and domination, but also for circuitously bringing an end to clear theorization, interpretation and analysis in literature. The subtext of Cohen's article is that the dissolution of the interpretive category of genres is not devoid of its own ideological underpinnings. Walter L. Reed reinforces this point further by demanding a more simple approach for studying novels:

Many recent poetics, of course, claim not to deal merely with the novel but with 'fiction', 'narrative', or even 'prose'. But since all these schemes give novels a place of prominence in the conceptual spectrum, it seems fair to address oneself initially to this historically significant type of prose fiction and ignore for the time being the wider reaches.[13]

Dorothy J. Hale makes the observation that 'novel theory now seems either dismissed or ignored.... Formal and generic descriptions of the novel have increasingly been subsumed by the almost hermetically sealed field of narratology.'[14] Revising this opinion later she stresses:

... current academic interest in the novel has never been stronger. Studies of the novel have never been so prolific or so influential. The last thirty years have shown us that even cultural critics who think they have nothing to do with literary theory (and less to do with novel theory) have more than ever to do with novel studies.[15]

A simple agreement, however, on studying the novel as a distinct generic category is not the end of all contention. What is equally important is *how* and *to what end* are 'genres' being employed in literary studies. For instance, studying the novel through its teeming multitude of sub-genres like the novel of chivalry, the romantic, picaresque, adventure, travel, sociological, historical, documentary novel, chronicle novel, saga, encyclopaedic, political, propaganda, didactic, philosophical, thesis, utopian, allegory, regional novel, novel of the soil, and so on, can also unsettle one's perspective about the novel. Georg Lukács argues in *The Historical Novel*:

The genre theory of later bourgeois aesthetics which splits up the novel into various 'sub-genres'—adventure novel, detective novel, psychological novel, peasant novel, historical novel, etc., and which vulgar sociology has taken over as an 'achievement' has nothing to offer scientifically.... This soulless and ossified, this thoroughly bureaucratic classification is meant as a substitute for the living dialectics of history.[16]

Lukács dates the tendency towards generic sub-divisions to the end of the nineteenth century and links it to the neo-conservatism of the bourgeoisie. He locates the emergence of the new discipline of sociology in this context. 'The single original methodological feature of the new science of sociology is that it separates knowledge of the "laws" of social behaviour from economics and renders them independent.'[17]

Fredric Jameson, too, expresses his discomfort with the proliferation of novelistic subtypes in *The Political Unconscious*, wherein he denounces various generic categories and classifications of the novel like Gothic, picaresque, *mémoire*, associative psychology, *Bildungsroman*, historical novel, *roman d'adventures* and others by declaring that they 'prove rewarding only as long as they are felt to be relatively arbitrary critical acts'.[18] He argues that such categories are part of a provisional and transient tendency in literary theory:

> ...in which the working categories of genre are themselves historically deconstructed and abandoned...all generic categories, even the most time-hallowed and traditional, are...understood (or 'estranged') as mere ad hoc, experimental constructs, devised for a specific textual occasion and abandoned like so much scaffolding when the analysis has done its work.[19]

Peter Hitchcock in his essay 'The Genre of Postcoloniality' (2003) also observes, 'Most recent literary theory has avoided dealing with the novel as genre, opting instead for a focus on subgenres or types, variations on the genre (sociological, philosophical, political, historical) or modes of writing (realism, postmodernism, and so forth) in which the novel as genre remains axiological.'[20] We do not intend to argue that conceptual categories like narrative or fiction are entirely irrelevant, or that many familiar generic subtypes of the novel are completely extraneous; just that when it comes to studying the development of the novel, using categories like narrative or fiction is like using a telescope to study a book, and using its multitude of novelistic subtypes is like using a microscope to read a book. Both, we believe, are ill suited for the object of study, and the novel perhaps merits a much simpler and more straightforward approach. Of course, the genre of the novel is challenging. On the one hand, it seems easily accessible and intelligible even to ordinary readers; on the other, it has continued to perplex the tallest of critics for generations. Some of the challenges of studying the novel historically are outlined by Michael McKeon in *The Theory of the Novel*:

> For the novel genre to be 'coherent'... [as a historical phenomenon] requires that it fulfil the demands that pertain to all historical things: namely, that it display both the continuity of an integral entity and, within the continuity, the discontinuity that confirms its existence over time and space, its capacity to change without changing into something else.[21]

In the course of this chapter, we shall try to grasp the nature of the novel in this sense, by interrogating the continuities in the rise and development of the novel in history in order to examine whether its changes are enough to qualify it by some other name.

The Novel in the Literary Canon

A sweeping survey of the three hundred odd years of the history of the novel reveals that it has had many ups and downs. Unlike today, the novel did not always enjoy the favour of the literary establishment. In its initial stages, the novel existed on the margins of official literary culture. In fact, it existed in considerable disrepute. J. Paul Hunter in *Before Novels* discusses this aspect of the early novel to note, 'Until quite late in the eighteenth century, the term "novel" was used very loosely and imprecisely (not that more recent use has been all that precise either), often implying little more than opprobrium or contempt.'[22] Lennard J. Davis also points out in *Factual Fictions* that the 'English novels of the seventeenth and early eighteenth centuries were perceived by many of the middle and upper classes as immoral and illicit'.[23] Pam Norris makes a similar observation that 'as an upstart literary form, the novel lacked the cultural capital or prestige of traditional forms like poetry or drama'.[24]

In such a context, early novelists took pains to deny that they were writing novels. Daniel Defoe's denials in this regard were among the most vociferous. Dissociating himself from novel writing, Defoe wrote in 1719 that *Robinson Crusoe* was a 'true story,' as opposed to novels which were lies 'created to corrupt men's hearts and their tastes'.[25] In 1722, he again reiterated that the 'private history' of Moll Flanders was very different from other kinds of writings like 'novels and romances'.[26] During these early decades, novels and novelists faced scores of polemical attacks through articles in periodicals, pamphlets and newspapers.[27] In spite of the fact that many early novelists claimed to be pioneers of new kinds of writings, none of them identified themselves as novelists per se. As a result, the novel took its own time to carve out a niche for itself in the literary world. Ian Watt elaborates upon this late stabilization of the genre of the novel to say, '[Novelists] did not even canonize the changed nature of their fiction by a change in nomenclature—our usage of the term 'novel' was not fully established until the end of the eighteenth century.'[28]

Consequently, early evidences of the theorization of the novel are by far too few, that too mostly by novelists themselves.[29] William Congreve was among the first to define the novel by its name in a familiar modern sense in the 'Preface' to *Incognita: or, Love and Duty Reconciled* (1713). He counterposed the novel against the prevalent romances to argue that in contrast to the 'lofty language, miraculous contingencies and impossible performances'[30] of the romances, 'novels are of a more familiar Nature;

Come near us, and represent to us Intrigues in Practice, delight us with Accidents and odd Events, but not such as are wholly unusual or unprecedented'.[31] Tobias Smollett, another novelist, described the characteristics of the novel in the preface to *Ferdinand Count Fathom* (1753), 'A novel is a large diffused picture, comprehending the characters of life, disposed in different groups, and exhibited in various attitudes, for the purpose of a uniform plan, and general occurrence, to which every individual figure is subservient.'[32] Novelist Clara Reeve not only differentiated between 'Novels' and 'Romances', she also gave the novel its first serious treatment in the elevated style of a 'classical dialogue' in *The Progress of Romance Through Times, Centuries and Manners* (1785). She went a step further to argue, 'The word *Novel* in all languages signifies something new. It was first used to distinguish these works from Romances, though they have lately been confounded together and are frequently mistaken for each other.'[33] A possible reason for this stated confusion over the nomenclature of the novel could be that towards the end of the eighteenth century, novels from other European languages were also getting translated into English and vice versa. Novels in many other languages were called *roman*, as derived from the romances. Thus, at the same historical juncture in England, similar kinds of writings were circulating under two different names—novel and *roman*.

Apart from these occasional attempts at characterizing and analysing the form of the novel, the only other known early theorizations were done by German romantic thinkers Johann Wolfgang von Goethe, Friedrich Schlegel and Friedrich August. They, however, did not contrast the novel to the romance. Goethe compared the novel to drama; Schegel distinguished it from classical writing, while August saw it as 'the genre which included all other genres'.[34] J. Paul Hunter explains these early attempts as he says, 'Some of the difficulty stems from the novel's inferiority complex. [Moreover], because of its obscure beginnings and insecure place in the hierarchy of literary forms and kinds, the novel historically has asserted itself by comparison to more established forms.'[35] Henry Fielding's 'Preface' to *Joseph Andrews* (1742) in which he calls his work a 'comic epic poem in prose' is another such example.

During the early nineteenth century, theorizations of the novel continued to remain quite sparse. While it cannot be denied that the novel met with unprecedented success and underwent what many consider to be its peak as a form, the novel continued to exist outside the pale of official literary culture. For most part of the century, critics did not find the novel deserving of serious critical attention. Paradoxically, even the occasional prefaces written about novels by novelists disappeared. Despite the novel coming into its own as a genre, as far as its theorizations were concerned, the nineteenth-century novelists took the success of the genre for granted and ignored it. The only significant change from the previous century was that polemical attacks against the novel became less strident and infrequent. Early nineteenth-century novelists largely did not show any signs of overt self-reflexiveness and allowed their works to speak for themselves. It was only in the latter part of the century that novelists once again started writing about their novels, but this time it was more in the nature of polemical 'debates' or 'disputes' on the techniques, content and purpose of their novels.

The fiercest debates took place in post-1848 France. French novelists differed between three distinct philosophies—'art for art's sake', i.e. detached or apolitical writing, 'commercial or bourgeois art', i.e. art according to the needs of the market, and 'realist or social art', i.e. political or committed writing.[36] These disputes strongly affected an entire generation of writers and critics all over Europe. Émile Zola's theory of 'Naturalism' transformed this debate into a full-blown pan-European literary controversy. Zola not only wrote about how novels should be written, but also elaborated upon which novels were good and which subjects were appropriate for them. These debates opened up a floodgate of literary reflections on the art of the novel. Walter Besant wrote 'The Art of Fiction' in defence of naturalism; Henry James refuted him by writing an essay by the same title, before long Robert Louis Stevenson joined in by writing 'A Humble Remonstrance', all these within the same year of 1884. Thomas Hardy targeted Zola to write 'The Science of Fiction' in 1891. Joseph Conrad elaborated upon the process of writing fiction in the 'Preface' to *The Nigger of the Narcissus* in 1897. Most of these debates, however, were as much about explanations and descriptions as they were about refutations and rebuttals. In spite of many such writings, the academic establishment did not yet embrace the novel with open arms. There is record of an incident in 1895 in which a course on the novel was offered to students at Yale University. This course generated a huge academic controversy which spilled over into sensational debates in newspapers. In no time, the course was cancelled and the instructor threatened with suspension.[37]

It is only by the early twentieth century that a distinct change in the attitude to the novel became discernable. The novel started gaining critical acceptance and respect as a literary genre. Walter L. Reed points out, 'As far as the poetics of the novel is concerned, there were no real attempts at official classification until the twentieth century.'[38] He elaborates:

> The most influential figure in the latter development is of course Henry James, although one might mention Proust and Mann as well. . . . James insists on the high

seriousness of the art of the novel . . . reveals his desire to represent the novel as a solid and enduring institution, at least as important to the present age as poetry and the drama.[39]

Perceptions about the novel began to undergo changes. The novel started earning its place in the official system of genres. By the 1920s, with the inclusion of the novel into university syllabi, things changed even more dramatically. An entirely new breed of people, i.e. novel scholars, now came into being.[40] The novel graduated into becoming one among the major genres. Walter Allen takes note of this improvement in the status of the genre of the novel in *The English Novel* (1954):

> The novel emerged from the underworld of taste and its development has been conditioned by this. Until quite recently, the only men who have taken the novel seriously have been novelists, and, often relatively uneducated men, they have frequently brought little to the study of it but their own experience as novelists, novelists, moreover, who interpreted their craft in no very exalted way.
>
> The notion of the novel as a literary form having something to do with art in the sense of being consciously made and shaped to an aesthetic end is quite new.[41]

Though the novel became an important literary genre, poetry and drama continued to dominate university syllabi. It was only after the Second World War that the novel truly arrived within the academia, in the sense of becoming its central and most important genre. W.B. Carnochan explains this development in his essay, 'The English Curriculum: Past and Present' (2000), by arguing:

> A hundred years ago, English departments might list perhaps one course in the novel, but poetry and drama . . . counted most. At mid-century, under the influence of New Criticism, poetry kept its preeminence. But after World War II, as literary criticism took a sociological turn, the novel gathered strength at the expense of poetry and drama.[42]

After the Second World War, the institutionalization of the novel in universities transformed not merely the status of the novel, but also the way in which it was written. German novelist, Thomas Mann, famously observed in his 1947 work, *Doktor Faustus*, 'Art, is becoming criticism'.[43] Early novelists, who were mostly journalists, now started turning into professors and critics.[44] By the 1960s, the novel came to occupy a commanding position within the literary establishment. So much so, that in 1967, Frank Kermode said, 'It happens in our phase of civility, the novel is the central form of literary art.'[45] In this phase, novel 'scholarship' progressively became more deeply entrenched in universities. As Peter Hitchcock says:

Throughout the sixties and into the seventies . . . the English literature establishment was vigorously formalizing elements discussed in criticism of the novel such as Ian Watt's *The Rise of the Novel*, F.R. Leavis's *The Great Tradition*, Northrop Frye's *Anatomy of Criticism*, Wayne C. Booth's *The Rhetoric of Fiction*, and Raymond William's *The English Novel from Dickens to Lawrence*.[46]

Simultaneously, a rival trend also began to manifest itself. Some literary critics started complaining about the near total domination of the field of literature by the novel. Hostility and resentment towards the novel's enhanced status started finding expression in certain quarters. By 1957, Northrop Frye wrote *Anatomy of Criticism* to pose a challenge to the 'novel-centred view of prose fiction'. Others too, followed suit. This turnaround in the general approach towards the novel has been noted by Michael McKeon in *Theory of The Novel* (2000):

. . . over the course of the last two centuries, the novel has become so dominant that its popularity has tended to obscure the importance, and the ongoingness, of other forms of fictional narrative. To speak of the novel, it came to appear, was to speak of narrative 'as such'. Four decades ago, however, there was a powerful reaction against this general tendency.[47]

By the late 1960s, critics like Robert Scholes and Robert Kellogg sought 'to put the novel in its place'.[48] Many critics started paying deliberate attention to other literary categories like prose-fiction and narrative. Approximately at the same point in time, some critics and novelists also started questioning 'high' canonical novels as opposed to 'low' novels. Ihab Hassan describes this new tendency in his book *The Postmodern Turn* to argue that 'Decanonization . . . [became the key feature of the literary posturing after the 1960s and it] applies to all canons, all conventions of authority . . . we decanonize culture, demystify knowledge, deconstruct the language of power, desire, deceit.'[49] Eric Hobsbawm also notes this shift in *Age of Extremes*:

[T]he boundary between what is and is not classifiable as 'art' 'creation' or artifice became increasingly hazy, or even disappeared altogether, . . . an influential school of literary critics at the *fin de siècle* thought it impossible, irrelevant and undemocratic to decide whether Shakespeare's *Macbeth* was better or worse than *Batman*.[50]

The form of the novel started undergoing a corresponding change. Novelists now tried to consciously embrace and integrate popular novels within the folds of the 'high' novel. They sought to collapse literary 'margins' into the 'centre'. Perhaps the most esteemed example of this trend is Italo Calvino's 1979 novel, *If on a winter's night a traveller,* which cleverly combines recognizable motifs from the 'spy' novel, 'murder mystery', 'romance', 'science fiction', 'adventure' novel, 'detective' novel, 'travel tale' and 'gangster' novel within the folds of a novel-within-novel mode of a highly stylized, self-referential and theoretically up-to-date novel. Calvino summed up the essence of his lifelong literary endeavour in a posthumously published work:

> After forty years of writing fiction, after exploring various roads and making diverse experiments, the time has come for me to look for an overall definition of my work. I would suggest this: my working method has more often than not involved the subtraction of *weight*. I have tried to remove *weight*, sometimes from people, sometimes from heavenly bodies, sometimes from cities; above all I have tried to remove *weight* from the structure of stories and from language. [51]

Apart from novelists, other artists also started changing the formal characteristics of their 'high' or 'canonized' art in order to include elements from 'low' or 'popular' arts within their works. As Linda Hutcheon writes in *A Poetics of Postmodernism*:

> [P]ostmodern painters, sculptors, video artists, novelists, poets, and film-makers join[ed] with these architects in collapsing the high/low art hierarchy of earlier times, in an attack on high art centralisation of academic interest, on the one hand, and, on the other, on the homogeneity of consumer culture which adapts, includes, and makes all seem accessible by neutralizing and popularising.[52]

This change in perspective was a manifestation of an aversion towards the elitism of the 'high' canon. It was also a result of the ideological triumph of the 'market' after the 1960s, and the ensuing commercialization of literature, wherein erstwhile 'low/mass' culture now gained in esteem. Paradoxically and ironically, this shift also included a fair degree of critical self-awareness. As Robert Mengham says, '[F]rom the late 1970s onwards the mutual dependence of fiction and critical theory began to figure largely in the production and reception of numerous texts'.[53] This was because during the 1960s 'literary theory' started making dramatic breakthroughs in the academic world. Postmodernism, too, started making its mark. Frederick Karl aptly links both these developments to say, 'Put succinctly: Postmodernism may be an invention of critics.'[54] Now, the canonized novel became even more overtly intellectualized and theoretical. By the late eighties the situation came to a point where refrains about the deliberate obscurity and unintelligibility of 'theoretically loaded' novels started getting voiced. Elizabeth Dipple complains in *The Unresolvable Plot* (1988), 'The task of reading many current novels has become a serious academic exercise . . . [and there is a] failure of complex experimental writers to win convinced American or international audiences inside or outside of the academy. . . .'[55] Novelist and critic Raymond Federman, in his collection of essays, *Critifiction* (1993), also expresses his exasperation at postmodernist fiction being 'stifled by academic theorizing'.[56] He articulates his suspicions to say, 'The question then: Is a novel labelled UNREADABLE because it is experimental (a priori or a posteriori)? Or is it labelled EXPERIMENTAL because it is left unread?'[57] This emerging state of affairs, conversely, was a further critique of the increasing institutionalization of the genre of the novel, particularly the canonized novel, within the extremely restricted and limited circles of only those who had access to higher education.

In recent years, another shift has become discernable in relation to the novel. Critics have started arguing that the novel is perhaps not as central to our civilization as has been made out to be. Linda Hutcheon, makes the following observation, 'In the early years of postmodernism, for instance, fiction seemed to be the genre that attracted the most attention from critics, including myself.... But what was particularly striking in the 1990s was the move to [study] the performative.'[58] Fredric Jameson also notes that the novel has seen no major innovation after the nouveau roman, and that the most distinctive new medium-cum-form of postmodernism undoubtedly is the 'videotext'.[59] With literature departments turning into culture-studies departments, novels have become uneasy in their ivory towers. Interestingly, debates about the end of 'theory', as well as the end of 'postmodernism' have also started coming to the fore.[60] Against this overall backdrop, it cannot yet be said that the novel has entirely fallen from grace, but it is undoubtedly poised at a juncture which does not look like its canonical ascendancy.

On the whole, we can say that literary perceptions about the novel have undergone dramatic reversals in the course of its history. During its initial stages, the novel started out by being a genre that existed outside the ambit of literary canonization. For most part of its existence, it was considered inappropriate and unbefitting for serious literary contemplation. It was only during the twentieth century that the novel started gaining acceptance and recognition within the official system of genres. By the mid-twentieth century, the novel came to occupy a distinct, assured and enviable place in the elite club of genres, enough to provoke hostile reactions, not on account of its 'low' character, but, on the contrary, on account of its 'high' character. In recent years, the spotlight has once again started shifting away from the novel. The novel has undeniably travelled a long way. It has occupied dramatically different positions in the literary canon in the course of its history. Let us now try to understand the factors that have caused and shaped these developments.

Bourgeois Culture and the Novel

So far, we have mainly tried to provide a brief outline of 'what' happened to the novel in history. Now, let us try to understand 'why' what happened,

happened. We have already argued in the last two chapters that the novel was and continues to be a quintessential middle class genre. In this section, we would continue the same argument that the trajectory of the genre of the novel can be best understood if the corresponding trajectories of capitalism and the development of 'bourgeois culture' are also kept in mind. We would discuss how the middle classes, on the whole, played an important role in legitimizing 'bourgeois culture' with the novel as a genre playing an important role in the process. Let us explicate how.

The novel was a product of the very same historical circumstances that threw up the middle classes themselves, viz., the transition from feudalism to capitalism. Its themes reflected all the main debates involved in this long drawn process of transition, particularly its moral and ethical dimensions. Unbound by any rules or codes, the novel incorporated within its fold new forms of print literature like character, travelogue, diary, letter, pamphlet, etc. During its early days, it emerged from low social origins, precisely the kind of origins that the middle classes came from. It represented either people who had recently bettered their social status and gained access to education, or those who were aspiring to improve their station in life. Its opposition to 'high' aristocratic literary forms was so overt that during its initial stages the novel displayed a deliberate preoccupation with 'low' themes. As Lennard J. Davis says, 'Indeed, without the appearance of the whore, the rogue, the cutpurse, the cheat, the thief, or the outsider it would be impossible to imagine the genre of the novel.'[61] Or, as J. Paul Hunter says, '[T]he early novel concentrates not on true extremes (the unique or near unique) but rather on people who slip beyond the norm and test the social fabric. Here are murderers, thieves, rapists, those who commit incest, and those who father bastards or malidentified offspring . . . '.[62] With such subjects and themes it is not so difficult to understand why the novel was treated with contempt by the literary establishment of those times, especially an establishment that was largely aristocratic in nature.

During its early years, the novel was an 'emergent' literary form, which represented the imaginative concerns of the still 'emergent' middle classes. In this phase, the novel fulfilled an important historical function. As Fredric Jameson says:

> . . . the novel play[ed] . . . a significant role in what can be called a properly bourgeois cultural revolution—that immense process of transformation whereby populations whose life habits were formed by other, now archaic, modes of production [we]are effectively reprogrammed for life and work in the new world of market capitalism.[63]

However, as we have already underscored, the novel, a typical middle class form, did not become part of the official culture too easily. This was because the middle classes themselves were not part of the establishment yet. As historians have observed, even by the late eighteenth century, the middle classes were '[d]ependent on the aristocracy for patronage . . . [and] bound to the landed elites in ties of deference'.[64] The novel came into its own only during the nineteenth century when the triumph of the bourgeoisie over the aristocracy seemed imminent. As David Daiches says, 'The nineteenth century was the great age of the English novel. This was . . . because this essentially middle-class form of literary art was bound to flourish increasingly as the middle classes rose in power and importance . . .'.[65] Several significant historical events took place during the mid-nineteenth century that led to and revealed the dramatic increase in the influence of the bourgeoisie. In 1846, the Corn Laws were repealed in England; a legislation that broke the backbone of the powerful landed aristocracy. By 1848, popular revolutions demanding liberal reforms started taking place simultaneously all over Europe—in Paris, Sicily, Naples, Vienna, Venice, Milan, Warsaw and Cracow.[66] These revolutions delivered a deathblow to an already declining feudalism.[67] The way was now paved for a capitalism that had been 'emergent' till then to establish itself as a 'dominant' system and for the bourgeoisie to become the dominant class. Serious efforts were made to replace old aristocratic cultural symbols with new bourgeois cultural signifiers. The new liberal bourgeois state played its due role in this entire process, especially putting to use the ideology of nationalism. The entire literary establishment began to get overhauled. By then the '[m]iddle-class cultural hegemony was evidenced by the gains of the life-style of respectability among all social strata, with its family-centred social life and insistence on sobriety, frugality, educational attainment, religious observance and sexual propriety'.[68] The reduction in the antipathy and hostility towards the form of the novel in this century was undoubtedly linked to this entire transformation. As the middle classes gained in prestige, the novel, too, gained in approval.

The middle classes, however, continued to play the same kind of role that we have described before. Neither were they like the bourgeoisie, i.e. the class that led from the front, nor were they like the peasantry or the emerging working class, i.e. the classes whose raw power fuelled the bourgeois liberal revolutions but which clearly didn't want to stop where the bourgeoisie, in fact, had. The middle classes occupied a more intermediate place in the capitalist system and were more like weather cocks. They became its self-appointed bearers of the cross. As a consequence, they debated the right and wrong of all occurrences. By nature, the middle classes always swam with the tide. Right now, the tide was in favour of capitalism and the bourgeoisie, and although a section of the middle classes were unhappy, its vast majority helped in defining, legitimizing and institutionalizing bourgeois culture as national culture. The novel played a crucial role in this process.

In this backdrop, new kinds of debates and deliberations came up within the literati. The upwardly mobile middle classes, drawing from the industrial and mercantile elites, now aspired to turn into sophisticated 'gentlemen' and 'gentlewomen', a new non-class identity. As David Cody points out '[B]y the latter part of the century, it was almost universally accepted that the recipient of a traditional liberal education based on Latin at one of the elite public schools—Eton, Harrow, Rugby, and so on—would be recognized as a gentleman no matter what his origins had been.'[69] The dominant bourgeoisie now sought to mould itself into the neo-elites. It imbibed many of the same aristocratic values which it had earlier opposed. This changing ethos is best captured by William Thackeray in his masterpiece, *Vanity Fair* (1847–8) or by Charles Dickens in his famous novel, *Great Expectations* (1860–1). Gustave Flaubert and Charles Baudelaire also reproduce the same spirit in their French novels in more overt ways. *Great Expectations* is particularly noteworthy for its protagonist Pip, who begins as an apprentice blacksmith aspiring to become a gentleman. A mysterious benefactor pays for his education. However, Pip mistakenly imagines that his real benefactress is Miss Havisham, an old aristocratic lady symbolic of the declining nobility. It is only later that Pip realizes, much to his initial embarrassment and shock, that the true source of his income is the outlawed Australian criminal from his childhood, Abel Magwitch. Although Pip tries to repay his moral debt to the dying Magwitch, his admiration and desire for becoming a sophisticated and refined gentleman, unlike Magwitch, remains intact. By the end of the novel, Pip realizes that the only true 'gentleman' he has ever known in his life is his blacksmith brother-in-law, Joe. He, therefore, gives up his snobbish ways and learns to value the inner worth of people as opposed to just appearances based on elite education, money and wealth. Interestingly, he plans to return to the marshes to become a blacksmith again, but circumstances force him to go away to Cairo where he ends up earning a lot of money. Returning after eleven years, he not only becomes a gentleman but also marries his childhood fancy, the aristocratic Estella. Such issues became the subject of novels.

As historians Belchem and Price say, 'Ideologically liberal, the bourgeoisie emerged as the hegemonic class by 1875. Thereafter, however, the always-variegated class fragmented further, as genteel capitalists intermarried with landed wealth and embraced conservative politics.'[70] It is not surprising to understand, therefore, why late Victorian culture is often associated with negative epithets like 'decadent', 'high', 'prudish', 'repressed', 'old-fashioned', etc.

New kinds of class differentiations began to surface. The middle classes started subdividing and stratifying into the 'upper' and the 'lower' middle classes. This was not a simplistic transition. Yet, on the whole, things changed so dramatically, that a novelist like Emile Zola, who advocated the writing of novels based on the lives of the poor and the downtrodden, ended up earning the ire of most of his colleagues and successors. Clearly, the bourgeoisie and the elite upper middle classes no longer wished to concern themselves with the lives of the underprivileged. By the turn of the century, with advances in capitalism—particularly in its more predatory form of imperialism—the middle classes grew in numbers on a scale that was unprecedented. The bourgeois state now became more aggressively nationalist, even as its economic growth became increasingly premised upon unprecedented levels of international trade, investment and financial activities through colonialism.

The size of the reading public also grew at an extraordinary rate. The novel witnessed a corresponding increase in circulation. However, this growth was paradoxical in nature. As Eric Hobsbawm says, 'The democratisation of culture through mass education—even through the numerical growth of culture-hungry middle and lower-middle classes—was itself sufficient to make elites look for more exclusive cultural status-symbols.'[71] Though the circulation and publication of novels increased manifold, novels themselves started getting subdivided into 'high' and 'low' novels. 'High' experimental novels emphasized technique and style and were rooted in the modernist movement, while 'low' novels were those associated with old-fashioned realism. This 'high—low' division was clearly a new development for the novel. Q.D. Leavis, in her study, *Fiction and the Reading Public* (1932), emphasizes how the novel was not always divided into such categories; in fact, before the twentieth century such hierarchical divisions and classifications were virtually non-existent:

> It would not be true to suggest a stratification of novel writers and novel readers in 1760, for example, when anyone who could read would be equally likely to read any novel, or every novel, published . . . even a century later the same conditions hold. . . . To illustrate the curiously inverse relation now existing between esteem and popularity. . . . The twentieth-century reader who would let this pass as a commonplace could only be brought to realize that it is indeed something new in English history . . .[72]

In order to understand the emergence of this inverse relation between 'esteem' and 'popularity' during the twentieth century, it is important to understand the nature of the modernist movement in arts. The early twentieth century modernist movement was quite unique in nature. The modernists were bitterly and evenly divided between rival progressive and conservative ideological impulses and usually wore their politics on their sleeves. Their differences became even more pronounced after the Russian Revolution, though on the whole they remained highly confined and restricted in the scope of their influence upon the wider people.

As Raymond Williams says, 'Modernism and the avant-garde, in any of their forms, have never involved, as producers or as publics, more than minorities: often very small minorities.'[73] Eric Hobsbawm also writes, 'It is the experimental avantgarde of the pre-war years which, outside a small community of the "advanced"—intellectuals, artists and critics and the fashion-conscious—was never to find a genuine, spontaneous welcome among the broad public.'[74] Malcolm Bradbury reiterates that the modernist movement was restricted to a handful of intellectuals, artists and critics living in 'cosmopolitan artistic enclaves . . . [or] culture-capitals like Berlin, Paris, London for a time, and perhaps more latterly New York'.[75] David Harvey echoes the sentiment, 'Modernism was "an art of cities" and evidently found "its natural habitat in cities".[76] In fact Bradbury further argues that modernism not only made a distinguished 'cult of the artist . . . [but also] a distinct "*class*" of artists'.[77]

At approximately the same point in time, from about the 1890s onwards, the process of overhauling universities also started in Europe. In this phase, universities started playing a crucial role in institutionalizing bourgeois culture as 'national' culture, especially in the context of the surcharged years preceding the First World War.[78] As Terry Eagleton says, by the 1910s, universities like Oxford and Cambridge were already seen as 'the bastions of ruling-class power'.[79] The canonization of the genre of the novel during the twentieth century was part of this entire process and ethos. The novel was canonized because it was clearly the most eminent literary creation of capitalism and bourgeois middle class culture. However, just because the novel was canonized does not mean that all novels were admitted into the corridors of 'culture'. An intense debate over 'good' and 'bad' novels also started within the academia. Conversely, novels also fed on these university-based debates. The deliberately obscure, self-reflexive, experimental novels written by the modernists served to consolidate literature as a new 'discipline' of study in universities.[80] A certain class of novels also became considerably more unintelligible and out of reach of the ordinary reader. A new kind of elitism and exclusivity started creeping into the form of the novel. This trend became evident through works like F.R. Leavis's *Mass Civilization and Minority Culture* (1930). Leavis made his point, 'In any period it is upon a very small minority that the discerning appreciation of art and literature depends.'[81] T.S. Eliot also theorized this elitism as literary 'taste'. Harry Levin makes the following observation about this transformation:

> [P]opularity was excluded, by definition, from the aims of the [modernist] writers . . . their names did not figure upon the best-sellers list of their day; many others did, which are now forgotten. The aura of obscurity or unintelligibility which may still occasionally tinge these intellectuals, in some degree, emanates

from their refusal to advertise themselves or to talk down to their audiences in the hope of enlarging it. That, for them, would indeed have been a treason of the clerks. Their ultimate quality, which pervades their work to the marrow, is its uncompromising intellectuality.[82]

Many modernists asserted their anti-populist positions along with their respective pro- or anti-capitalist positions. Some of them were anti-populist because they were against the stranglehold of market forces in arts and literature; they were against the arts being converted into commodities for mass consumption. However, others were anti-populist because they were just blatantly anti-democratic. As Fredric Jameson says, 'Indeed, it can be argued that the emergence of high modernism is itself contemporaneous with the first great expansion of a recognizably mass culture . . .'.[83] Modernist trends like Dadaism, which were vehemently anti-elitist and anti-bourgeois, could not make real breakthroughs with the masses. On the whole, popularity largely evaded both progressive and conservative experimental artists (except a few) during the early twentieth century.

The canonization of the novel during the early twentieth century took place in this overall backdrop. The novel was canonized largely through university departments; although only eighteenth and nineteenth centuries novels were included in the syllabi. Twentieth century contemporary novels were largely left out. However, the notable point for us about this process of canonization is the fact that the division of the novel into high and low novels also started taking place simultaneously.

The post-Second World War scenario was characterized by governments playing a significantly enhanced role in the fields of culture and literature by overtly constituting, patronizing and regulating many bodies associated with painting, literature, architecture, film, television, radio, etc.[84] Against the backdrop of the Cold War, the ideological preferences of Western governments and government-sponsored universities became very clear.[85] Frederic Jameson argues, 'In the aesthetic realm, indeed, the process of cultural 'universalisation' (which implies the repression of the oppositional voice, and the illusion that there is only one genuine 'culture') is the specific form taken by what can be called the process of legitimation in the realm of ideology and conceptual systems'.[86] This same process was at work during the 1950s for canonizing twentieth-century literature. Academicians chose to canonize only 'high' modernism in university syllabi, and ignored both the progressive avant-gardes as well as the realists, who were very much part (perhaps the more dominant part) of early twentieth-century literature. Many critics have made this observation in their studies. Aijaz Ahmad elaborates on this view in *In Theory*:

. . . the *triumph* of modernism is indicated today precisely in the fact that realist texts produced during that same period and in the same Euro-American spaces now find no significant place in the literary curricula and critical discourses pertaining to that period and place, regardless of the number, the worth or social influence of such texts in their own time.[87]

Raymond Williams also writes, 'After Modernism is canonized, however, by the post-war settlement and its accompanying, complicit academic endorsements.... The marginal or rejected artists become classics of organized teaching ...'.[88] Even authors with fascistic sympathies like Yeats, Lewis, Pound, Eliot and Lawrence were canonized, but the progressive avant-gardes and the realists were obliterated from memory.[89] Perhaps the most notable example of this tendency was *The Great Tradition* (1948) written by F.R. Leavis. In it, Leavis nominated only Jane Austen, George Eliot, Henry James, Joseph Conrad, and D. H. Lawrence to the novel canon, leaving out Charles Dickens on the excuse that he was a mere 'entertainer'. Thus, universities became very important sites of ideological contestations. They defined and redefined modern literary history, and made conservative bourgeois culture seem like universal culture and good taste. It is at this juncture that novels and scholarship about novels started displacing poetry and drama from their esteemed positions in literature and literary criticism.

Meanwhile, in advanced capitalist countries, there was an explosive growth in the size of the middle classes and in their economic prosperity during the years of the 'Golden Age' from 1950 to 1973. By and large, the middle classes benefited from this prosperity, but a section of the educated youth in the universities were uncomfortable with the proliferation of blatant consumerism and commercialization, and the ideological intolerance towards dissent in the backdrop of the Cold War. A wave of opposition and rebellion spread among the students of Europe, America, Africa, Mexico, and Japan, etc. This dissent manifested itself through the watershed student movements of 1968. These movements were an attempt in history to critique and transcend capitalism as a system in order to build something new. These movements also perhaps symbolized the last major dissent that emerged from the heart of capitalism against capitalism for a long time.[90] While they fizzled out very fast, they left a huge negative impact upon intellectuals and artists. Pierre Bourdieu states that 'the collapse of illusions' after 1968 was very similar to the situation after 1848, when writers vigorously invoked and asserted the autonomy of intellectuals in a 'radically elitist' way.[91] The proliferation of disengaged academic 'theory' and postmodernist intellectualism after 1968 was very likely an outcome of these disappointments. Alex Callinicos also argues:

> The political odyssey of the 1968 generation is, in my view, crucial to the widespread acceptance of the idea of a postmodern epoch.... This conjuncture—the prosperity of the Western new middle class combined with the political

disillusionment of many of its most articulate members—provides the context of the proliferating talk of postmodernism.[92]

Martin McQuillan, Graeme Macdonald, Robin Purves and Stephen Thomson also explain the emergence of 'theory' in the Western academia in their book, *Post Theory: New Directions in Criticism* (1999):

Theory wants more than anything to be thought of as 'Radical'... It is also a wished-for Political activism.... The rise of Theory as an institutional practice is contemporaneous with the 'decline' of the political left.... Furthermore ... there is some connection between 'market-led' educational reforms and the eminence of Theory within the academy.... Not only is the university itself a site of political contest both in terms of what is taught and in terms of the struggle for control of access to education and 'academic freedom', it is the university in its production and demarcation of the limits of knowledge which defines the possibilities of any institutionalized, or otherwise, activity of thinking.... 'Theory', its rhetoric, is *that which can be applied*, without having to bother *applying itself.* [93]

The arrival of 'theory' in the Western academia by the 1970s impacted the novel canon in a particular way. Because theory basically represented a 'conversation among academic professionals',[94] canonized novels now withdrew into the in-house circle of universities. One of the earliest theorists of postmodernism, Susan Sontag, articulates this emerging trend in 'One Culture and the New Sensibility' to say:

Art does not progress, in the sense that science and technology do. But the arts do develop and change. For instance, in our own time, art is becoming increasingly the terrain of specialists. The most interesting and creative art of our time is not open to the generally educated; it demands special effort; it speaks a specialized language.[95]

Eric Hobsbawm also takes up the same theme in *Age of Extremes*, Speaking generally, the decisive development of twentieth-century culture, the rise of a revolutionary popular entertainment industry geared to the mass market, reduced the traditional forms of high art to elite ghettoes, and from the middle of the century their inhabitants were essentially people who had enjoyed a higher education.[96]

It is in this overall backdrop that postmodern novelists started advocating for a break in the 'high-low' hierarchy in literature. The sheer ferocity of their claims implied that unlike ever before, the novel, in fact, become subdivided into two types—the novel for the common reading public, i.e. the 'popular' novel, and the novel for the specialized and sophisticated reader, i.e. the 'crtically acclaimed' novel. In this case, it is useful to invoke what Fredric Jameson argues in another context, 'Yet it is commonplace that transgressions, presupposing the laws or norms or taboos against which they function, thereby end up precisely reconfirming such laws.'[97] For all their well-intentioned claims of doing away with high and low divisions in literature, postmodern novelists have not managed to bridge the gap between their novels and their reading public in the manner of the realist novelists like Balzac, Dickens or Tolstoy. Although attempts to create hybrid novels by mixing high and low genres do reveal the anxieties of the 'high' establishment in sustaining the sheer restrictedness and elitism of its existence, yet basic statistics of sales show that but for a few exceptions such intentions have not materialized into reality for most critically acclaimed postmodern novelists.

The ascendancy of theory within the academia also meant that canons were scrutinized in greater detail, but they were not fundamentally changed. 'Derrida', 'Kristeva', 'Foucault' or 'Said' could be applied to the same old Austen or Dickens to revolutionize the meaning of their novels/texts. Any radical restructuring was, therefore, largely left undone. A separate canon for popular fiction did come up within the academia; however, as Bob Ashley seeks to remind in his anthology titled, *The Study of Popular Fiction: A Source Book* (1989), there remains a deep 'theoretical' problem with the existence of the category of popular fiction itself within the academia:

> The very notion of a method for the study of popular fiction may be questioned. There may be an anxiety lest one simply constructs an alternative tradition, even an 'alternative canon', separate and distinct from that of main-stream literature.... And it may further be argued that to remove work on popular texts to a separate terrain, with its own distinctive methodology, is to endorse its marginalisation, to legitimize Literature in its tendency to ignore.[98]

Theoretical and novelistic avowals against high-low hierarchy, therefore, instead of obliterating hierarchical differences also ended up reinforcing and fortifying them. This must be understood in another context. By the mid-1970s the forces of free market and neoliberalism started gaining ground in policymaking circles. As Steven Connor says:

> From the 1960s onwards, it became plain that the careful quarantining of culture from commerce was unsustainable; from the early 1980s onwards, as more and more cultural institutions were taken out from under the wing of government and exposed to the tender mercies of the market-place, the dream of the autonomy of art from society and the culture industry survived only as nostalgic desire or utopian vision.[99]

With the withdrawal of the state from crucial areas related to education, market forces stepped in. The 'market' derived a lot of its cultural, ideological and social legitimacy from sponsored universities, academies and research institutions. In such a context, literary arguments finding inherent 'merit' in the literary market started emanating from the universities. Claims for doing away with literary hierarchies in the late twentieth century, therefore, were not only about integrating the really marginalized, oral, folk or other arts into the canon, but were also about integrating 'mass' literatures entrenched in the successes of the market into the canon. As Raymond Williams says, 'We have all learned, on the pulse, the material realities of that long capitalist appropriation of the popular, and its scarcely less disturbing indifferences to the genuinely different.'[100]

Thus, on the whole, the history of the canonization of the genre of the novel was deeply entrenched in the changing nature of the literary 'establishment' itself. The process of the novel becoming the part of the literary establishment or the official system of genres was integrally tied to and coincided with the process of the bourgeoisie itself, becoming part of the establishment. The middle classes swayed in their artistic and other preferences with the ascending bourgeoisie. The novel, as a genre, remained outside the ambit of canonization as long as the bourgeoisie themselves were outside the establishment. It became a part of the canon as soon as the bourgeoisie became dominant and started reconstituting the literary canon. Crucially, the canonization of the novel coincided with the division of the genre into 'high' and 'low' novels, a bifurcation, that enabled the novel to progress from being an 'unimportant' to a 'more important' to the 'most important' literary genre. While it now began to reach an increasing number of people, the canonized novel at the same time also became more and more elite.[101]

Over the past couple of decades, the politics of canonization has come under a lot of scrutiny. However, in spite of self-critical reconstitutions of the canon by the literary establishment, aimed at including novels by women writers, black writers, postcolonial writers,[102] etc., the canon is yet to undergo a restructuring which may be sufficient for entirely doing away with the high-low hierarchization of the novel. This is because, the literary establishment, entrenched in bourgeois culture, has consistently found motivation in the tendency to distinguish its reading habits from an ever-increasing vast multitude of common readers, whether in the guise of 'taste' or in the guise of 'intellectualism' or 'theory'. The 'high' canonized novel has undoubtedly become uncomfortable in its restrictedness, but that has not necessarily made the canon more accommodative in any radical or far-reaching way.

On the other hand, instead of examining the canonized novel, if we were to look at the genre of the novel as a whole, we would find that it still continues to be consumed in vast numbers by the ever-growing educated middle classes. The novels that the middle and the lower-middle classes read are standard products of an increasingly standardizing market, and cannot be valorized or celebrated uncritically. Nonetheless, their lack of canonization neither means that they are not being written, nor that they are not being read. Perhaps, the sheer volume of such novels has ensured that in spite of nearly a hundred years of canonization, the establishment still hasn't managed to entirely tame the genre of the novel. Even though elite literary establishments have sought to turn the novel into their own genre, the novel has not entirely divorced itself from its modest social origins. The quintessential middle class form may certainly be facing challenges in recent times from other mediums like film and the Internet, but it continues to be the most dominant literary genre of print.

Death of the Novel and the Ever-novel Form

There is another aspect that must be kept in view while trying to understand the novel's development in history—its uncertain and insecure existence as a genre. Over the last century, the novel has continually been plagued by predictions about its exhaustion or death. These predictions started coming to the fore in the early twentieth century, just about the time when the novel started improving its literary acceptability as a genre, and they continue to plague the novel till date. In this section, we shall try to understand why the novel seems to exhaust itself every few years and yet manages to reinvent itself each time and remain new.

It was during the early twentieth century, that Tolstoy, upon watching a film, famously expressed doubts over the future, of the novel, arguing that writers were now more likely to write for the screen rather than for the book. André Breton called for the end of the novel in 1924 condemning its tendency to generate consent and familiar reassurance among its readers. José Ortega y Gasset announced the death of the novel in 1925, putting the blame on new mass/democratic societies which were an anathema to the novel. George Orwell predicted the demise of the novel in 1939 through his essay, 'Inside the Whale', finding it incompatible with totalitarian dictatorships. Alain Robbe-Grillet also tried to address the 'state of stagnation' in the novel through his essay 'A Future for the Novel'. Debates about the end of the novel resounded again during the 1960s, this time it was mass media that was put in the dock for affecting reading habits. By 1965, such predictions became so common that Frank Kermode was prompted to say, 'The special fate of the novel, considered as a genre, is to be always dying.'[103] In 1967, John Barth wrote his famous essay 'The Literature of Exhaustion' arguing that conventional literary modes of the novel had been 'used up'. Once again, in 1969, American novelist, Ronald Sukenick, wrote *The Death of the Novel and Other Stories*. During the 1970s, debates about 'metafiction' or 'surfiction' assumed that novels were already dead and that contemporary writings merited an entirely new nomenclature. In 1983, Milan Kundera announced the death of the novel under socialism, finding it incompatible with 'Totalitarian Truth'. He also argued that the reductive and unifying spirit of mass media was 'contrary to the spirit of the novel'.[104] In 1988, Linda Hutcheon emphasized, '... postmodernist fiction has also been called the death of the novel by so many critics that a list would run on for pages'.[105] Robert Steiner claimed in 1996 that the novel was dead prompting a retort by Salman Rushdie who located the vitality of new novels in the postcolonial world.[106] Debates about computer *hypertexts* also predicted and continue to predict the demise of the novel. In 2004, V.S. Naipaul announced, 'I have no faith in the survival of the novel. It is almost over.'[107]

Such predictions have consequently led a large number of novelists and critics over the last hundred years to also express relief over the novel's endurance and continuity as a genre. If we were to start enlisting writers and critics who have celebrated the novel's longevity, or tried to provide prescriptions for its revival, the list would run into hundreds. Irrespective of the specific instances of such opinions, however, doubts about the novel's endurance continue to be expressed, that too, to an extent not found for any other genre in literature. Those making these predictions fall into two distinct types. There are those who associate the novel's demise to outmoded novelistic techniques and content, and argue that the novel's exhaustion is internal in nature. And there are those who link the end of the novel to external factors like developments in cinema, television, video and the Internet, and their effects on book reading as a whole. Irrespective of the specific reasons associated with these different types of announcements or predictions, what can be underscored is the fact that throughout the twentieth century the novel has constantly run into a crisis of survival, customarily seeming to be at the brink of death, yet repeatedly reinventing itself.

If we examine the other side of this coin, we find that the novel has rejuvenated itself time and again by calling itself a 'New' form. When the genre of the novel originated in England, it was named 'novel', literally meaning new. Samuel Richardson wrote that his works belonged to a 'new species of writing',[108] while Henry Fielding, too, described his novels as 'a new province of writing'.[109] During the early twentieth century, when Henry James discussed innovative novelistic techniques devised by his contemporaries, he called this type of fiction—'The New Novel'—in an essay by the same name in 1914. When Robbe-Grillet announced fresh approaches to writing novels by getting rid of 'order', 'chronology' and 'omniscient narration', he again made use of the epithet 'new' to describe, what he called, the *Noveau Roman* or what was translated into English as the 'New Novel'. His collection of essays was also titled *For A New Novel* (1963). Novelists like Philippe Sollers and Jean-Marie Le Clezio of the *Tel Quel* group[110] advanced the project of the 'New Novel' further by emphasizing the inability of writers to put their inner or outer worlds into words. In fact they innovated yet another style of writing fiction calling it the 'New New Novel'. As Linda Hutcheon says, 'If the *nouveau roman* is self-mirroring auto-representation, then *Tel Quel's* works are anti-representation.'[111] *Put together, these different stages of the development of the novel can thus be documented as—the novel, the new novel, the noveau roman/ new novel and the new new novel.* Thus, somehow, alongside the predictions of death, the novel has also been strongly associated with newness in all its different senses, of being innovative, recent, original, anti-traditional, latest, fresh and different. Without separately going into the details of each, let us first try to understand the reasons behind the novel's constant newness.

As we have already discussed, the basic temper of the novel was forged by the new system of capitalism. Part of the novel's newness lay in the fact that it broke the formal rigidities imposed upon literature by earlier genres, that evolved as a flexible new type of genre. Part of it lay in the ethos of the new era itself, which was based upon a strong sense of historical progress and invested value in the 'new' instead of the 'old'. By the eighteenth century, perceptions changed to such an extent that unlike ever before, 'Originality then became a common term of praise of art and literature.'[112] The novel embodied this proclivity for the new, both in its form as well as in its content. It imbibed a forward-looking ethos as well as an anti-traditional approach. By dealing with contemporary times and ordinary characters, it broke new grounds in literary writing. However, the novel was path breaking in yet another way and in order to understand this, we must take into account the fact that before the novel's times, oral forms of story-telling were dominant and prevalent. The novel was the first major literary genre to break away from oral storytelling traditions in order to become an important literary genre of print. Let us examine this point in some detail.

The modern technology of print was invented in Germany during the mid-fifteenth century; however, the mass use of print took a long time to establish itself. As Elizabeth L. Eisenstein says in her book *The Printing Revolution in Early Modern Europe* (1983) even till quite late after the establishment of printing presses, oral transmissions remained the preferred mode of communication. In fact, even the much older technology of manuscripts was not very prevalent. As Eisenstein explains, 'Outside certain transitory special centres, moreover, the texture of scribal culture was so thin that heavy reliance was placed on oral transmission even by the literary elites.'[113] Even after considerable advancements in printing, the remnants of orality in literature remained very pronounced and took a long time to give way to an autonomous and self-contained 'print culture'. The most explicit proof of this phenomenon was that repetitions and adaptations of the same 'stock' stories continued in different narrative literary forms till well into the seventeenth century, be it drama, verse or prose.[114] Walter J. Ong notes in *Orality and Literacy* (1982), 'In oral tradition, there will be as many minor variants of a myth as there are repetitions of it . . . But the formulas and themes are reshuffled rather than supplanted with new material.'[115] Walter Benjamin also writes, 'storytelling is always the art of repeating stories, and this art is lost when the stories are no longer retained'.[116] The novel was the first major literary genre to break away from this tradition of repeating old stories. Benjamin elaborates:

> The earliest symptom of a process whose end is the decline of storytelling is the rise of the novel at the beginning of modern times. What distinguishes the novel from the story (and from epic in the narrower sense) is its essential dependence on the book. The dissemination of the novel became possible only with the invention of printing . . . What differentiates the novel from all other forms of prose literature—the fairy tale, the legend, even the novella—is that it neither comes from oral tradition nor goes into it.[117]

Walter J. Ong also differentiates the novel from oral traditions to say, 'The print world gave birth to the novel . . .,'[118] while emphasizing that the novel is different from oral storytelling mainly because it does not rely upon 'oral episodic narratives'. One of the main distinguishing features of the novel was that it largely put an end to presenting variants, reworkings or adaptations of the same old stories to the reading public. By engaging with the lives of ordinary people located in the here and now, novels basically introduced new and unique stories of individuals into the literary realm. As Wallace Martin says, 'It was in fact by breaking away from conventional forms and imaginary situations that the novel came into existence . . . The shift from anonymous repetition of traditional tales to original stories filled with circumstantial detail [marked its emergence].'[119] Thus, apart from many other factors, an important demarcating factor for the emergence of the novel also was the sheer originality of its stories.

Obvious links can also be drawn between the novel's engagement with newness or novelty and the emergent philosophical ethos which invested value in the 'new' instead of in the 'old'. It also privileged a sense of historical progress as opposed to stagnation or continuum. However, the reasons behind the continuing endurance of 'innovation' and 'novelty' in the novel also lay in the predilection of capitalism for favouring innovative and novel products, including literary products, for success in the market. Let us understand this view in some detail. It is true that pitched philosophical debates involved in the transition from feudalism to capitalism paved the way for establishing the worth and merit of 'originality' and 'novelty'. However, this entire philosophical ethos was an important ideological asset for capitalism only as long as feudalism (representing tradition) remained an important challenge for it. Once, the dominance of capitalism was established, it gave up its complete antipathy towards 'tradition' and established its own elite culture in the vocabulary of 'customs', 'classics' and 'conventions', though to be fair, tradition never became a dominant feature of capitalism. However, an enduring reason for the prevalence of novelty as a virtue in the modern age has been the centrality of the 'market' for capitalism. The market has always sustained itself on the ideology of innovation and novelty, selling everything from goods to culture in the name of the latest fad. As Pam Norris says, 'Novels also were the first literary products to discover a mass market and they made some of their writers a great deal of money.'[120]

The development of print culture, which gave birth to the novel, was based upon the simultaneous emergence of a literary 'market'. In the new marketplace, the skills of writers could be sold for a price and they could earn a living without necessarily having to depend upon aristocratic and feudal patrons. They could also make a living without necessarily having to follow classical rules of writing. Writers like Henry Fielding and Dr Johnson always lamented the manner in which upstarts like Samuel Richardson or Daniel Defoe could earn a living in the same marketplace without having received any formal training in the classics.[121] Many authors also revelled in this newfound freedom from old constraints and restrictions. However, almost as soon as writers discovered their economic independence and self-reliance, they also started discovering the tyranny of the marketplace and the new dependencies and limits that it imposed. Many learnt it the hard way that the marketplace did not turn them into their own masters; rather book traders and publishers assumed the role of their erstwhile noble patrons and became as exacting and demanding as their predecessors had been. The development and growth of print culture meant that writing became a 'profession' and literary books a 'commodity'. The unease created by this new situation was and continues to remain a running strain for many writers and artists. Novelists throughout the history of the novel have expressed this tension and lament over the commercialization of art. Authors have also especially attacked other authors by insinuating that while they themselves were writing for the sake of art, others were writing for money. A subtle double-irony has always accompanied this topic of discussion by novelists. Let us take a look at a few examples.

Daniel Defoe, one of the earliest beneficiaries of this transformation wrote rather critically in 1725,'Writing . . . is become a considerable Branch of the English Commerce. The booksellers are the Master Manufacturers or Employers. The several Writers, Authors, Copyers, Sub-writers, and all other Operators with Pen and Ink are the workmen employed by the said Master Manufacturers.'[122] Henry Fielding also complained about falling literary standards due to the use of cheap writers as a substitute for quality writers—'paper merchants, commonly called booksellers [force the public to] . . . drink cider water . . . because they can produce no other liquor'.[123] Goldsmith also condemned the devaluing of literary merit in the new marketplace in 'The Distress of a Hired Writer' (1761) lamenting 'that fatal revolution whereby writing is converted to a mechanic trade; booksellers, instead of the great, become the patrons and paymaster's [sic] of men of genius'.[124] He felt that the older system of feudal patronage was much better than the new marketplace. In 1837, Balzac wrote an entire novel on the changing face of writing and publishing entitled *Lost Illusions*. He created the character of Lucien who seeks to defend 'pure poetry' and goes to Paris for this purpose. He, however, gets ruined in the process. In the course of his misfortunes, a seasoned publisher enlightens him:

> In short, my dear fellow, in literature you will not make money by hard work, that is not the secret of success; the point is to exploit the work of somebody else. A newspaper proprietor is a contractor, we are the bricklayers. The more mediocre the man, the better his chance of getting on among mediocrities; he can play the toad-eater, put up with any treatment, and flatter all the little base passions of the sultans of literature. . . . The austerity of your conscience, clear as yet, will relax when you see that a man holds your future in his two hands, when a word from such a man means life to you, and he will not say that word. For, believe me, the most brutal bookseller in the trade is not so insolent, so hard-hearted to a newcomer as the celebrity of the day.[125]

Interestingly, David, another character in the novel, who tries his hand at developing cheap paper for printing, is the one who manages better success between the two friends. In 1859, novelist Gustave Flaubert also wrote, 'And though I have great needs (which I never mention), I would rather be a wretched monitor in a school than write four lines for money.'[126] In 1891, George Gissing wrote his most successful novel called *New Grub Street*, in which he wrote, 'Literature nowadays is a trade. Putting aside men of genius, who may succeed by mere cosmic force, your successful man of letters is your skilful tradesman. He thinks first and foremost of the markets; when one kind of goods begin to go off the slackly, he is ready with something new and appetising.'[127] In 1979, Italo Calvino, too, grieved over the fate of the author as a 'brand' for promoting sales in the market. The dramatized novelist of his novel, *If on a winter's night a traveller*, writes:

Strange people circulate in this valley: literary agents awaiting my new novel, for which they have already collected advances from publishers all over the world; advertising agents who want my characters to wear certain articles of clothing and drink certain fruit juices; electronic technicians who insist on finishing my unfinished novels with a computer.[128]

In 1996, Salman Rushdie voiced his dissatisfaction as well—'The pressures of monopoly and bureaucracy, of corporatism and conservatism, limiting and narrowing the range and quality of what gets published, are known to every working writer.'[129] This lament has not been exclusive to novelists alone. Critics have also made similar observations about the stranglehold of the market over creativity. Ken Worpole, a critic of popular fiction notes in *Reading by Numbers*, 'No longer does the writer type away at an original idea which becomes a novel submitted to the publisher; rather, the publisher, or agent, goes to the writer with the idea of the novel . . . in many publishing houses the editorial department has shrunk as the rights, sales, publicity and marketing departments have grown'.[130] Other artists, especially poets, too, have expressed similar disappointments about writing in the era of capitalism. However, our reason for singling out the novel in this context is that the novel has been the first *major* literary genre (apart from genres associated with journalism), which made its mark in the literary world through its successes in the marketplace.[131] Thus, apart from philosophical reasons, it is this integral link of the novel to the market that has made it rely upon emphasizing its 'novelty' and 'innovation' in the course of its developments, so much so, that the novel has embodied this spirit explicitly in its developing nomenclature.

This valuing of innovation or novelty by the market, however, has not always been about real innovations. Very often, it has also been about *fetishizing* the new. Many literary critics have made observations about the vacuousness of the aesthetic value of novelty in literature. Richard Hoggart writes about this phenomenon that 'there is an obsession with fashion and novelty: to be the latest thing is thought in itself sufficient recommendation'.[132] Harry Levin makes similar observation in his 1960 article, 'What was Modernism?' He writes, 'There is no inherent reason why time's latest offspring should be the last; on the other hand, there is an irrepressible tendency to canonize—at least for a day—the very latest thing.'[133] Malcolm Bradbury also concurs, 'Not to be *new* is, in these days to be nothing . . . novelty is an achieved convention'.[134] Fredric Jameson explains this same tendency in his 1991 work *Postmodernism*:

What has happened is that aesthetic production today has become integrated into commodity production generally: the frantic economic urgency of producing fresh waves of ever more novel-seeming goods (from cloning to airplanes), at ever greater turnover, now assigns an increasingly essential structural function and position to aesthetic innovation and experimentation.[135]

An interesting development since the mid-twentieth century has been that certain critics have started highlighting the lack of originality or innovation in contemporary novels. Irving Howe, an early critic of postmodern fiction says, '...younger writers,...feel that at whatever peril to their work and careers they must grapple with something new in contemporary experience, even if, like everyone else, they find it extremely hard to say what that "newness" consists of'.[136] Harry Levin also says, 'Since more and more combinations have been tried, more and more possibilities have been exhausted ... the problems of experimentation have become harder and harder.'[137] Edward Said points out in *The World, the Text, and the Critic* (1984), that today's 'writer thinks less of writing originally, and more of rewriting'.[138] The same opinion is also expressed by Italo Calvino through the character of a dramatized reader, 'With me, more and more often I happen to pick up a novel that has just appeared and I find myself reading the same book I have read a hundred times'.[139] Umberto Eco, writing about his novel, *The Name of the Rose*, claims that 'I discovered what writers have always known (and have told us again and again): Books always speak of other books, and every story tells a story that has already been told.'[140] Tim Woods writes in *Beginning Postmodernism*, 'Yet if there is one note which dominates all these descriptions of postmodernist fiction, it is exhaustion ... that it is impossible to write an original work.'[141] And Bran Nicole also notes in *Postmodernism and the Contemporary Novel*, 'In postmodernity we are no longer able to appreciate the particularity of our historical location, we can no longer create original works of art.'[142]

Some critics and novelists take this line of argument a bit further to express a sense of choking-up in the very act of writing itself. For instance, Robert Scholes says in 'The Fictional Criticism of the Future':

Once we knew that fiction was about life and criticism was about fiction—and everything was simple. Now we know that fiction is about other fiction, is criticism infact, or metafiction. And we know that criticism is about the impossibility of anything being about life, really, or even about fiction, or, finally, about anything.[143]

Raymond Federman explains this tendency to say that in today's times 'writers write simply to reveal the impossibility of writing in a postmodern era'.[144] Terms like paranoia, rhizomatic reading or schizophrenia have become common in analysing or understanding postmodern fiction.

Thus, while most novels continue to be sold in the name of novelty, a creative exhaustion of possibilities has also come to the fore. This condition can be understood through two notions. One is the development of a highly centralized publishing industry, which imposes a sameness upon the products for its global market, and the other is the theory of 'intertextuality' premised upon the ideas of Derrida, Foucault, Barthes, Kristeva and others. Let us elaborate.

Over the last few decades the publishing industry has become more monopolistic in nature. Big multinational publishing giants have expanded the scope of their business by increasingly investing in the book markets of different countries. Very often this development has been celebrated for making it possible for local readers to read a novel simultaneous to its release in the West. Often it has also been celebrated for making it possible for local writers, especially third world writers, to make a splash in the global market. The globalized publishing industry has periodically focussed upon 'Latin American writers', 'African American women writers', 'Indian writers', 'Canadian writers', 'Australian writers', etc., and made a novelty out of them. They have also claimed to bring the world closer through this act. However, this entire process has undoubtedly resulted in also making the products of these publishing houses all the more 'same'. As Milan Kundera writes in *The Art of the Novel* in 1986:

> But alas, the novel too is ravaged by the termites of reduction, which reduce not only the meaning of the world but also the meaning of works of art. Like all of culture, the novel is more and more in the hands of mass media; as agents of the unification of the planet's history, the media amplify and channel the reduction process; they distribute throughout the world the same simplifications and stereotypes easily acceptable by the greatest number, by everyone, by all mankind.[145]

Raymond Williams also describes this process in *The Politics of Modernism* (1989) to say:

> What was being addressed was a real development of universal distribution and of unprecedented opportunities for genuine and diverse cultural exchange. What was ideologically inserted was a model of an homogenized humanity consciously served two or three centres: the monopolising corporations and the elite metropolitan intellectuals. One practiced homogenization, the other theorized it.[146]

Describing the scenario of British publishing houses over the last few decades, Steven Connor says in *The English Novel in History* (1996):

> Since the 1970s, British publishers, who had hitherto been able to resist the pressure of large American corporations, have become more and more vulnerable to

takeovers and mergers. The 1980s saw a simultaneous increase in the size of publishers and a remorseless reduction in their numbers. Increasingly publishing houses found themselves either part of large publishing conglomerates, which demanded high-volume sales from every unit of production, or part of multinational companies, whose publishing sections were only a small part of a range of different activities ... it also meant that their product became increasingly difficult to distinguish from other commodities and the techniques used to promote and sell them.[147]

Thus, to some extent the exhaustion of novelty or innovation in novel writing has also been induced by the fact that choices regarding publications are increasingly being made by a small number of very large publishing houses, which decide upon what to supply to the reading public. Genuine variety and diversity, therefore, have to quite an extent been compromised.

On the other hand, the current sense of exhaustion in the novel is also an outcome of an accompanying philosophical trend whose roots can be traced to the views forwarded by Derrida, Foucault, Barthes, Kristeva and others. These scholars argue that the only means of knowing the world are textual, rather than material. In Derrida's famous words in *Of Grammatology*, 'There is nothing outside the text.' Accordingly anything that we know of the world today, or whatever we may know of it tomorrow is derived from existing textual knowledge. Even the limits of imagination are conditioned by what has already been imagined and expressed through texts. Therefore, all stories are an outcome of the stories that have already been told. Among the most significant works in this regard are Julia Kristeva's 'Word, Dialogue and Novel' and Roland Barthes's 'The Death of the Author', both written during the late 1960s. Both these essays effectively put a serious question mark on the claims to originality and creativity by authors and writers. Kristeva, of course, famously coined the term 'intertextuality' in order to concretize this entire concept of the inevitable interdependence of all new texts upon earlier texts. These critical ideas have had a corresponding impact upon the novel. Instead of claiming to write new stories, writers themselves have started positing their works as intertextual works. Narrating stories has now become all about deliberately giving a new spin to old tales. As Linda Hutcheon explains, 'The stories which *The Name of the Rose* retells are both of literature (by Conan Doyle, Borges, Joyce, Mann, Eliot, and so on) and those of history (medieval chronicles, religious testimonies). This is the paradoxically doubled discourse of postmodern intertextuality.'[148] This theoretical tendency has also been embraced by the culture industry. Remix music albums or film remakes are the most prominent examples of this trend. Thus, for the first time since the inception of the novel, novelists have started claiming helplessness over the inability to write anything original or tell original tales. I have already discussed how recent historical tendencies in the West have been those of preferring a sense of historical continuum over the sense of progress. The theory of intertextuality, i.e. that the new is not so different from the old, smoothly merges into this tendency. In fact, of late, this tendency has intensified. Both mass industry as well as critically acclaimed novelists have been pursuing an illusive creative 'originality' for quite some time now and critical discussions have increasingly moved to novels emerging from outside the West.

While the current sense of exhaustion in the novel in the West can be located in this context, in order to understand the periodic 'deaths' predicted for the novel throughout the twentieth century, it may be useful to note the striking resemblance between the trajectory of the novel and the crisis-ridden character of capitalism itself. Many scholars have argued that economic cycles of the 'boom' and 'slump', or 'growth' and 'slowdown' are systemic to capitalism.[149] In spite of frequent predictions about imminent end, capitalism, too, has repeatedly managed to sustain and revive itself. This tendency of capitalism caused Georg Lukács to remark in *Studies in European Realism* (approx. 1938), '[Capitalism] is like the hydra of the legend which grows a new head every time one of its heads is chopped off.'[150] Of late, in the neoliberal era, capitalism has been finding its sustenance through periodic growth stories often occurring outside the West, i.e. Japan and Latin America during the 1980s, South-East Asia during the 1990s, and China and India in current times. We do not intend to propose an exact one-to-one correspondence between the crisis-ridden system of capitalism and recurrent predictions about the novel's death or its renewals; however, the structural parallels between the two are too hard to miss. That the cultural form of the middle classes has also been finding itself going through crests and troughs, with some authors regularly running out of content or form, and others discovering fresh cause for rejuvenation, is a reflection of the novel as a barrowmeter of middle class mood. Unlike poetry[151] or drama, it is the novel that has witnessed enormous success on the one hand and incessantly invited such announcements and predictions over the last hundred years, on the other.

Some critics have been claiming that no major innovations have taken place in the form of the novel over the last few decades. With the collapse of many erstwhile socialist countries in the 1990s, Francis Fukuyama declared in *The End of History and the Last Man* (1992),

> [Today] we cannot picture to ourselves a world that is *essentially* different from the present one, and at the same time better. Others, less reflective ages also thought of themselves as the best, but we arrive at this conclusion exhausted, as it were, from the pursuit of alternatives we felt *had* to be better than liberal democracy.[152]

Thus, even the celebration of the triumph of capitalism has been accompanied by a sense of an end or death of radically new possibilities. Literary critics and novelists have started taking a special interest in examining 'dystopias' as opposed to utopias, i.e. a unique civilizational malady in which contemporary writers are unable to imagine a beautiful or ideal future.[153] Now, with the recent economic crisis, the situation has only become worse.

Current observations about the novel's exhaustion must be taken into account against this overall backdrop. The novel emerged in an ethos that celebrated novelty and innovation, firmly believed in the concept of progress and was aggressively anti-traditional in its temper. As J. Paul Hunter explains, the early novel was, 'Self-conscious about innovation and novelty.... The repeated claims of novelty and innovation, whether about the specifics of a single book or about new variations for the species itself, taken together are a strong reminder of how odd the novel looks among traditional literary forms.'[154] The novel always celebrated this spirit of novelty in the course of its developments. Of late, however, novels have been written in an ethos that is anti-thetical to this spirit of the early novel and to the spirit of early capitalism, carrying deep scepticism about the possibility of novelty and innovation in narration. The stranglehold of the monopolistic publishing industry has also had a deep influence. Though novelty still continues as the mantra of the literary market, it exists often in terms of a fetish. The present times do not carry a sense of historical progress, rather there is an emphasis on an endless continuum of history. The anti-traditional approach of the novel, too, has run into trouble with the emergence of concepts like intertextuality, and theories about the impossibility of originality, which theoretically link even the latest novel with others that have come before.

Today, therefore, the novel is poised at an interesting juncture. Has the novel run out of words, techniques and content? Ralph Fox says in *The Novel and The People*, '[T]he novel is the most important gift of bourgeois, or capitalist, civilisation to the world's imaginative culture.'[155] It is difficult not to agree. As long as capitalism and the middle classes exist, the novel is likely to continue in some *avatar* or the other. The history of the novel over the last century has been all about constant alternation between exhaustion and rejuvenation. A large part of the novel's constantly having to die has got to do with its insatiable longing to relentlessly renew itself. What shape its innovations take in the coming days would depend to a very large extent upon the turn that the middle classes take towards the world around them. Would they look for new possibilities or would they resign themselves to a dystopic future of the world? It is these developments that would go a long way in determining the character of the novel in the days to come.

Early, Realist, Modernist and Postmodern Novels

Till now, we have largely examined the development of the novel 'externally'. In this section, we will study the 'internal' developments of the novel in history, i.e. examine changes in theme, content, technique and form. At the very outset, it is important to note that one of the most popular typologies for documenting the development of the Western novel is its classification into early, realist, modernist and postmodern novels. Let us briefly recall some of the basic characteristics of these different stages.

Early novels written during the late seventeenth and early eighteenth centuries were mostly about experimenting with various available genres of writing, ranging from church sermons, ballads and travelogues to private diaries and letters evolving new ways of narrating the emerging bourgeois subject's stories. These novels were path breaking in their choice of subjects, dealing with ordinary people of modest or low social origins instead of nobles, kings or gods. Their narrators were self-conscious (though not self-reflexive in the postmodern sense) and struggled to establish the credibility of their stories. They went to great lengths to explain how they had been able to gain insights into the 'true' stories of other people's lives, very often, private lives. Most authors employed devices like epistolary forms, diary or journal entries, dramatized narrators, etc., in order to make their stories seem believable and tangible. They created individual 'characters' in great detail by giving them distinctive psychological and physical attributes. These characters largely remained constant throughout the course of their novels. The plots mostly comprised of the varying experiences of these unchanging characters against the backdrop of changing circumstances.

By the nineteenth century, the form of the novel underwent further modifications and developed into a more comprehensive genre for narrating the tale of individual subjects. In this phase, the novel came to be dominated by realism. Realist novels showed a marked preference for 'omniscient' narration, which was a more holistic technique of narration developed to its full by nineteenth century novelists. First-person biographical accounts of individuals progressing from childhood to youth to finding professional and/or personal happiness also became frequent. Considerable emphasis was now placed upon depicting socio-historical settings of novels in great detail. Plots gradually evolved structures with distinct beginnings, middles and ends. Realist narrations largely remained chronological and their endings usually tried to neatly tie the loose ends together into a closure. A two-fold development took place in these novels simultaneously; on the one hand, circumstances underwent change, on the other hand, characters also transformed through their diverse experiences.

Plots were usually about transformations in both socio-historical settings as well as individual characters.

By the late nineteenth and early twentieth centuries, realist novels started giving way to modernist novels. However, modernism was not a homogenous movement or tendency. Many major novelists of the early twentieth century did not switch over to modernist techniques of writing. They continued in the tradition of realism. Even those who used modernist techniques did not use all its techniques simultaneously or towards the same end. Yet, modernist innovations included many features. Chronological narratives gave way to non-chronological narratives. Closures were abandoned in favour of more open-ended narratives. The focus shifted away from characters located in particular socio-historical contexts to fragmented interior lives. In many novels of the main plot revolved around developments in the inner lives of individuals, very often in spite and irrespective of their socio-historical contexts. Symbolism, imagism, stream-of-consciousness and other techniques evolved and were employed to emphasize the difficulty and indeterminacy of representing life. Point-of-view narratives also emerged to further underline the breakdown of unified and reliable accounts of truths. A sense of anguish or nostalgia for lost wholesomeness or unity became the characteristic tone of these novels. Relativity in moral and intellectual outlook also gained ground.

After the mid-twentieth century, the techniques and themes of 'high' modernism further evolved to give way to postmodern novels or fiction. Postmodern novels lay emphasis on the breakdown of the possibility of representing the real. They were against all accounts claiming to be authoritative or reliable, and stressed plurality of meaning. Instead of nostalgia for lost narratives, however, they foregrounded irony and black humour. They also displayed narcissist tendencies in the persona of their dramatized narrators and characters. Postmodern novels were acutely self-referential and self-reflexive, both in their themes as well as techniques. Their characters were a-social beings devoid of identifiable character traits. The authority of authors or novelists also progressively declined. Readers were deliberately invited by novelists to participate more actively in the creation and interpretation of texts. Intertextuality was also used to highlight the textual constructedness of everything. Novelists took conscious positions against the division of literature into 'high' and 'low' genres, and emphasized the creation of hybrid novels. Parody and pastiche were also employed as common techniques. Put simply, postmodern novels have been theorized into five major types—*nouveau roman, metafiction, surfiction, fabulation and historiographic metafiction.* Nouveau romans mainly emphasize the lack of any deep, coherent or definitive meaning in this world. Metafictions are self-referential fictions about fiction itself, i.e. they make a commentary on their own form and technique. Surfictions propose that far from trying to make fiction imitate reality it is more important to understand that life itself is fictional. Fabulations denote a form of writing similar to magic realism, and are fantastic, mythical, nightmarish, strange, tragic yet comic at the same time. Historiographic metafiction comprises of novels which revisit the socio-historical instead of evading it; however, the revisiting is always mediated through irony or a basic scepticism about the authenticity of histories and historiographies.

The typology of early, realist, modernist and postmodern novels is pertinent to this study and we shall employ it in the Jamesonian sense to denote the 'cultural dominant' of the novel in successive ages. However, using this typology is not without its own perils. For instance, the category of 'modernist novels' is highly problematic, because what is largely recognized as the 'modernist novel' today undoubtedly represents only a selective 'high modernist' canon that was put in place during the late 1940s and 50s. This explains the persistence of debates about continuities or similarities between 'modernism' and 'postmodernism' in literary theory. Contrary to such debates, no comparable confusions or ambiguities exist about continuities between realism and modernism in literature. The relationship between modernism and postmodernism is akin to the relationship between early and realist novels. They are different, yet they denote the deepening of the same continuing essence. Historically, during the early twentieth century, realism was waning from being a 'dominant' to a 'residual' form, while modernism was just emerging. It was after the mid-twentieth century that high modernism gave way to postmodernism as the 'dominant' tendency, while realism became truly 'residual'. Let us take a brief look at some prevalent views about modernism and postmodernism.

Several scholars argue that modernism and postmodernism share more in common between them than has usually been assumed. For instance, David Lodge in his 1977 work, *The Modes of Modern Writing* opines, 'Critical opinion varies about how significantly *new* postmodernism really is . . . genuinely revolutionary [or] . . . "marginal developments of older modernism". Both opinions are tenable—both are in a sense "true".'[156] Jean-Francois Lyotard famously states in *The Postmodern Condition* (1979), 'What then is the postmodern? . . . It is undoubtedly a part of the modern. . . . Postmodernism . . . is not modernism at its end but in its nascent state, and this state is constant.'[157] Linda Hutcheon in *A Poetics of Postmodernism* (1988) argues, '. . . modernism literally and physically haunts postmodernism, and their interrelations should not be ignored'.[158] In a subsequent work, *The Politics of Postmodernism* (1989) she reiterates, 'Contrary to the tendency of some critics to label as typically postmodern both American surfiction and the French texts of *Tel Quel*, I would see these as extensions of modernist notions of autonomy and auto-referentiality and thus as "late modernist".'[159] Alex Callinicos in *Against Postmodernism* (1989) goes a step further to emphasize, 'I doubt very much that Postmodern art represents a qualitative break from Modernism of the early twentieth century.'[160] He emphasizes that they both share common features or traits, viz., 'Aesthetic Self-consciousness or Self-Reflexiveness', 'Simultaneity, Juxtaposition, or Montage', 'Paradox, Ambiguity, and Uncertainty' and 'Dehumanisation and the demise of the Integrated Subject or Personality'.

Most critics, however, hold the complicated cultural category of postmodernism responsible for such theoretical ambiguities. Contrary to this view, we believe that postmodern tendencies which emphasize self-reflexivity, pluralism, loss of nostalgia, constant irony, black humour, breakdown of representation and language, narcissism, lack of meaning and totality, intertextuality, hybridity, etc., are easier to understand because of their homogeneity; while the myriad and ideologically contested positions of modernism are more difficult to come to terms with, more so because of a largely successful historiographic exercise in the decades following the Second World War which managed to strait jacket the ideological and aesthetic diversity of early twentieth-century arts and literatures.[161]

Without going into further details of this debate, let us just say that most critics view modernism and postmodernism as oppositional and different. Common entries in literary dictionaries, on web sites or in postmodern anthologies bear testimony to this opinion. For instance, Brian McHale in his landmark study *Postmodernist Fiction* (1987) summarizes his entire study to say, 'This is essentially a one-idea book . . . That idea simply stated: postmodernist fiction differs from modernist fiction just as a poetics dominated by ontological issues differs from one dominated by epistemological issues.'[162] David Harvey in *The Condition of Postmodernity* (1990) also argues, 'Somewhere between 1968 and 1972 . . . we see postmodernism emerge as a full-blown though still incoherent movement out of the chrysalis of the anti-modern movements of the 1960s.'[163] Such inconsistencies in views about the typology of modernism and postmodernism are not very easy to resolve. Therefore, it is better to refer to these conceptual categories with a pinch of salt.

Other interesting typologies of the development of the novel also exist. For instance, a subtext to the dominant typology of the development of the novel is the trajectory of 'popular' novels. Brian McHale says, 'Science fiction, we might say, is to Postmodernism what detective fiction was to Modernism'.[164] The phenomenon of 'spy' fiction, too, existed during the Cold War era, i.e. a period ranging from what could be called late modernism to early postmodernism. 'Gothic' novels also had their moments, most notably during the late eighteenth, late nineteenth and late twentieth centuries.[165] Moreover, 'romantic' novels also enjoyed unrivalled popularity throughout the history of the novel. Recently the typology of the Western novel has changed from national to postcolonial to globalized novels. The study of the development of the Western novel, therefore, definitely merits a more exhaustive examination of all these and perhaps more categories like women's novels, etc. However, as we have already mentioned before, the purpose for studying the development of the novel is not to document the multiple and diverse ways in which the novel has developed in history, but rather to discern and sift out the generic essence of the novel irrespective and in spite of its diversifications and modifications.

In an earlier chapter on the rise of the novel, we have already sought to establish that an important generic feature of the novel is its plastic, elastic, incorporative and inclusive form. In this section too, we would continue to argue that across its development, it is the incorporative generic character of the novel that constitutes its essential genre-giving principle. However, the real question is not whether the novel is flexible and incorporative as a genre, but whether there is any logic or pattern to the generic incorporations made over time in the novel. After all, a viable definition of any phenomenon cannot be that it has no defining boundaries or limits, or that it is 'free to the point of arbitrariness or total anarchy'.[166] In an effort to understand the development of the novel, therefore, we would concentrate upon trying to discern the pattern of the myriad generic incorporations made by the novel. Other critics have also raised similar questions about the novel, although without offering any answers. For instance, Marthe Robert asks in *Origins of the Novel*, 'Indeed, if the genre is undefined and virtually indefinable, can it constitute a form recognisable as such?'[167] J. Paul Hunter also notes in *Before Novels*, 'The novel's imperialism—its ability to take over features from other species and assimilate them into a new form—is well known, but we have to be clearer about what those feature are and where they come from.'[168] Let us, therefore, explore these questions in some detail. In the chapter on the rise of the novel, we linked the flexible and inclusive character of the novel to the roots of its inception in the flexible and incorporative system of capitalism and the socially diverse origins of the middle classes. In this section also then we would continue to follow the same line of argument by taking into account two important aspects of the development of capitalism, i,e. increasing centralization of its politico-economic system and the simultaneous fragmentation of its social and individual life.

We have already tried to argue how from the days of its inception, capitalism was an ever-expanding system that steadily spread to all parts of the globe. Terry Eagleton writes in *The Illusions of Postmodernism* (1996), 'Capitalism is the most pluralistic order history has ever known, restlessly transgressing boundaries and dismantling oppositions, pitching together diverse life-forms and continually overflowing the measure.'[169] In its initial years, capitalism emerged in England and then emerged and re-emerged in other European nations. By the mid-nineteenth century, it had become the dominant system of Europe integrating both rural as well as urban areas within its life forms. Simultaneously, the process of colonization not only intensified but also came to be indispensable to the sustenance of capitalism. By the twentieth century, elaborate worldwide networks of 'drain of wealth' were deeply entrenched. As Edward Said explicates, 'Primarily, as we look back at the nineteenth century, we see that the drive toward empire in effect brought most of the earth under the domination of a handful of powers.'[170] Eric Hobsbawm also testifies, 'Between 1876 and 1915 about one-quarter of the globe's land surface was distributed or redistributed as colonies among half-dozen states.'[171] Ania Loomba elaborates, 'By the 1930s, colonies and ex-colonies covered 84.6 per cent of the land surface of the globe'.[172] This tendency to centralize profits from around the world produced conflicts which led to the First and the Second World Wars. It also augmented international economic transactions on an unprecedented scale. The two World Wars had an interesting outcome. On the one hand, they triggered a process of decolonization. On the other, they weakened most capitalist nations and only a single nation emerged as the most powerful. Eric Hobsbawm writes of this, 'Only the USA came out of the world wars very much as it had gone into them, only rather stronger. For all others the wars meant upheaval.'[173] After the mid-twentieth century, the process of decolonization witnessed acceleration. After the 1970s, with the advent of neoliberal policies the world also started turning more and more into a single economic unit. By the 1990s, the world became what is now popularly called a global village. Economic and political power became concentrated in the hands of the United States. Simultaneously, mini-growth stories of capitalism also started shifting to different parts of the world. We are emphasizing this point about the development of capitalism only so that the spread of capitalism is not viewed merely as a process of spread and extension, but also as a process of concentration and centralization. It is in the context of this view that we would subsequently try to theorize the development of the novel and its form.

Contrary to this actual process of centralization, the emphasis in most artistic, theoretical and critical discourses over the last hundred years has been on quite the opposite—fragmentation and the lack of any identifiable centre in the world. The modernist movement in arts and literature was strongly associated with this tendency. W.B. Yeats's famous lines—'Things fall apart; the centre cannot hold'—almost became the motto of modernism.

The modernist emphasis on points-of-view and multiplicity of meanings also served the same philosophical end associated with fragmentation and breakdown. Ironically, these were the same times which historically represented the peak period of colonialism. The emphasis on fragmentation also became an important part of postmodern theorizations. Major postmodern theorists celebrated 'fragmentations' and 'decentring'. For instance, the influential method of 'deconstruction' forwarded by Derrida sought to do away with the assumption that the structure of texts had a unifying centre. Derrida tried to 'disperse' meanings instead of integrating them. Explaining the genesis of postmodernism, Linda Hutcheon argues in *A Poetics of Postmodernism*, 'Umberto Eco has suggested that postmodernism is born at the moment when we discover that the world has no fixed centre and that, as Foucault taught, power is not something unitary that exists outside of us.'[174] *The intensification of this philosophical trend during the twentieth century is extremely ironical. The more the real world became centralized (even to the extent of having a single instead of multiple centres), the more the philosophical discourses about fragmentation and decentring proliferated in theory.* Linda Hutcheon, of course, associates the process of decentring and fragmentation to political and cultural decolonization and to assertions by hitherto marginalized sections and groups. She says, 'Outside of North America too, then, there are texts which overtly challenge cultural notions of the centrality of the metropolis, for both France and Britain had former colonial empires, with strong centralized cultures that are now being upset by their own history, as Arab, African, East and West Indian voices demand to be heard.'[175] Many critics and thinkers, however, criticize views which celebrate fragmentation. In their opinion, fragmentation is something to be overcome and combated. For instance, Edward Said in *Culture and Imperialism* (1993) argues that:

> Imperialism consolidated the mixture of cultures and identities on a global scale. But its worst and most paradoxical gift was to allow people to believe that they were only, mainly, exclusively, white, or Black, or Western, or Oriental.... No one can deny the persisting continuities of long traditions, sustained habitations, national languages, and cultural geographies, but there seems no reason except fear and prejudice to *keep on insisting on their separation and distinctiveness*, as if that was all human life was about.[176]

Approaches to the concept of 'fragmentation' vary drastically among philosophers and thinkers and the concept merits some examination in order to understand the development of the novel over the years.

Hegel was among the first influential modern philosophers to theorize fragmentation. He associated the new modern age with the breakdown of totality. In his book, *Phenomenology* (1808), he used the concept of alienation to proclaim that the 'World Spirit' or world consciousness had lost its unity of thought in modern times. He attributed this to the shattering of symmetry between mind and matter. People were now alienated from nature and viewed it as something outside of them. He argued that this stage of alienation or fragmentation of the World Spirit was a degraded stage because it destroyed the ability of human beings to think in terms of totality. He proposed that the only way to overcome this alienation was to always seek the knowledge of the 'whole' rather than of just a part. Ludwig Feuerbach, a student of Hegel, extended this concept of alienation to the realm of religion in his book, *The Essence of Christianity* (1841), wherein he professed that inherently all human beings were good. But due to religion, they projected all good qualities upon an imaginary being, 'God', and thought of themselves as worthless. Religion, he said, alienated people from their own goodness. Feuerbach, thus, viewed religion as an obstacle in the way of people attaining this realization and gaining true insights into the nature of man.[177]

The concept of alienation, however, is most famously associated with Karl Marx, who linked the growing sense of alienation and fragmentation to the conditions produced by capitalism. Marx attributed alienation to various factors. One of his arguments was that under capitalism the worker was alienated from his own labour .because he did not have any control over the fate of the product of his labour or over the production process. He was merely a wage labourer. Moreover, the process of production under capitalism itself was fragmented. For instance, in the process of making a shoe in a capitalist enterprise, various people were involved. One person designed the shoe, one labourer prepared the leather for it, one just cut the leather in a particular shape, one nailed the sole to the shoe, one worked only with glue, one coloured or polished it, and another finally put it in a box. The net outcome of such a process was that a particular worker could just nail the left sole of the shoe for his entire life without having an integrated sense of creating a whole pair of shoes. Thus, Marx attributed the sense of alienation to the emergence of narrower specializations in the field of production. He also associated alienation or fragmentation with 'commodity fetish', i.e. a process wherein things and relationships got transformed into market relations, a tendency that afflicted not merely the working classes but all classes of people under capitalism. In the *Communist Manifesto* (1848) he explained,'The bourgeoisie has stripped of its halo every occupation hitherto honoured and looked up to with reverent awe. It has converted the physician, the lawyer, the priest, the poet, the man of science, into its paid wage labourers.'[178] In *Capital I* (1859) Marx elaborated that under a system of generalized commodity production 'the definite social relation between men themselves . . . assume . . . the fantastic form of a relation between things'.[179] Marx takes up the idea further in *Theories of Surplus Value* (1863) to describe the new role of the writer as, 'A writer is a worker not in so far as he produces ideas, but in so far as he enriches the publisher, in so far as he is working for a wage.'[180] Ralph Fox explained this process of 'commodity fetish' in the realm of literature and art to write:

No less deeply did they [creative artists] feel the levelling of their work through the capitalist market. Money makes all things equal—a Michael Angelo to so much oil or soap, if it is purchased by a millionaire with a fortune made from these useful and homely commodities, a play by Shakespeare to a quantity of manure, should a season be run in the West End on the charity of a shareholder in the Imperial Chemical Industries.[181]

Georg Lukács also theorized the same concept of fragmentation/alienation/commodity fetish by calling it 'reification'. He maintained that, 'Just as the capitalist system continuously produces or reproduces itself economically on higher and higher levels, the structure of reification progressively sinks more deeply, more fatefully and more definitively into the consciousness of man.'[182] He linked this fragmentation of consciousness to the development of the genre of the novel in *Theory of the Novel* by stating that 'The novel is the epic of an age in which the extensive totality of life is no longer directly given, in which the immanence of meaning in life has become a problem, yet which still thinks in terms of totality'.[183] Unlike other forms the novel, he explained, is 'an expression of this transcendental homelessness'.[184] Subsequently, another literary critic, Lucien Goldman, used the concept of reification to theorize the novel. In *Towards a Sociology of the Novel* (1964) he argued, '[R]eification as a permanent psychological process [has been] working for several centuries uninterruptedly in Western Market societies.'[185] He proposed that there exists 'an intelligible relation or a homology between the history of reificational structures and the history of fictional structures'.[186] His entire book was an exposition of the homologies existing between the literary form of the novel and 'the everyday relation between man and commodities in general, and by extension between men and other men, in a market society'.[187]

Let us now try to employ this concept in the analysis of the development of the novel. We have already linked the genesis of the novel to the historical genesis of capitalism. One of the first few changes that capitalism brought about in the consciousness of people was to give rise to an 'individual subject'. This was a new realization in history. The emergence of individualism led to an opinion that 'only individuals are real, but the wholes of which they are parts such as social groups, political societies and the like, have no independent reality over and above that of their components and the interrelations and interactions amongst these'.[188] There have been many theorists of the rise-of-the-novel debate that have shown links between the emergence of the novel and the growth of individualism. The most notable among them is Ian Watt who opines that '[T]he modern novel is closely allied on the one hand to the realist epistemology of the modern period, and on the other to the individualism of its social structure.'[189] It is not a coincidence, therefore, that all early novels were based upon an abstraction of the individual and his/her life from the socio-historical 'whole'.

By the nineteenth century, the individual fragmented further to divide into phases of childhood, youth and old age. Before the nineteenth century, most early novels did not devote attention to details of the evolution of characters from the days of their childhood, the way the *bildungsromans* did. Of course, in today's times these phases of life have fragmented even further to involve phases like pre-teens, late teens, mid-life, mid-life crisis and so on, notions that were non-existent in earlier times. During the nineteenth century, there was also a deepening of consciousness regarding the division of an individual between the private and the public, the physical and the mental, the intellectual and the emotional, as well as the objective and the subjective. These details were used to fill out the characters of novels and situate them a more complicated backdrop. The interplay of these distinguishable aspects in different characters created the grounds for interesting plots in novels. The novels of Charles Dickens, Jane Austen or William Thackeray exemplify this. The sense of the socio-historical was also consciously perceived as important. The social was now not just taken into account, but also presented as an important and developing factor in novels. It was no longer just an incidental aspect but an objective reality viewed as such.

By the late nineteenth century, the alienation of the individual from the socio-historical deepened. Increasingly, the socio-historical was relegated to the role of a lifeless background or context. Georg Lukács makes this criticism in all his studies about the development of realism. Lukács argues that this also happens in 'naturalism', which represents a degraded stage of the novel in which the social becomes just a lifeless average. The socio-historical now began to be dealt with a sense of aesthetic distance by novelists and therefore, the conceptions about 'life' changed considerably. Further fragmentation of the individual continued into the twentieth century. Now the focus of novels shifted to a large extent to the interior lives of people. This interiority, simultaneously, included within itself a sense of the emotional as well as the intellectual. This new type of interior life was now popularly called the *psychological*. Fredric Jameson elaborates upon this in *The Political Unconscious* by saying that, 'The conditions of possibility of psychoanalysis become visible, one would imagine, only when you begin to appreciate the extent of psychic fragmentation since the beginnings of capitalism, with its systematic quantification and rationalization of experience, its instrumental reorganization of the subject as much as of the outside world.'[190] The psychological, too, became very complex. Not only was it at odds with 'exterior' life, but it was also at odds with the subconscious and the unconscious. The unconscious was a new discovery and had a life of its own. As a result, the behaviour of individual characters became arbitrary and ambiguous for the unconscious could assert itself at any time. Also, the interior life of characters could be one at one moment and another, the next. The interior became so important that opinions about the external began to get mediated by it. Thus, the socio-historical was left with very little life of its own and was slowly subordinated to the psychological. The evolution of the technique of stream-of-consciousness was an outcome of these developments wherein the random or associative leaps in thought were narrated. The act of writing further became fragmented between content and form. Now, authors increasingly started discussing their techniques and style with a considerable degree of self-consciousness. Novelists like Virginia Woolf, James Joyce, Henry James and Conrad show such tendencies in their novels. Modernist techniques of point-of-view, non-chronological narratives, symbolism and imagism evolved to give suitable expression to this highly fragmented state of consciousness. It is in this backdrop that one can understand the very strong sense of anguish, which became characteristic of the modernist movement to represent the loss of wholeness and unity. This inability to have any reliability or stability in the world increased steadily, and led to the pits of anguish during the Existentialist or Absurd movement in Europe.

Many critics associate fragmentation centrally with modernism. According to Ihab Hassan, 'Alienation of the self from society used to be, and in a sense remains, the basic assumption of the modern novel'.[191] Fredric Jameson also argues, 'That modernism is itself an ideological expression of capitalism, and in particular, of the latter's reification of daily life, may be granted a local validity'.[192] Subsequently, he asserted again, 'Indeed, their [modernist] work was said to represent a new "inward turn" and the opening up of some new reflexive deep subjectivity: the "carnival of interiorized fetishism," Lukács once called it'.[193] David Harvey also reiterates, 'Modernity, therefore, not only entails a ruthless break with any or all preceding historical conditions, but is characterized by a never-ending process of internal ruptures and fragmentations within itself'.[194]

This process of fragmentation was intensified further during the century. Slowly the very act of writing became full of perils. The use of language by humans turned into one of the most complicated and disabling phenomenon. The act of thinking, speaking, and writing became more complicated. By now people were ironically conscious and self-conscious about everything—thoughts, emotions, speech, writing, etc. Patricia Waugh describes this phase to say, '. . . language soon becomes a 'prisonhouse' from which the possibility of escape is remote. Metafiction is set out to explore this dilemma.'[195] Fredric Jameson writes that 'The "discovery" of Language is at one with its structural abstraction from concrete experience, with its hypostasis as an autonomous object, power, or activity . . . as a thing in itself.'[196] The modernist anguish accompanying this acute sense of fragmentation was abandoned in postmodernism for a more playful irony. An apt example of this playful irony is evident in *Tin Drum* (1959) by Gunter Grass. The dramatized narrator of *Tin Drum*, Oskar Matzerath ponders while writing a novel in a mental asylum:

> You can begin a story in the middle and create confusion by striking out boldly, backward and forward. You can be modern, put aside all mention of time and distance and, when the whole thing is done, proclaim, or let someone else proclaim, that you have finally, at the last moment, solved the space-time problem. Or you can declare at the very start that it's impossible to write a novel nowadays, but then, behind your own back so to speak, give birth to a whopper, a novel to end all novels. I have also been told that it makes a good impression, an impression of modesty so to speak, if you begin by saying that a novel can't have a hero anymore *because there are no more individualists, because individuality is a thing of the past, because man- each man and all men together—is alone in his loneliness and no one is entitled to individual loneliness, and all men lumped together make up a 'lonely mass' without names and without heroes.*[197]

By this time, the interior had become so prevalent that it could transform the external at will. Novels like Gunter Grass's *Tin Drum* or Salman Rushdie's *Midnight's Children* exhibit this skill explicitly. The dramatized narrators of these novels, namely Oskar and Saleem Sinai, transform the history of Germany and the history of the Indian subcontinent according to their own whims and fancies. By the late twentieth century, novelists and critics started celebrating the figure of the exiled or rootless intellectual, who did not belong anywhere and lived in complete alienation. They argued that this rootless individual was at an advantage because he could interpret and understand the world without any prejudices or attachments. Postmodern fragmentation, however, also had its own discomforts. As Bran Nicol states in *Postmodernism and the Contemporary Novel* (2002) that, 'It is striking how readily postmodern theory turns to the language of psychopathology—schizophrenia, hysteria, narcissism, paranoia, etc.—to explain the postmodern "condition".'[198]

All in all, if one looks at the development of the novel in history, one would not be wrong in concluding that the novel parallels and represents the process of reification or fragmentation of life under capitalism.[199] Fredric Jameson says of this, 'The realm of separation, of fragmentation, of the explosion of codes and the multiplicity of disciplines is merely the reality of the appearance: it exists, as Hegel would put it, not so much in itself as rather for us, as the basic logic and fundamental law of our daily life and existential experience in late capitalism'.[200] The novel's techniques have developed in accordance with providing an appropriate expression to this increasing fragmentation. However, the crucial question in this regard is about the approach adopted towards understanding this process. On the one hand are those who view fragmentation as an enabling process, as an indicator of acquiring greater knowledge about the complications of life. For instance, modernist and postmodern novelists ridicule realist novelists for not being aware of the problems of representation in the same way as them, for being naïve, ignorant and simplistic. Such critics attack the very possibility of acquiring 'whole' knowledge and celebrate the fragmented as a higher stage of knowledge. For example, Linda Hutcheon argues:

> And, in addition, if elitist culture has indeed been fragmented into specialist disciplines, as many have argued, then hybrid novels like these work both to address and to subvert that fragmentation through their pluralizing recourse to the discourses of history, sociology, theology, political science, economics, philosophy, semiotics, literature, literary criticism, and so on.[201]

On the other hand are those who view fragmentation as disabling, as a process which destroys the capacity of human beings to live wholesome lives. Such critics criticize intellectuals and artists who make no attempt to transcend this fragmentation in order to grasp the 'whole'. Once again Fredric Jameson tackled this issue in *The Political Unconscious*:

> ...the program to which the various contemporary ideologies of pluralism are most passionately attached is a largely negative one: namely to forestall that systematic articulation and totalization of interpretive results which can only lead to embarrassing questions about the relationship between them and in particular the place of history and the ultimate ground of narrative and textual production.[202]

They also view fragmented narratives of modern and postmodern novels as somewhat inferior to realist narratives. Fredric Jameson argues that the 'Great Writer' has disappeared under postmodernism.[203] Eric Hobsbawm also laments, 'Naturally it [the novel] continues to be written in vast quantities, bought and read. Yet if we look for the great novels and great novelists of the second half of the century, which took an entire society or historical era as their subject, we find them outside the central regions of Western culture.'[204] Lucien Goldman also writes, '...the novel can be characterized as the story of a search for authentic values in a degraded mode, in a degraded society, and that this degradation, in so far as it concerns the hero is expressed principally through the mediatization, the reduction of authentic values to the implicit level and their disappearance as manifest realities'.[205]

Instead of getting into detailed debates about how this increasing fragmentation should be perceived by novelists and critics, we would just conclude by saying that there is a little bit of truth in both these views, and a suitable balance between both is merited in understanding the development of the novel. However, we do not share the view that fragmentation in the realm of philosophy or discourse is independent of the process of fragmentation unleashed by capitalism. Unfortunately, the dominant view in literary theory is that fragmentation at the level of consciousness leads to fragmentation in real life. we would prefer a more dialectical approach in understanding this phenomenon and its relation to the development of the novel.

Let us now return to the main task of this chapter, i.e. to try and discern the nature of the generic incorporations made in the novel over a period of time. We have already discussed how during its initial stages the early novel borrowed extensively from various genres like ballads, sermons, letters, diaries, travelogues, ethnographies, etc. At this early stage, the novel looked like it was incorporating all kinds of genres within its form. However, the novel evolved in times when oral forms were fast weakening and bourgeois print culture was taking over.[206] As J. Paul Hunter notes in *Before Novels*, 'Some historians of English folklore claim that no fairy tales survived into the mid-eighteenth century, and they all agree that the native tradition atrophied severely in the face of disuse and active suppression.'[207] The change in the situation during the nineteenth century is also noted by Eric Hobsbawm in *The Age of Capital*:

> With the triumph of city and industry an increasingly sharp division grew up between the 'modern' sectors of the masses, i.e. the urbanized, the literate, and those who accepted the content of hegemonic culture—that of the bourgeois society—and the increasingly undermined 'traditional' ones. Increasingly sharp, because the heritage of the rural past became increasingly irrelevant to the pattern of urban working-class life: in the 1860s and 1870s the industrial workers in Bohemia stopped expressing themselves through folksong and took to music-hall song, doggerel ballads about a life which had little in common with their fathers.... The hegemony of the official culture, inevitably identified with the triumphant middle class, was asserted over the subaltern masses.[208]

Other scholars also talk about similar developments. Jameson is one who opines,'... the older kind of folk and genuinely 'popular' culture which flourished when the older social classes of a peasantry and urban *artisanat* still existed and which, from the mid-nineteenth century on, has been gradually colonized and extinguished by commodification and the market capitalism'.[209] This is not to suggest that oral forms disappeared completely or that the subaltern masses did not invent their own cultural forms to resist and critique the emerging bourgeois culture, but just that the consolidation of bourgeois print culture was the dominant trend of these times. In the overall backdrop of the transition from feudalism to capitalism, the novel emerged in an oppostional spirit to pre-capitalist cultures and genres. The novel was not averse to dealing with people of low social origins or marginalized sections, but only so long as they were part of a process of consolidating bourgeois culture, not otherwise. Thus, while the novel was generically open to modern evolving genres, it was not equally open to older genres representing a contradictory cultural ethos. This tendency was apparent both in the early novel as well as the realist novel.

By the time the modernist movement got underway, the novel started integrating artists from all over Europe and America, and borrowing liberally from the colonies, both in subject as well as form. But unlike earlier novels, modernist novels were more overt, obvious, explicit and conscious while incorporating these influences. It is not a coincidence that these assimilations began during the late nineteenth century and not before, when capitalism was still mainly trying to consolidate the nation state as an entity, even though it crucially depended on colonization for that entire process. As Raymond Williams writes in 'The Metropolis and the Emergence of Modernism' (1985), 'The most important general element of the innovations in form is the fact of immigration to the metropolis, and it cannot too often be emphasized how many of the major innovators were, in this precise sense, immigrants.'[210] Or, as Bernard Bergonzi notes in 'The Advent of Modernism; 1900–20' (1970), 'In its broadest sense the Modern Movement was international and embraced all the arts.... Conrad was Polish, and Ford was half-German ...; Yeats was Irish, and Pound and Eliot were Americans.... The dominance of alien talents in the Modern Movement, whether Continental or Celtic or American [is remarkable].'[211] Daniel Bell also writes in *The Cultural Contradictions of Capitalism* (1976), 'Modern culture is defined by this extraordinary freedom to ransack the world storehouse and to engorge any and every style it comes upon.'[212] Aijaz Ahmad emphasizes the same point in *In Theory*, 'The felt experience of the elite artist, in this same phase of modern capital, was that he too could now draw upon a whole range of cultural artefacts from around the globe (Indian philosophy, African masks, Cambodian sculpture).'[213] Stephen Slemon also reiterates in 'Modernism's last post' (1991) that modernism was 'unthinkable had it not been for the assimilative power of Empire to appropriate the cultural work of a heterogeneous world "out there" and to reproduce it for its own social and discursive ends . . . .'[214]

It is precisely in this context that we can understand the way in which assimilations happened in the novel during the early twentieth century. The assimilations were not random or without reason. While modernism was an expression of fragmentation and a loss of totality, Western artists looked for this lost wholesomeness both in their own pasts as well as in the colonies or in tribal and primitive societies, etc. But these assimilations were partly to reconfirm the cultural lag of these places and their people, and partly to address the Western sense of alienation. Without understanding the stage of imperialism or the acute fragmentation in the lives of Western bourgeois subjects, it is impossible to understand the generic assimilations in the novel. Those made from the colonies largely reconfirmed to the Western readerships that the loss of totality of meaning and fragmentation of truth were indeed the deepest and most advanced levels of knowledge. For instance, in Joseph Conrad's novel *Lord Jim* (1900) the main narrator, dramatized as the sailor Marlow, knows all about the wisdom of the East, the Africas and the Caribbeans because he has travelled across the world. By temperament, Marlow is drawn to scrutinize and understand the motives of men and he tries to understand Jim. However, after all his efforts and assistance from people from diverse places and cultures he concludes, 'I wanted to know—and to this day I don't know, I can only guess.'[215] Thus, although the form of the novel was open, it was so only to give expression to the fragmented urban angst of the Western bourgeois subject. Moreover, the rural Western subject was already getting out of sight.

If one looks at the development of postmodernism, one finds that in the second half of the twentieth century conscious efforts were made to assimilate diverse generic forms into the novel. we have already discussed the aspect of mixing high and low genres in a previous section of this chapter. Here, we will look at another aspect of postmodern novels, i.e. their engagement with the postcolonial. Aijaz Ahmad notes that from the 1960s onwards an interest in 'empire, colony, nation, migrancy, post-coloniality, and so on'[216] intensified in the West. So much so, that today many critics argue that no credible canon of postmodern novel can be constituted without including novels by writers like Marquez, Fuentes, Achebe, Rushdie, Naipaul, etc. Ostensibly, postmodern discourses are characterized not only by the West visiting the colonies, but also by the colonies visiting the West in the field of literature, especially with regards to the novel. Many critics point to this diversity by especially emphasizing the emergence of 'postcolonial' theoretical discourses in Western literature. As Tim Woods notes in *Beginning Postmodernism*, 'Although one might be tempted to suggest that postmodern fiction is largely an American and European affair, it was not exclusively so. The debate about the extent to which postmodernism has engaged with postcolonial texts is deeply involved and complicated.'[217] However, many critics also believe that postcolonial discourses serve a greater purpose in the West than for the Third World. As Kwame Anthony Appiah argues in 'Is the Post- in Postmodernism the Post- in Postcolonial?' (1991):

> Postcoloniality is the condition of what we might ungenerously call a *comprador* intelligentsia: a relatively small, Western-style, Western-trained group of writers and thinkers, who mediate the trade in cultural commodities of world capitalism at the periphery. In the West they are known through the Africa they offer; their compatriots know them both through the West they present to Africa and through an Africa they have invented for the world, for each other, and for Africa.[218]

Ania Loomba also argues in *Colonialism/Postcolonialism* (1998), 'But many "Third World" academics continue to be wary of even this transformed theory, including postcolonial theory, because of its perceived distance from situations in their part of the world, and because of its supposed overlaps with "postmodernism".'[219] Aijaz Ahmad also notes:

> ...to offer a *symptomatic* reading of an ideological location which makes it possible for Rushdie to partake, equally, of the postmodernist movement and the counter-canon of 'Third World Literature'... the actual authors who are accorded central importance in this evolving counter-canon—Garcia Márquez, Fuentes, Rushdie, among others—we find, first, that these critical positions are framed by the cultural dominance of postmodernism itself...[220]

In the context of the writings of Salman Rushdie, Aijaz Ahmad claims that his novels are centrally dependent upon the 'rootless' individual who serves the purpose of reassuring the Western fragmented subject and the cosmopolitan third world reader about the philosophical fundamentals of postmodernism. We would further argue that only those 'postcolonial' texts find a premier place in the West, which reconfirm Western philosophical concerns. For instance, *One Hundred Years of Solitude* (1967) by Gabriel Garcia Márquez is an important novel of the postcolonial/postmodern canon. While the allegorical novel is subversive and oppositional in its own political context of censorship and repression, for the West it reconfirms some important postmodern moorings of inescapable solitude amidst a history that does not progress but rather moves in circles. The entire narrative of this novel is arranged around this point. Due to an interesting narrative device, we discover at the end of the novel that actually the end is the real beginning of the story. In the course of the novel, different characters make several such observations. Let us recount one such conversation:

'What did you expect? He murmured. 'Time passes.'

'That's how it goes,' Ursula said, 'but not so much.'

When she said it she realized that she was giving the same reply that Colonel Aureliano Buendía had given in his death cell, and once again she shuddered with evidence that time was not passing, as she had just admitted, but that it was turning in a circle.[221]

We can recount numerous other such instances in the course of the novel. There are also examples of other parts of the novel in which questions of subjectivity, interiority, the primacy of perception over material reality, the lack of coherent meaning, the impossibility of accessing totality, etc., are presented in the text. However, most of these conclusions are presented not in any overt conformity to the West but rather as opposed to and in spite of the West. Thus, the novel works with a double irony. This double bind is also pointed out by Rushdie vis-à-vis his novel *Midnight's Children* (1981) which he notes was read for its 'magic' in the West and for its 'realism' in India.

All in all, the development of the genre of the novel can be better understood against the template of the development of fragmented consciousness under capitalism. The assimilative character of the novel derives its character from the roots of its inception in the equally assimilative system of capitalism and the negotiating middle ground of the middle classes. As Fredric Jameson says, 'For we all know that capitalism is the first genuinely global culture and has never renounced its mission to assimilate everything alien into itself.'[222] This generic flexibility, in our view, is also found in other art forms emerging under capitalism. However, the novel is unique because it is the first and the most eminent literary form to display this characteristic right from its inception. The generic assimilations are not arbitrary or random. They follow the pattern created by the needs and material conditions of the bourgeoisie. The Western novel starts borrowing on a considerable scale from the colonies only when capitalism reaches the stage of imperialism, not before. Earlier, the novel develops in opposition to pre-capitalist oral and other forms, and the colonial is like a subconscious. By the modernist turn, the novel starts looking for a lost wholeness in the colonies or just reiterates the loss of totality through references to the colonies. Later, by postmodern times, it becomes open to incorporating oral, mythic and folk elements, especially through third world writers. The novel does so in times that represents the stage of '. . . late capitalism, in which all the earlier modes of production in one way or another structurally coexist'.[223] All pre-capitalist modes of production in this stage are entirely subordinated to the highly centralized system of capitalism. Thus, the novel in this phase traverses at will through the entire ambit of cultural diversity available in the world. Also, in the phase of neoliberalism, periodic economic growth stories in different parts of the world become routine to the logic of capitalism. The novel, too, begins displaying a periodic interest in Latin America, Afro-American women writers, India, etc. Yet, the centre appropriates only that which fits its purpose. In the postmodern stage only those novels from the Third World find legitimacy in the West, which connect with its philosophical moorings; the rest remain ignored.

All in all, from this appraisal of various theoretical views on the novel, it is possible to reiterate that the form of the novel and its various developments can be studied and understood in relation to the evolution of the middle classes in modern capitalist history. The slow ascendancy of the form in the literary canon, its various literary inventions, successive predictions about its 'death' and constant rejuvenations, as well as the orientation of incorporations from other literary and non-literary genres, can all be located in middle class histories. Despite various innovations, the genre of the novel is not yet divorced from the predilections of this class. This appraisal also shows, that the 'novel' continues to remain a pertinent and relevant literary concept. Therefore, trends that take recourse to studying only the sub-genres of the novel, or which discount the novel altogether in order to replace it with conceptual categories like fiction, narrative or text, emanate more from particular theoretical positions rather than from the nature of the genre itself.

Notes

1. Frank Kermode, 'Literary Fiction and Reality,' 1967; Hoffman, Michael J. and Patrick D. Murphy, eds., *Essentials of the Theory of Fiction,* Durham and London: Duke University Press, 1988, p. 222.
2. Wallace Martin, *Recent Theories of Narrative*, Ithaca and London: Cornell University Press, 1986, p. 44.
3. Walter L. Reed, *An Exemplary History of the Novel: The Quixotic Versus the Picaresque,* Chicago and London: The University of Chicago Press, 1981, p. 3.
4. Lorna Martens, *The Diary Novel*, Cambridge: Cambridge University Press, 1985, p. 23.
5. It has been argued by many critics that rule-bound genres have become important in literary history only in times when the establishment has been threatened by some new social impulse that is democratic, be it in and about 68-8 BC (Horace) Rome or during the late seventeenth and early eighteenth centuries. Hayden White argues, 'Everyone recognizes that the notion of generic purity is a supreme value among aristocratic, conservative, and reactionary social groups and political parties.' Therefore,

the assertion of the importance of genres has been a means to argue for the superiority of select political or social groupings, especially when their predominance has been under threat. See Joseph Farrell, 'Classical Genre in Theory and Practice'; Hayden White, 'Anomalies of Genre'; Michael B. Prince, 'Mauvais Genres' in *New Literary History: Theorising Genres II*, vol. 34, Summer 2003.

6. Martin, op. cit., p. 15.
7. Umberto Eco,'Postmodernism, Irony,The Enjoyable', 1985; Nicol Bran, ed., *Postmodernism and the Contemporary Novel: A Reader,* Edinburgh: Edinburgh University Press, 2002, p. 110.
8. E.M. Forster, *Aspects of the Novel*, Harmondsworth: Penguin Books, 1964, p. 19.
9. Ibid., pp. 30–1.
10. Ibid., p. 28.
11. Ralph Cohen, 'Do Postmodern Genres Exist?' 1988; *Postmodern Literary Theory: An Anthology*, ed. Niall Lucy, Oxford: Blackwell Publishers, 2000, p. 293.
12. Ibid., p. 295.
13. Reed, op. cit., pp. 1–2.
14. Dorothy J. Hale, *Social Formalism: The Novel in Theory from Henry James to the Present*, Stanford and California: Stanford University Press, 1998, p. 2.
15. Dorothy J. Hale, *The Novel: An Anthology of Criticism and Theory, 1900-2000,* Malden and Oxford,Victoria: Blackwell Publishing, 2006, p. 4.
16. Lukács, *The Historical Novel*, 1936–7, tr. Hannah and Stanley Mitchell, Lincoln and London: University of Nebraska Press, 1962, p. 240.
17. Ibid., p. 177.
18. Frederic Jameson, *The Political Unconscious: Narrative as a Socially Symbolic Act,* Ithaca and New York: Cornell University Press, 1981, p. 145.
19. Ibid., p. 145.
20. Peter Hitchcock, 'The Genre of Postcoloniality', in *New Literary History: Theorizing Genres I*, vol. 34, Summer no. 2, 2003, p. 310.
21. Michael McKeon, *Theory of the Novel: A Historical Approach,* Baltimore and London: The John Hopkins University Press, 2000, p. xiv.
22. Novelists were accused of promoting immorality and licentiousness in society, particularly due to their deliberate choice of low subjects. See J. Paul Hunter, *Before Novels: The Cultural Contexts of Eighteenth-Century English Fiction*, New York and London: W.W. Norton & Co., 1990, p. 25.
23. Lennard J. Davis, *Factual Fictions: The Origins of the English Novel,* Philadelphia: University of Pennsylvania, 1983, p. 131.
24. Pam Morris, *Realism,* London and New York: Routledge, 2003, pp. 3–4.
25. Qtd. in Marthe Robert, *Origins of the Novel,* 1972; tr. Sacha Rabinovitch, Sussex: The Harvester Press, 1980, p. 3.
26. Cited in Davis, *Factual Fictions*, p. 131.
27. See Davis, *Factual Fictions*; Hunter, *Before Novels* and McKeon *Origins*.
28. Ian Watt, *The Rise of the Novel,* 1957; London: Penguin Books, 1968, p. 10.

29. Janet Barron and David Nokes say, 'As late as 1711 *The Tatler* was still using the word "novelist" to mean a newspaperman.' See 'Market, Morality and Sentiment: the Eighteenth-century Novel', *Bloomsbury Guides to English Literature: The Novel from its Origins to the Present Day*, ed. Andrew Michael Roberts, London: Bloomsbury, 1994, p. 22.
30. Davis, *Factual Fictions*, pp. 103–4.
31. Qtd. by J. A. Cuddon, *The Penguin Dictionary of Literary Terms and Literary Theory,* London: Penguin Books, 1991, pp. 603–4.
32. Qtd. by Harry Blamires, ed., *A Short History of English Literature,* London: English Language Book Society and Methuen & Co Ltd., 1979, pp. 247–8.
33. Clara Reeve, 'The Progress of Romance', in *The Nineteenth-Century Novel: A Critical Reader,* ed., Stephen Regan, London and New York: The Open University, 2001, p. 14.
34. Reed, op. cit., p. 8.
35. Hunter, op. cit., p. 29.
36. See Pierre Bourdieu, *The Rules of Art: Genesis and Structure of the Literary Field*, 1992; tr. Susan Emanuel, Stanford and California: Stanford University Press, 1995, p. 71.
37. See Eric Leuschner, 'Anthologizing the Novel', in *The Minnesota Review*, n.s., vol. 55, no. 7, 2002.
38. Reed, op. cit., p. 9.
39. Ibid., p. 8.

    See also Steven Connor who says, 'Theory of the novel arrived comparatively late in its history, with the work of Henry James,' *The English Novel in History: 1950–1995*, London and New York: Routledge, 1996, p. 28.
40. Novel scholarship was directly linked to reforms in the English literature syllabi of two major British universities during the early twentieth century—Cambridge and Oxford. The novel was included in their literary syllabi along with classical writings and Shakespeare. The related changes were quite dramatic. As Terry Eagleton says, 'In the early 1920s it was desperately unclear why English was worth studying at all; by the early 1930s it had become a question of why it was worth wasting your time on anything else,' *Literary Theory: An Introduction*, Oxford: Basil Blackwell, 1983, p. 31.

    See also Peter Barry, *Beginning Theory: An Introduction to Literary and Cultural Theory*, Manchester and New York: Manchester University Press, 2002, pp. 11–38.
41. Walter Allen, *The English Novel,* London: Penguin Books, 1991, pp. 17–18.
42. W.B. Carnochan, 'The English Curriculum: Past and Present', *PMLA* 115, 2000, pp.1958–61.
43. Harry Levin, 'What Was Modernism?' 1960; Tim Middleton, ed., *Modernism: Critical Concepts in Literary and Cultural Studies*, vol. 2, London and New York: Routledge, 2003, p. 146.

44. Davis says, '. . . Eliza Haywood was a journalist; Defoe and fielding wrote and edited newspapers; Aphra Behn was also the writer of political pieces, as was Mary Manley; Bunyan was a pamphleteer; Swift . . . wrote journalistic pieces . . . Like these writers, Richardson printed newspapers, pamphlets, and other pieces,' *Factual Fictions*, p. 175.

    See also, Eric Hobsbawm, *Age of Extremes*, pp. 509–10.
45. Frank Kermode, 'Literary Fiction and Reality', 1967, in Hoffman and Murphy, eds., p. 220.
46. Hitchcock, op. cit., pp. 309–10.
47. McKeon, *Theory*, pp. xiii–xiv.
48. Robert Scholes and Robert Kellogg, *The Nature of Narrative*, New York: Oxford University Press, 1966, p. 3.
49. Ihab Hassan, *The Postmodern Turn: Essays in Postmodern Theory and Culture*, Ohio State University Press, 1987, p. 169.
50. Eric Hobsbawm, *Extremes*, p. 500.
51. Italo Calvino, *Six Memos for the Next Millennium*, 1988, http://www.kirjasto.sci.fi/calvino.htm
52. Linda Hutcheon, *A Poetics of Postmodernism: History, Theory, Fiction*, New York and London: Routledge, 1988, p. 61.
53. Robert Mengham, ed., *An Introduction To Contemporary Fiction: International Writing in English Since 1970*, Cambridge: Polity Press, 1999, p. 1.
54. Frederick Karl, 'Modern and Postmodern, Modernism and Postmodernism', 1985, in Middleton, eds., vol. 4, p. 12.
55. Elizabeth Dipple, *The Unresolvable Plot,* New York and London: Routledge, 1988, pp. 10–11.
56. Raymond Federman, *Critifiction: Postmodern Essays,* New York: State University of New York Press, 1993, p. 124.
57. Ibid., p. 66.
58. Linda Hutcheon, *The Politics of Postmodernism*, 1989; London and New York: Routledge, 2005, pp. 167–8.
59. Frederic Jameson, *Postmodernism, or, The Cultural Logic of Late Capitalism,* London and New York: Verso, 1991, p. xv.
60. See Martin McQuillan et al., eds., *Post Theory: New Directions in Criticism*, Edinburgh: Edinburgh University Press, 1999.

    Federman says, 'Postmodern fiction came and went, and *there is nothing to compare it to now*,' p. 109.

    Nicol also says in *Postmodernism and the Contemporary Novel*, 'Yet now, however, there is a sense that the term is finally showing signs of "stopping moving"—or at least that major new definitions of postmodernism have, for the time being ceased appearing', p. 2.
61. Davis, *Factual Fictions*, p. 175.
62. Hunter, op. cit., p. 37.
63. Jameson, op. cit., p. 152.
64. Richard J. Soderlund, 'Middle Classes', in *The Penguin Dictionary of Nineteenth-Century History*, ed. John Belchem and Richard Price, London: Penguin Books, 1996, p. 381.

65. David Daiches, *A Critical History of English Literature*, vol. IV, 1960; New Delhi: Allied Publishers Pvt. Ltd., 2002, p. 1049.
66. John Belchem and Price Richard, eds., *The Penguin Dictionary of Nineteenth-Century History*, London: Penguin Books, 1996, p. 692.
67. The outcome of most of these revolutions was a compromise between the ascendant bourgeoisie and the decadent yet durable aristocracy, in favour of the principles of 'liberalism' and the 'free market'.
68. Belchem and Price, eds., p. 382.
69. David Cody, 'The Gentleman', *The Victorian Web: literature, history, and culture in the age of Victoria*, 1998, http://www.victorianweb.org/history/Gentleman.html
70. Belchem and Price, op. cit., p. 131.
71. Eric Hobsbawm, *The Age Of Empire: 1875–1914,* London: Abacus, 1987, p. 221.
72. Q.D. Leavis, *Fiction and the Reading Public*, 1932, in Ashley, ed., pp. 44–5.
73. Raymond Williams, *The Politics of Modernism: Against the New Conformists*, London and New York: Verso, 1996, p. 77.
74. Hobsbawm, *Empire*, p. 221.
75. Malcolm Bradbury, 'Modernity in Modern English Literature', 1971, in Middleton, ed., vol. 3, p. 72.
76. David Harvey, 'Modernity and Modernism', 1990, in Middleton, ed., vol. 4, p. 282.
77. Bradbury, op. cit., p. 72 (emphasis mine).
78. See Barry, op. cit., pp. 11–38. See also Eagleton, *Literary Theory*.
79. Eagleton, *Literary Theory*, p. 29.
80. Terry Eagleton describes various aspects of this prolonged academic transformation and reconstitution of university education in his book *Literary Theory: An Introduction* (1983). Eagleton argues how literature came to occupy an important place within the academia—'In the early 1920s it was desperately unclear why English was worth studying at all; by the early 1930s it had become a question of why it was worth wasting your time on anything else' (p. 31). Also, 'the definition of an academic subject was what could be examined, and since English was no more than idle gossip about literary taste it was difficult to know how to make it unpleasant enough to qualify as proper academic pursuit' (p. 29). Modernism with its deliberately difficult techniques certainly helped in this entire project.
81. F.R. Leavis, *Mass Civilization and Minority Culture*, Cambridge: The Minority Press, 1930, pp. 3–4.
82. Levin, op. cit., p. 156.
83. Jameson, *Postmodernism*, p. 63.
84. See John Holloway, 'The Literary Scene; Literary Institutionalism', in *The Present: Volume 8 of the New Pelican Guide to English Literature*, ed. Boris Ford, London: Penguin Books, 1990, pp. 73–8. Holloway explains this shift in the context of England.
85. After the First World War, capitalism's conflict with 'socialism' further intensified, and 'fascism' emerged as a major civilizational challenge. By the

end of the Second World War, fascism was defeated and the West emerged from a deep crisis of decades of massacres, killings and destruction. The post-Second World War years, heralded the era of national liberation and decolonization for the colonized nations. By the 1970s 'no territories of any significant size remained under direct administration by former colonialist powers or their settler regimes, except in Central and Southern Africa—and of course, in embattled Vietnam' (Hobsbawm, *Extremes*, p. 222). Advanced capitalist nations lost their direct economic and political control over the worldwide web of profit making through colonial rule. However, new ways of keeping this economic web alive were devised. Bourgeois governments of most of the newly independent nations (in spite of avowals of non-alignment) were slowly drawn into economic complicity. As Eric Hobsbawm says, 'Some time in the early 1970s such a transnational economy became an effective global force' (*Extremes*, p. 277). Meanwhile, intense ideological, economic and political battles (largely non-military) were fought with socialism throughout the decades of the Cold War. By the 1970s, socialist economies became discernibly weak. By 1989, socialism started politically collapsing in many nations. In 1991, the Soviet Union also collapsed. This changed many things for capitalism. Eric Hobsbawm describes the decades of the nineties to say, '. . . the globe has now become far more of a single operational unit . . . In fact, for many purposes, notably in economic affairs, the globe is now the primary operational unit and older units such as the "national economies", defined by the politics of territorial states, are reduced to complications of transnational activities. The stage reached by the 1990s . . . [is that of the] the "global village" . . .' (*Extremes*, p. 15).

86. Jameson, op. cit., p. 87.
87. Aijaz Ahmad, *In Theory: Classes, Nations, Literatures*, New Delhi: Oxford University Press, 1999, pp. 123–4.
88. Raymond Williams, *The Politics of Modernism: Against the New Conformists*, London and New York: Verso, 1996, p. 34.
89. John R. Harrison, 'The Anti-Democratic Intelligentsia', 1966, in Middleton, ed., vol. 2, p. 190.
90. The only other movement has been the protests against the Iraq War in the advanced capitalist countries. Now with the recent economic crisis in the advanced capitalist countries since 2008, movements against austerity measures in Europe or 'Occupy Wall Street' movements in the US and elsewhere have begun to stir.
91. Pierre Bourdieu, *The Rules of Art: Genesis and Structure of the Literary Field*, 1992; tr. Susan Emanuel, Stanford and California: Stanford University Press, 1995, p. 341.
92. Alex Callinicos, *Against Postmodernism: A Marxist Critique*, Cambridge: Polity Press, 1989, p. 168.
93. Martin McQuillan, Graeme McDonald, Robin Purves and Stephen Thomson, eds., *Post-Theory: New Directions in Criticism*, Edinburgh: Edinburgh University Press, 1999, pp. x–xii.

94. Ahmad, p. 2.
95. Susan Sontag, 'One Culture and the New Sensibility', 1965, Nicol, ed., p. 154.
96. Hobsbawm, *Extremes*, p. 509.
97. Jameson, op. cit., p. 68.
98. Bob Ashley, ed., *The Study of Popular Fiction: A Source Book*, London: Pinter Publishers, 1989, p. 5.
99. Steven Connor, *The English Novel in History: 1950–1995,* London and New York: Routledge, 1996, p. 24.
100. Williams, *Politics of Modernism*, p. 118.
101. The publishing industry contributed to this process in their own way. As Steven Connor says, 'Central to the paperback revolution was the establishment of Penguin Books by Allen Lane in 1935.... Initially, Penguin Books achieved its readership for classics and literary texts by not announcing them as such.... Following the establishment of 'quality paperback' in the USA in the 1950s, an idea whose success depended on a hugely expanding college market, British publishers in the 1970s began to distinguish literary texts or classics from their other products by marketing them in larger format, more expensive editions and series, thus removing them from the kind of distribution outlets where they had previously been available alongside other less exalted kinds of reading' (pp. 14–15).
102. Aijaz Ahmad in 'Salman Rushdie's Shame: Postmodern Migrancy and the Representation of Women', a part of *In Theory* argues that 'the authors who are accorded central importance in this evolving counter-canon' write texts that are complicit in their appropriation by postmodernism (p. 125).
103. Frank Kermode, 'Life and Death of the Novel', The New York Review of Books, vol. 5, no. 6, 28 October 1965, http://www.nybooks.com/articles/article_preview? article_id=12720.
104. Milan Kundera, *The Art of the Novel*, 1986; tr. Linda Asher, London: Boston: Faber & Faber, 1988, pp. 17–18.
105. Hutcheon, *Poetics*, p. 40.
106. Salman Rushdie, 'In Defense of the Novel, Yet Again', 1996; Eleanor McNees, ed., *The Development of the Novel: Literary Sources and Documents,* East Sussex: Helm Information, 2006, pp. 347–53.
107. Seehttp://www.erinoconnor.org/archives/2004/10/a_very_easy_dea.html. In 1995, another important American novelist, William Browning Spenser wrote his award winning short story, *The Death of the Novel.*
108. Samuel Richardson, *Selected Letters*, qtd. by Davis, *Factual Fictions*, p. 182.
109. Fielding, qtd. by Davis, *Factual Fictions*, p. 197.
110. The *Tel Quel* group involved almost all the major luminaries of the structuralist and later poststructuralist movement at some or the other stage in their lives—Roland Barthes, Derrida, Foucault, Julia Kristeva, etc.
111. Linda Hutcheon, *Narcissistic Narrative: The Metafictional Paradox,* New York and London: Methuen, 1980, p. 14.
112. Raymond Williams, *Keywords,* New York: Oxford University Press, 1983, p. 230.

113. Elizabeth L. Eisenstein, *The Printing Revolution in Early Modern Europe*, New York: Cambridge University Press, 1983, p. 7.
114. See Lennard Davis, *Factual Fictions*, where he argues that many forms of print like ballads, *newes,* novellas or news claimed to be new, recent or latest; however, during the late sixteenth and seventeenth centuries it was still virtually impossible for any reader to imagine a narrative as being actually recent. Claims could be made; but there was no guarantee of a text of recentness. Older stories were still used (pp. 49–70).
115. Walter J. Ong, *Orality and Literacy: The Technologizing of Word*, London and New York: Methuen, 1982, p. 42.
116. Walter Benjamin, 'The Storyteller', in Ashley, ed., p. 66.

    Ngugiwa Thiong'o also describes a similar transformation in the African art of storytelling to say, 'There were good and bad story-tellers. A good one could tell the same story over and over again, and it would be fresh to us, the listeners.' However, it was the colonial print culture that brought an end to this culture. See 'The Language of African Literature', in Ashcroft, Griffiths and Tiffin, eds., p. 287.
117. Benjamin, op. cit., p. 66.
118. Ong, op. cit., pp. 148–9.
119. Martin, op. cit., p. 18.
120. Norris, op. cit., pp. 3–4.
121. See Watt, op. cit., pp. 55–9.
122. Ibid., p. 55.
123. Ibid., p. 56.
124. Ibid., p. 55.
125. The Project Gutenberg EBook of *Lost Illusions*, by Honore De Balzac http://www.gutenberg.org/cache/epub/13159/pg13159.html. Also qtd. by Lukàcs, *European Realism* 50.
126. Qtd. by Bourdieu, *Rules of Art*, p. 85.
127. George Gissing, *New Grub Street*, 1891; Hertfordshire: Wordsworth Classics, 1996, p. 4.
128. Italo Calvino, *If on a winter's night a traveller*, 1979; London: Vintage, 1998, p. 183.
129. Rushdie, *In Defence*, p. 353.
130. Ken Worpole, 'From *Reading by Numbers: Contemporary Publishing and Popular Fiction'*, in *The Study of Popular Fiction: A Source Book*, ed. Bob Ashley, London: Pinter Publishers, 1989, pp. 8–9.
131. See Ian Watt (58–60) where he argues that the economic criterion led to the predominance of prose over verse because authors were paid on a per sheet basis. Verbose novels, therefore, were the most paying genre for authors who wanted to make a living. Novels, thus, proliferated due to the favourable terms offered by the market.
132. Richard Hoggart, 1957; *The Uses of Literacy*, in Ashley, ed., p. 62.
133. Levin, op. cit., p. 142.
134. Bradbury, op. cit., pp. 73– 89.

135. Jameson, *Postmodernism*, pp. 4–5.
136. Irving Howe, 'Mass Society and Postmodern Fiction', 1959, in Nicole, ed., p. 148.
137. Levin, op. cit., p. 144.
138. Said qtd. in Hutcheon, *Narrative*, p. xvi.
139. Calvino, *If on a winters* ..., p. 197.
140. Hutcheon, *Poetics*, p. 128.
141. Tim Woods, *Beginning Postmodernism*, Manchester and New York: Manchester University Press, 1999, p. 52.
142. Nicol, op. cit., p. 5.
143. Robert Scholes, 'The Fictional Criticism of the Future', 1975, qtd. in Bran Nicol, ed., p. 1.
144. Federman, op. cit., p. 5.
145. Kundera, op. cit., p. 17.
146. Williams, *Politics of Modernism*, p. 132.
147. Connor, op. cit., pp. 17–18.
148. Hutcheon, *Poetics*, p. 128.
149. Many economists and philosophers argue that capitalism is a crisis-ridden system. Notable among them are Karl Marx, Joseph Schumpeter, Joan Robinson, Ernest Mandel, Paul Baran, Paul Sweezy and Robert Brenner. They argue that since the days of its inception, capitalism has followed the cycle of boom and slump, and that economic stagnation and crisis are inherent to the development of capitalism. I must mention here, however, that this is not the dominant view about capitalism. Most bourgeois economists do not accept crisis to be an inherent component of the development of capitalism.

    As Eric Hobsbawm says, 'The so-called "trade cycle" of boom and slump was familiar to all businessmen from the nineteenth century.... In the past, waves and cycles, long, medium and short, had been accepted by businessmen and economists rather as farmers accept the weather, which also has its ups and downs.' *Age of Extremes*, pp. 86–7.
150. Georg Lukács, *Studies in European Realism,* 1930; tr. Alfred Kazin, New York: The Universal Library, 1964, p. 241.
151. Predictions about the end of poetry were made at the beginning of the modern age, i.e. just about the time when the novel started emerging. Hegel, most notably argued that the new age was prosaic in nature, therefore, it would be impossible for poetry or art to survive in it. During the twentieth century, both poetry and drama continue to survive in considerably weakened forms. This has produced anxieties, but no fresh or repeated speculations about the possibility of their very existence.
152. Francis Fukuyama, 'From *The End of History and the Last Man*', 1992, in *Revolutions of the Word: Intellectual Contexts for the Study of Modern Literature*, ed. Patricia Waugh, London: Arnold, 1997, p. 123.
153. There has been a lot of critical interest in the study of Utopias during the last one decade. Critics have invented the category of Dystopias,

symbolizing the inability to imagine a beautiful future. It is not a coincidence that over the last two decades, economists have also been talking about a progressive slowdown in the Western economy.

154. Hunter, op. cit., pp. 24–5.
155. Ralph Fox, *The Novel and the People,* Moscow: Foreign Language Publishing House, 1956, p. 82.
156. David Lodge, 'Postmodernist Fiction', 1977, in Nicol, ed., p. 257.
157. Jean-Francois Lyotard, Answering the Question: What is Postmodernism?' in *Modern Literary Theory,* ed. Philip Rice and Patricia Waugh, London: Arnold Publishers, 2002, p. 335.
158. Hutcheon, *Poetics*, p. 61.
159. Ibid., p. 27.
160. Alex Callinicos, *Against Postmodernism: A Marxist Critique,* Cambridge: Polity Press, 1989, p. 5.
161. An excellent five-volume anthology in this regard is *Modernism* by Tim Middleton.
162. Brian McHale, *Postmodernist Fiction,* London and New York: Routledge, 1987, p. xii.
163. David Harvey, *The Condition of Postmodernity,* Cambridge: Basil Blackwell, 1989, p. 293.
164. Brian McHale, 'Change of Dominant from Modernist to Postmodernist Writing', 1986, in Nicol, ed., p. 290.
165. Jerrold E. Hogle, 'The Gothic at our Turn of the Century: Our Culture of Simulation and the Return of the Body', in *The Gothic*, ed. Fred Botting, Cambridge: D.S. Brewer Publications, 2001, p. 153.
166. Marthe Robert, *Origins of the Novel,* 1972; tr. Sacha Rabinovitch, Sussex: The Harvester Press, 1980, p. 5.
167. Ibid.
168. Hunter, op. cit., p. 58.
169. Terry Eagleton, *The Illusions of Postmodernism*, Oxford: Blackwell Publishers, 1996, p. 133.
170. Said, op. cit., p. 20.
171. Hobsbawm, *Empire*, p. 59.
172. Ania Loomba, *Colonialism/Postcolonialism*, London and New York: Routledge, 1998, p. xiii.
173. Hobsbawm, *Extremes*, p. 55.
174 Hutcheon, *Poetics*, p. 86.
175. Ibid., p. 72.
176. Said, op. cit., p. 336 (emphasis mine).
177. See 'alienation', *Sociology*, pp. 12–15.

    See also, 'alienation', *Penguin Dictionary of Philosophy*, ed. Thomas Mautner, London: Penguin Books, 1997, pp. 13–14.
178. Karl Marx and Frederick Engels, 'Manifesto of the Communist Party', 1848; tr. 1888 in *A World to Win: Essays on the Communist Manifesto*, ed. Prakash Karat, Delhi: Left Word, 1999, p. 91.

179. Qtd. by Callinicos, op. cit., p. 149.
180. Qtd. by Terry Eagleton, *Marxism and Literary Criticism*, London and New York: Routledge, 2002, p. 56.
181. Fox, op. cit., p. 78.
182. Georg Lukács, *History and Class Consciousness*, tr. Rodney Livingstone, New Delhi: Rupa & Co., 1993, p. 93.
183. Lukács, *Theory*, p. 56.
184. Ibid., p. 41.
185. Lucien Goldman, *Towards a Sociology of the Novel*, 1964; tr. Alan Sheridon, London: Tavistock Publications Ltd., 1975, p. 135.
186. Ibid., p. 135.
187. Ibid., p. 7.
188. See 'Individualism', *Dictionary of Philosophy*, pp. 272–3.
189. Watt, op. cit., p. 64.
190. Jameson, *Unconscious*, p. 62.
191. Ihab Hassan, 'The Pattern of Fictional Experience', 1961; *Modern American Fiction*, ed. A. Walton Litz, London, Oxford and New York: Oxford University Press, 1967, p. 320.
192. Jameson, op. cit., p. 236.
193. Jameson, *Postmodernism*, p. 311.
194. Harvey, p. 268.
195. Patricia Waugh, 'From *Metafiction*', ed. Nicol, 1984, p. 240.
196. Jameson, *Unconscious*, pp. 63–4.
197. Günter Grass, *The Tin Drum*, tr. Ralph Manheim, London: Vintage Classics, 1998, p. 3 (emphasis mine).
198. Nicol, op. cit., p. 6.
199. It may be worthwhile to explore if any dissenting tradition exists in novel writing where authors have sought to create wholesomeness in the lives of their characters in reaction to the growing fragmentation of the individual subject. Some sentimental novelists and the globally popular Brazilian novelist Paulo Coelho immediately come to mind. However, we are not aware if such a running thread has indeed been traced.
200. Jameson, op. cit., p. 40.
201. Hutcheon, *Poetics*, pp. 20–1.
202. Jameson, op. cit., p. 32.
203. Jameson, *Postmodernism*, p. 307.
204. Hobsbawm, *Extremes*, pp. 511–12.
205. Goldman, *Sociology*, p. 6.
206. The history of the development of the colonial novel is somewhat different. While the novel in the West developed after over three hundred years of the evolution of print forms, the novel in the colonies was among the forms that transported print culture to the colonies. Thus, in the colonies, the novel emerged in times when oral forms were vibrantly alive, while in the West it emerged in conditions when oral forms were already considerably weakened.

207. Hunter, op. cit., p. 142.
208. Hobsbawm, *Extremes*, pp. 352–3.
209. Jameson, *Postmodernism*, p. 63.
210. Raymond Williams, 'The Metropolis and the Emergence of Modernism', 1985, in Middleton, ed., vol. 4, p. 9.
211. Bernard Bergonzi, 'The Advent of Modernism: 1900–1920', 1970, in Middleton, ed., vol. 2, p. 260.
212. Daniel Bell, 'Urbanization and Mass Society', 1976; *Revolutions of the Word: Intellectual Contexts of the Study of Modern Literature*, ed. Patricia Waugh, London: Arnold, 1997, p. 104.
213. Ahmad, op. cit., p. 129.
214. Stephen Slemon, 'Modernism's last post', 1991; qtd. in Middleton, ed., vol. 5, p. 320.
215. Joseph Conrad, *Lord Jim*, New York and Ontario: New American Library, 1961, pp. 63–4.
216. Ahmad, op. cit., p. 3.
217. Woods, op. cit., p. 63.
218. Kwame Anthony Appiah, 'Is the Post- in Postmodernism the Post- in Postcolonial?' 1991;Padmini Mongia, ed., *Contemporary Postcolonial Theory: A Reader,* Delhi: OUP, 1997, pp. 62–3.
219. Loomba, op. cit., p. xii.
220. Ahmad, op. cit., p. 125.
221. Gabriel Garcia Márquez, *One Hundred Years of Solitude*, 1967; tr. Gregory Rabassa, London: Penguin Books, 1996, p. 341.
222. Frederic Jameson, 'Beyond the Cave: Demystifying the Ideology of Modernism,' 1975; Francis Mulhern, ed., *Contemporary Marxist Literary Criticism,* London and New York: Longman, 1992, p 171.
223. Jameson, op. cit., p. 100.

CHAPTER FIVE

The Novel in India

Some Aspects

As discussed in the previous chapter, the development of the novel in the West, especially over the past few decades, is intricately linked to the non-Western novel. In this chapter, we will examine some aspects of the novel in India. No easy generalizations are possible, as the novel exists in a multilingual field encompassing at least twenty-two official Indian languages and hundreds of others seeking their place under the sun. In each language, the novel has a story of its own, both independent as well as interdependent. The emergence and development of the novel over time has been informed by several sources—literary and non-literary, Western and non-Western as also, powerful living oral and performative traditions.[1]

Only a handful of scholars have attempted to tackle the novel in its multilingual domain. Sisir Kumar Das's two mammoth volumes—*A History of Indian Literature, 1800–1910 Western Impact: Indian Response* (1991) and *A History of Indian Literature, 1911–1956 Struggle for Freedom: Triumph and Tragedy* (1995)—provide a rare literary history of a wide array of writings across languages and genres. Another stalwart, Meenakshi Mukherjee, started by studying Indian-English novels but increasingly devoted herself to bridging the gaps in literary knowledge between multilingual, bilingual and monolingual (English) India. In her last book, she observed that Indian fiction still remained an 'elusive terrain'. In our times the numbers of edited volumes, anthologies and collections of essays on novels across Indian languages have grown. Greater attention is being paid to translations as well as the multilingual pool of myths, archives, texts and literary traditions that have informed novels. Recent theories have also acquired a distinctly composite flavor in the West, especially through the contributions of Franco Moretti, who is mapping a field in which the novel can be studied in the multilingual/multi-continental terrain of the entire globe.[2] To employ an analogy—while most theorists of the novel are doing deep sea diving on particular shares, Franco Moretti is sailing the seven seas, and the likes of

Meenakshi Mukherjee are demarcated by their navigation of the inland waterways—rivers, streams, canals and backwaters. Despite a wide array of studies in recent years, a comprehensive story of the novel in India is mostly yet to be told. In this chapter, we will try to explore a few select aspects and debates about the novel in India based on the resources available in English.

Like in the West the dating of the novel in India, too, is a matter of dispute. Most critics agree that Bangla novelist Bankim Chandra Chatterjee was the first major novelist of India. But the 'first novel' is variably traced to Pyari Chand Mitra's Bengali novel *Alaler Gharer Dulal* (1858) or Baba Padmanji's Marathi novel *Yamunaparyatan* written in the same year. Sisir Kumar Das traces the emergence of the novel a little earlier to Hannah Katherine Mullens' *Phulmani O Karunar Bibaran* (1852) in Bengali. Priyamvada Gopal discusses two early works of Anglophone fiction, namely, Kylas Chunder Dutt's *A Journal of Forty-Eight Hours of the Year 1945* (1835) and Soshee Chunder Dutt's *The Republic of Orissa: A Page from the Annals of the 20th Century* (1845) as the first experiments. Meenakshi Mukherjee dates the novel further back to Insha Allah Khan's *Rani Ketaki Ki Kahani* (1801) in Hindi, while T.W. Clark locates the first novel to the same year, but to a different work in Bengali, *Pratapadityacaritra*. Qurratulain Hyder labels Hasan Shah's Urdu novel *Nashtar* (1790) as the first novel, while Rebecca Reuben W. argues the same for Banabhatta's *Kadambari* written as far back as the seventh century AD. Novels have also variably been traced to earlier works in other languages including Sanskrit. Without repeating what we have posited earlier vis-à-vis the rise of the novel debate in Europe, let us just reiterate that the resolution of this debate depends on both how one demarcates the 'novel' from within the larger body of 'narratives' as well as what is one's approach to history.

The fiercest debate regarding the novel in India, however, has centered on the extent or degree of colonial influence. Some scholars have argued that colonialism along with the introduction of the English were decisive in the evolution of the novel in various Indian languages. For instance, T.W. Clark, a philologist and Orientalist scholar, examined the rise of the novel in Bengali, Marathi, Urdu, Hindi, Tamil and Malayalam in an edited collection of essays titled *The Novel in India: It's Birth and Development* (1970). He mainly gave credit to Professor William Carey (1791–1834), a Christian missionary at the Fort William College, for preparing the ground for the emergence of the novel through pioneering work in developing script and vocabulary in several vernacular languages as well as in guiding the evolution of prose fiction. The technique of the novel, according to Clark, was evolved through a 'struggle to develop a prose style of literary merit, and of slow acquiring, chiefly by reading the works of Western authors . . .'.[3]

While mapping this rise, he looked for evidence of British style realism and dismissed other writings as not quite novels. He argued, in fact, that Indian classical and traditional forms were a hindrance to the full development of the novel and that early Indian novelists based their writings largely on available British models.

Many early novelists, in fact, made such overt claims. For instance, Bankim Chandra Chatterjee wrote in the preface to Bengali novel *Rajani* (1877) that his characters were based on Lord Lytton's *The Last Days of Pompeii* and Wilkie Collin's *Woman in White*. Malayalam writer O. Chandu Menon claimed that *Indulekha* (1889) was modeled on Benjamin Desraeli's *Henrietta Temple*, while Urdu novelist Mirza Hadi Ruswa acknowledged that he found inspiration for *Umrao Jan Ada* (1899) in G.M. Reynold's *Rosa Lambert*. Not many critics, however, agree that the novel was an outcome just of British handholding.

Meenakshi Mukherjee provides a counterpoint in *Realism and Reality* (1985), arguing that unlike in the West, the social conditions in India could not sustain themes like love, linear time, individualism and detailed time-space coordinates. She suggests that, 'It is a critical platitude to say that the Indian novel has a derivative form, imitated from the West. This is only superficially true. A form cannot be superimposed upon a culture which lacks the appropriate conditions to sustain its growth.'[4] Priya Joshi further confirms in *In Another Country* (1995) that despite British efforts to promote certain types of novels in India, the novel was indigenized and often operated in oppositional ways through selection by Indian readers, who preferred melodramatic and sensational novels as opposed to realist ones. She identifies in this the latent seeds of subversion against British authority. Sisir Kumar Das also concludes that the novel in India was born out of an anguished and dual approach of the Indian middle classes towards the British, and was deeply influenced by oral forms as well as translations of traditional texts.

Others like Qurratulain Hyder, a foremost Urdu-English novelist, completely deny the influence of English novels in shaping the genre in India. In the foreword to her English translation of Hasan Shah's *Nashtar* (1790), Hyder emphasized that Shah did not know the English language and therefore, his novels proved the 'original' emergence of the novel in India completely 'uninfluenced' by English novels. Tabish Khair suggested that Subandhu's *Vasavadatta*in Sanskrit or Shah's *Nashtar* in Urdu revealed the 'possibility of the autonomous development of a non-European novel', but not the novel per se.[5] Makarand Paranjape in *Towards a Poetics of the Indian English Novel* (2000) went a step further to argue that Western parameters and theories were insufficient and inappropriate for providing an aesthetic for appreciating and theorizing novels in India.

However, despite the assertions of uniqueness, the early novel in India can also be located in the broader context of all colonial novels. For instance, Frantz Fanon argued in *The Wretched of the Earth* (1961) that the works of native writers can be classified into three distinct phases. In the first phase, 'the native intellectual gives proof that he has assimilated the culture of the occupying power'.[6] His writings are inspired by European culture and reflect unqualified assimilation. In the second phase, an estranged native intellectual gets disturbed and 'decides to remember what he is',[7] invoking memories of childhood or a bygone era. In the third phase, the native 'turns himself into an awakener of the people'[8] and enters a fighting phase. From writing exclusively for the oppressor, the native intellectual increasingly addresses his own people. The national culture that arises therewith is 'the sum total of all these appraisals: it is the result of internal and external tensions exerted over society as a whole and also at every level of that society'.[9]

Fredric Jameson in 'Third-World Literature in the Era of Multinational Capitalism' (1986) forwarded the view that all third world literatures shared similar trajectories. They were a reminder of 'our own outmoded stages of our own first-world cultural development' and seemed 'as though already-read'.[10]

> All third-world texts are necessarily…allegorical, and in a very specific way: they are to be read as what I will call *national allegories*, even when, or perhaps I should say, particularly when their forms develop out of predominantly Western machineries of representation, such as the novel.[11]

Aijaz Ahmad countered this argument in his essay, 'Jameson's Rhetoric of Otherness and the "National Allegory"' (1987), by providing the example of Urdu novels:

> I cannot think of a single novel in Urdu between 1935 and 1947, the crucial year leading up to decolonization, which is in any direct or exclusive way about 'the experience of colonialism and imperialism'. All the novels I know from that period are predominantly about other things: the barbarity of feudal landowners, the rapes and murders in the houses of religious 'mystics', the stranglehold of moneylenders upon the lives of peasants and the lower petty bourgeoisie, the social and sexual frustrations of school girls, and so on.[12]

Offering a more generalized explanation for the emergence of the novel in the colonies, Franco Moretti concluded in 'Conjectures on World Literature' (2000) that Jameson's model of a compromise between 'foreign form' and 'local materials' was incomplete because the compromise was not binary but more 'triangular' in nature between 'foreign form, local material—and local form'.[13]

Despite many claims and counterclaims, questions of nation formation and nationalism have dominated theorizations of the colonial novel in India. For instance, Namwar Singh, a noted Marxist critic of Hindi literature linked the emergence of the novel in India to the nationalist turn, 'The year 1857 as the year of the First War of Indian Independence in India assumes importance here, because the novel emerged in India only after this major political event, that was not a coincidence.'[14] The emergence and popularity of historical novels, starting with in Bangla and then in several other languages during the second half of the nineteenth century, has often also been linked to the emergent nation searching for its past. Priyamvada Gopal in *The Indian English Novel* (2009) drew a distinction between English and *bhasha* novels to argue that whatever be the case with the novel in indigenous Indian languages, at least the anglophone novel in the subcontinent has 'returned repeatedly to a self-reflexive question: "What is 'India(n)?"'[15] Dilip M. Menon, however, departs from the national paradigm in 'No. Not the Nation' to ask, 'So is the Indian novel an artifact of the universal rendition of modernity, i.e. the narration of the nation, or does it express more the anxieties of a distorted colonial modernity?'[16] In another essay, 'A Place Elsewhere', he examines low-caste Malayalam novels to argue that it were religious reform and anti-slavery discourses that left a greater impact on the form of the novel than nationalism. Susie Tharu and K. Lalita, too, map the trajectory of women's representation in novels in the backdrop of the evolving nationalist discourse. In their two volume set, *Women Writing in India* (1991), they discuss at length how during the nineteenth century the focus shifted from the Hindu widow to women's education to the figure of the middle-class housewife or the *bhadramahila* defined vis-à-vis the 'crude and licentious behavior of lower-class women'.[17] And while till the 1880s, the central fictional relationship remained between husband and wife, by the 1920s a new fictional relationship between mother and son began to take center stage in the backdrop of nationalist discourses around the motherland.

The novel has also been variably examined vis-à-vis themes of East-West encounter, tradition and modernity, literacy and circulation figures, language debates, indigenous literary traditions, gender and domesticity, caste, etc. But our main concern is rooted in the singular perceived lack of linking the novel in India to the trends and predilections of the Indian middle classes. In this chapter, we will try to do precisely that. We do not seek to examine the novel of any one single language. Rather, the aim is to explore the possibility of a theoretical framework that may help us to understand novels across the linguistic divide in India. For that, we will also examine the recent success of the Indian-English novel.

The Indian-English novel, which 'arrived' on the world stage in the

1980s, is fraught with many debates. The privileged status of English vis-à-vis other languages of India has been a continued ground for discontent. For instance, Harish Trivedi writes,'Indian writing in English is to Indian literature rather like the creamy layer on top of a large jug . . . all that lies below represents a serious omission.'[18] While some scholars have argued that the Indian-English novel is less 'authentic' than *bhasha* novels, others find it to be equally if not more representative, since unlike other languages, English is not restricted to any specific 'region' of the country. The antipathy towards English has witnessed a decline in recent years with the emergence of 'Hinglish' and other macaronic variants. As Aijaz Ahmad reiterated, 'English is simply one of India's own languages now.'[19] On the other hand, questions have also started emerging in the globalized era over whether the anti-English movements of the previous decades had, in fact, served to keep certain castes and classes of people outside the corridors of power. Noting this shift in the approach towards the English language, Meenakshi Mukherjee notes that 'the most articulate champions of English today no longer come from the urban Westernized sector of society but from among the Dalits'.[20]

With a significant number of Indian-English writers based or settled abroad, their location, too, has been a matter of debate. The basic contention is whether their location warrants the label—'Indian'. While a few celebrated writers continue to live in India, many others live abroad and some are removed from India by more than one generation (some like Naipaul by even three). Writers like V.S. Naipaul or Bharati Mukherjee choose not to be labeled as Indian-English writers. Ruth Jhabvala does not favour any labels. Arundhati Roy has made her preference for an independent, mobile republic well known. Rushdie perhaps has embraced his status as an Indian born writer most enthusiastically even while many in India continue to question the validity of his claim. Many Indian-English writers are also demarcated by the time they divide between living in India and the West. Focusing on their location T. Vijay Kumar asks whether '"India" exists only in narratives that are imagined abroad?' as other writers in English 'write locally rather than nationally or globally'.[21] Harish Trivedi discusses voluntary migration by Indian English writers to argue that, 'The post-colonial project of writing back thus turns out to be writing back not to the centre but to the former colony one has exiled or displaced oneself from while occupying the centre.'[22]

The unease is also focused on content and ideology. For instance, Aijaz Ahmad faults Rushdie for his politics which is marked by an antipathy to solidarity and 'inability to believe in any community of actual praxis'.[23] While heaping high praise on Arundhati Roy's *The God of Small Things* he emphasizes that the book is damaged by how it panders to anti-communist sentiments in order to assert that 'resistance can only be individual and fragile…that the personal is the only arena of the political'.[24] Tabish Khair identifies crucial omissions or lacunae in Indian-English fiction relating to issues of caste and working class landscapes beyond the domestic since the writers are often bourgeois elites. He notes that they are more self-consciously and dramatically positioned between India and the West than most Indians but remain the most privileged section of *Babus* who are Westernized, urban, and English educated. Meenakshi Mukherjee argues that postcolonial discourses by migrant intellectuals are shaped by their desire to belong to an international community and that 'concerns like social injustices, erosion of democracy, and threat of fundamentalism'[25] may be more central to our local contexts than race, hybridity or mimicry.

As outsiders both 'in' and 'for' the West, Indian-English writers have often been viewed as transporting perspectives from the periphery to the core, tackling the challenges of existence therein, or crossing over to cast nostalgic or disingenuous backward glances at India. Others are marked by their explicit disenchantment with migration to the West. Despite postcolonial/postmodern attempts to eulogize the exile, the non-rooted artist or the hybrid who does not belong and is arguably more akin to many, there is no getting away from being 'Indian' for the globalized Indian-English novelist. For the writer in other Indian languages, there is both a dialogue with English as also a coming to terms with being ignored.

In the course of this chapter, we will focus on four interesting observations made by critics about the novel in India, (1) that melodrama, sensation and historical modes were more prevalent than realism in early colonial novels across several Indian languages; (2) that the novel developed into a popular form relatively late in south India despite better literacy rates, an earlier introduction to print and more diverse and sustained European influence in the region; (3) that after a promising beginning, the novel became a minor form of fiction compared to the short story in Urdu; and (4) that the recent generation of globally acclaimed Indian-English novelists continue to create unease in India. We will try to examine the 'why' of these critical observations by primarily linking the novel to the Indian middle classes, who, we believe, have some unique characteristics that have shaped the novel in India.

Departures in the Early Novel

In *Realism and Reality*, Meenakshi Mukherjee outlines three significant categories of early novels—novels of purpose with a focus on social reform or missionary enterprise; historical and supernatural fiction; and realist novels. Among them, she notes that the novels of romance, fantasy, legend, magical happenings, sensation and marvel were by far the most popular and numerous. She explains that this was so because the conditions necessary for sustaining realism in novels like individualism, love, social mobility, etc., were not present in India. While individualism was the backbone of the novel in England, in 'the rigidly hierarchical familial and social structure of nineteenth-century India, individualism was not an easy quality to render in literature'.[26] The theme of love too, she insists, was difficult to depict because man-woman relationship was bound in restrictive conventions of marriage and could only be portrayed in historical romances. 'The Indian novelist had to operate in a tradition-bound society where neither a man's profession nor his marriage was his personal affair. His life was mapped out by his family or his community or his caste . . . one of the problems of the early novelist was to reconcile two sets of values.'[27] Moreover, the description of nature and objects was stylized, treatment of time was often mythic, and realistic accounts of people or objects were rare. She concludes that theories of the Western novel based either on the argument of emerging bourgeoisie and capitalism, or individualism and social mobility could not be easily transferred to the historical context of India.

This theme was explored further by Priya Joshi in *In Another Country* by examining consumption patterns, library records and import of British novels to India during the nineteenth century. Joshi found that instead of Dickens or Thackeray, Indian readers preferred sensational and melodramatic novelists like Reynolds who were 'voraciously—discussed, copied, translated, and "adapted" avidly into Indian languages and eventually into the Indian novel . . .'.[28] Joshi also notes that novels written in various regional Indian languages relied heavily on elements of history, fantasy, magic, myth and the supernatural; that the use of realist techniques was rare and many Indian writers self-reflexively struggled with the techniques of realism. Joshi offers another set of possible explanations. First, she finds merit in Terry Eagleton's view that realism is primarily a 'metropolitan' form which presumes the stability of a comprehensible world running on the logic of cause and effect whereas the condition in the colonies involves 'political instability, sustained social unrest, and a very different class structure . . . [which is] amenable neither to the rise of the realist novel nor its popularity among readers'.[29] Second, Joshi argues that print culture and orality co-existed well beyond the nineteenth century in India. With oral symbolic and allegorical forms still existing, the necessary preconditions for the rise of a more objective realism were not created. Joshi also draws a distinction between novels written by Indians in regional languages and those written in English. While in the former '. . . a receding domestic literary tradition (the epic) was refashioned and made usable by the consumption of an imported form (the novel)',[30] the latter was based on emulated forms and techniques of British novels instead of engaging deeply with Indian realities and literary traditions to indigenize the novel. She suggests that this is why it took so much longer for an indigenized novel to emerge in English and its popularity followed only after that turn.

Elsewhere in her essay 'India, 1850–1900', Joshi also argues that the melodramatic mode gained popularity in India because it helped restore moral order through its use of the binaries of vice and virtue. 'The melodramatic mode provided the pleasure and satisfaction of experiencing wholeness, victory, and retribution for all the wrongs that were, in reality or imagination, visited on the community of readers.'[31] Such tropes, she proposes, helped imagine a political landscape in which the liberation struggle was fashioned. Readers in nineteenth-century India had 'an affection for romance and melodrama . . . [because] the melodramatic mode, with its narratology of stark social and moral contrasts, was more effective in interpellating Indian readers than a realism that depended on metropolitan conditions for its legitimacy—and indeed, for its legibility'.[32]

In his exhaustive survey of literary writings across several languages, Sisir Kumar Das too makes a passing reference to the fact that during its initial stages the novel in India was dominated either by the didactic or the marvelous modes. He, however, offers no explanations for the same.

These observations made by the above critics give rise to an important question. What accounts for the conditions in colonial India that gave rise to an emergent Indian middle class which became very fond of reading novels, but with considerably different concerns and preferences compared to their European counterparts? Das notes that by 1885 the novel had become the most popular literary genre in India; Joshi, too, writes that the novel became an instant success and was at least three to four times more popular than other forms in print in the late nineteenth century. The conditions were definitely not different enough to give rise to some entirely distinct class of people or a form of writing other than the novel. So, obviously there were some similarities with Europe. Of late, however, especially in historical writings about colonial India, the differences between class formation in colonial India and the West have been overemphasized and the causal linkages between the emergence of the middle class and industrial capitalism often dismissed as 'economism'. What has rightly been attacked is the view that developments in colonial India were part of some 'incomplete' process of capitalist class formation that required completion. It is argued instead that developments in India must be examined and judged on their own merit. Let us investigate if there is, in fact, a case for linking the rise of industrial capitalism in India, albeit different from the West, and the rise of the middle classes as well as early novels in India.

Partha Chatterjee in his 1991 essay 'The Nationalist Elite' demarcates the colonial Indian middle classes from those in Europe by emphasizing that the social world in India was not peopled by 'individuals' and there was no 'audience-oriented subjectivity', or distinction between man-bourgeois, man-citizen or private-public. Rather, the middle class, who he terms as 'the principal agents of nationalism', constituted a 'private' domain as different from and in resistance to Western modernity.[33] His crucial point of insistence is the distinction from Western style modernity of the European middle classes. Sanjay Joshi in his book *Fractured Modernity: Making of a Middle Class in Colonial North India* (2001) takes a different view of Indian modernity, proposing that the 'definition and power of the middle class in colonial India came from its propagation of modern ways of life'.[34] This modernity, however, was 'fractured' and involved contradictory impulses of reason and sentiment, tradition and radical change, liberty and authoritarianism, equality and hierarchy, simultaneously. Instead of occupation or education, he attributes the consolidation of the middle classes to their enterprises in the field of culture and the project of 'self-fashioning'. Unlike Chatterjee, Joshi sees strong similarities between the colonial middle classes and their counterparts in the West, insisting that the 'ideal type' of Western modernity didn't even exist in the West. The 'fractured modernity' of Lucknow, he proposes, provides reason to rethink the conceptions of modernity in the West as well. Elsewhere, in the introduction to *The Middle Class in Colonial India* (2010) he uses the term 'middle class-ness' in lieu of middle class, and critiques the elusive quest for an 'authentic' middle class evidenced in opinions throughout colonial India. These two different arguments by the two are made in the context of intensive studies of the middle classes in Bengal and Lucknow, respectively. However, Dipesh Chakrabarty in *Rethinking Working-Class History: Bengal, 1890–1940* (1989) makes a similar argument about the working classes. He demarcates the working classes of colonial Bengal by the predominance of pre-bourgeois relations based on kinship and community ties. The common thread in the readings of these historians is that the new emergent classes in colonial India did not have typical 'bourgeois' characteristics as in Europe, but bore anti-modern, traditional or pre-bourgeois values alongside 'modernity'.

It is a fact of history that colonialism introduced both a different variety of feudalism as well as capitalism in India. Let us examine this process in some detail before attempting to understand the early novel in India. With the East India Company obtaining the Diwani of Bengal in 1764 after the historic Battle of Plassey in 1757, the Company introduced proprietary rights over land in parts of Bengal, Bihar, Orissa and north Madras through the Permanent Settlement in 1793, wherein land was auctioned off to the highest bidder on the basis of taxes fixed for perpetuity. Prior to the British 'no class of landed feudal nobility with proprietary rights over land ever existed'.[35] While holding powers over revenue collection, neither the Mughal kings nor their intermediaries were owners of land. A new loyal class of landlords/zamindars was drawn from among the descendants of civil servants, revenue collectors, merchants and non-traditional ruling classes, not necessarily from among the traditional aristocratic elites. The Company also introduced the Ryotwari and Mahalwari systems of land ownership and revenue collection in other parts of India.[36]

The Company supported the establishment of the Calcutta Madrasah in 1780 and the Benares Sanskrit College in 1791. The foundation of the Asiatic Society in 1784 dedicated to oriental research, and the establishment of Fort William College in 1800 for training British officers in Indian languages, were decisive. The Serampore Press in Bengal undertook the task of recording and printing traditional and modern Indian languages and literatures. Many early Indologists promoted education in classical languages and Vedic texts with a sense of a shared Indo-European heritage.

By 1813, the monopoly of the East India Company in India ended and free trade policies were introduced. In 1817, John Stuart Mill published the *History of British India*—a strong departure from prevailing Orientalist views, for in it, Mill argued that Indian society lacked progress, reason and good governance and had remained primitive, rude and immoral. Evangelicals tended to agree with Mill and proposed that only Christianity could provide the solution to the ills plaguing Indian society. The desire for Western education, enlightenment and social reform among the aspiring classes resulted in the foundation of the Hindu College in 1817 by Raja Ram Mohan Roy along with his European friends who made a plea to the British for English education in the sciences and literatures rather than in classical texts and languages. The emergence of social reform movements and the establishment of newspapers and journals got underway with some regional variations. 'The first vernacular newspaper, *The Bengali Gazette*, began in 1816. Bombay had its first Indian press in 1861; Madras had its first Indian-owned newspaper, the *Madras Mail*, in 1868.'[37] The first professional classes like civil servants, doctors, lawyers, educationists started emerging in this period. But this development was not without its own set of tensions; social reformers clashed with the traditionalists, Anglicists with the Indologists.

The British approach underwent a shift from Indologist/Orientalist to Anglicist, i.e. from those who held some sympathy/respect towards Indian culture and languages, to those who derided native languages, culture and beliefs. The Anglicists found cause in modernizing and reforming Indian society through English education. Macaulay's *Minute on Indian Education* of 1835 famously sought to 'form a class who may be interpreters between us and the millions whom we govern; a class of persons, Indian in blood and colour, but English in taste, in opinions, morals and in intellect'. The beginning of English education also started bilingualism in the Indian education system as also the privileging of English language. By 1837, Persian was abolished as the official language of administration and was replaced by English. Many Indians established their own schools to impart education in Indian languages, and many continued to petition the British to expand the English education system in India. Debates over women's education started gaining ground. The first free school for girls was established in Calcutta in 1847. The Wood's *Education Despatch* of 1854 widened the scope of state funded education and led to the establishment of universities in the three Presidencies of Madras, Bombay and Calcutta in 1858.

During this period, the introduction of free trade policies from 1813 onwards led to a steep decline in Indian industries and exports, which were slowly overwhelmed by British imports in the backdrop of the Industrial Revolution in Britain. While some from the Indian merchant classes made gains in trading activities with the British, most who traded in indigenous products like handicrafts, spices, textiles, shipping, paper, and iron smelting started suffering losses. The peasantry, 'too', suffered and 'In the first half of the nineteenth century, there were seven famines, with an estimated total of 1½ million deaths from famine.'[38] In this phase, a nascent educated middle class started emerging in colonial India that revolved around the colonial administration and Western education.

The Revolt of 1857 was a major watershed in changing both the British approach to India and vice-versa. It shook the Company's rule to its core and an alarmed British Crown took over the reins of power by 1858. Starting with the sepoy mutiny in Meerut which was fuelled by issues of religious sanctity, twenty years of relentless wars, no increase in salary and limited promotion options, the revolt soon spread to 'almost all over North India, as well as Central and Western India. South India remained quiet and Punjab and Bengal were only marginally affected'.[39] Landlords and princes who faced annexation or threat of annexation due to non-payment of taxes joined the revolt. Peasants, artisans, religious priests, pre-bourgeois industrialists, small merchants and traders who were all in acute distress, united with over two lakh rebellious army men to try and reinstate an ailing Bahadur Shah Zafar as the Emperor of India. However, almost half of the Indian soldiers and major sections of 'merchants, intelligentsia and Indian rulers not only kept aloof but actively supported the British'.[40] The popular uprising was crushed. While constant peasant uprisings against local oppressors were the hallmark of this period, the Revolt of 1857 was the first stirring of nationalism in India. As K.N. Panikkar observes, 'The Revolt of 1857 was both a culmination and a beginning.'[41] It was an expression of the anger and distress faced by the people, but it lacked a vision of laying the foundations for a new system. Characterizing the rise of nationalism in India, Prabhat Patnaik also writes:

> Nationalism is conventionally associated with the emergence of the bourgeoisie.... In the third world context however, there is a curious development.... Since nationalism emerges in opposition to imperialism, which penetrates these societies long before they have equipped themselves with a modern bourgeois class, its first stirrings manifest themselves through the actions and perceptions of representatives of the pre-bourgeois order.[42]

Early moorings of the nascent middle classes in India can be better understood if they are located in this context. Significant sections of the emerging middle classes were drawn from among the new landed elites, merchants and privileged castes who largely benefited from British policies or trade, found employment in colonial administration or at least believed in the benign role of the colonialists. They were steeped in the neo feudal-colonial order and were often pro-British. However, large-scale repression in the aftermath of 1857 marked the beginnings of deep angst among them. The Proclamation of Queen Victoria that promised to protect all traditional beliefs and practices put an end to the possibility of further social reform like the earlier anti-sati legislation. Restrictions on freedom of press through the Licensing Act of 1857 started creating disillusionment (by 1870 the Act was amended to further add sections on sedition). Strict racial hierarchies and segregation began to be imposed. Another set of changes started occurring in south India. The Zamorin of Calicut, Maharaja of Cochin and Maharaja of Travancore in Kerala entered into pacts with the British. The Rajas of Rudukkottai, Tanjore, Arcot and Mysore subordinated their authority to the British. The Peshwa of Poona and Nizam of Hyderabad did the same.[43]

The popularity of the novel in Indian languages can be traced to the period subsequent to the revolt. A didactic and realist Bengali novel about a cheat, *Alaler Gharer Dulal*, was published in a magazine for women in 1858. A realist contemporary Marathi novel *Yamuna Paryatan* was followed by a didactic romance *Muktamala* in 1861. Bankim Chandra Chatterjee, who began his career by writing an English novel *Rajmohan's Wife* (1864), soon abandoned English and took to writing in Bengali, much like Michael Madhusudan Dutt who had done the same prior to him. After a string of popular novels, his Bangla novel *Anandamath* (1882) based on the Sannyasi rebellion during the Bengal famine of the 1770s fuelled Hindu nationalist imagination and started the modern discourse around the 'motherland'. Novels began to appear at a rapid pace in this period in various languages. Translations also gained momentum. Earlier, Lieutenant-Colonel James Tod's historiographical account, *Annals and Antiquities of Rajasthan*, had been published in two volumes in 1829 and 1831. Meenakshi Mukherjee argues that the book profoundly influenced the intelligentsia of Bengal during the latter half of the nineteenth century. 'Over a hundred narrative texts published in Bangla between 1858 and 1920 drew their raw material'[44] from this single book about the heroic past of Rajasthan. She explains that the interest in mythic history was fuelled both by British historical writings and emerging nationalist moorings to write from an indigenous point of view. Historical and pseudo-historical novels were more suited to traditional elements of storytelling like myth, romance and fantasy in comparison to realistic fiction. And since any direct challenge to British authority in print was not easy, novelists turned to the past to write about Hindu challenge to Muslim rule. The Muslims, too, wrote about their glorified past going back to Moorish domination of the Mediterranean or Spain. But as is noted by many critics including Mukherjee, not all novels were about nationalism or history. Not all were fantastic or magical, a fair number were also realist, contemporary and domestic. The post-1857 period, however, was also significant for another reason—the emergence of a domestic industrial bourgeoisie in India.

In this phase, industrial investments started gathering momentum, both by the British as well as Indians. Railways, post and telegraph expanded at a rapid pace. Plantations and commercial agriculture increased. In 1859, the Indigo Plantation Revolt erupted in Bengal. Dinabandhu Mitra's historic play *Neel Darpan* was a watershed in building middle class opinion for the revolt. Powerful peasant and tribal revolts occurred at regular intervals. For the first time, the intelligentsia in Calcutta and Bombay began to mobilize opinion in favour of these uprisings. Cotton mills, coal mines and jute mills grew at a rapid pace. Coffee plantations started expanding in southern India. A.R. Desai notes that between 1850 and 1855 the first cotton mill, a few jute mills and coal mines were set up; by 1894–5, the number of cotton mills reached 144; there were 29 jute mills and 123 coal mines. Needless to say, Europeans owned most of these industries. However, as Jawaharlal Nehru writes in *The Discovery of India* (1946), 'Slowly India recovered from the after-effects of the revolt of 1857–8. Despite British policy, powerful forces were at work changing India, and a new social consciousness was arising.'[45] Nehru identifies the development of industry and the rise of nationalism as the two most significant advances of this period and attributes the development of domestic industries to the removal of duties on imported machinery in 1860.

The Banias and Parsis who were traditionally engaged in trading and money lending initiated this process. Domestic industrialists emerged in Bombay and Ahmedabad. The Marwaris of Maharashtra, Gujarat and Rajasthan started setting up industries in various parts of India, including

Calcutta. By 1875, the Bombay Millowner's Association was formed. The India Tea Association was formed in 1881. The Indian Jute Mills Association came up by 1884, and by 1891 the Ahmedabad Millowners' Association was formed.[46] A new commercial and industrial bourgeoisie (we use the term bourgeoisie in the same sense that the middle class is used, i.e. with some differences from the West) started taking shape in India. This path of capitalist development in India was different from the West in that it occurred under colonial rule and influence. It was also different in another major respect. Unlike the early European bourgeoisie, the Indian bourgeoisie often had entrenched landed interests of its own and crucially depended upon the zamindars who invested in banks for capital.[47] As noted before, even in the West the links between the bourgeoisie and the landed elites were not entirely severed, but the dominant spirit of Western bourgeois revolutions was anti-feudal. The case was different in India. B.T. Ranadive elaborates on this, 'In Europe the rising bourgeoisie had to defeat the feudal ideology and fight the Roman Catholic Church ... [t]his was not so in India.'[48] The moorings of this emerging Indian bourgeoisie were anti-colonial but not decisively against either landed interests or against the feudal-traditional-kinship-caste based social order.

This was the second phase of the development of the middle class in India. With domestic industrial development, a new middle class whose livelihood, aspirations and interests were increasingly tied to bourgeois development started gaining in numbers. Education in the 'vernaculars' picked up. Women's education now gained grounds in different parts of India. Muslims who had largely kept away from Western style education witnessed the establishment of the nationalist Deoband Dar-ul-Uloom in 1868 and the Muhammadan Anglo Oriental College at Aligarh in 1875. Jyotirao Phule in Maharashtra pioneered education for women and the lower castes along with his wife Savitribai Phule. Despite this, the overall size of the middle class remained small. Judith E. Walsh notes that by the late 1880s the English educated elites were generally referred to as the 'middle classes' though they comprised only about 0.3 per cent of the Indian population.[49] A shift from English educated middle classes to those educated in Indian languages started taking place. K.R. Srinivasa Iyengar records in *Indian Writing in English* (1962) that 'even in 1834–5, 32,000 English books sold in India, as against 13,000 in Hindi, Hindustani and Bengali, and 1,500 in Sanskrit, Persian and Arabic'.[50] By 1911, the tables were turned and literacy figures reached 1 per cent for English and 6 per cent for the vernaculars. It is important to take into account that the spread of education was not merely linked to some esoteric awareness about the benefits of education, which could be the luxury of a few, but was also crucially dependent upon the availability of livelihood avenues based on that education. It is in this crucial regard that the development of domestic industrial capitalism was decisive for the spread of education in the 'vernaculars' and the emergence of professional classes trained in the 'vernaculars'. As Partha Chatterjee notes, the middle class or the agents of nationalism constructed a new form of public discourse 'through a modern vernacular . . .'.[51] It was not just a question of 'vernacular' education; however, the English-educated middle class also underwent a change in political attitude alongside other major developments. By 1885 the Indian National Congress (INC) came into being consisting of professionals from Calcutta, Bombay and other parts of India. This period was also a time of intensified agrarian crisis. 'In the second half of the nineteenth century, there were twenty-four famines (six between 1851 and 1875, and eighteen between 1876 and 1900), with an estimated total, according to official records, of over 20 million deaths.'[52] Major tribal rebellions took place. Despite this backdrop, the initial demands of the INC were linked to the interests of the bourgeoisie and Western-educated classes. They included representation in legislative councils, more representation for Indians in civil services, separation of judiciary, promotion of Indian industries, and abolition of unfair tariffs and excise duties.[53] The seeds of the subsequent success of an Indian style bourgeois nationalism during the national liberation movement from among competing ideologies of religious, communal, revivalist, pre-bourgeois varieties to more radical, secular, democratic varieties were sown during this period in the late nineteenth century.

In a sociological appraisal of the contemporary middle classes of India, Surinder S. Jodhka and Assem Prakash identify three 'moments' in the history of Indian middle class development—first, in the colonial period that led to the emergence of the new middle class; second, at the turn of freedom from colonial rule in 1947; and third, during the 1980s with the decline of the Nehruvian state, political churning and changing geo-political economy that ushered in economic reforms in India. In the colonial period, historians also identify the nationalist turn in the late nineteenth century as an important turning point for the colonial middle classes. Sumit Sarkar writes:

> The basic pattern was of an English-educated 'middle class' reared by British rule, engaging in various renaissance activities, and eventually turning against their masters and so giving birth to modern nationalism—out of frustrated selfish ambitions, ideals of patriotism and democracy derived from Western culture, or natural revulsion against foreign rule, the imputed motive in each case depending on the viewpoint of the scholar.[54]

This change in the orientation of the middle classes can also be understood if it it is linked to the rise of domestic industrial capitalism in colonial India.

To recall, the rise of the colonial middle classes involved a two-fold process. Initially, during the early nineteenth century, a Western-educated nascent middle class emerged, which in its livelihood and other concerns revolved around the colonial administration. Subsequently, after the 1860s, with domestic industrial development, a domestically-educated middle class versed in the 'vernaculars' also found an increasing basis for expansion. It was the nature of capitalist development in colonial India, however, anti-colonial but not anti-feudal, that shaped the character of all the new emergent classes—the industrial bourgeoisie, the middle classes as well as the working classes, none of whom were born out of any radical opposition to feudalism, the past, kinship ties, caste, religion or other pre-bourgeois modes of social organization; and all of whom were bearers of a 'fractured modernity'. They navigated several contradictions as well as a spectrum of values ranging from traditional, conservative, revivalist, communal, casteist to secular, progressive, radical, reformist, scientific and rationalist. This is not to say that they did not undergo bourgeois stirrings or experience social mobility, but that they acquired their peculiar characteristics from the manner of capitalist development in colonial India. This also became the character of the Indian national movement where communal, revivalist and conservative ideologies found expression alongside progressive and secular ideologies.

The emergence of the early novel in India can be better understood in this milieu. Historically, it is only in this second phase of colonial middle class development that the novel started finding a foothold among a wider readership. In various languages, the novel aided the emergent middle classes in making sense of the world as well as their place in it. The themes picked up by early novels ranged from magical, fantastic, fabulous and historical, to contemporary, realist, didactic and domestic. The form of the novel incorporated generic characteristics from a range of diverse living genres, both oral and print. Some early novels displayed strong elements of realism, treatment of love theme, individualism, linear time, ordinary characters, rationality, social reform and secularism. But most novels tended to deal with the past; created stock and heroic characters, relied upon supernatural and chance elements, invoked religion, and were more traditional in form. The novel's flexible form was opposed to the earlier codified forms of literature; however, the novel in India was not fundamentally opposed to the content and form of earlier genres. This characteristic was in keeping with the nature of the growing middle classes, their integral relation to emerging bourgeois culture, and the bourgeoisie's interconnections with pre-bourgeois forms of social organization. The bourgeoisie in India was both forward looking as well as traditional in its values right from its inception, and so were the middle classes. The novel, too, was modern as well as traditional both in its form and content. In this phase, the fact that a larger bulk of novels were sensational, fantastic, melodramatic and historical (more legendary) compared to realist novels can be read as a barometer of the ideological/intellectual concerns of the Indian middle classes of the late nineteenth century.

To return to the arguments put forward by Priya Joshi and Meenakshi Mukherjee, respectively, it would be incorrect to identify the paucity of realism in early novels in India to only a difference between novels in English and the vernaculars, or as rooted only in early nationalist awakening and a desire for a past. Neither were the vernaculars entirely devoid of realist novels, nor was emergent nationalism only about reviving dignity through the historical past. While it is true that Western theories of bourgeois development cannot be transported to India to understand the development of the novel, abandoning all theories of bourgeois development to understand the emergence of the novel may not be suitable either.

We have argued in the context of the earlier discussion on realism in the Western novel that realism was both an ethic as well as an aesthetic with some major characteristics—a focus on depicting the common people and ordinary lives, an emphasis on depicting the socio-historical context, an endeavor to locate cause-and-effect and an effort to capture totality. We have also stated that realist trends gained in the European novel only when the middle classes actively involved themselves in progressive causes. Modern progressive values that could sustain realism in literary writings took a considerable time emerging in India. While the bourgeoisie and the middle classes in the West became increasingly progressive in their effort to gather ranks to overthrow feudalism, the bourgeoisie and middle classes opened up to progressive values in India very cautiously in the process of building wider alliances with different classes and sections of the people in the course of building the anti-colonial freedom movement. In this context, it is easier to understand why realism that was relatively marginal in early Indian novels gained momentum by the 1930s, championed by the stalwarts of the Progressive Writers' Association, who attacked social injustices, inequality and backwardness in their writings. It was not a coincidence that this happened in a context when the national liberation movement acquired a pan-Indian mass character. As the middle classes became increasingly involved in the powerful, progressive national liberation movement, the finest realist novels got written in different languages. While a few gems of realist writings were produced in different languages throughout the late nineteenth century, the realist novel overtook the revivalist, historical (legendary) and fantastic novel in sheer numbers and popularity only when progressive and democratic ideologies overtook the intellectual concerns of the middle classes in a much wider way. This happened only by the 1930s.

What we seek to argue is not that colonial class development provides some all-purpose key to unlock the mysteries of the novel and its form in India, but that ignoring it altogether may not serve the purpose either. However, just the coincidence in the timing of the two developments—of the novel and domestic industrial bourgeoisie—hardly suffices as conclusive proof of the links between the two. So, let us put this thesis to two more tests—that of understanding the late popularity of the novel in south India and the relative marginality of the novel in comparison to the short story in Urdu.

Late Popularity in South India

Scholars have noted a crucial regional variation in the emergence of the novel in India—the late popularity and development of the novel in south India. T.W. Clark, in his appraisal of the rise of the novel in several Indian languages, notes that both prose forms as well as the novel developed late in southern Indian languages. He offers a simple explanation for the same—'Madras and Kerala had no William Carey to give the lead'.[55] R.E. Asher examines early novels in Tamil and Malayalam in the same volume. He argues that the development of prose fiction in Tamil was significantly different from other modern Indian languages because, Tamil was an ancient language with a long-standing literary tradition. He notes that the Tamil Renaissance began well during the nineteenth century with Tamil writers becoming conscious of creating something new. A few early novels emerged in the late nineteenth century but subsequently the novel form declined and did not witness resurgence till after several decades. With regard to the Malayalam novel, Asher observes that Malayali literature was ripe with lively controversies about religion, politics and literature because of the diverse population of Kerala as well as its high literacy levels. He finds the first Malayali novel *Indulekha* (1889) by O. Chandu Menon to be remarkable and outstanding, but notes that subsequent to this first novel, the genre of the novel itself developed late in Kerala.

In *Realism and Reality* Meenakshi Mukherjee discerns some shared factors between early novels across different regions based on Puranic heritage, hierarchical social structure, colonial education, disjunction of agrarian life, etc., but finds it better to steer clear of schematic categorizations because the variables in early novels were too many, starting with the nomenclature itself. For instance, the novel was called *upanyas* in Hindi, a term coined in 1862. In Marathi it took the name *kadambari*, coined in 1829. In Urdu it was called *naval* since 1868, *naval-katha* in Gujarati, *novel* in Tamil and Malayalam, and *vachanaprabandha*, loosely translated as prose fiction, in Telugu. Emphasizing these differences, she writes:

> The novel did not develop at the same pace in every language, nor was the influence of English evident in the same degree. Considering the fact that the trading centers at Calcutta, Bombay and Madras had an earlier and greater exposure to Western ways of life and thought than other parts of India and considering that the three universities in India were established simultaneously in these cities in 1858, at least in Bengali, Marathi and Tamil the development of modern literature should have followed similar lines. But in actual fact the variables were many . . .[56]

In *Perishable Empires*, Mukherjee again raises the same question and wonders, '. . . why novels in Bangla, Marathi and Tamil happened to evolve differently despite early British presence in the three coastal cities and the simultaneous establishment of universities'.[57] However, she concludes that this '. . . would be a separate area of research'.

Priya Joshi also locates the lag in the popularity of novels in south India by tracing consumption patterns. She notes that nearly 80 per cent or more of print imports to India arrived in the two ports of Calcutta and Bombay. Publishing in India in various languages increased remarkably during the second half of the nineteenth century. 'The largest number of titles published in a single year was in the Bengal Presidency: 2,425 titles in 1888, and the smallest number, 218 titles, was published in 1871 in the Madras Presidency.'[58] Mapping the record of registration of books in the three Presidencies between 1867 and 1901 Joshi notes that the highest numbers were in Bengal and the lowest in Madras.

Sisir Kumar Das brings forth the same aspect in another way. He notes that the establishment of printing presses in India started in Tranquber and Madras and reached Serampore and Calcutta much later.[59] The first Indian language to be printed was Tamil in 1551, in Lisbon, in a Roman alphabet typeset.[60] But in spite of an early introduction to the print form, the novel emerged relatively late in Tamil. Das argues that the reasons for this were many, but points to an obvious difference between Calcutta and Bombay, and Madras Presidencies. While there were similarities in the '[social reform] movements in Bengal, Maharashtra and Gujarat, . . . [which] are reflected in similar patterns of growth in literature. Similar social movements in Madras started a little later and took more time to gather momentum'.[61] This, he suggests, was because the critical spirit and the freedom of relative social mobility required for writing novels were not present in Madras. He observes that after the publication of its first novel, 'Tamil . . . took a couple of decades to exploit the potentiality of the genre'.[62] Even, Telugu saw 'sporadic original writings for several decades'.[63] 'Between *Indulekha* and the death of C.V. Raman Pillai in 1922 there were very few novels published in Malayalam.'[64] Similarly, 'The growth of the Kannada novel into a serious art-form was also rather slow.'[65]

In view of the above observations, some facts acquire relevance here because the story of bourgeois and middle class development in south India, was a bit different. While examining industrial development in south India Amiya Kumar Bagchi makes a pertinent observation, 'The whole of South India remained extremely industrially backward compared with Bombay and Bengal . . . What little industry there was up to the First World War was controlled mostly by British businessmen with some Indian collaborations in a few cases.'[66] He notes that till 1914, leading business houses in the Madras Presidency were engaged in trading rather than industrial activities. David Washbrook emphasizes that Madras did not develop a 'large expatriate-based commercial and industrial system'.[67] He also notes that the English, Portuguese, Dutch, Danish, French and German mission and trade were all present in south India and strict racial hierarchies took 'a very long time reaching South India'.[68] While discussing provincial differences in early industrial development in India, Jawaharlal Nehru notes that after the Chettys of Madras, who were leaders of banking and business from ancient times, there were no significant business houses in the south. Rather than industrialists, 'Madras, highly intellectual, has produced and still produces distinguished philosophers, mathematicians, and scientists.'[69] Sumit Sarkar takes Suntharalingam's view into account to reiterate that the commercial elites of the 1850s like the Chettys of Madras gave way to administrative and professional elites in south India.[70] Implicit in this observation is that the industrial elite did not develop at the same pace in colonial south India. Ch. M. Naidu in *Nationalism in South India* (1998) finds that 'by the end of the nineteenth century most of the native industries had already decayed beyond recovery or were on the verge of complete ruin'.[71] He argues that the demand for industrial development in Madras was a major factor in building nationalism in the region during the early decades of the twentieth century. B.R. Tomlinson also records that landlords and others with capital started investing in industry in Madras only after the 1930s.[72] The late rise of a domestic industrial bourgeoisie in south India is significant because unlike the commercial or mercantile bourgeoisie, the industrial bourgeoisie was not necessarily comprador or dependent upon colonial interests for its prosperity. It could and indeed over time did develop a relative independence of its own.

The figures for the spread of education in this period point to another set of significant facts. By the late 1880s, Madras was already ahead of Bengal and Bombay in education, a record that the region has consistently maintained since then. Comparing education figures of different regions of India, Sumit Sarkar points out:

> The Public Service Commission report of 1886—7 found 18,390 "educated natives" in Madras, 16,639 in Bengal, 7,196 in Bombay—but only 3,200 in the United Provinces, 1,944 in Punjab, 608 in the Central Provinces, and 274 in Assam.... It is certainly true that the traditional "literary" castes tended to take more easily to the new education. Thus 84.7 percent of Hindu College students in Bengal came from the three *bhadralok* castes of Brahman, Kayastha, or Vaidya in 1883–4. Brahman students predominated in Madras, Bombay, or Poona, Kayasthas were prominent in UP.[73]

That the education records of the southern states were better than the others during the nineteenth century are often attributed to investments made by princely states or the missions in education. However, education was overwhelmingly restricted to the traditional scholarly castes of the Brahmins. Sarkar notes that 'Brahman domination was less clear-cut in northern and eastern India, with other high-caste groups serving as buffers' but Brahmins constituted nearly 70 per cent of all graduates from the Madras University between 1870 and 1918.[74] At a time when north India was dealing with issues of Hindu–Muslim rift, in south India it was caste that came to occupy the centre stage. Powerful anti-Brahmin social reform movements in Madras led by Periyar gained momentum by the 1920s resulting in a range of affirmative actions in the southern princely states, including reservations, much before India's independence.

Southern India was also marginally better in its approach to the education of women. Madras University was the first to open its doors to women in 1876. Themes revolving around women in early novels as well as novels written by women can both be found in southern languages; Priya Joshi discusses two serialized novels of Krupa Sattianandhan in English at length, *Saguna: A Story of Native Charistian Life* (1887–8) and *Kamala: A Story of Hindu Life* (1893–4). O. Chandu Menon's *Indulekha* also created one of the most powerful women characters of early novels in India.

However, despite better literacy rates, including those of women, an earlier introduction to print, as well as more diverse European influence in south India, the late popularity of the novel in this region confirms that none of these factors were decisive in creating a foothold for the novel among readers. Rather, the novel gained popularity in the period between the 1920s and 30s when a domestic industrial bourgeoisie started taking roots in the southern states and gave a fillip to the development of a new middle class that was more composite in caste composition as well. It was only then that the pathways for wider upward social mobility through education and employment were created. Without domestic bourgeois stirrings, therefore, it appears that the novel could not truly come into its own.

Paucity in Urdu

Another interesting variation in the novel is its relative paucity in Urdu after a promising early start during the late nineteenth century. It is generally acknowledged that the early exponents of the Urdu novel were Nazir Ahmad, Ratan Nath Sarshar and Abdul Halim Sharar who wrote didactic novels and adventure novels based on the *quissa* and *daastan* traditions, and historical novels in the romance tradition set in medieval Spain and elsewhere, respectively. It is Mirza Mohammed Hadi Ruswa's *Umrao Jan Ada* (1899), however, which is universally acknowledged as the first fully formed novel. Written in the realist tradition, the novel is about an aged courtesan who narrates the events of her life and in the process debates with a group of young men about women, moral values, literature, etc. Set in the backdrop of the 1857 Revolt, the novel is critical of the old decadent system and traverses across different social sections. It was romance and didactic traditions; however, that continued to pre-dominate Urdu novels for quite a few decades. Munshi Premchand, the next major Urdu novelist, who wrote during the early twentieth century, took the novel away from its fantastic, historical and urban setting to provincial and rural setting. But he increasingly shifted to writing short stories in both Urdu and Hindi.

By the 1930s, the Progressive Writers decisively changed the trend of Urdu fiction. Firmly entrenched in realism, the new generation of writers threw up a string of radical poets and short story writers. The publication of *Angare*, a collection of short stories in 1932 transformed the Urdu literary landscape. A generation of stalwarts of the Urdu short story like Ghulam Abbas, Sadat Hasan Manto, Rajinder Singh Bedi, Krishan Chander, Ismat Chugtai, etc., soon made their mark. Since then, the Urdu short story has never looked back. It is not the case that Urdu novels were not written in India anymore—the novels of Qurratulain Hyder and others appeared at regular intervals; but on the whole the novel was slowly overshadowed by the short story. As early as in 1945, in *A Critical Survey of the Development of the Urdu Novel and Short Story*, Shaista Akhtar Banu Suhrawardy compared Urdu short stories to novels to conclude that 'The "afsana" [short story], a still later arrival, is even more securely established, and its achievements have been even more remarkable . . . the short story has a more promising future than the novel.'[75] While making a cautious prediction, she still heaped praise on the inherent superiority of the novel form. Her intuitive forecast, however, came true; by now, it is commonly observed in the context of Urdu literature that *ghazal is to poetry what the short story is to fiction*.

Ralph Russell in his essay, 'The Development of the Modern Novel in Urdu' also comments on the arrested development of the Urdu novel that, 'Some of the factors that hold back the development of the novel are undoubtedly economic. Urdu writers work in a community where the standard of living is low and the percentage of illiteracy is still very high.'[76] M. Asaduddin in 'First Urdu Novel,' while contrasting the achievements of the Urdu short story with that of the novel remarks, 'the achievement of Urdu novel (Indian) in the twentieth century is rather a lack-luster affair'.[77] Asaduddin endorses Nirmal Verma's view that the failure of Urdu writers to dive into the abyss of impersonal, a-historical and myth laden memories accounts for the lack of any 'Great Tradition of the Urdu Novel'. In *A History of Urdu Literature*, Ali Jawad Zaidi notes that the short story made a late appearance as a literary form in Urdu but 'grew into the most popular form of fiction'.[78] He also notes that the size of Urdu readership was limited by the fact that 'vast majority of readers belong to the lower middle classes'.[79] While making a case for not ignoring minor forms of early Urdu fiction, Christina Oesterheld of her essay 'Entertainment and Reform: Urdu Narrative Genres in the Nineteenth Century' explains the shift away from the longer *dastaan* tradition as a probable outcome of the lack of leisure time. But she is perplexed by the shift away from the much shorter *quissa* as well. She asks, 'Why were they replaced by novels, and later short stories, by the rest of the reading public?'[80] In passing, she too refers to the subsequent prominence of the short story in Urdu but offers no explanations for the same.

Before we make our suggestion, it is important to situate the Urdu language in context. In many ways, the history of Urdu language is quite unique. Unlike many other languages of India it is not confined to any specific geographical region. English education and Western influence were very contentious issues among early Urdu writers. During the nineteenth century, the evolution of Urdu literature witnessed a bifurcation into the Western influenced Delhi school and the more indigenous Lucknow school; early Urdu novelists came from both these schools. By the end of the nineteenth century, however, the language became a part of the raging communal controversy. Sumit Sarkar notes that '"communalism" proper was acquiring, for the first time in the 1880s and 90s, something like an all-India dimension and the two principal issues were the Urdu-Devanagri controversy and cow protection'.[81] Despite the fact that both Urdu and Hindi had roots in spoken Hindustani, Urdu was now beginning to get bracketed with the Muslims and Hindi with the Hindus.

Alok Rai records that the controversy over Urdu precipitated after 1877, when the knowledge of Urdu was made compulsory for official employment in northern India. Following this, throughout the 1880s and

1890s there were demands for the replacement of Urdu with Hindi in the Devanagari script. The order for compulsory requirement of Urdu was withdrawn in 1896 and by 1900 the use of Devanagari was permitted by the British in the north-Western regions. Rai calls this decision 'a crucial, even inaugural, moment in a durable and long-running process of the invention and exacerbation of animosities'.[82] Pondering over the discomforting link between Urdu and the Muslims, he asks:

> . . . are Hindi and Urdu two names of the same language, or are they two different languages? does Urdu become Hindi if it is written in the Nagari script? is Hindi Hindu? is Urdu Muslim, even though Muslims in distant Malabar have been known to claim it as their mother tongue? The only reasonable, *and maddening*, answer to all these questions is, well, yes and no.[83]

Shamsur Rahman Faruqi, a foremost contemporary Urdu critic and writer, argues that 'In independent India, severe punishment was meted out to Urdu, because it was equated with a language that divided up the country.'[84] He notes that the language experienced a decline and is now confined largely to religious schools in 'ignorance of the true spirit of Urdu's cultural tradition'.[85] The changed status of Urdu, he argues, must be acknowledged:

> It is neither wrong nor discreditable, I feel, that we now begin to declare, unequivocally and openly, that Urdu is the language of the Muslims of north India. I also oppose the apologetic view whereby Urdu is presented as the language equally of Hindus and Sikhs. Let's be honest. Today Urdu belongs only to Muslims. Yes, it was the language of Hindus and Sikhs at one time. But no more.[86]

Many practitioners of Urdu continue to plead that the language must not be associated with any particular religious community. Others locate the decline of Urdu language to the decline of the Muslim community in India. Yet others associate the decline of Muslims to the treatment meted out to Urdu.

Whatever be the case, the saga of the decline of Urdu as well as the Muslims of India began in the nineteenth century. Judith E. Walsh notes that 'Northern Indian Muslim elites saw their control over positions in regional government services steadily declining in the second half of the 19th century, from 65 percent in 1857 to 35 percent by the early 20th century, as Muslims lost ground to English-educated applicants from Hindu trading, money lending, and professional communities.'[87] The controversies continued even after independence. In 1951 Hindi was declared the sole official language in Uttar Prdesh with Urdu losing out its place.[88] Even as late as 1978, the then Home Minister of India, Charan Singh, held Urdu responsible for the partition of India.[89]

Writing in 1990, Mushirul Hasan in 'Adjustment and Accommodation: Indian Muslims After Partition' argues, 'Today, the language of Mir and Ghalib survives lazily in the alleys and by-lanes of Muslim localities and is grasping for breadth in government-sponsored academies. Both in the Nehruvian and post-Nehruvian era, Urdu has been deliberately stifled, nay destroyed, by prejudices against a language as well as a community.'[90] Among the many recommendations made by the Prime Minister-appointed Justice Sachar Committee in 2006 for improving the socio-economic and educational status of the Muslim community, the promotion of Urdu-medium education figured prominently.

Assuming that the fate of Urdu in Indian history is inextricably linked to the Muslims, an interesting fact regarding the stymied bourgeois development of the Muslims in colonial India presents itself. There are two basic stories—one that views the Muslims as having always been backward in industry, and another that finds certain developments in the decades of the 1920–30s to be decisive. Jawaharlal Nehru links the industrial backwardness of the Muslims to their lack of English education by suggesting that 'Moslems were thus, in the second half of the nineteenth century, backward in English education and therefore in contacts with Western thought, as also in government service and in industry.'[91] Others like Timur Kuran and Anantdeep Singh in 'Economic Modernization in Late British India: Hindu–Muslim Differences' (2010) suggest that the Islamic beliefs and practices of the Muslims of India that prevented investments in emerging capitalist enterprises were responsible for their economic backwardness.

Gyanendra Pandey in his study of political developments in colonial Uttar Pradesh traces the economic decline of the Muslims to the decades of the 1920s and 30s. He argues that these developments contributed to intensifying the political schism between religious communities in the run-up to independence. Recording them in the city of Kanpur he notes:

> Business and industry dominated the economic and political life of the city. As has been noted, the First World War provided a considerable stimulus to these activities.... To a large extent those who thus accumulated wealth were Hindus, though Muslims also had their share in two limited but fairly lucrative fields—the leather trade and haberdashery. As it happened, however, even those Muslims who had some place in the commercial and industrial life of the city proved to have less luck than their Hindu fellows. The leather trade ... inevitably slumped after the war ... the handloom industry was extremely hard pressed ... the economic fluctuations of the 1920s and 1930s ... made important groups of Muslims feel especially deprived. Some of them were even led to believe that their loss was the Hindu's gain.[92]

B.T. Ranadive emphasizes the same shift, but in a more generalized context of the whole India. In *India's Freedom Struggle* (1986) he writes:

> The Indian bourgeoisie arose mainly out of the Hindu trading and other sections. In the earlier years, in Bombay, certain big bourgeois groups arose out of the Muslim merchant class; but by 1930, the year of the international crisis of capitalism, they disappeared. Jinnah's earlier years perhaps represented the advance of the Muslim bourgeoisie.... Besides, in the 1930s, the biggest Muslim industrial groups—the Currimbhoy Ibrahim group—went bankrupt. Muslim capital now remained mainly in trade and commerce.[93]

These observations suggest that the emergence of a nascent industrial bourgeoisie among the Muslims of colonial India did indeed take place. However, this process suffered a setback during the 1920s and 30s. The timing of this decline coincides remarkably with the fate of the novel, which was soon overtaken by the short story in fiction.

The industrial backwardness of the Muslims in India continued even after these decades. Asghar Ali Engineer in his essay 'Muslim Middle Class and its Role' (2001) writes:

> The Indian Muslims, unlike the Hindus, never developed modern entrepreneurial class. The Muslim ruling classes right up to partition of the country in 1947 remained feudal. There was no modern industrialist worth the name among Muslims then or even now.[94]

In 'Problems of the Muslim Minority in India' (1976), Irfan Habib, Iqtidar Alam Khan and K.P. Singh identify the economic and industrial backwardness of the Muslim minorities as one of the major areas of continued grievance in post-independence India.[95] The *Sachar Committee Report* published in 2006 records a declining trend in graduation attainment rates between Muslims and other communities and concludes that the bulk of the Muslim population in India is engaged in artisanal activity, petty trade or petty industry. They note that no sizable middle class among the Muslims of India has come to the fore; the fate of Urdu language and literature is rooted in this overall context where a mass of Urdu reading middle class born out of bourgeois development simply does not exist.

How does one situate the trajectory of the Urdu novel in this context? The Urdu novel has experienced some exceptional practitioners of the form right from the nineteenth century to the more recent *Makaan* (1989) by Paigham Afaqui or *Kai Chand the Sar-e-Aasman* (1998) by Shamsur Rahman Faruqi. The early Urdu novel made its appearance in the late nineteenth century at a time when Urdu was more prevalent. 'As late as the decade 1881–90, 4380 Urdu books had been published in U.P. as compared to 2793 in Hindi while the corresponding circulation figures for newspapers were 16,256 for Urdu and 8002 for Hindi. Even Premchand wrote mainly in Urdu down to 1915, till he found publishers difficult to obtain.'[96] Something changed in this period. The language was increasingly identified with the Muslims. The nascent development of an industrial bourgeoisie among

Muslims also got stymied. While educated sections continued to grow among Muslims, their growth was painfully slow and not necessarily related to bourgeois stirrings. Even in contemporary India, a significant number of Muslims who undertake higher education in universities do not engage in employment based on their qualifications, but return to petty trade and more traditional forms of livelihood. Despite education they do not transform in what can legitimately be called a 'middle class'. The small elite among Muslims who have no knowledge of Urdu have switched almost entirely to English.

Unlike novels, the Urdu short story that found a foothold among readers does not presuppose a comprehensive bourgeois individualistic appraisal of society. It caters to those who can read, and can carry bourgeois as well as non-bourgeois sensibilities. During much of the twentieth century, the short story seems to have helped the Urdu reading public come to terms with fragments of modernity. Without industrial bourgeois development among the Muslims of India, the novel in Urdu appears to have turned into a relatively minor literary form and has just not found the suitable conditions to flourish.

The three cases put together—the growing popularity of the novel after the 1860s in various Indian languages alongside the development of a domestic industrial bourgeoisie; the late popularity of the novel in the south with the late development of an industrial bourgeoisie; and the stymied development of the novel in Urdu after the 1920s–1930s alongside the stymied development of industrial bourgeoisie among the Muslims of India—make a case for linking the rise and development of the colonial novel to domestic bourgeois development. This is not to argue for some simple one-to-one correlation between the two. Rather, ignoring this fact altogether in trying to understand the rise or even the form and content of the novel may not do justice to the history of the colonial novel. The fact that the middle classes navigated a range of concerns ranging from revivalist to rationalist cast its shadow on the early novel, its form as well as content, which too ranged from traditional to more modern.

The aim is to cautiously suggest that further investigation is required in the two-fold development of the middle classes in colonial India, besides and alongside the nationalist turn. Also, that greater investigation is also required in tracing the similarities in the moorings of all the new classes formed by capitalist development in colonial India—the industrial bourgeoisies, the middle classes as well as the working classes. And that more differentiation needs to be drawn between those professional middle classes that were a byproduct only of education and those whose rise accompanied the development of domestic industrial capitalism in India, in order to make better sense of the colonial novel. Based on the evidence presently available, it appears safe to say that linking the colonial novel to the specific characteristics of capitalist development in India may help understand both its rise as well as the preferences of its early innovators in both form and content. The concern to avoid 'economism' in recent scholarship must not make us susceptible to prejudices of another kind.

Unease with the Globalized Indian-English Novel

The final point of enquiry is the unease within India with Indian-English writers, especially the generation that emerged after the 1980s—more specifically after the dazzling entry made by Salman Rushdie's *Midnight's Children* in 1981. Since then, growing numbers of Indian-English writers have made their mark globally. Many now feature regularly on international awards lists. Unlike the early practitioners who were self-conscious and uncomfortable in their use of English, the current generation of writers have made English their own, changed it and made the world reckon with the changes. Even while they have embraced and have been embraced by the global English speaking world, they continue to generate polarized opinions in India with many viewing them as 'inauthentic' and 'overrated', especially vis-à-vis *bhasha* writers. Of course, Rushdie's controversial comment in 'Damme, This is the Oriental Scene for you!' (1997) only added fuel to fire—'prose writing—both fiction and nonfiction—created in this period by Indian writers working in English is proving to be much stronger and more important body of work than most of what has been produced in the eighteen 'recognized' languages of India'.[97] In 2002, V.S. Naipaul too made similar dismissive comments about *bhasha* literature. The unease is clearly mutual.

In order to understand this state of affairs, let us first place the Indian-English novel in context. The present generation of writers represent the second coming of the Indian novel in English after the first generation of the 1930s. R.K. Narayan, Raja Rao and Mulk Raj Anand emerged almost simultaneously after the 1930s when the national liberation movement started acquiring a pan-Indian mass character. The spread of the freedom struggle connected the English speaking regional elite through common nationalist moorings, created a situation where the novel in English could find a wider readership as well as voice. The second generation of Indian-English writers, too, was located at a particular turn in post-independence history—the period when the ruling elite of India started moving away from Nehruvianism and third-world nationalism towards neoliberal globalization. Aijaz Ahmad in his essay 'On Post Modernism' (2011) provides a broad schematization of the post-independence period:

> ... between Independence and the Emergency, let us say—as a phase of Indian Modernity, in continuation with the pre-47 Independence Movement ... [t]he

second phase begins with the declaration of Emergency when a full-blown crisis of the Congress paradigm manifested itself in the suspension of liberal democracy itself . . . the 1975–1990 years can be regarded as a transitional phase between one (so-called 'Nehruvian') paradigm to another ('neoliberal'), we can say that the period between 1991 up to the present has witnessed the consolidation of the latter paradigm, with much turbulence during the 1990s, then more smoothly during the period just behind us.[98]

The turn away from Nehruvianism based on welfare state and planned economy to neoliberalism was not easy either for the nation or the middle classes. It was several decades in the making. After the enthusiasm of the early years, after independence, by the 1960s, disillusionment with the hopes generated by India's freedom started setting in. By the early 1970s, amidst growing political discontent, Prime Minister Indira Gandhi tried to garner dwindling public support with the slogan of poverty eradication (*garibi-hatao*). During the Emergency of 1975–7 the government tried to orient itself leftwards. It amended the Indian Constitution to include socialism as one of the key state principles and nationalized several strategic sectors. These half-hearted efforts, however, were discredited because of the accompanying excesses, repression and authoritarianism. The people rose up to defend democracy. After the Emergency, the first non-Congress government of the Janata Party assumed power at the Centre. But it was unstable and ideologically, too, divided. In 1980, Indira Gandhi again returned to power but this time with distinct rightward and Hindu religious overtones. This was the beginning of the shift of the Indian ruling elite away from secularism and other Nehruvian values, a trend which only intensified in the years to come and created massive social schisms to culminate in the decisive ushering in of neoliberal policies in 1991 and the demolition of the Babri Masjid in 1992.

The 1980s was a decade of prolonged anguish. Nascent sections of the Indian elite started advocating for free market capitalism as a panacea for the ills plaguing India. Located in the middle, the middle classes were torn between the pulls of an aspiring bourgeoisie and the pauperized under-classes. Could they turn their backs on the poor or should they come to their aid? Were they to try and carry the goals of the freedom struggle forward, could they be carried forward, or were they to make peace with their principles and their conscience? The bourgeoisie, too, was divided between the globalizing big and the apprehensive middling and trading sections. The under classes were also pulled apart. Regional aspirations, separatist movements and chauvinist concerns gained political grounds, with the most alarming being the rise of the Hindu right wing. The year 1984 saw the assassination of Indira Gandhi by Sikh separatists, and 1991 witnessed the assassination of Rajiv Gandhi by the LTTE. A fundamental challenge was posed to secularism from the virulent Ram Janmabhoomi movement. The late 1980s also saw the turbulent implementation of Mandal Commission recommendations with vehement opposition from upper-caste elites.

In the 1980s, another development made its presence felt in the intellectual life of India. This was the emergence of the Subaltern Studies group in 1982 which slowly started gaining in influence and international reputation. Sumit Sarkar, one of its initial members, locates the early moorings of this group in his essay 'The Decline of the Subaltern in *Subaltern Studies*' (1997):

> *Subaltern Studies* emerged in the early 1980s in a dissident-Left milieu, where sharp criticism of orthodox Marxist practice and theory was still combined with the retention of broad socialist and Marxian horizon. There were obvious affinities with the radical-populist moods of the 1960s and 1970s, and specifically with efforts to 'write histories from below'.[99]

Subsequently, Sarkar dissociated himself from the later phase of this group arguing that the early trends of writing better Marxist histories increasingly paved way for a 'neo-traditionalist anti-modernism'. He criticized the group for undercutting civil, secular, democratic, feminist and liberal individual rights along with class in their repudiation of the Enlightenment, while maintaining silence on the ideology of the free market, which too was derived from the Enlightenment.

Aijaz Ahmad also characterizes the Subaltern School by its anti-Nehruvianism and extreme opposition to universalism, rationalism, secularism and nationalism. Their broad rubric of anti-statism, he concludes, 'only serves the ideology of market fundamentalism'.[100] The Nehruvian era, he argues, was debunked by a combined intellectual onslaught from Anglo-American neoliberal scholarship, the Hindu communalists as well as Indian postmodernists which included the subalterns.

Let us now digress a bit to examine three Indian-English novels before trying to locate the unease with them in a broader context.

Midnight's Children

The dazzling entry made by Salman Rushdie's *Midnight's Children* in 1981 was sandwiched between the emergence of the Subaltern Studies group in 1982 and the beginning of the rightward shift within India's ruling elite. It had elements of convergence with both. Like the Subalterns, Rushdie, too, wrote a history from below relying on unusual sources like gossip, memory, oral accounts, myths, legends, literature, journalism, mass media, popular culture, etc., to cover the history of the subcontinent starting from the

Jallianwallah Bagh massacre, the role of the Muslim league, to the partition riots, five year plans, state reorganization, Sino-Indian and Indo-Pak wars, the liberation of Bangladesh, and the Emergency. It was not a coincidence that both Rushdie and the Subaltern Studies group shared common roots in Cambridge history. Saleem Sinai's fictional autobiography was essentially a commoner's claim on history. The claim made on behalf of an individual, not a collective, aptly relied upon magic realism. A symbolic historian, Saleem, a pickle factory worker, undertook the task of preserving both memory and fruit, of changing flavor in degree, to give it shape, form and meaning so that, 'One day, perhaps, the world may taste the pickles of history.'[101]

Rushdie's magic realism was admittedly inspired by Gunter Grass, Gabriel García Márquez and the oral traditions of India. Magic realism has been employed variously by various writers. Grass used it to bring forth a repressed narration of the epochal violence of the World War II and the trauma of Germany's fascist history. Márquez and many Latin American writers employed it to come to terms with the unreasonable and irrational in their societies, to create elaborate allegories in times of censorship and repression. It was not surprising, therefore, that Rushdie's novel, too, was written during the Emergency. But in his hands, magic realism was strictly a rationalist's tool, employed not to confront the unfamiliar or the traditional, but to make strange and magical much of which was otherwise reasonable. The novel had a telling self-reflexive comment on his art—'the magicians were people whose hold on reality was absolute; they gripped it so powerfully that they could bend it every which way in the service of their arts; but they never forgot what it was'.[102] The attraction of *Midnight's Children* lay not in its magic, but in the trick of magic, the performance of the magician. In that, Rushdie was more like an illusionist than a magician. Within the novel, Saleem's caretaker and future wife Padma provides a consistent foil to Saleem's narrative exuberance with her skepticism. By the end, even Saleem doesn't believe in his fantastic tale and admits that 'There have been illusions in my life; don't think I am unaware of the fact.'[103]

Born at the stroke of midnight on 15 August 1947, Saleem's future is tied to India's future both literally and metaphorically. A thousand and one children born within the first hour of India's independence are bestowed with diverse miraculous powers and comprise the midnight's children. Among them Saleem is demarcated by his powers of telepathy making him a relay station like the All India Radio. His abilities also periodically switch on and off like the radio. Nehru's letter at his birth is ominous—'Your life, which will be, in a sense, the mirror of our own ...'.[104] An Anglo-Indian by birth, a bastard child of a departing Englishman and a servant woman who could not survive childbirth, Saleem is switched in his cradle by Mary Periera with the child of a Kashmiri couple. The other child Shiva, who is denied his rightful place and never discovers the truth, remains Saleem's adversary. Saleem's son, Aadam Aziz, the bastard child of Shiva and Saleem's wife Parvati, is a child of the Emergency, born with grotesque ears and a steely will and determination. These hybrid births are reflective of the postcolonial angst as well as the emergent ambidexterities of neoliberalism. Mothered and fathered by many, Saleem neither tries to chase his authentic family history linked to his biological parents, nor correct historical wrongs.

Spanning an entire timespan between 1917 to 1978, through Kashmir to Amritsar, Agra, Delhi, Bombay, Pakistan, Bombay, Karachi, the Rann of Kutch, Bangladesh, Sundarbans, Delhi, Benares, Delhi and back to Bombay, the city of Saleem's birth, the narrative spares and endorses none. Through the travails, Rushdie is decisive in damning India's post-independence history, an act that he accomplishes through Saleem—'[T]he nearly-thirty-one-year-old myth of freedom is no longer what it was. New myths are needed; but that's none of my business.'[105] This disengagement was also a sign of things to come—the political cynicism of India's middle classes and their subsequent turning away from the underclasses to aspire for a self-serving upward mobility. Rushdie's protagonist analyses his mistake—'Politics, children: at the best of times a bad dirty business. We should have avoided it . . . But too late. Can't be helped. What can't be cured must be endured.'[106]

It is Indira Gandhi's wrath during the Emergency that drains the children of all hope till they disappear into the 'healing privacy of the crowds'.[107] An early prophesy about Saleem is fulfilled—'He will be old before he is old! *And he will die . . . before he is dead*.'[108] Haunted by the ghosts of his past, a disintegrating Saleem concludes that neither he nor the subsequent generations would be able to avoid the 'annihilating whirlpool of the multitudes, and . . . live or die in peace'.[109] In that, the novel predates a kind of 'end of history' refrain. At the last leg of the autobiography, it is not just Saleem but India that stands exhausted, direly in need of 'new myths', with a dystopia looming large. The dystopia symbolized Rushdie's approach towards the emergent myths, poised to be born, not out of optimism, but deep disenchantment and failures.

In many ways, Rushdie's novel was inaugural in the literary and intellectual articulation of the disenchantment with Nehruvianism, a theme that was repeated by many subsequent Indian-English novelists. *Midnight's Children* captured a crucial historic juncture, acted as a potent bridge, opened up a new conversation with the globalizing West, a conversation which was simultaneously positioned in the West as much as it was in

India. It voiced the moorings of the middle classes of India, disillusioned and wearied by the goals of the freedom struggle. It also offered a new ideological perspective laced in cynicism, disengagement and playful irony. Getting past the sheer brilliance of the elaborately contrived plot and numerous innuendos, the conclusions Saleem reaches can be discerned—abandon politics, give up all hopes for a utopian future, discard the masses-and-classes/capital-and-labour/us-and-them paradigms, adopt a grotesque narcissism, and renounce the logic of cause-and-effect.

In Rushdie's own words, the novel was an attempt to reclaim his Indian origins. In doing so, Rushdie, as old as his protagonist Saleem Sinai, shared the dilemmas faced by many other third-world novelists who also found their hopes and aspirations fading away. Some turned leftwards and took more proactive political positions, many turned cynical, and many others shifted rightwards. By debunking third-world nationalism, Rushdie's novel carried one of the necessary intellectual preconditions for inaugurating the new 'myth' of neoliberal globalization in India. Rushdie's dystopia was not tragic but surreal, ironic, satiric and comic. As events in Saleem's personal life became magnified to propel the history of the subcontinent, history itself wreaked havoc on him and his family with perverse consequences. While the novel has often been discussed for its teeming history—mythic, oral and political—the power of the novel also lay in capturing the plight of a nation poised at a crucial historic turn, and at the same time inaugurating its future.

Like the subalterns after him, Rushdie's most intimate ideological engagement, too, was with the Left, only to depart and move away. While the novel begins and engages itself with Lenin's *What Is To Be Done?* on Saleem's grandfather's shelf, his grandfather's radical friends and atheism, the radical Joseph D'Costa, Mary Periera's crime prompted by a brief impulse of enforcing class justice, the Communist Nasir Qasim (Nadir Khan), the split within the Indian Communists, and the Communist Picture Singh, the head of the conjurer's ghetto; by the end—'Communism had seeped out of them.'[110] Saleem's resolve to 'save' India could not fructify for—'we simply could not think our way out of our pasts'.[111]

Rushdie had his own omissions and commissions. Gandhi hardly featured except through oblique references to hunger strikes or vows of silence in domestic squabbles, or a deliberately mistaken reference to his date of death. In the history of the subcontinent there were hardly any farmers. In a country that was soon to see issues of social justice and backward caste assertions take the political center stage, there was hardly any mention of caste. But then Rushdie did not make claims to capturing totality. In fact, he expressed the characteristic postmodern suspicion of totality. His protagonist Saleem wondered, '... is this an Indian disease, this urge to encapsulate the whole of reality? Worse: am I infected, too?'[112]

Over the years much has been written and discussed about Rushdie's prose, his innovative use of Indian English, and his élan with puns, parodies, innuendos. His narrative is rich in references and potent in its invocation of myths. Rushdie delights in his tongue-in-cheek parodies because his irony is always a double irony. It is as much an irony on the narration and the narrator, as on the characters and history. If one conclusion is drawn, the corollary is also often true.

The second coming of the Indian-English novel was poised at this globalizing juncture. Contentious as neoliberalism was in India, it was interesting that both Rushdie as well as the Subaltern Studies group found affinity with neoliberalism's postmodern varieties of dissent, and that both were positioned equally in India as in the West. Over the years, successive generations of globalizing and postmodernizing Indians have read and taken delight in *Midnight's Children*. Rushdie wrote many more remarkable novels by bending history to the service of fiction, but in no other work could he anticipate the historic turn and the future as potently as he did in this novel. While Rushdie became very controversial with the publication of *The Satanic Verses*, the overall unease with his variety of writing is rooted in the fact that even after thirty years there is still no consensus in India on debunking Nehruvianism. Despite high economic growth, there is still no consensus on neoliberalism. And despite the increasing influence of postmodernism in the academia, there is still no consensus on its philosophical moorings either. With the world today getting increasingly wary of neoliberal globalization and it once again seems to be in need of new myths. Rushdie, as an artist in living 'exile' could once grasp the unfolding history of India with remarkable perception and intuition. It remains to be seen whether he would keep on revisiting the same history or seek to create the new myths of the future. But for that, he may have to shed his entrenched positions and live up to the claims of being a true exile.

The God of Small Things

Arundhati Roy's *The God of Small Things*, published in the fiftieth year of India's independence in 1997, turned its author into an overnight sensation. The novel was written between 1992 and 1996, which were turbulent years in India's history. The decade witnessed the ushering in of neo-liberal policies in 1991, the demolition of the Babri Masjid in 1992 and unprecedented corruption scandals rocking the country. By the year 1996, the first BJP-led NDA government came to power at the Centre for thirteen days causing major alarm among secular sections, followed by a short-lived alliance stitched together against the communal formation with some initiative from the Communists. During the same years the issue of social justice against upper caste domination began making its presence felt more powerfully in politics. The main discourse at the global level at that time was about the collapse of erstwhile socialist countries and the 'end of history'. The novel, published in 1997, received the Booker prize and immediately began to polarize opinion in India—partly for its style and philosophy, partly for its sexual frankness, for attacking the Communists and for upsetting the Syrian Christian community.

Written in a poignantly feminine voice, the novel, like Rushdie's, is also dystopic. Roy's dystopia, however, is tragic and traumatic, not playful. Like in *Midnight's Children* here, too, there is a pickle factory which produces some hybrid variety of pickle. There is also a kind of telepathy between the Siamese twins, Rahel and Estha, who can hear each other's thoughts. Sections of the narrative toy with magic realism and the contempt for politics is also a shared feature. Like with Rushdie, it is the loss of childhood that is regretted the most, yet unlike his narrative, Roy's novel is mostly about the longing for love. Roy's plot goes much beyond Rushdie's flirtations with incest. And while history is also very important for Roy, her narrative does not teem with historical details; rather, her's is more of the a-historical variety of history.

In the novel the laws of 'History' are juxtaposed against the anarchy of 'Nature.' The symbolism of the 'History House' of the English pedophile Kari Saipu embodies Roy's disdain for the historical as opposed to the natural. It is significant that in the general milieu of pessimism prevailing both in India and the world, where the triumph of capitalism over socialism hardly made things any better, Roy's history did not stand for any optimism about the future, nor for any nostalgia for the past. Nature, in the novel, acts as a foil to all man-made laws aimed at imposing order. It also has its unpredictability, anarchy and rhythms.

The plot of *The God of Small Things* revolves around how—'Things can change in a day.'[113] Starting with the return of thirty-one year old Rahel to Ayemenem in Kerala, after a gap of twenty-three years, to meet her twin brother Estha, the narrative takes us back and forth in time to the mystery of that fateful day in 1969, the day of 'Terror', which spelled catastrophe for the seven year old twins, their mother and her untouchable lover. The narrative culminates in the consummation of two relationships twenty-three years apart—that of Rahel and Estha, and their mother, Ammu and Velutha. The twins incestuously share 'not happiness, but hideous grief'.[114] And Ammu and Velutha bear the disastrous consequences of violating 'Love Laws. That lay down who should be loved. And how. And how much.'[115]

The 'natural' Ayemenem provides the backdrop to the bid by people across generations to escape from the 'social' Ayemenem and return, but to no avail. Ammu is compelled to return to Ayemenem from Delhi after her father's retirement, tries to escape through an inter-religious marriage to Calcutta only to suffer an abusive husband and return from the tea estates of Shillong and Assam with her 'half-Hindu hybrid' twins. Similarly, Velutha, the untouchable carpenter, disappears from Ayemenem for four years. It is not clear if he had joined the naxalites, had been in prison or was just working in another town. Rahel, Ammu's daughter, spends a few happy days in Ayemenem before the catastrophic day of 'Terror' leads to separation from her mother and brother. Expelled from schools, she grows up to move to Delhi to complete a degree in architecture, drifts into marriage with an American, goes to Boston, gets divorced, does odd jobs in New York and Washington, finally to return to Ayemenem after her brother Estha is sent back by their Baba before his migration to Australia. Estha's childhood bid to escape to Africa to become a 'Mobile Republic' is doomed by the accidental drowning of Sophie Mol. Chacko, Ammu's brother, a Rhodes Scholar, returns from Oxford after marriage and divorce, to teach at the Madras Christian College. Returning to Ayemenem after his father's death, he immigrates permanently to Canada after his daughter's drowning. Eighty-three year old Baby Kochamma, too, joins a seminary in Madras in her youth and converts to Roman Catholicism in her elusive pursuit of a visiting Irish monk, Father Mulligan, only to find him becoming a Vaishnavaite at Rishikesh. It is clear that no one in the novel finds any companionship or fulfillment. The angst and futility of migration both across national borders as well as within the country, remains a running theme in the novel with no one being at home and everybody sort of living in exile. Written a decade and a half after *Midnight's Children* the novel dissociated the state of exile from the specificities of location to make it a more general state of being. Roy's approach towards migration also emerged from the hindsight of a couple of years of familiarity with globalization.

Issues of caste, patriarchy and sexuality were central to Roy's scheme of things, with many characters living ambidextrous lives in a postcolonial setting. Pappachi, the patriarch, is extremely violent towards his wife and daughter, and refuses to believe Ammu that any Englishman could want to covet another's wife. On the other hand, he helps Velutha train as a carpenter to gain a German design sensibility in his school for the untouchables. Mammachi, the matriarch, is scathing in her class and caste biases and grudges her English daughter-in-law, Margaret, for being a shopkeeper's daughter. She is also livid and unforgiving towards Ammu for her affair with Velutha. Ammu's self-proclaimed Marxist brother, Chacko, reveres his ex-wife, but also flirts with women workers in his pickle factory on the pretext of organizing Party classes and has no qualms in denying Ammu her share in the family property. Vellya Paapen, the father of Velutha, exposes his son's affair for what he considers is insolence. Comrade Pillai, the 'chameleon' and 'professional omeletteer' is secretly resentful of Velutha for the unease he creates among other workers by his caste, refuses to intervene in the hour of crisis, but is eager to utilize Velutha's killing for his designs on the pickle factory. Inspector Thomas Mathew, a Congressman, has no qualms in being lawless, brutal and opportunistic. All are complicit in their shared patriarchy and intolerance for the untouchables. In her enthusiasm to expose the hypocrisies of the world, however, Roy made some avoidable references to Communist leader, E.M.S. Namboodiripad which were not based on fact. In combination with the overplayed influence of the Peking-inspired Naxalites in Kerala, Roy's scathing dislike for the CPI(M) was located in the general middle class disdain for politics, a more specific petty-bourgeois radical urge for idealism, and the wider global anti-communist mood. The overall pessimism and simmering anger of her world view sought a better world, albeit with no solutions in sight.

All families and relationships in the novel are dysfunctional, with only two brief sexual relations providing some fulfillment. But even these are marred by social taboos, on account of caste and incest. The unions, in any case, are built upon ruins. In the case of the twins, the unspoken trauma of the telepathically shared sexual abuse of Estha by the Orangedrink Lemondrink Man forms the basis of their bond, alongside the subsequent blame for Sophie Mol's accidental drowning, as well as the compulsion of Estha (who is silenced into unspeakable grief) to testify falsely against Velutha. Ammu is attracted to Velutha for '[s]he hoped that under his careful cloak of cheerfulness, he housed a living, breathing anger against the smug, ordered world that she so raged against'.[116] With Velutha's resistance to her breaking down, the two are drawn into a fatalistic relationship—'instinctively they stuck to the Small Things. The Big Things ever lurked inside. They knew that there was nowhere for them to go. They had nothing. So they stuck to the small things.'[117] In the novel, the realm of the sexually forbidden embodies Roy's protest as well as search for reprieve.

The other poignant reference is to a Kathakali performance by artists returning from the city. The performance, watched in rapture by the young twins, Rahel and Estha, is full of danger, madness, and complete despair—it is 'To apologize to the gods for corrupting their stories. For encashing their identities. Misappropriating their lives.'[118] The enactment of Karna's story from the Mahabharata invokes a child abandoned by his mother Kunti because he is born out of love laws and dies unfairly to keep his promise to her. The killing of Dushashana by Bhim is ominous of the ensuing injustice, violation, violence and catastrophe. The performance is, entirely personal for the artists and the connect felt by the twins, too, intensely personal.

Roy's indignation towards caste is very powerful and comprises a major theme of the novel. Roy holds everyone to task for the prevalence of caste oppression in society—those who believe in the caste system and practice it, those who do not object, as well as those who submit and endure. No one is left untouched by the consequences. The Syrian Christian Church, the State, the Communists and the family, all are complicit. Accused of rape, murder and kidnapping, Velutha is brutalized and killed as he holds no chance against the forces at play. His description in the novel, though sublime, is more as the eroticized 'other'—all body and soul, retaining a boyish smile from his childhood and a bearer of many virtues and sensitivities. Only those who are thick skinned and willing to trample upon others to serve their own ends, like Baby Kochamma or Comrade Pillai can live in relative peace. Others are doomed to live and hurt.

In the novel, Roy captured an entire mood of deep discontent and anguish prevailing in India. But the ultimate culprits identified in the novel—history and love laws—were too vague and general. Roy's simmering indignation towards injustice was accompanied by a sense of helplessness and loss. The protest was private, sexual and in silence. The characters lived and suffered in the margins. It was only apt that her language and prose were highly symbolic. In literary history, symbolism has always been a device employed in times that lack clarity. Her evocative symbolism provided the basis for connecting with the readership over a gloomy commentary on the world. The Indian Communists, who bucked the worldwide trend of socialist reverses, received her maximum contempt for not submitting to the general environment of pessimism.

Roy wove the entire drama within the confines of a local town and one family. The tragedy was simultaneously collective, a-historical as well as intensely personal. Roy rejected meta-narratives and the big picture in favour of 'small things'. By being local, she connected with the global. However, over fifteen years later, it must be said that Arundhati Roy, particularly in her essays, has increasingly been engaging with the big picture. She is tracing the roots of individual miseries to systemic causes. The streak to protest by offending average sensibilities remains, as does her powerful symbolism. But as an activist-writer, whether she will choose to embrace only the margins, or will harbor real ambitions to make the margins grow, will determine the nature of her next novel in the making.

Sea of Poppies

The trajectory of Amitav Ghosh as a writer is different from the previous two authors. He first earned his reputation in India to then slowly acquire an international one. Like *Sea of Poppies*, many of his previous novels, too, were historical novels. *Sea of Poppies*, published in 2008, was followed by

River of Smoke in 2011, both parts of the Ibis trilogy, the third part of which is still awaited. After exploring many bye lanes and alleyways of history, Ghosh, in this novel, took on the core issue of empire. His ability to reflect potently on the present through the medium of an allegorical novel, was what made this historical fiction remarkable on a standalone basis.

Sea of Poppies came out in the same year as debutant Aravind Adiga's *The White Tiger* and both novels competed for the Man Booker Prize. Both were about India and China and were published in the backdrop of the global economic crisis, with the two countries bucking the trend and continuing their growth stories. Adiga's novel was a contemporary racy pastiche, full of quotable quotes and sensational events screaming out of newspaper headlines. In it, a low caste driver, murderer and entrepreneur in his own right, exposed the underbelly of India's growth story (much like the movie *Slumdog Millionaire*) through his letters to the Chinese Premier. Adiga pricked the conscience of his Indian middle class readership sitting uneasy on a heap of hypocrisies and injustices. Adiga's novel was different in many regards from Ghosh's; the most crucial being that Ghosh was firmly anti-imperialist while Adiga was still rooting for neoliberalism. Predictably, *The White Tiger* won the award. The investigation of myriad hypocrisies, injustices and oppressions also permeates Ghosh's novel. It goes to Ghosh's credit that his criticism of contemporary imperialism also came with an inward glance; a critical eye upon India, connecting the dots between a multitude of home grown problems and the workings of the empire.

The novel is about the Anglo-Chinese Opium Wars with the action starting in 1838 India. Ghosh introduces a host of characters who, under varying compulsions and motivations, converge on a ship, the Ibis, which sets sail for Mauritius from Calcutta. Most of those who board the ship remain unmindful of its true purpose in the scheme of the impending war. The novel ends with the Ibis, carrying various victims, collaborators and fortunes seekers navigating a raging storm on the high seas near Singapore, with some of its passengers jumping ship.

The work of a very deliberate artist, the novel is structured into three neat parts—Land, River and Sea—divided into seven chapters each. The novel begins with the vision of a large ship seen by Deeti, the peasant woman, 'at once blind and all-seeing', while bathing in the Ganga. A sketch of the ship immediately finds place in her private shrine. The Ibis and the characters are then introduced one by one as those who would ultimately become part of her pantheon. The first part predictably traces the unfolding lives of various characters on land, the second navigates the river and the third is set on the seas.

Deeti, married to a crippled Rajput ex-sepoy, an opium addict, employed at the opium factory in Ghazipur, northern Bihar, is escaping persecution from family members after his death. Dramatically rescued from her sati pyre by Kalua, an untouchable from the same village, the two are united in love by their respective sexual violations and sheer desire for survival. Her escape with the low caste Kalua is a point of no return. The opium factory is owned by the East India Company and the harvest is meant for illicit trade to China, already being resisted by the Chinese Emperor. A war may be imminent. Starting at the opium producing fields, through the opium factory in Ghazipur via opium traders and opium transporting ships, the novel puts us on route to the destination of opium trade in China.

The author introduces a host of diverse characters. An enthusiastic twenty three year old American, Zachary Reid, the son of a Maryland freed woman, reaches India on board the Ibis, a former slave ship, charting a difficult eleven months long journey from Baltimore, through Patagonia and Mauritius to Hoogly. Serang Ali, the head of the *laskars*, the crew of the Ibis, has his own hidden motivations. Benjamin Burnham, a powerful Evangelical trader, the new owner of the Ibis, owns one of the biggest estates in Calcutta and operates a fleet of ships. Jailed at Port Blair as a child, educated at the missions, having started off as a clerk at a trading firm to obtain a free merchant indenture from the East India Company in 1817, he began by transporting convicts to move on to bidding for opium auctions in China. By 1838, he has amassed a fortune. A free trade fundamentalist, he does not believe in leaving crucial decisions to the British Parliament and is planning to make the Ibis a part of a secret expedition to take on the Celestials.

The brunt of his philanthropy and charity is felt by Miss Paulette Lambert, the orphaned daughter of a French botanist, who was born in India and is more at ease in the local dress, language and customs. Adopted by the Burnhams after her father's death, she neither shares their racism nor zeal, and her growing troubles carry the full ideological import of the historic transition of power from the Orientalists to the Evangelical Anglicists in India. Nobo Krishna Panda, the agent of the Burnhams is a moneylender, facilitator and intermediary who is fluent in English and manages to climb up the social ladder by his endless ability to tolerate abuse. A Vaishnavite by faith, the mystic in him slowly takes over and he remains one of the prime movers of the plot as well as its chief source of humor.

The highly educated Raja Neem Rattan Halder, the Zamindar of Raskhali, experiences a dramatic turn of events. Inheriting the curse of family investments in immovable wealth, he loses his estate within two years to tragically find himself in the curious company of Ah Fat, an addict and the illegitimate son of a Parsi businessman and a Dan girl from Guangzhou.

Jodu or Azad Naskar is a spirited young Muslim boatman who grew up serving the Lamberts with his mother. Miss Paulette is like a sister to him. After his mother's death, he longs to sail the sea. These and many other characters converge on the Ibis. Among them are also indentured labourers and *girmitiyas* (peasants) who are made to exchange their names for money and disappear. Others like Heeru or Munia are driven by personal troubles. Each of these characters is revealed to have a backstory. This interesting ensemble of characters drives the plot forward and Ghosh brings his historical and anthropological expertise to bear on many interesting details, including recreating the pidgin-creole language of the *lascars*.

Some shortcomings, however, remain. Similar to Roy's Velutha, the portrayal of Kalua, the powerful giant, does not move much beyond the agency of body and instinct. While Ghosh is sensitive to the history of peasant distress in colonial India, there are no fleshed out peasant characters. Deeti, the peasant woman is too resourceful and brave, and does not undergo the prevarications of the rooted peasantry before migration. Issues of caste, gender and sexuality are more central to her character than class. In fact, all of Ghosh's characters are too resourceful to paint a realistic picture and resolve many contradictions almost too easily. But it has to be granted that Ghosh wrote this novel in the general milieu of 'yes, we can', a fever that was gripping the United States and also the rest of the world. In depicting Raja Neel's turmoil, Ghosh returns with his tried and tested formula to focus on the loss of hygiene to depict the loss of social status. While remaining a powerful symbolic purge, Ghosh's repertoire has to be expanded. Yet, these are minor glitches in an otherwise commendable novel.

One can read *Sea of Poppies* just for its interesting plot and history, but Ghosh essentially created an allegory for the present. He admittedly wrote the novel with a sense of simmering rage against the Iraq war. Providing the key to reading the novel he commented, 'Oil is the opium of today.' By revisiting the history of the Opium Wars, Ghosh made a scathing commentary on contemporary wars, capitalism, free trade and evangelicalism. Without compromising on historical accuracy, the similarities he dug up were uncanny. For instance, for Burnham free trade was almost like one of God's commandments and he believed—'war, when it comes, will not be for opium. It will be for a principle: for freedom—for the freedom of trade and for the freedom of the Chinese people.'[119] The parallels with the Iraq war that was allegedly waged to secure the 'freedom' of the Iraqi people were hard to miss. The havoc created by the heady cocktail of free trade and 'clash of civilizations' doctrine, was critiqued by Ghosh by exposing the motivations of the nineteenth-century colonial empire. Burnham, at least, was very clear that 'British rule in India could not be sustained without opium—that is all there is to it, and let us not pretend otherwise.'[120] Opium was introduced as an ominous force early in the novel. By allowing the nineteenth-century Empire to reflect on twenty-first-century imperialism, Ghosh created a remarkable piece of fiction.

At the time when Ghosh was writing the novel, Barack Obama's race for Presidency had already gained momentum in the United States. The mood had turned anti-war with the American people demanding a course correction from the Bush era. The mixed race character of Zachary Reid in the novel embodied all the promise held out by Barack Obama. In the same year, in the backdrop of the economic crisis in the US it appeared that the drama may shift to the growing economies of China and India. Within India, the high-pitched debate over the Indo-US Nuclear Deal was at its peak. Through his historical plot Ghosh integrated these debates; and through his Indian characters, Ghosh interrogated whether India would become a junior partner of the empire, a collaborator in its injustices, or would it chart out a different path? The novel was infused with all the promise held out by that moment.

By now, the situation has changed. While the economic slowdown of Western economies continues, the growth momentum of India and China has subsided. The Presidency of Barack Obama has only confirmed how difficult it is to change the course of imperialism. The Indo-Us Nuclear Deal has been signed and sealed and the entire high pitched debate has turned into a kind of anti-climax. By the time, Ghosh published the second part of the trilogy in 2011, *River of Smoke*, the anthropologist in Ghosh took over and the script got lost in too many details. We all know that the historic Opium Wars ended with the humiliation of China and the triumph of the empire. Is this the story that Ghosh would want to script today? It is up to Ghosh's resourcefulness to dig up aspects from the past to reflect on the dynamics of the Empire, India and China of today to create his third novel. While *Sea of Poppies* remains a remarkable historical novel on a standalone basis, it can be argued that it is the vision of the final part of the trilogy that would really cement Ghosh's status as one of the great novelists of our times.

~

We have examined these three novels briefly because we consider them to represent three different responses of the middle classes to contemporary times. Rushdie, a first generation migrant to the West made his place by rejecting third-world nationalism and riding the tide of postmodernism. He brilliantly anticipated the unfolding turn in India's history. Arundhati Roy, wrote poignantly about the global and Indian dystopias. Amitav

Ghosh created his finest novel when he combined the debate raging at the heart of imperialism as well as in India. While, Rushdie is a magic realist with great interest in politics, Arundhati Roy is a symbolist with an assumed subalternity, and Amitav Ghosh is a realist who harbours interest in history, culture and political economy. All three writers belong to different literary traditions as well as diverse traditions of dissent—Rushdie, with his confirmed political disenchantment, Roy with her defiance, and Ghosh with his determined resourcefulness. All three are rooted as much in the debates in India as in the West.

Theorizing the evolution of Indian-English novelists, Mukherjee argued in 1990 that the second generation betrayed an anxiety of Indianness. She drew a distinction between the first and second generations of Indian-English novelists as well as Indian-English and *bhasha* writers:

> If the anxiety of Indianness in Raja Rao, Anand and Narayan came out of their own desire to be rooted, the anxiety of the new generation who can thrive on easy international accessibility may be attributed to the pressures of the global market place which demand that . . . [their writings] be perceived as a national allegory. . . . The writer in an Indian language may not perceive the thirdness of his world as acutely as the average writer in English does, because the first world of the Hindi, Marathi and Bengali writer may well be where he/she lives.[121]

By 2008, she revised her opinion to write that 'In the decentered post-modern novels of today, colonialism and nationalism, the twin impulses of earlier fiction seem to have spent themselves, dissolving to some extent the clear-cut "self and other" oppositions.'[122] Characterizing this generation of writers as 'Third World cosmopolitans', Timothy Brennan also suggested, 'We have for some time now been witnessing a shift from a binary otherness to a single, internally rich and disparate plurality: a variety of levels within and sites between, rather than the lonely outposts on either side of the belief's wall.'[123] He viewed this cosmopolitanism as largely employed in the service of maintaining imperial cultural hegemony.

Yet, neat schematizations of Indian-English novels do not easily hold. For instance, while characterizing Indian-English writing as 'babu fictions' Tabish Khair made an exception for Amitav Ghosh. Mukherjee, too, found Vikram Seth and Amitav Ghosh to be bereft of the anxiety of Indianness. She credited Vikram Seth for being more akin to the *bhasha* traditions and for not giving in to the terms of the market; and observed that Amitav Ghosh did not attempt to prove anything or frame his writings as a metaphor or deal with issues of marginality or hybridity, interrogating instead the concept of a totalizing India. Many, including her, have also expressed surprise at why an Indian-English novel like Kiran Nagarkar's *Cuckold* (1997) could not receive its due share of attention abroad.

Mukherjee made her disappointment evident: '... the literary republic also has its frontiers, passports, and I would like to add, mysterious ways of issuing and denying visa'.[124]

In our times the scenario within Indian-English writing has evolved further. With the phenomenon of Chetan Bhagat and others, Indian-English writing has found a foothold within India on an unprecedented scale. A sizable home grown readership for English has evolved. In recent years, translations, too, have increased manifold from Indian languages to English as well as English to Indian languages. After the decades spent in discussing women's writing, the literary phenomenon of Dalit writers is the current center of discussion. As yet Dalit writings comprise more of autobiographies than novels. So, while significant sections of the English readership in India are still reading and enjoying the 'cosmopolitan' sensibility of Rushdie and Arundhati Roy, large numbers have started voraciously consuming Chetan Bhagat who represents the concerns of those who are not yet globalized but aspire to be. And, emerging Dalit writers in English are recording the experiences of a first generation that is still 'becoming' middle class while living under the shadow of globalization. These writers do not exist in independent or mutually exclusive universes but are critically aware of each other. The contemporary novel in India exists in such a terrain. It is no longer valid to assume that the English speaking population of India is some unitary and homogenous entity. The simple binaries of Indian-English and *bhasha* writings may no longer hold.

It makes better sense to situate Indian-English and *bhasha* writings in the context of the stratification of the middle classes in India under neoliberalism, rather than in the sole domain of language and literary traditions. Much has been made about the rise of the middle classes in contemporary times. With high growth, the middle classes have experienced unprecedented prosperity and expansion. While some sections of the Indian middle classes are linked to the most advanced outposts of global capitalism, others are still joining middle class ranks as first generation learners everyday. The language, intellectual make-up and literary concerns of these different sections are considerably different and so are the novels they read. They are also bearers of several contradictory values and beliefs. The caste composition of the middle classes still remains skewed in favour of the upper castes, and customary practices like dowry and son-preference continue unabated.

Other classes and fields are affected too. For instance, it is commonsensical to now refer to the schism that exists between 'national' and 'regional' politics in India. Yet, regional politics is not of a homogenous variety. In cinema, the discussion is often focused on movies aimed at multiplex and single screen theatre releases with all the accompanying connotations of urban-small town, experimental-formula, art-mass entertainment, etc. The Indian State has its own set of accompanying hypocrisies wherein it decriminalizes same sex relationships in the capital city of Delhi at one stage but refuses to confront 'honour' killings by Khap Panchayats in neighbouring Haryana. The list can go on.

While the debate often manifests itself in terms of binaries, what it conceals is a wider spectrum. While one end of the spectrum often finds the other 'elite', 'inauthentic' or 'out of touch with Indian reality,' the other finds the former 'backward' and 'outdated'. A writer like Rushdie has nothing but impatience for much of what is being written in India, but others find him presenting an inauthentic account of India. Issues of sexual frankness in Arundhati Roy's writings are perceived as an elite luxury by many.

A reflection of this unease can also be found in literary theorizations. For instance, examining the entire scenario of novel writing in India, Mukherjee found the repeated invocation of myths to be one of its most perplexing characteristics. In her 2006 essay 'Epic and Novel in India' she wrote:

> Thus epics in India do not belong to the past alone—they are also part of contemporary consciousness.... Not only do novelists in many Indian languages continue to reinterpret specific incidents and derive symbols, narrative structures, and moral dilemmas from this inexhaustible reservoir; even in public life and political action the rhetoric from these epics is used to sway emotions and to aid and abet violence, and tropes from these provide material for constructing alternative ideas of the nation in currently raging ideological battles across the country.[125]

On the other hand in his 2011 essay 'On Post Modernism' Aijaz Ahmad found the popularity of postmodernism in India 'ironical' because postmodern analysis presupposes structures of advanced capitalism or at least the existence of post-industrial societies, which cannot be found in a primarily agrarian society like India.[126]

The range is perhaps best manifested in the kind of marriages and relationships that we witness in middle class India today. There are marriages arranged by family members based on strict enforcement of class-community-caste based choices which involve customs like matching *kundlis*, horoscopes and the constellation of stars; arranged marriages within caste-community constraints wherein periods of courtship simulating love marriages are permitted by family members; own-choice marriages where caste-community-class conveniently converge in the exercise of individual choice; own-choice marriages across caste-community-class divide that are faced with varying degrees of violence including killings, social boycott and hostility from families; own choice marriages across caste-community divide that are accepted by family; marriages in accordance with religious rituals; civil marriages without religious or customary rituals; short term live-in relationships wherein partners part ways by mutual consent for marriages in accordance with respective family wishes; sustained long term live-in relationships, as well as same-sex relationships. All these types exist in India today. Their sheer range reveals the underlying complex value systems of the contemporary middle classes. The generation of young novelists writing since Chetan Bhagat is negotiating precisely these relationships in their writings. It is only a matter of time before a work from such a writer would combine critical acclaim with popularity.

If we factor in *bhasha* sensibilities, the range of values and ideologies of the middle classes of India get even more complicated. In keeping with their colonial origins, the Indian middle classes still negotiate several contradictions in their daily life and live with a 'fractured modernity'. Revivalist to rationalist concerns still remain alive. But today, it cannot be said that *bhasha* novels do not already have an entrenched postmodern tradition. Many *bhasha* writers, too, are negotiating issues of migration, some cross-border but most across regions in India. Elements of nostalgia, the pain of uprooting as well as the desire to belong in urban cosmopolitan locales can all be traced in *bhasha* writings. Yet others are still writing more locally in small town milieus. The theoretical and conceptual universes of Indian-English and *bhasha* writings do not exactly overlap, but there are elements of both convergence and divergence.

The debate between Indian-English and *bhasha* writings is symptomatic of the deeper unease rooted in the stratification of the middle classes in neoliberal India. A simplistic English-*bhasha* divide or unitary categories of Indian-English and *bhasha* fictions no longer capture the contemporary scenario which is much more nuanced and layered. Both Indian-English novels and *bhasha* novels have evolved to cater to multiple sections and sensibilities of the middle classes. The challenge for the novelists of today, be it of English or of other Indian languages, is to be able to capture a totality extending from the frontiers of globalized life to the farthest reaches of our society populated by millions of poor, exploited and marginalized people living with decisively different concerns and values. Without this, the novels produced from one end of the spectrum would continue to seem alien and disconcerting to the other.

This brief examination of a few aspects pertaining to the emergence and development of the novel in India seeks to make this limited point that the middle classes remain pertinent and relevant to understanding novels today. As the middle classes have grown in size and diversity, however, discussions about their links with the novel have receded. The middle classes are often taken for granted in literary theory and ignored. There is, no doubt, a great need to enrich our understanding of the middle classes in order to make better assessments about the novel and to understand novels better to make sense of this increasingly influential class. Novel studies provide an interesting intersection for both—for understanding novels and their evolving literary techniques and concerns, as well as for comprehending the middle classes and their negotiations with the world around them.

Notes

1. In *Indian Literary History: Essays on the Nineteenth Century*, ed. Stuart Blackburn and Vasudha Dalmia, there are discussions on many nineteenth century forms considered relatively minor today like *quissa, dastaan, katha, charit, kavya*, Tamil poetic and performative traditions, Parsi theatre, etc., which were flourishing to a greater extent than the novel and impacted the novel.
2. See, Franco Moretti, *The Novel: Volume One, History, Geography and Culture* and *The Novel: Volume Two, Forms and Themes*, Princeton and Oxford: Princeton University Press, 2006.
3. T.W. Clark, ed., *The Noble in India: Its Birth and Development*, London: George Allen and Calwin Ltd., 1970, p. 18.
4. Meenakshi Mukherjee, *Realism and Reality: The Novel and Society in India*, New Delhi: Oxford University Press, 1985, 2005, p. 99.
5. Tabish Khair, *Babu Fictions: Alienation in Contemporary Indian English Novels*, Oxford India Paperbacks, Oxford University Press, 2001, 2011, p. 41.
6. Frantz Fanon, *The Wretched of the Earth*, tr. Constance Farrington, Harmondsworth: Penguin Books, 1963, 1982, p. 178.
7. Ibid., p. 179.
8. Ibid.
9. Dilip M. Menon, 'No. Not the Nation: Lower Caste Malayalam Novels of the Nineteenth Century', in *Early Novels in India*, ed. Meenakshi Mukherjee, p. 50.
10. Frederic Jameson, 'Third-World Literature in the Era of Multinational Capitalism', 1986; Brydon, Diana, ed., *Postcolonialism: Critical Concepts in Literary and Cultural Studies*, vol. II, London & New York: Routledge, 2000, p. 542.
11. Ibid., p. 45.
12. Aijaz Ahmad, *In Theory: Classes, Nations, Literatures,* New Delhi: Oxford University Press, 1999, p. 118.
13. Franco Moretti, 'Conjectures on World Literature', in *New Left Review* 1, January–February 2000.

14. Namwar Singh, 'Reformulating the Question', in *Early Novels in India*, ed. Meenakshi Mukherjee, Sahitya Akademi, 2002, 2005, p. 4.
15. Priyamvada Gopal, *The Indian English Novel: Nation, History, Narration*, Oxford: Oxford University Press, 2009, p. 6.
16. Ibid.
17. Susie Tharu and K. Lalita, eds., *Women Writing in India*, New Delhi: Oxford University Press, 1991, p. 8.
18. Harish Trivedi, 'India and Post-colonial Discourse', in *Interrogating Post-colonialism: Theory, Text and Context*, ed. Harish Trivedi and Meenakshi Mukherjee, Shimla: Indian Institute of Advanced Study, 1996, p. 239.
19. Ahmad, *In Theory*, p. 77.
20. Meenakshi Mukherjee, *Elusive Terrain: Culture and Literary Memory*, New Delhi: Oxford University Press, 2008, 2011, p. 4.
21. T. Vijay Kumar, 'Introduction', in *Focus India: Postcolonial Narratives of the Nation*, ed. T. Vijay Kumar, Meenakshi Mukherjee, Harish Trivedi and C. Vijayshree, Delhi: Pencraft International, 2007, p. 12.
22. Trivedi, op. cit., p. 243.
23. Ahmad, *In Theory*, p. 158.
24. Aijaz Ahmad, 'Reading Arundhati Roy *Politically*' in *Arundhati Roy's God of Small Things*, ed. Alex Tickell, London and New York: Routledge, 2007, p. 119.
25. Mukherjee, *Elusive Terrain*, pp. 187–8.
26. Mukherjee, *Realism*, p. 7.
27. Ibid.
28. Priya Joshi, *In Another Country: Colonialism, Culture, and the English Novel in India*, New York: Columbia University Press, 2002, p. 4.
29. Ibid., p. 131.
30. Ibid., pp. xviii–xix.
31. Ibid., p. 505.
32. Joshi, 'The Novel', p. 505.
33. Partha Chatterjee, 'The Subalternity of the Nationalist Elite' in *The Middle Class in Colonial India*, Sanjay Joshi ed. , Oxford, New York: Oxford University Press, 2010, pp. 94–118.
34. Sanjay Joshi, *Fractured Modernity: Making of a Middle Class in Colonial North India*, Oxford and New York: Oxford University Press, 2001, p. 2.
35. A.R. Desai, *Social Background of Indian Nationalism*, Bombay: Popular Prakashan, 1948, 1976, p. 37.
36. The British did not replicate the Permanent Settlement in other parts of India. They opted for Ryotwari settlements in Bombay, Sind, Berar, Madras, Assam and some other areas wherein taxes and rents were imposed upon individual cultivators who became owners of their land for a period of thirty years. Mahalwari settlements were created in some northern parts of India wherein the British entered into settlements with groups of villages/mahals. This meant that land became a property, which was owned, purchased, sold and mortgaged. Two forms of property were thus created—landlordism and individual peasant ownership. A new class of moneylenders emerged all

across India at a rapid pace. Cash payment of taxes generally had a ruinous impact on the peasantry.

37. Judith E. Walsh, *A Brief History of India*, New York: Facts On File Inc., 2006, p. 127.
38. R.P. Dutt, *India Today*, Calcutta: Manisha, 1940, 1986, p. 125.
39. Bipan Chandra, *India's Struggle for Independence*, New Delhi: Penguin Books, 1989, p. 31.
40. Ibid., p. 38.
41. K.N. Panikkar, 'From Revolt to Agitation: Beginnings of the National Movement', in *Five Essays: Indian People in the Struggle for Freedom*, New Delhi: SAHMAT, 1998, p. 25.
42. Prabhat Patnaik, 'Introduction', in *Five Essays*, p. 5.
43. E.M.S. Namboodiripad, *A History of Indian Freedom Struggle*, Trivandrum: Social Scientist Press, 1986, p. 44.
44. Mukherjee, *Elusive Terrain*, pp. 154–5.
45. Jawaharlal Nehru, *The Discovery of India*, Jawaharlal Nehru Memorial Fund-Oxford University Press, 1946, 1996, p. 330.
46. Desai, p. 206.
47. Ibid., p. 205.
48. B.T. Ranadive, 'India's Freedom Struggle',in *Social Scientist*, vol. 14, no. 159–60, August–September 1986, p. 93.
49. Walsh, op. cit., p. 133.
50. K.R. Srinivasa Iyengar, *Indian Writing in English*, New Delhi: Sterling Publishers Private Ltd., 1962, 2011, p. 28.
51. Chatterjee, op. cit., p. 95.
52. Dutt, op. cit., p. 125.
53. Panikkar, op. cit., p. 34.
54. Sumit Sarkar, *Modern India, 1885-1947,* Chennai: Macmillan India, 1983, 2011, p. 5.
55. Clark, op. cit., p. 10.
56. Mukherjee, *Realism*, p. 15.
57. Meenakshi Mukherjee, *The Perishable Empire: Essays on Indian Writing in English*, Oxford India Paperbacks: Oxford University Press, 2000, 2005, p. 23.
58. Joshi, *In Another Country*, pp. 144–5.
59. Sisir Kumar Das, *A History of Indian Literature 1800–1910: Western Impact: Indian Response*, New Delhi: Sahitya Akademi, 1991, 2000, p. 33.
60. Stuart H. Blackburn in *Print, Folklore, and Nationalism in Colonial South India*, Delhi: Permanent Black, 2003, records that the first book to be printed in any Indian language was in Tamil, in 1577. He argues, that while the print technology was brought to the West coast in 1556, it led to 'no large-scale conceptual shifts, no new mentalities, no "logic of print".' (10)
61. Das, *Western Impact*, p. 113.
62. Sisir Kumar Das, *A History of Indian Literature 1800–1910: Struggle for Freedom: Triumph and Tragedy*, New Delhi: Sahitya Akademi, 1995, p. 278.

63. Das, *Struggle*, p. 280.
64. Ibid., p. 281.
65. Ibid., p. 282.
66. Amiya Kumar Bagchi, *Private Investment in India: 1900–1939*, New Delhi: Orient Longman and Cambridge University Press, 1972, 1980, p. 189.
67. David Washbrook, 'South India 1770–1840: The Colonial Transition', in *Modern Asian Studies*, vol. 38, no. 3, Cambridge University Press, 2004, p. 492.
68. Ibid., pp. 479–516.
69. Nehru, op. cit., p. 334.
70. Sumit Sarkar, '"Middle-class" Consciousness and Patriotic Literature in South Asia', in *A Companion to Postcolonial Studies*, ed. Henry Schwarz and Sangeeta Ray, Malden, Oxford and Victoria: Blackwell Publishing, 2000, 2005, p. 254.
71. Ch. M. Naidu, *Nationalism in South India: Its Economic and Social Background (1885–1918)*, Delhi: Mittal Publications, 1998, p. 80.
72. B.R. Tomlinson, *The New Cambridge Economy of India, Vol. 3: The Economy of Modern India, 1860–1970*, Cambridge, New York and Melbourne: Cambridge Histories Online @ Cambridge University Press, 1993, 2008, p. 183.
73. Sarkar, 'Middle-Class', pp. 252–3.
74. Sarkar, *Modern India*, p. 58.
75. Shaista Akhtar Banu Suhrawardy, *A Critical Survey of the Development of the Urdu Novel and Short Story*, London: Longmans, Green & Co., 1945, p. 304.
76. Clark, p. 140.
77. M. Asaduddin, 'First Urdu Novel: Contesting Claims and Disclaimers', in *Early Novels in India*, ed. Meenakshi Mukherjee, New Delhi: Sahitya Akademi, 2002, 2005, p. 142.
78. Ali Jawad Zaidi, *A History of Urdu Literature*, New Delhi: Sahitya Akademi, 1993, pp. 390–1.
79. Ibid., p. 441.
80. Christina Oesterheld, 'Entertainment and Reform: Urdu Narrative Genres in the Nineteenth Century', in *India's Literary History: Essays on Nineteenth Century*, ed. Stuart Blackburn and Vasudha Dalmia, Delhi: Permanent Black, 2004, p. 205.
81. Sarkar, *Modern India*, p. 79.
82. Alok Rai, *Hindi Nationalism*, India: Orient Longman, 2001, 2007, p. 20.
83. Ibid., p. 4.
84. Samsur Rahman Faruqi in an interview to Ather Farouqui, 'The Problem of Urdu in India—Political or Existential?: An interview with S.R. Faruqi', tr. M.U. Memon in Annual of Urdu Studies 10 (1995), p. 158.
85. Ibid., p. 164.
86. Ibid., p. 162.
87. Walsh, op. cit., p. 137.

88. Mushirul Hasan, 'Adjustment and Accommodation: Indian Muslims After Partition', in *Social Scientist*, vol. 18, no. 207–8, August–September 1990, p. 60.
89. A.G. Noorani, *The Muslims of India: A Documentary Record*, Oxford India Paperbacks: Oxford University Press, 2003, 2011, pp. 336–7.
90. Hasan, op. cit., p. 61.
91. Nehru, op. cit., p. 334.
92. Gyanendra Pandey, *The Ascendancy of the Congress in Uttar Pradesh: Class, Community, and Nation in Northern India, 1920–1940*, London: Anthem Press, 2002, pp. 110–11.
93. Ranadive, op. cit., pp. 106, 110.
94. Asghar Ali Engineer, 'Muslim Middle Class and its Role', in *Secular Perspective*, 16–31 May 2001.
95. Irfan Habib, Iqtidar Alam Khan and K.P. Singh, 'Problems of the Muslim Minority in India', in *Social Scientist*, vol. 4, no. 47, June 1976, p. 68.
96. Sarkar, *Modern India*, p. 85.
97. Salman Rushdie, 'Damme, This is the Oriental Scene for You!' in *The Development of the Novel*, ed. McNees Eleanor, vol. 1, East Sussex: Helm Information, 2006, p. 355.
98. Aijaz Ahmad, 'On Post Modernism', in *The Marxist*, XXVII 1, January–March 2011, pp. 24–7.
99. Sumit Sarkar, 'The Decline of the Subaltern in *Subaltern Studies*' in *Writing Social History*, Delhi, Calcutta, Chennai and Mumbai: Oxford University Press, 1997, p. 83.
100. Ahmad, 'On Post Modernism', pp. 37–8.
101. Salman Rushdie, *Midnight's Children*, New York: Avon Books, 1982, p. 550.
102. Ibid., p. 476.
103. Ibid., p. 509.
104. Ibid., p. 285.
105. Ibid., p. 546.
106. Ibid., p. 518.
107. Ibid., p. 525.
108. Ibid., p. 99.
109. Ibid., p. 552.
110. Ibid., p. 531.
111. Ibid., p. 137.
112. Ibid., p. 84.
113. Arundhati Roy, *The God of Small Things*, India: India Ink, 1997, p. 192.
114. Ibid., p. 328.
115. Ibid.
116. Ibid., p. 176.
117. Ibid., p. 338.
118. Ibid., p. 229.
119. Amitav Ghosh, *Sea of Poppies*, New Delhi: Penguin Books, 2009, p. 115.
120. Ibid.

121. Meenakshi Mukherjee, 'The Anxiety of Indianness: Our Novels in English', *Economic and Political Weekly*, vol. 28, no. 48, 27 November 1993, pp. 2610–11.
122. Ibid., p. 180.
123. Timothy Brennan, *At Home in the World: Cosmopolitanism Now*, Cambridge: Harvard University Press, 1997, p. 2.
124. Mukherjee, *Elusive Terrain*, p. 13.
125. Mukherjee, *Epic*, p. 603.
126. Ahmad, 'On Post Modernism', p. 14.

Bibliography

Abercrombie, Nicholas, Stephen Hill and Bryan S. Turner, eds., *The Penguin Dictionary of Sociology*, London: Penguin Books, 1994.

Abrams, M.H., *A Glossary of Literary Terms*, New Delhi: Macmillan, 2004.

Adorno, Theodor W., 'Culture Industry Reconsidered', in *The Study of Popular Fiction: A Source Book*, ed. Bob Ashley, London: Pinter Publishers, 1989.

Adorno, Theodor W. and Max Horkheimer, *The Dialectic of Enlightenment*, London: Verso, 1979.

Ahmad, Aijaz, *In Theory: Classes, Nations, Literatures*, New Delhi: Oxford University Press, 1999.

———, 'Reading Arundhati Roy *Politically*', in *Arundhati Roy's God of Small Things*, ed. Alex Tickell, London and New York: Routledge, 2007.

———, 'On Post Modernism', in *The Marxist*, XXVII 1, January–March 2011.

Albinski, Nan Bownan, *Women's Utopias in British and American Fiction*, London and New York: Routledge, 1988.

Allen, Walter, *The English Novel*, London: Penguin Books, 1991.

Allott, Miriam, *Novelists on the Novel*, London and Hexley: Routledge and Kegan Paul, 1980.

Althusser, Louis, *For Marx*, tr. Ben Brewster, London: Allen Lane and The Penguin Press, 1969.

Anderson, Benedict, *Imagined Communities: Reflections on the Origin and Spread of Nationalism*, London: New Left, 1991.

Appiah, Kwame Anthony, 'Is the Post- in Postmodernism the Post- in Postcolonial?' 1991; Padmini Mongia, ed., *Contemporary Postcolonial Theory: A Reader*, Delhi: Oxford University Press, 1997.

———, 'The Postcolonial and the Postmodern', 1992; Bill Ashcroft, Gareth Griffiths and Helen Tiffin, eds., *The Post-Colonial Studies Reader*, London and New York: Routledge, 2003.

Armstrong, Nancy, *Desire and Domestic Fiction: A Political History of the Novel*, New York and Oxford: Oxford University Press, 1987.

———, *How Novels Think: Limits of Individualism from 1719–1900*, New York: Columbia University Press, 2005.

Asaduddin, M., 'First Urdu Novel: Contesting Claims and Disclaimers', in *Early Novels in India*, ed. Meenakshi Mukherjee, New Delhi: Sahitya Akademi, 2002, 2005.

Ashcroft, Bill, Gareth Griffiths and Helen Tiffin, eds., *The Empire Writes Back*, London and New York: Routledge, 1989, 2005.

———, *The Post-Colonial Studies Reader*, London and New York: Routledge, 2003.

Ashley, Bob, ed., *The Study of Popular Fiction: A Source Book*, London: Pinter Publishers, 1989.

Auerbach, Eric, *Mimesis: The Representation of Reality in Western Literature*, 1946; tr. Willard R. Trask, Princeton, New Jersey: Princeton University Press, 1974.

Azim, Firdous, *The Colonial Rise of the Novel*, London and New York: Routledge, 1993.

Baccolini, Raffaella and Ton Moylan, eds., *Dark Horizons: Science Fiction and Dystopian Imagination*, London and New York: Routledge, 2003.

Bagchi, Amiya Kumar, *Private Investment in India: 1900–1939*, New Delhi: Orient Longman and Cambridge University Press, 1972, 1980.

Baker, Ernest A., *The History of the English Novel*, London: H.F.G. Witherby, 1924.

Baker, Stephen, *The Fiction of Postmodernity*, Edinburgh: Edinburgh University Press, 2000.

Bakhtin, Mikhail, *Problems of Dostoevsky's Poetics*, 1929; ed. and tr. Caryl Emerson, United Kingdom: Manchester University Press, 1984.

———, 'Discourse in the Novel (1934–5)', in *The Dialogic Imagination: Four Essays*, ed. Michael Holquist, tr. Caryl Emerson and Michael Holquist, Austin: University of Texas Press, 1981.

———, 'Epic and Novel: Toward a Methodology for the Study of the Novel', 1941; Michael J. Hoffman and Patrick D. Murphy, eds., *Essentials of the Theory of Fiction*, Durham and London: Duke University Press, 1988.

———, 'Forms of Time and of the Chronotope in the Novel' (1934–8), in *The Dialogic Imagination: Four Essays*, ed. Michael Holquist, tr. Caryl Emerson and Michael Holquist, Austin, University of Texas Press, 1981.

Balzac, Honore de, *Lost Illusions*, http://www.gutenberg.org/cache/epub/13159/pg13159.html.

Baran, Paul A. and Paul M. Sweezy, *Monopoly Capital*, Calcutta: K.P. Bagchi & Co., 1994.

Barron, Janet and David Nokes, 'Market, Morality and Sentiment: the Eighteenth-century Novel', in *Bloomsbury Guides to English Literature: The Novel from its Origins to the Present Day*, ed. Andrew Michael Roberts, London: Bloomsbury, 1994.

Barry, Peter, *Beginning Theory: An Introduction to Literary and Cultural Theory*, Manchester and New York: Manchester University Press, 2002.

Barth, John, 'The Literature of Replenishment', in *Essentials of the Theory of Fiction*, ed. Michael J. Hoffman and Patrick D. Murphy, Durham and London: Duke University Press, 1988.

———, 'The Literature of Exhaustion', in *Postmodernism and the Contemporary Novel: A Reader*, ed. Bran Nicol, Edinburgh: Edinburgh University Press, 2002.

Barthes, Roland, *S/Z*, tr. Richard Miller, Malden, MA: Blackwell Publishing, 2002.

———, 'Writing and the Novel', 1953; Hoffman, Michael J. and Patrick D. Murphy, eds., *Essentials of the Theory of Fiction*, Durham and London: Duke University Press, 1988.

Baudrillard, Jean, *Simulations*, tr. Paul Foss, Paul Patton and Philip Beitchman, New York: Semiotext[e], 1983.

———, 'The Order of Simulacra', in *Modern Literary Theory*, ed. Philip Rice and Patricia Waugh, London: Arnold Publishers, 2002.

Becket, Samuel, 'Dante . . . Bruno . . . Vico . . . Joyce', 1929; Vassiliki Kolocotroni, Jane Goldman, and Olga Taxidou, eds., *Modernism: An Anthology of Sources and Documents*, Edinburgh: Edinburgh University Press, 1998.

———, 'Proust', 1931; Vassiliki Kolocotroni, Jane Goldman, and Olga Taxidou, eds., *Modernism: An Anthology of Sources and Documents*, Edinburgh University Press, 1988.

Behn, Aphra, *Oroonoko or, the History of the Royal Slave*, 1688; Duffy, Maureen, ed., *Oroonoko and Other Stories*, London: Metheun, 1986.

Belchem, John and Richard Price, eds., *The Penguin Dictionary of Nineteenth Century History*, London: Penguin Books, 1996.

Bell, Daniel, 'Urbanization and Mass Society', 1976; Waugh, Patricia, ed., *Revolutions of the World: Intellectual Contexts for the Study of Modern Literature*, London: Arnold, 1997.

———, *The Cultural Contradictions of Capitalism*, New York: Basic Books, 1976.

Benjamin, Walter, 'The Work of Art in the Age of Mechanical Reproduction', in *Illuminations*, tr. Harry Zhon, London: Jonathan Cape, 1970.

———, 'The Storyteller' qtd. in Bob Ashley, *The Study of Popular Fiction: A Source Book*, London: Pinter Publishers, 1989.

Bergonzi, Bernard, 'The Advent of Modernism: 1900–1920', 1970; Tim Middleton, ed., *Modernism: Critical Concepts in Literary and Cultural Studies*, vol. 2, London and New York: Routledge, 2003.

Berman, Marshall, *All That is Solid Melts Into Air*, London: Verso, 1983.

Black, Jeremy and Roy Porter, eds., *The Penguin Dictionary of Eighteenth-Century History*, London: Penguin Books, 1994.

Blackburn, Stuart H., *Print, Folklore, and Nationalism in Colonial South India*, Delhi: Permanent Black, 2003.

Blackburn, Stuart and Vasudha Dalmia, eds., *Indian Literary History: Essays on Nineteenth Century*, Delhi: Permanent Black, 2003.

Blamires, Harry, ed., *A Short History of English Literature*, London: English Language Book Society and Methuen & Co Ltd., 1979.

Booth, Wyne C., *The Rhetoric of Fiction*, Chicago and London: The University of Chicago Press, 1983.

Botting, Fred, ed., *The Gothic*, Cambridge: D.S. Brewer Publications, 2001.

Bourdieu, Pierre, *The Field of Cultural Production: Essays on Art and Literature*, Cambridge: Polity Press, 1993.

———, *The Rules of Art: Genesis and Structure of the Literary Field*, 1992; tr. Susan Emanuel, Stanford and California: Stanford University Press, 1995.

Bradbury, Malcolm, 'Modernity in Modern English Literature', 1971; Middleton,

Tim. ed., *Modernism: Critical Concepts in Literary and Cultural Studies*, vol. 3, London and New York: Routledge, 2003.

———, *The Modern British Novel*, London: Secker & Warburg, 1993.

Bradbury, Malcom and James McFarlane, *Modernism 1890–1930*, London: Penguin, 1991.

Brecht, Bertold, 'The Modern Theatre is The Epic Theatre', 1930; Vassiliki Kolocotroni, Jane Goldman, and Olga Taxidou, eds., *Modernism: An Anthology of Sources and Documents*, Edinburgh: Edinburgh University Press, 1998.

Brennan, Timothy, *At Home in the World: Cosmopolitanism Now*, Cambridge: Harvard University Press, 1997.

Breton, André, 'The First Manifesto of Surrealism', 1924; Vassiliki Kolocotroni, Jane Goldman, and Olga Taxidou, eds., *Modernism: An Anthology of Sources and Documents*, Edinburgh: Edinburgh University Press, 1998.

Brydon, Diana, ed., *Postcolonialism: Critical Concepts in Literary and Cultural Studies, Volume II*, London and New York: Routledge, 2000.

Calvino, Italo, *Six Memos for the Next Millennium*, Cambridge and Massachusetts: Harvard University Press, 1988.

———, *If on a winter's night a traveler*, London:Vintage, 1998.

Capote, Truman, *In Cold Blood*, New York:Vintage, 1965.

Carnochan, W.B., 'The English Curriculum: Past and Present,' *PMLA* 115 (2000): 1958–61.

Chakrabarty, Dipesh, *Rethinking Working-Class History: Bengal, 1890–1940*, Princeton: Princeton University Press, 1989.

Chandra, Bipan,*India's Struggle for Independence*, New Delhi: Penguin Books, 1989.

Chatman, Seymour, *Coming to Terms: The Rhetoric of Narrative in Fiction and Film*, Ithaca and London: Cornell University Press, 1990.

Chatterjee, Partha, 'The Subalternity of the Nationalist Elite', in *The Middle Class in Colonial India*, ed. Sanjay Joshi, Oxford and New York: Oxford University Press, 2010.

Clark, Katerina and Michael Holquist, *Mikhail Bakhtin*, Cambridge, Massachusetts, and London: Harvard University Press, 1984.

Clark, T.W., ed., *The Novel in India: Its Birth and Development*, London: George Allen &Unwin Ltd, 1970.

Cody David, 'The Gentleman', in *The Victorian Web: literature, history, and culture in the age of Victoria*, 1998, http:victorianweb.org/history/gentleman.html.

Cohen, Ralph, 'Do Postmodern Genres Exist?' 1988; Lucy, Niall, ed., *Postmodern Literary Theory: An Anthology*, Oxford: Blackwell Publishers, 2000.

Colliers Encyclopedia, vol. 17, London and New York: Macmillan Educational Co., 1987.

Compton-Rickett, Arthur, *A History of English Literature*, London, Edinburgh, Paris, Melbourne, Johannesburg, Toronto and New York: Thomas Nelson & Sons Ltd., 1963.

Connor, Steven, *The English Novel in History: 1950–1995*, London and New York: Routledge, 1996.

Conrad, Joseph, *Lord Jim*, New York and Ontario: New American Library, 1961.

Cuddon, J.A., *The Penguin Dictionary of Literary Terms and Literary Theory*, London: Penguin Books, 1991.

Daiches, David, *A Critical History of English Literature*, 4 vols., 1960; New Delhi: Allied Publishers Pvt. Ltd., 2002.

Damrosch, David, *What is World Literature?*, Princeton and Oxford: Princeton University Press, 2003.

Danow, David K., *The Thought of Mikhail Bakhtin: From Word to Culture*, London: Macmillan, 1991.

Das, Sisir Kumar, *A History of Indian Literature 1800–1910: Struggle for Freedom: Triumph and Tragedy*, New Delhi: Sahitya Akademi, 1995.

———, *A History of Indian Literature 1800–1910: Western Impact: Indian Response*, New Delhi: Sahitya Akademi, 1991, 2000.

Davis, Lennard J., *Factual Fictions: The Origins of the English Novel*, Philadelphia: University of Pennsylvania, 1983.

———, *Resisting Novels: Ideology and Fiction*, New York and London: Methuen, 1987.

Davis, Robert Con and Ronald Schliefer, *Contemporary Literary Criticism: Literary and Cultural Studies*, New York and London: Longman, 1986.

Day, Geoffrey, *From Fiction to the Nove*l, London and New York: Routledge and Kegan Paul, 1987.

Defoe, Daniel, *The Life and Adventures of Robinson Crusoe*, 1719; Angus Ross, ed., Harmondsworth: Penguin Books, 1965.

Dentith, Simon, *Bakhtinian Thought: An Introductory Reader*, London and New York: Routledge, 1995.

Desai, A.R., *Social Background of Indian Nationalism*, Bombay: Popular Prakashan, 1948, 1976.

Dickens, Charles, 'These Melancholy Shades of Life', 1841; Travers, Martin, ed., *European Literature From Romanticism to Postmodernism: A Reader in Aesthetic Practice*, London and New York: Continuum, 2001.

Dipple, Elizabeth, *The Unresolvable Plot*, New York and London: Routledge, 1988.

Doody, Margaret Anne, *The True Story of the Novel*, New Brunswick and New Jersey: Rutgers University Press, 1996.

Duranty, Louis-Edmond, 'Demanding from the artist useful truth', 1856; in Travers, Martin, ed., *European Literature From Romanticism to Postmodernism: A Reader in Aesthetic Practice,* London and New York: Continuum, 2001.

Dutt, R.P., *India Today*, Calcutta: Manisha, 1940, 1986.

Eagleton, Terry, *After Theory*, New York: Basic Books, 2003.

———, *Literary Theory: An Introduction*, Oxford: Basil Blackwell, 1983.

———, *The English Novel: An Introduction*, Malden, Oxford and Victoria: Blackwell Publishing, 2005.

———, *Marxism and Literary Criticism*, London and New York: Routledge, 2002.

———, *The Illusions of Postmodernism*, Oxford: Blackwell Publishers, 1996.

Eco, Umberto, 'Postmodernism, Irony: The Enjoyable', 1985; Bran Nicol, ed., *Postmodernism and the Contemporary Novel: A Reader*, Edinburgh: Edinburgh University Press, 2002.

———, *The Limits of Interpretation*, Bloomington and Indianapolis: Indiana University Press, 1990.

Eisenstein, Elizabeth L., *The Printing Revolution in Early Modern Europe*, New York: Cambridge University Press, 1983.

Encyclopedia Britannica, vol. 7, 15th edn., Chicago, London, Toronto, Geneva, Sidney, Manila and Seoul: Helen Hemingway Benton Publications, 1974.

Engineer, Asghar Ali, 'Muslim Middle Class and its Role', in *Secular Perspective*, 16–31 May 2001.

Engles, Friedrich, 'Letter to Margaret Harkness', 1888; Travers, Martin, ed., *European Literature from Romanticism to Postmodernism: A Reader in Aesthetic Practice*, London and New York: Continuum, 2001.

Ermarth, Elizabeth Deeds, *Realism and Consensus in the English Novel: Time, Space and Narrative*, Edinburgh: Edinburgh University Press, 1998.

Fanon, Frantz, *The Wretched of the Earth*, tr., Constance Farrington, Harmondsworth: Penguin Books, 1963, 1982.

Farouqui, Ather, 'The Problem of Urdu in India—Political or Existential?: An interview with S.R. Faruqi', tr. M.U. Memon in *Annual of Urdu Studies*, vol. 10, 1995.

Federman, Raymond, *Critifiction: Postmodern Essays*, New York: State University of New York Press, 1993.

Fielding, Henry, *Joseph Andrews*, 1742; London: Penguin Books, 1985.

———, *The History of Tom Jones, A Foundling*, 1749; Hertfordshire: Wordsworth Classics, 1999.

Ford, Boris, ed., *The New Pelican Guide to English Literature*, 9 vols., London: Penguin Books, 1983.

Forster, E.M., *Aspects of the Novel*, Harmondsworth: Penguin Books, 1964.

Foucault, Michel, *The Archaeology of Knowledge and the Discourse on Language*, tr. A.M. Sheridan Smith, New York: Pantheon, 1972.

———, *Discipline and Punish: The Birth of the Prison*, tr. Alan Sheridan, New York: Pantheon, 1978.

Fowles, John, 'Fiction is Woven into All', 1969; Travers, Martin, ed., *European Literature From Romanticism to Postmodernism: A Reader in Aesthetic Practice*, London and New York: Continuum, 2001.

Fox, Ralph, *The Novel and the People*, Moscow: Foreign Language Publishing House, 1956.

Frank, Joseph, 'Spatial from in Modern Novel', 1945; Hoffman, Michael J. and Patrick D. Murphy, eds., *Essentials of the Theory of Fiction*, Durham and London: Duke University Press, 1988.

Frye, Northrop, *Anatomy of Criticism: Four Essays*, Princeton and New Jersey: Princeton University Press, 1957.

Fukuyama, Francis, *Fromthe End of History and the Last Man*, 1992; in Patricia Waugh ed., *Revolutions of the Word: Intellectual Contexts for the Study of Modern Literature*, London: Arnold, 1997.

———, *The End of History and the Last Man*, London: Penguin, 1992.

Gallagher, Catherine, *Nobody's Stories: The Vanishing Acts of Women in the Marketplace 1670–1820*, Berkeley and Los Angeles: University of California Press, 1994.

Gasset, Jose Ortega Y., '*From Mediations on Quixote*', 1914, and 'Notes on the Novel', 1925; Michael McKeon, ed., *Theory of the Novel: A Historical Approach*, Baltimore and London: The John Hopkins University Press, 2000.

———, 'The Crowd Phenomenon', an extract from his book *The Revolt of the Masses*, 1929; Tim Middleton, ed., *Modernism: Critical Concepts in Literary and Cultural Studies*, vol. 1, London and New York: Routledge, 2003.

Ghosh, Amitav, *Sea of Poppies*, New Delhi: Penguin Books, 2009.

Gilber, Sandra and Susan Gubar, *The Madwoman in the Attic: The Woman Writer and the Nineteenth Century Literary Imagination*, New Haven: Yale University Press, 1978.

Gillie, Christopher, *Longman Companion to English Literature*, London: Longman, 1972.

Gissing, George, *New Grub Street*, 1891; Hertfordshire: Wordsworth Classics, 1996.

Goldman, Lucien, *Towards a Sociology of the Novel*, 1964; tr. Alan Sheridon, London: Tavistock Publications Ltd., 1975.

———, *Cultural Creation in Modern Society*, 1971; tr., Bart Grahl, Oxford: Basil Blackwell, 1977.

———, *Method in the Sociology of Literature*, tr. and ed., William Q. Boelhower, Oxford: Basil Blackwell, 1981.

Gopal, Priyamvada, *The Indian English Novel: Nation, History, Narration*, Oxford: Oxford University Press, 2009.

Grass, Günter, *The Tin Drum*, tr. Ralph Manheim, London: Vintage, 1998.

Greaney, Michael, *Contemporary Fiction and the Uses of Theory*, Hampshire and New York: Palgrave Macmillan, 2006.

Habib, Irfan, Iqtidar Alam Khan and K.P. Singh, 'Problems of the Muslim Minority in India', *Social Scientist*, vol. 4, no. 47, June 1976.

Hägg, Thomas, *The Novel in Antiquity*, Oxford: Basil Blackwell, 1983.

Hale, Dorothy J., *Social Formalism: The Novel in Theory from Henry James to the Present*, Stanford, California: Stanford University Press, 1998.

———, *The Novel: An Anthology of Criticism and Theory, 1900–2000*, Malden, Oxford, Victoria: Blackwell Publishing, 2006.

Hardy, Thomas, 'The Science of Fiction', 1891; Kolocotroni, Vassiliki, Jane Goldman, and Olga Taxidou, eds., *Modernism: An Anthology of Sources and Documents*, Edinburgh: Edinburgh University Press, 1998.

Harrison, John R., 'The Anti-Democratic Intelligentsia', 1966; Tim Middleton, ed., *Modernism: Critical Concepts in Literary and Cultural Studies*, vol. 2, London and New York: Routledge, 2003.

Harvey, David, *The Condition of Postmodernity*, Cambridge: Basil Blackwell, 1989.

———, 'Modernity and Modernism', 1990; Tim Middleton, ed., *Modernism: Critical Concepts in Literary and Cultural Studies*, vol. 4, London and New York: Routledge, 2003.

Hasan, Mushirul, 'Adjustment and Accommodation: Indian Muslims After Partition', in *Social Scientist*, vol. 18, nos. 207–8, August–September 1990.

Haslett, Moyra, 'A Question of Form: the Realism/Modernism Debates', in *Marxist Literary and Cultural Theories*, London: Macmillan Press Ltd., 2000.

Hassan, Ihab, 'The Pattern of Fictional Experience', 1961; A. Walton Litz, ed., *Modern American Fiction: Essays in Criticism*, London, Oxford and New York: Oxford University Press, 1967.

———, *The Postmodern Turn: Essays in Postmodern Theory and Culture*, Columbus: Ohio State University Press, 1987.

Hawthorn, Jeremy, *Studying the Novel: An Introduction*, London and New York: Edward Arnold, 1992.

Head, Dominic, *The Cambridge Companion to Modern British Fiction, 1950–2000*, Cambridge: Cambridge University Press, 2002.

Hegel, G.W.F., *Aesthetics: Lectures on Fine Art*, 1842, tr. K.M. Knox, London: Oxford University Press, 1975.

Heiserman, Arthur, *The Novel Before the Novel*, Chicago and London: Chicago University Press, 1977.

Henderson, Philip, 'The Function of the Novel', 1936; Tim Middleton, ed., *Modernism: Critical Concepts in Literary and Cultural Studies*, vol. 2, London and New York: Routledge, 2003.

Hill, Christopher, *Writing and Revolution in Seventeenth Century England*, Brighton: The Harvester Press: 1985.

Hirschkop, Ken and David Shepherd, *Bakhtin and Cultural Theory*, Manchester and New York: Manchester University Press, 2001.

Hitchcock, Peter, 'The Genre of Postcoloniality', in *New Literary History: Theorizing Genres I*, vol. 34, Summer no. 2, 2003.

Hobsbawm, Eric, *The Age of Capital: 1848–1875*, London: Abacus, 1975.

———, *Age of Extremes: The Short Twentieth Century—1914–1991*, London: Abacus, 1994.

———, *The Age of Revolution 1789–1848*, London: Abacus, 2002.

———, *The Age Of Empire: 1875–1914*, London: Abacus, 1987.

Hoffman, Michael J. and Patrick D. Murphy, eds., *Essentials of the Theory of Fiction*, Durham and London: Duke University Press, 1988.

Hoggart, Richard, *The Uses of Literacy*, 1957; in Bob Ashley, ed., *The Study of Popular Fiction: A Source Book*, London: Pinter Publishers, 1989.

Hogle, Jerrold E., 'The Gothic at our Turn of the Century: Our Culture of Simulation and the Return of the Body', in *The Gothic*, ed. Fred Botting, Cambridge: D.S. Brewer Publications, 2001.

Holloway, John, 'The Literary Scene; Literary Institutionalism', in Ford, Boris, ed., *The Present: Volume 8 of the New Pelican Guide to English Literature*, London: Penguin Books, 1990.

Holquist, Michael, *Dialogism: Bakhtin and his World*, London and New York: Routledge, 1990.

Houlgate, Stephen, ed., *The Hegel Reader*, Oxford: Blackwell, 1998.

Howe, Irving, 'Mass Society and Postmodern Fiction', 1959; Bran Nicol, ed., *Postmodernism and the Contemporary Novel: A Reader*, Edinburgh: Edinburgh University Press, 2002.

Hunter, J. Paul, *Before Novels: The Cultural Contexts of Eighteenth-Century English Fiction*, New York and London: W.W. Norton & Co. 1990.

Hutcheon, Linda, *Narcissistic Narrative: The Metafictional Paradox*, New York and London: Methuen, 1980.

———, *A Poetics of Postmodernism: History, Theory, Fiction*, New York and London: Routledge, 1988.

———, *The Politics of Postmodernism*, 1989; London and New York: Routledge, 2005.

Huyssen, Andreas, *After the Great Divide*, Basingstoke: Macmillan, 1988.

Iyengar, K.R. Srinivasa, *Indian Writing in English*, New Delhi: Sterling Publishers Pvt. Ltd., 1962, 2011.

James, Henry, 'The Art of Fiction', 1884; Hoffman, Michael J. and Patrick D. Murphy, eds., *Essentials of the Theory of Fiction*, Durham and London: Duke University Press, 1988.

———, 'The New Novel', 1914; Tim Middleton, ed., *Modernism: Critical Concepts in Literary and Cultural Studies*, vol. 1, London and New York: Routledge, 2003.

Jameson, Frederic, *The Political Unconscious: Narrative as a Socially Symbolic Act*, Ithaca and New York: Cornell University Press, 1981.

———, 'Beyond the Cave: Demystifying the Ideology of Modernism', 1975; Francis Mulhern, ed., *Contemporary Marxist Literary Criticism*, London and New York: Longman, 1992.

———, 'Third-World Literature in the Era of Multinational Capitalism', 1986; Brydon, Diana, ed., Postcolonialism: Critical Concepts in Literary and Cultural Studies, vol. II, London and New York: Routledge, 2000.

———, *Postmodernism, or, The Cultural Logic of Late Capitalism*, London and New York: Verso, 1991.

Jay, Martin, *The Dialectical Imagination: A History of the Frankfurt School and the Institute of Social Research 1923–1950*, Heinemann and London: Heinemann Educational Books, 1973.

Joshi, Priya, *In Another Country: Colonialism, Culture, and the English Novel in India*, New York: Columbia University Press, 2002.

———, 'India, 1850–1900', in *The Novel: Volume One History, Geography and Culture*, ed. Franco Moretti, Princeton and Oxford: Princeton University Press, 2006.

Joshi, Sanjay, ed., *The Middle Class in Colonial India*, Oxford and New York: Oxford University Press, 2010.

———, *Fractured Modernity: Making of a Middle Class in Colonial North India*, Oxford and New York: Oxford University Press, 2001.

Joyce, James, *A Portrait of the Artist as a Young Man*, New Delhi: Peacock Books, 2000.

Juserand, J.J., *The English Novel in The Times of Shakespeare*, New York: A.M.S. Press, 1965.

Karl, Frederick R. and Marvin Magalaner, *A Reader's Guide to Great Twentieth-Century English Novels*, London: Thames and Hudson, 1973.

Karl, Frederick, '*Modern and Postmodern, Modernism and Postmodernism*', 1985; Tim Middleton, ed., *Modernism: Critical Concepts in Literary and Cultural Studies*, vol. 4, London and New York: Routledge, 2003.

Karl, Frederick R., *A Reader's Guide to the Contemporary English Novel*, London: Thames and Hudson, 1961.

Kearns, Katherine, *Nineteenth Century Literary Realism: Through the Looking-Glass*, Cambridge: Cambridge University Press, 1996.

Kermode, Frank, 'Life and Death of the Novel', in The New York Review of Books, vol. 5, no. 6, 28 October 1965.

———, 'Literary Fiction and Reality', 1967; Hoffman, Michael J. and Patrick D. Murphy, eds., *Essentials of the Theory of Fiction*, Durham and London: Duke University Press, 1988.

Kettle, Arnold, *An Introduction to the English Novel*, London: Hutchinson's University Library, 1951.

Khair, Tabish, *Babu Fictions: Alienation in Contemporary Indian English Novels*, Oxford India Paperbacks: Oxford University Press, 2001, 2011.

Kolocotroni, Vassiliki, Jane Goldman, and Olga Taxidou, eds., *Modernism: An Anthology of Sources and Documents*, Edinburgh: Edinburgh University Press, 1998.

Kumar, T. Vijay, Meenakshi Mukherjee, Harish Trivedi and C. Vijayshree, eds., *Focus India: Postcolonial Narratives of the Nation*, Delhi: Pencraft International, 2007.

Kundera, Milan, *The Art of the Novel*, 1986; tr. Linda Asher, London and Boston: Faber and Faber, 1988.

Kuran, Timur and Anantdeep Singh, 'Economic Modernization in Late British India: Hindu-Muslim Differences', in Economic Development and Cultural Change, vol. 61, 2013.

LaCapra, Dominick, *History, Politics, and the Novel*, Ithaca and London: Cornell University Press, 1987.

Landow, George P., *Hypertext: The Convergence of Contemporary Critical Theory and Technology*, Baltimore and London: The John Hopkins University Press, 1992.

Lawrence, D. H., 'Morality and the Novel'; qtd. in Sharma K.K., *Tradition in Modern Novel-Theory*, New Delhi: Abhinav Publications, 1978.

Leavis, F.R., *Mass Civilization and Minority Culture*, Cambridge: The Minority Press, 1930.

Leavis, Q.D., 'From *Fiction and the Reading Public*', 1932; Bob Ashley, ed., *The Study of Popular Fiction: A Source Book*, London: Pinter Publishers, 1989.

Leuschner, Eric, 'Anthologizing the Novel', in *The Minnesota Review*, nos. 55–7, 2002.

Levi, Primo, *The Periodic Table*, tr. Raymond Rosenthal, New York: Schocken Books, 1984.

Levin, Harry, 'What Was Modernism?' 1960; Tim Middleton, ed., *Modernism: Critical Concepts in Literary and Cultural Studies*, vol. 2, London and New York: Routledge, 2003.

Levine, George, 'Realism Reconsidered', 1974; Michael J. Hoffman and Patrick D. Murphy, eds., *Essentials of the Theory of Fiction*, Durham and London: Duke University Press, 1988.

———, *The Realistic Imagination: English Fiction from Frankenstein to Lady Chatterly*, Chicago and London: University of Chicago Press, 1981.

Litz, A. Walton, ed., *Modern American Fiction: Essays in Criticism*, London, Oxford and New York: Oxford University Press, 1967.

Lodge, David, *Language of Fiction: Essays in Criticism and Verbal Analysis of the English Novel*, London: Routledge and Kegan Paul, 1966.

———, 'Postmodernist Fiction', 1977; Bran Nicol, ed., *Postmodernism and the Contemporary Novel: A Reader*, Edinburgh: Edinburgh University Press, 2002.

———, *Essays on Fiction and Criticism*, London and New York: Routledge, 1990.

———, *The Novelist at the Crossroads, and Other Essays on Fiction and Criticism*, Ithaca: Cornell University Press, 1971.

Loomba, Ania, *Colonialism/Postcolonialism*, London and New York: Routledge, 1998.

Lovell, Terry, *Consuming Fiction*, London: Verso, 1987.

Lovett, Robert Morss, 'The Novel To-Day', in Tim Middleton, ed., *Modernism: Critical Concepts in Literary and Cultural Studies*, vol. 1, London and New York: Routledge, 2003.

Lucy, Niall, ed., *Postmodern Literary Theory: An Anthology*, Oxford: Blackwell Publishers, 2000.

Lukács, Georg, *The Historical Novel*, 1936–7; tr. Hannah and Stanley Mitchell, Lincoln and London: University of Nebraska Press, 1962.

———, *Studies in European Realism*, 1930; tr. Alfred Kazin, New York: The Universal Library, 1964.

———, *History and Class Consciousness*, tr. Rodney Livingstone, New Delhi: Rupa & Co., 1993.

———, *Soul and Form*, tr. Anna Bostock, London: Merlin Press, 1974.

———, *The Theory of the Novel*, tr. A. Bostock, London: Merlin Press, 1971.

Lyotard, Jean-Francois, *The Postmodern Condition: A Report on Knowledge*, Minneapolis, MN: University of Minnesota Press; Manchester: Manchester University Press, 1979.

———, 'Answering the Question: What is Postmodernism?' in *Modern Literary Theory*, ed. Philip Rice and Patricia Waugh, London: Arnold Publishers, 2002.

———, 'Narrative, Knowledge and Representation', in *Postmodernism and the Contemporary Novel: A Reader*, ed. Bran Nicol, Edinburgh: Edinburgh University Press, 2002.

Macherey, Pierre, *A Theory of Literary Production*, tr. Geoffry Wall, London and New York: Routledge and Kegan Paul, 1986.

Márquez, Gabriel Garcia, *One Hundred Years of Solitude*, 1967; tr. Gregory Rabassa, London: Penguin Books, 1996.

Martens, Lorna, *The Diary Novel*, Cambridge: Cambridge University Press, 1985.

Martin, Wallace, *Recent Theories of Narrative*, Ithaca and London: Cornell University Press, 1986.

Marx, Karl and Frederick Engels, 'Manifesto of the Communist Party,' 1848; tr. 1888; in Prakash Karat, ed., *A World to Win: Essays on the Communist Manifesto,* Delhi: LeftWord, 1999.

Matthews, J.H., *Surrealism and the Novel,* Ann Arbor: The University of Michigan Press, 1969.

Mautner, Thomas, ed., *Penguin Dictionary of Philosophy*, London: Penguin Books, 1997.

McDermott, Hubert, *Novel and Romance: The Odyssey to Tom Jones*, London: Macmillan Press, 1989.

McHale, Brian, 'Change of Dominant from Modernist to Postmodernist Writing', 1986; Bran Nicol, ed., *Postmodernism and the Contemporary Novel: A Reader,* Edinburgh: Edinburgh University Press, 2002.

———, *Constructing Postmodernism*, London and New York: Routledge, 1992.

———, 'POSTcyberMODERN-punkISM', in *Postmodern Literary Theory: An Anthology*, ed. Niall Lucy, Oxford: Blackwell Publishers, 2000.

______, 'What Was Postmodernism?' in *electronic book review*, http://www.electronicbookreview.com/thread/fictionspresent/tense.

———, *Postmodernist Fiction*, London and New York: Routledge, 1987.

McKeon, Michael, *The Origins of the English Novel: 1600-1740*, Baltimore: The John Hopkins University Press, 1987.

———, *Theory of the Novel: A Historical Approach*, Baltimore and London: The John Hopkins University Press, 2000.

McNees, Eleanor, ed., *The Development of the Novel: Literary Sources and Documents,* East Sussex: Helm Information, 2006.

McQuillan, Martin, Graeme McDonald, Robin Purves and Stephen Thomson, eds., *Post-Theory: New Directions in Criticism*, Edinburgh: Edinburgh University Press, 1999.

McSweeney, Kerry, *Four Contemporary Novelists: Angus Wilson, Brian Moore, John Fowles, V.S. Naipaul*, London: McGill-Queen's University Press, 1983.

Mengham, Robert, ed., *An Introduction to Contemporary Fiction: International Writing in English Since 1970*, Cambridge: Polity Press, 1999.

Menon, Dilip M., 'No. Not the Nation: Lower Caste Malayalam Novels of the Nineteenth Century', in *Early Novels in India*, ed. Meenakshi Mukherjee, New Delhi: Sahitya Akademi, 2002, 2005.

Middleton, Tim, ed., *Modernism: Critical Concepts in Literary and Cultural Studies*, 5 vols., London and New York: Routledge, 2003.

Miles, Rosalind, *The Female Form: Women Writers and the Conquest of the Novel*, London and New York: Routledge and Kegan Paul, 1987.

Miller, D.A., *The Novel and the Police*, Berkeley, Los Angeles, and London: University of California Press, 1988.

Moglen, Helene, *The Trauma of Gender: A Feminist Theory of the Novel*, Berkeley, Los Angeles and London: University of California Press, 2001.

Mongia, Padmini, *Contemporary Postcolonial Theory: A Reader*, Delhi: OUP, 1997.

Moretti, Franco, *Modern Epic: The World System from Goethe to Garcia Marquez*, tr. Quintin Hoare, London and New York: Verso, 1996.

———, 'Conjectures on World Literature', *New Left Review* 1, January–February, 2000.

———, *The Novel: Volume One, History, Geography and Culture* and *The Novel: Volume Two, Forms and Themes*, Princeton and Oxford: Princeton University Press, 2006.

Morris, Pam, *Realism*, London and New York: Routledge, 2003.

Morson, Gary Saul and Caryl Emerson, eds., *Rethinking Bakhtin: Extensions and Challenges*, Evanston and Illinois: Northwestern University Press, 1989.

Mowat, R.B., *The Victorian Age*, London: Senate, 1995.

Mukherjee, Meenakshi, *Elusive Terrain: Culture and Literary Memory*, New Delhi: Oxford University Press, 2008, 2011.

_______, 'The Anxiety of Indianness: Our Novels in English', *Economic and Political Weekly,* vol. 28, no. 48, 27 November 1993.

_______ , ed., *Early Novels in India*, New Delhi: Sahitya Akademi, 2002, 2005.

_______, 'Epic and Novel in India', in *The Novel: Volume One History, Geography and Culture, ed. Franco Moretti,* Princeton and Oxford: Princeton University Press, 2006.

———, *Realism and Reality: The Novel and Society in India*, New Delhi: Oxford University Press, 1985, 2005.

———, *The Perishable Empire: Essays on Indian Writing in English*, Oxford India Paperbacks: Oxford University Press, 2000, 2005.

Mulhern, Francis, ed., *Contemporary Marxist Literary Criticism*, London and New York: Longman, 1992.

Naidu, Ch. M., *Nationalism in South India: Its Economic and Social Background (1885–1918)*, Delhi: Mittal Publications, 1998.

Naipaul, V. Shiva, *Journey to Nowhere: A New World Tragedy*, New York: Penguin Books, 1982.

Namboodiripad, E.M.S., *A History of Indian Freedom Struggle*, Trivandrum: Social Scientist Press, 1986.

Nehru, Jawaharlal, *The Discovery of India*, New Delhi: Jawaharlal Nehru Memorial Fund-Oxford University Press, 1946, 1996.

Nicol, Bran, ed., *Postmodernism and the Contemporary Novel: A Reader*, Edinburgh: Edinburgh University Press, 2002.

———, *Cambridge Introduction to Postmodern Fiction*, Cambridge: Cambridge University Press, 2009.

Noorani, A.G., *The Muslims of India: A Documentary Record*, Oxford India Paperbacks: Oxford University Press, 2003, 2011.

Oesterheld, Chrsitina, 'Entertainment and Reform: Urdu Narrative Genres in the Nineteenth Century', in *India's Literary History: Essays on Nineteenth Century*, ed. Stuart Blackburn and Vasudha Dalmia, Delhi: Permanent Black, 2004.

Ong, Walter J., *Orality and Literacy: The Technologizing of Word*, London and New York: Methuen, 1982.

Pandey, Gyanendra, *The Ascendancy of the Congress in Uttar Pradesh: Class, Community, and Nation in Northern India, 1920–1940*, London: Anthem Press, 1978, 2002.

Panikkar, K.N., 'From Revolt to Agitation: Beginnings of the National Movement', in *Five Essays: Indian People in the Struggle for Freedom*, New Delhi: SAHMAT, 1998.

Pasco, Allan H., *Inner Workings of the Novel: Studying a Genre*, New York: Palgrave Macmillan, 2010.

Patnaik, Prabhat, 'The Concept of the Mode of Production and the Theory of Imperialism', in *The Great Divergence: Hegemony, Uneven Development, and Global Inequality*, ed. K.S. Jomo, New Delhi: Oxford University Press, 2006.

———, 'Introduction', in *Five Essays: Indian People in the Struggle for Freedom*, New Delhi: SAHMAT, 1998.

Phelps, Gilbert, *A Short Guide to the World Novel: From Myth to Modernism*, London: The Folio Society, 1987.

Prendergast, Christopher, ed., *Debating World Literature*, London and New York: Verso, 2004.

Prince, Michael B., 'Mauvais Genres', in *New Literary History: Theorising Genres II*, vol. 34, Summer no. 3, 2003.

Rai, Alok, *Hindi Nationalism*, India: Orient Longman, 2001, 2007.

Ranadive, B.T., 'India's Freedom Struggle', in *Social Scientist*, vol. 14, nos. 159–60, August–September 1986.

Reed, Walter L., *An Exemplary History of the Novel: The Quixotic Versus the Picaresque*, Chicago and London: The University of Chicago Press, 1981.

Reeve, Clara, 'The Progress of Romance', in *The Nineteenth-Century Novel: A Critical Reader*, ed. Stephen Regan, London and New York: The Open University, 2001.

Rice, Philip and Patricia Waugh, eds., *Modern Literary Theory*, London: Arnold Publishers, 2002.

Rielly, Jim, *Shadowtime: History and Representation in Hardy, Conrad and George Eliot*, London and New York: Routledge, 1993.

Rimmon-Kenan, Schlomith, *Narrative Fiction: Contemporary Poetics*, London and New York: Routledge, 2003.

Roberts, Andrew Michael, ed., *Bloomsbury Guides to English Literature: The Novel from its Origins to the Present Day*, London: Bloomsbury, 1994.

Robbe-Grillet, Alain, 'Towards a New Novel', 1963; Martin Travers, ed., *European Literature from Romanticism to Postmodernism: A Reader in Aesthetic Practice*, London and New York: Continuum, 2001.

Robert, Marthe, *Origins of the Novel*, 1972; tr. Sacha Rabinovitch, Sussex: The Harvester Press, 1980.

Roy, Arundhati, *The God of Small Things*, India: India Ink, 1997.

Rushdie, Salman, 'Damme, This is the Oriental Scene for You!' in *The Development of the Novel, Volume I*, ed. Eleanor McNees, East Sussex: Helm Information, 2006.

———, 'In Defense of the Novel, Yet Again', 1996; McNees, Eleanor, ed., *The Development of the Novel: Literary Sources and Documents*, East Sussex: Helm Information, 2006.

———, *Midnight's Children*, New York: Avon Books, 1982.

Russel, John, *Reciprocities in the Nonfiction Novel*, Athens and London: The University of Georgia Press, 2000.

Sachar Committee: Social, Economic and Educational Status of the Muslim Community of India, Prime Minister's High Level Committee, Cabinet Secretariat: Government of India, 2006.

Said, Edward, *Beginnings: Intention & Method*, New York: Columbia University Press, 1985.

———, *Culture and Imperialism*, New York: Vintage Books, 1994.

———, *Orientalism: Western Conceptions of the Orient*, London: Penguin Books, 1995.

Sarkar, Sumit. *Modern India, 1885–1947*. Chennai: Macmillan India, 1983, 2011.

———, '"Middle-class" Consciousness and Patriotic Literature in South Asia', in *A Companion to Postcolonial Studies*, ed. Henry Schwarz and Sangeeta Ray, Malden, Oxford, Victoria: Blackwell Publishing, 2000, 2005.

———, 'The Decline of the Subaltern in *Subaltern Studies*', in *Writing Social History*, Delhi, Calcutta, Chennai and Mumbai: Oxford University Press, 1997.

Schlauch, Margaret, *Antecedents of the English Novel: 1400–1600*, London: OUP, 1963.

Scholes, Robert and Robert Kellogg, *The Nature of Narrative*, New York: Oxford University Press, 1966.

Scott, Walter, 'The art of copying from nature', 1815; Martin Travers, ed., *European Literature from Romanticism to Postmodernism: A Reader in Aesthetic Practice*, London and New York: Continuum, 2001.

Seth, Vikram, *The Golden Gate: A Novel in Verse*, New York: Random House, 1986.

Sharma, K.K., *Tradition in Modern Novel-Theory*, New Delhi: Abhinav Publications, 1978.

Showalter, Elaine, *A Literature of Their Own: British Women Novelists from Bronte to Lessing*, Princeton and New Jersey: Princeton University Press, 1999.

Singh, Namwar, 'Reformulating the Question', in *Early Novels in India*, ed. Meenakshi Mukherjee, New Delhi: Sahitya Akademi, 2002, 2005.

Smith, Andrew and Jeff Wallace, eds., *Gothic Modernisms*, Houndmills, Basingstoke, Hampshire and New York: Palgrave Publishers Ltd, 2001.

Sontag, Susan, 'One Culture and the New Sensibility', 1965; Bran Nicol, ed., *Postmodernism and the Contemporary Novel: A Reader*, Edinburgh: Edinburgh University Press, 2002.

Spencer, Jane, *The Rise of the Woman Novelist*, Oxford and New York: Basil Blackwell, 1986.

Steinberg, S.H., *Five Hundred Years of Printing*, Baltimore: Penguin, 1981.

Sterne, Laurence, *A Sentimental Journey*, 1768; Graham Petrie, ed., London: Penguin Books, 1986.

Stone, Lawrence, *The Family, Sex and Marriage in England, 1500–1800*, London: Weidenfeld & Nicolson, 1977.

Stubbs, Patricia, *Women and Fiction: Feminism and the Novel, 1880–1920*, Sussex: Harvester Press, 1979.

Suhrawardy, Shaista Akhtar Banu, *A Critical Survey of the Development of the Urdu Novel and Short Story*, London: Longmans, Green & Co., 1945.

Sutherland, John, *Bestsellers: Popular Fictions of the 1970's*, London, Boston and Henley: Routledge and Kegan Paul, 1981.

Swingewood, Alan, *The Novel and Revolution*. London and Basingstoke: The Macmillan Press Ltd, 1975.

Tharu, Susie, and K. Lalita, eds., *Women Writing in India*, New Delhi: Oxford University Press, 1991.

The Concise Oxford Dictionary of English Literature, 2nd edn., rev. by Dorothy Eagle, Oxford and New York: Oxford University Press, 1988.

The Encyclopedia Americana, vol. 20, Danbury and Connecticut: Grolier Incorp, 1983.

Thiong'o, Ngugiwa, 'The Language of African Literature', in *The Post-Colonial Studies Reader*, ed. Bill Ashcroft, Gareth Griffiths and Helen Tiffin, London and New York: Routledge, 2003.

Tickell, Alex, ed., *Arundhati Roy's God of Small Things: A Routledge Study Guide*, London and New York: Routledge, 2007.

Todorov, Tzvetan, *Mikhail Bakhtin: The Dialogic Principle*, tr. Wlad Godzich, Manchester: Manchester University Press, 1984.

Tomlinson, B.R., *The New Cambridge Economy of India, Vol. 3: The Economy of Modern India, 1860–1970*, Cambridge, New York and Melbourne: Cambridge Histories Online @ Cambridge University Press, 1993, 2008.

Travers, Martin, ed., *European Literature from Romanticism to Postmodernism: A Reader in Aesthetic Practice*, London and New York: Continuum, 2001.

Trilling, Lionel, 'Manners, Morals, and the Novel', 1950; Michael J. Hoffman, and Patrick D. Murphy, eds., *Essentials of the Theory of Fiction*, Durham and London: Duke University Press, 1988.

Trivedi, Harish, and Meenakshi Mukherjee, eds., *Interrogating Post-colonialism: Theory, Text and Context*, Shimla: Indian Institute of Advanced Study, 1996.

W.B. Carnochan, 'The English Curriculum: Past and Present', in *PMLA* 115, 2000, pp. 1958–61.

Walsh, Judith E., *A Brief History of India*, Facts On File Inc., New York, 2006.

Washbrook, David, 'South India 1770–1840: The Colonial Transition', in *Modern Asian Studies*, vol. 38, no. 3, 2004.

Watt, Ian, *The Rise of the Novel*, 1957; London: Penguin Books, 1968.

———, *Myths of Modern Individualism: Faust, Don Quixote, Don Juan, Robinson Crusoe*, New York: Cambridge University Press, 1996.

Waugh, Patricia, *Metafiction: The Theory and Practice of Self-Conscious Fiction*, London: Routledge, 1984.

———, *Revolutions of the World: Intellectual Contexts for the Study of Modern Literature*, London: Arnold, 1997.

Weber, Max, *The Protestant Ethic and the Spirit of Capitalism*, tr. Talcott Parsons and Anthony Giddens, London and Boston: Unwin Hyman, 1930.

Williams, Raymond, *The Long Revolution*, Westport and Connecticut: Greenwood Press Publishers, 1961.

———, 'The Metropolis and the Emergence of Modernism', 1985; Yim Middleton, ed., *Modernism: Critical Concepts in Literary and Cultural Studies*, vol. 4, London and New York: Routledge, 2003.

———, *Keywords*, New York: Oxford University Press, 1983.

———, *Marxism and Literature*, Oxford: Oxford University Press, 1977.

———, *The Country and the City*, New York: Oxford University Press, 1973.

———, *The Politics of Modernism: Against the New Conformists*, London and New York: Verso, 1996.

Woods, Tim, *Beginning Postmodernism*, Manchester and New York: Manchester University Press, 1999.

Woolf, Virginia, 'Modern Fiction', 1919; Tim Middleton, ed., *Modernism: Critical Concepts in Literary and Cultural Studies*, London and New York: Routledge, 2003.

______, *A Room of One's Own*, http://gutenberg.net.au/ebooks02/0200791h.html

———, 'Mr. Bennet and Mrs. Brown', 1924; Hoffman, Michael J. and Patrick D. Murphy, eds., *Essentials of the Theory of Fiction*, Durham and London: Duke University Press, 1988.

———, 'The Narrow Bridge Of Art', 1958; Lawrence Rainey, ed., *Modernism: An Anthology*, Malden, MA and Oxford: Wiley-Balckwell, 2005.

Worpole, Ken, 'From *Reading by Numbers: Contemporary Publishing and Popular Fiction*', in *The Study of Popular Fiction: A Source Book*, ed. Bob Ashley, London: Pinter Publishers, 1989.

Zaidi, Ali Jawad, *A History of Urdu Literature*, New Delhi: Sahitya Akademi, 1993.

Zhdanov, Andrey Alexandrovich, 'On Socialist Realism', 1934; Martin Travers, ed., *European Literature from Romanticism to Postmodernism: A Reader in Aesthetic Practice*, London and New York: Continuum, 2001.

Zola, Emile, 'Naturalism on the Stage', 1871; Vassiliki Kolocotroni, Jane Goldman, and Olga Taxidou, eds., *Modernism: An Anthology of Sources and Documents*, Edinburgh: Edinburgh University Press, 1998.

———, 'The Experimental Novel', 1893; Stephen Regan, ed., *The Nineteenth-Century Novel: A Critical Reader*, London and New York: The Open University, 2001.

Index